SUMMARY

OF THE

ART OF WAR,

OR,

A NEW ANALYTICAL COMPEND

OF THE

PRINCIPAL COMBINATIONS OF STRATEGY, OF GRAND
TACTICS AND OF MILITARY POLICY.

BY

BARON DE JOMINI,

GENERAL-IN-CHIEF, AIDE-DE-CAMP GENERAL TO HIS MAJESTY THE EMPEROR
OF ALL THE RUSSIAS.

TRANSLATED FROM THE FRENCH

BY

MAJOR O. F. WINSHIP, ASS'T. ADJ'T. GENERAL, U. S. A.
LIEUT. E. E. McLEAN, 1ST INFANTRY, U. S. A.

NEW-YORK.

Published for the Proprietors,

BY G. P. PUTNAM & CO., 10 PARK PLACE.

1854.

TO HIS MAJESTY,

THE EMPEROR OF ALL THE RUSSIAS.

————◦—◦✳◦—◦————

SIRE,

    YOUR IMPERIAL MAJESTY, *in his just solicitude for all that can contribute to the progress and the propagation of the sciences, deigned to order the translation into the Russian language of my* TREATISE UPON GRAND MILITARY OPERATIONS, *for the institutes of the crown.*

    Eager to respond to the benevolent views of YOUR MAJESTY, *I believed it my duty to augment this work by an* ANALYTICAL COMPEND, *which would serve as a compliment to it. This first essay, published in* 1830, *accomplished the object for which it had been written: but I have since thought that by enlarging somewhat its frame, it would be possible to render it more useful and to make of it a work complete in itself: I trust I have obtained that result.*

    Notwithstanding its small compass, this Summary now contains all the combinations which the general of an army and the statesman can make for the conduct of a war: never was so important a subject treated within limits at the same time more compact and more in the reach of all readers.

    I take the liberty of doing homage through this Summary to YOUR IMPERIAL MAJESTY, *begging him to be pleased to receive it with indulgence. My wishes would be crowned if this work could merit the suffrages of a judge so enlightened, of a monarch so versed in the important art which elevates and preserves empires.*

           I am, with veneration,
              SIRE,
          YOUR IMPERIAL MAJESTY'S
           Most humble and faithful servant,
             GENERAL JOMINI.

ST. PETERSBURG, 6th March, 1837.

TABLE OF CONTENTS.

ADVERTISEMENT.

THERE is perhaps some temerity in publishing a work upon war, at the moment when the apostles of perpetual peace alone are heard. But the industrial fever and the increase of riches expected from it, will not always be the only divinities to which societies will sacrifice. War is ever a necessary evil, not only for elevating or saving States, but yet for guaranteeing even the social body from dissolution, as the illustrious Ancillon has so judiciously observed in his brilliant picture of the revolutions of the European political system.

I am decided then upon the publication of this Summary, preceding it by some explanations upon the divers metamorphoses which it has undergone, and upon the motives which have prompted them.

His Majesty the Emperor having ordered the translation of my Treatise upon grand military operations, which had never been terminated as a complete work, I resolved first to fill the omissions in it by writing, in 1829, the Analytical Compend of the principal combinations of war. Executed rather precipitately, and conceived with the only object of serving as an appendant to my aforesaid Treatise, this first essay ought not to be considered as a separate work.

Called last year to give it some developments in order to make it serve for the instruction of an august prince, I rendered it sufficiently complete to accord it a *brevet d'emancipation* and to make of it a work independent of every other.

Several new articles on wars of opinion and national wars, upon the supreme direction of the operations of war, upon the *moral* of armies, upon lines of defense, upon zones and lines of operations, upon strategic reserves and transient bases, finally upon strategy in mountain warfare, on the manner of judging of the movements of the enemy and on grand detachments, have made of it an altogether new work, without speaking of the numerous ameliorations made in the other articles. Despite those changes, however, it appeared at first under its old title; but, yielding to the opinion of the publishers themselves, I was convinced of the necessity of giving it a new one in order to distinguish it from the partial essays which had preceded it. I named it then *Summary of the art of war, or new analytical compend, (precis de l'art de la guerre on nouveau tableau analytique,)* &c.

I give the second edition of this Summary, as my last word upon the great speculative combinations of war; it will be augmented still by several interesting articles on the bases and fronts of operations, on logistics (*la logistique*) or the practical art of moving armies, on remote grand invasions, on strategic lines, and manœuvres for turning lines of battle. Besides that, almost all the other articles have received new developments.

Not having been able to extend farther investigations upon the practical details of the art to which my limits and my object are equally opposed, I have indicated the works in which those details are found taught as far as feasible. It is to the proper application of the speculative combinations of grand warfare that all those details ought to tend ; but every one will naturally proceed to this application according to his character, his genius, his capacity ; here precepts become difficult and serve only as approximate landmarks.

I shall be happy if my readers find in this book the essential bases of those combinations, and if they accept it with kindness. I ask pardon for its style, above all for the constant repetition of technical expressions ; now that the art of making phrases has become so common, every one has the right to be difficult ; but the real merit of a didactic work, full of complicated definitions, is incontestably that of being perspicuous : now, to succeed in this, it is necessary to make up one's mind to those frequent repetitions of words and even of ideas which nothing could replace, and not to aim at elegance of phrases.

I shall be reproached perhaps with having pushed rather far the mania for definitions ; but I own I make a merit of it : for in order to lay down the basis of a science until now little known, it is essential to have an understanding before all upon the different denominations that must be given to the combinations of which it is composed ; otherwise it would be impossible to designate them and to qualify them. I do not dissemble that some of mine might yet be ameliorated, and as I have no pretension to infallibility, I am quite ready to be the first to admit those which should be more satisfactory. Finally, if I have often cited the same events as examples, I have decided to do so for the convenience of readers who have not all the campaigns in their memory or in their library. It will suffice thus to be acquainted with the events cited in order to render the demonstrations intelligible ; a greater series of proofs will not be wanting to those who are acquainted with modern military history.

G. J.

MARCH 6th, 1837.

TRANSLATORS' PREFACE.

In offering to the public a translation of the "*Precis de l'art de la Guerre*" of General Jomini, the undersigned are conscious that they have assumed a responsibility which should have devolved upon some officer of acknowledged professional attainments and experience, and the only motive they can plead in excuse of an enterprise so worthy of abler pens, is an earnest desire to see placed within the reach of every military reader, a book from which they themselves have derived so much interesting and valuable instruction.

It is indeed strange that the works of the greatest military historian and critic of the age, have not, long since, all been translated into the English language ; and the undersigned can only account for this omission upon the supposition that these works are necessarily very expensive, owing to the little encouragement they receive from the general reader. Otherwise, the circumstance that no one has yet been found in either the British or United States Army to undertake a labor which would reflect so much credit upon himself and render such an important service to the profession, must be regarded as reflecting upon the industry and enterprise of the officers of those armies.

It is possible that the undersigned are mistaken in their assumption that Jomini's works are not translated into English, but if so, they can only reply that, after the most careful inquiries of the book sellers in this country, they have been able neither to find, nor hear of any such translations.

It has often been urged, in discouragement of such enterprises, that those who are the most likely to read foreign military books prefer the originals to translations. This objection is opposed to our experience and common sense, and is founded at best upon the assumption that a translator is less capable and less careful to render the author's meaning than will be the majority of his readers. It is true that the French language, particularly, is a part of the course of instruction of every military school ; but it is equally true that it is lost almost as soon as it is attained when the necessity or the will for its acquisition ceases to operate. Moreover, military studies are by no means confined to military colleges; and in this country, especially, students in the art of war are to be found in nearly all the occupations of life.

To those students, whether in the military profession or not, the undersigned feel confident that they risk nothing in commending the book of which the following pages are an unpretending, but, as they trust, a faithful translation. Nothing has been added to, or subtracted from the original except a small map intended to illustrate the author's views upon lines of operations. This map and the single paragraph in the text referring thereto, have been omitted; the former increasing the cost of the work without a corresponding benefit. The same information can be conveyed to the intelligent reader by the ordinary school atlases of the country.

It is not for the undersigned to go into any particular details as to the merits of the author, either as a writer or as a soldier; they have been recognized by the highest military authorities in Europe, and rewarded in a conspicuous manner by the greatest military power in Christendom; a power remarkable for discovering this kind of merit and for turning it to its own account, whether found in a native or a foreigner.

General Jomini learned the art of war in the school of experience, the best and only finishing school of the soldier. He served with distinction in nearly all the campaigns of Napoleon, and it was mainly from the gigantic military operations of this matchless master of the art, that he was enabled to discover its true principles and to ascertain the best means of their application in the infinity of combinations which actual war presents. Those principles, he has laid down with so much clearness and precision, has illustrated them with so much force, and has supported them by so many incontestable facts drawn from the military history of all ages, that the reader rises from the perusal of his arguments with an irresistible conviction that he is at last possessed of the true secret of success in war, and that henceforth the chances of this great game of nations can be calculated with something approaching to certainty.

With such a guide then as Jomini, the military student is in no danger of being lost in the labaryuth of confused and conflicting maxims and systems of war; for with him everything is tried by the touchstone of a few distinct regulating principles, and whatever does not stand this test is unceremoniously rejected.

In conclusion, the most that the undersigned have to apprehend is, that they may not in every instance have rendered the author's ideas in all their force and integrity. If they shall be found to have succeeded in this, they will have accomplished all they could desire and more than they have a right to expect. Meanwhile they are not without hope that this, their first undertaking of the kind, will at least have the effect to stimulate their brother officers of the army and militia to similar and more important enterprises. We may then reasonably expect to see, ere long, those vast stores of military science and literature which are hoarded up in the French and German languages, opened in all their rich and varied profusion to the American student. A consummation all the more to be desired that the policy of our government, in accordance with the universal sentiment and practice of the Anglo-Saxon race, confides the defense of our territory to the citizen soldiery; thereby rendering it imperative to have choice works upon all the branches of the military art, in order, as far as possible, to make science supply the place of practical skill and experience in actual war.

O. F. WINSHIP.
E. E. McLEAN.

TROY, N. Y., August 15th, 1853.

NOTICE OF THE PRESENT THEORY OF WAR,

AND OF ITS UTILITY.

THE summary of the art of war, which I submit to the public, was written originally for the instruction of an august prince, and in view of the numerous additions which I have just made to it, I flatter myself that it will be worthy of its destination. To the end of causing its object to be better appreciated, I believe it my duty to precede it by a few lines upon the present state of the theory of war. I shall be forced to speak a little of myself and my works; I hope I shall be pardoned for it, for it would have been difficult to explain what I think of this theory, and the part which I may have had in it, without saying how I have conceived it myself.

As I have said in my chapter of principles, published by itself in 1807, *the art of war has existed in all time*, and *strategy* especially was the same under Cæsar as under Napoleon. But the art, confined to the understanding of great captains, existed in no written treatise. The books all gave but fragments of systems, born of the imagination of their authors, and containing ordinarily details the most minute (not to say the most puerile,) upon the most accessory points of tactics, the only part of war, perhaps, which it is possible to subject to fixed rules.

Among the moderns, Feuquires,[*] Folard and Puységur had opened the quarry: the first by very interesting, critical and dogmatical accounts; the second by his commentaries upon Polybus and his treatise upon the

---

[*] Feuquieres was not sufficiently appreciated by his cotemporaries, at least as a writer; he had the instinct of strategy as Folard, that of tactics, and Puy-ségur that of *la logistique.*

column; the third by a work which was, I believe, the first logistic essay, and one of the first applications of the oblique order of the ancients.

But those writers had not penetrated very far into the mine which they wished to explore, and in order to form a just idea of the state of the art in the middle of the 18th century, it is necessary to read what Marshal Saxe wrote in the preface to his Reveries.

" War," said he, " is a science shrouded in darkness, in the midst of which we do not move with an assured step; routine and prejudices are its basis, a natural consequence of ignorance.

" All sciences have principles, war alone has yet none; the great captains who have written do not give us any; one must be profound to comprehend them.

" Gustavus Adolphus has created a method, but it was soon deviated from, because it was learned by routine. There are then nothing but usages, *the principles of which are unknown to us.*"

This was written about the time when Frederick the Great preluded the Seven Years War by his victories of Hohenfriedberg, of Soor, &c. And the good Marshal Saxe, instead of piercing those obscurities of which he complained with so much justice, contented himself with writing systems for clothing soldiers in woolen blouses, for forming them upon four ranks, two of which to be armed with pikes; finally for proposing small field pieces which he named *amusettes*, and which truly merited that title on account of the humorous images with which they were surrounded.

At the end of the Seven Years War, some good works appeared; Frederick himself, not content with being a great king, a great captain, a great philosopher and great historian, made himself also a didactic author by his instructions to his generals. Guichard, Turpin, Maizeroy, Menil-Durand, sustained controversies upon the tactics of the ancients as well as upon that of their own time, and gave some interesting treatises upon those matters. Turpin commented Montécuculi and Vegetius; the Marquis de Silva in Piedmont, Santa Cruz in Spain, had also discussed some parts with success; finally d'Escremeville sketched a history of the art, which was not devoid of merit. But all that by no means dissipated the darkness of which the conqueror of Fontenoy complained.

A little later came Grimoard, Guibert and Lloyd: the first two caused progress to be made in the tactics of battles and in *la logistique.** This latter raised in his interesting memoirs important questions of strategy, which

---

* Guibert, in an excellent chapter upon *marches*, touches upon strategy, but he did not realize what this chapter promised.

he unfortunately left buried in a labyrinth of minute details on the tactics of formation, and upon the philosophy of war. But although the author has resolved none of those questions in a manner to make of them a connected . system, it is necessary to render him the justice to say that he first pointed out the good route. However, his narrative of the Seven Years War, of which he finished but two campaigns, was more instructive (for me at least,) than all he had written dogmatically.

Germany produced, in this interval between the Seven Years War and that of the Revolution, a multitude of writings, more or less extensive, on different secondary branches of the art, which they illumined with a faint light. Thielke and Faesch published in Saxony, the one, fragments upon castrametation, the attack of camps and positions, the other a collection of maxims upon the accessory parts of the operations of war. Scharnhorst did as much in Hanover; Warnery published in Prussia a pretty good work on the cavalry; Baron Holzendorf another on the tactics of manœuvres. Count Kevenhuller gave maxims upon field warfare and upon that of sieges. But nothing of all this gave a satisfactory idea of the elevated branches of the science.

Finally even Mirabeau who, having returned from Berlin, published an enormous volume upon the Prussian tactics, an arid repetition of the regulation for platoon and line evolutions to which some had the simplicity to attribute the greater part of the successes of Frederick! If such books have been able to contribute to the propagation of this error, it must be owned however that they contributed also to perfecting the regulations of 1791 on manœuvres, the only result which it was possible to expect from them.

Such was the art of war at the commencement of the 19th century, when Porbeck, Venturini and Bulow published some pamphlets on the first campaigns of the Revolution. The latter especially made a certain sensation in Europe by his Spirit of the System of Modern Warfare, the work of a man of genius, but which was merely sketched, and which added nothing to the first notions given by Lloyd. At the same time appeared also in Germany, under the modest title of an introduction to the study of the military art, a valuable work by M. de Laroche-Aymon, veritable encyclopedia for all the branches of the art, strategy excepted, which is there scarcely indicated; but despite this omission, it is none the less one of the most complete and recommendable of the classic works.

I was not yet acquainted with the last two books, when, after having quitted the Helvetic service as chief of battalion, I sought to instruct myself by reading, with avidity, all those controversies which had agitated

the military world in the last half of the 18th century; commencing
with Puységur, finishing with Menil-Durand and Guibert, and finding
every where but *systems* more or less complete of the tactics of battles,
which could give but an imperfect idea of war, because they all contra-
dicted each other in a deplorable manner.

I fell back then, upon works of military history in order to seek, in
the combinations of the great captains, a solution which those systems
of the writers did not give me. Already had the narratives of Frederick the Great commenced to initiate me in the secret which had caused
him to gain the miraculous victory of Leuthen (Lissa). I perceived that
this secret consisted in the very simple manœuvre of carrying the bulk of
his forces upon a single wing of the hostile army; and Lloyd soon came
to fortify me in this conviction. I found again, afterwards, the same cause
in the first successes of Napoleon in Italy, which gave me the idea *that by
applying, through strategy, to the whole chess-table of a war (à tout
l'échiquier d'une guerre), this same principle which Frederick had applied
to battles, we should have the key to all the science of war.*

I could not doubt this truth in reading again, subsequently, the campaigns of Turenne, of Marlborough, of Eugéne of Savoy, and in comparing them with those of Frederick, which Tempelhoff had just published
with details so full of interest, although somewhat heavy and by far too
much repeated. I comprehended then that Marshal de Saxe had been
quite right in saying that in 1750 there were no principles laid down upon
the art of war, but that many of his readers had also very badly inter-
preted his preface in concluding therefrom that he had thought that those
principles did not exist.

Convinced that I had seized the true point of view under which it was
necessary to regard the theory of war in order to discover its veritable
rules, and to quit the always so uncertain field of personal systems, I set
myself to the work with all the ardor of a neophyte.

I wrote in the course of the year 1803, a volume which I presented, at
first, to M. d'Oubril, Secretary of the Russian legation at Paris, then to
Marshal Ney. But the strategic work of Bulow, and the historical narrative of Lloyd, translated by Roux-Fazillac, having then fallen into my
hands, determined me to follow another plan. My first essay was a didactic treatise upon the orders of battle, strategic marches and lines of
operations; it was arid from its nature and quite interspersed with historical citations which, grouped by species, had the inconvenience of presenting together, in the same chapter, events often separated by a whole
century; Lloyd especially convinced me that the critical and argumenta-

tive relation of the whole of a war had the advantage of preserving connection and unity in the recital and in the events, without detriment to the exposition of maxims, since a series of ten campaigns is amply sufficient for presenting the application of all the possible maxims of war. I burned then my first work, and re-commenced, with the project of giving the sequel of the seven years war which Lloyd had not finished. This mode suited me all the better, as I was but twenty-four years old and had but little experience, whilst I was about to attack many prejudices and great reputations somewhat usurped, so that there was necessary to me the powerful support of the events which I should allow to speak, as it were, for themselves. I resolved then upon this last plan, which appeared moreover, more suitable to all classes of readers. Doubtless a didactic treatise would have been preferable, either for a public course, or for re-tracing with more ensemble the combinations of the science somewhat scattered in the narration of those campaigns ; but, as for myself, I confess I have profited much more from the attentive reading of a discussed campaign, than from all the dogmatic works put together ; and my book, published in 1805, was designed for officers of a superior grade, and not for schoolboys. The war with Austria supervening the same year, did not permit me to give the work all the care desirable, and I was able to execute but a part of my project.

Some years afterwards, the Arch Duke gave an introduction to his fine work by a folio volume on grand warfare, in which the genius of the master already showed itself. About the same time appeared a small pamphlet on strategy by Major Wagner, then in the service of Austria ; this essay, full of wise views, promised that the author would one day give something more complete, which has been realized quite recently. In Prussia, General Scharnhorst commenced also to sound those questions with success.

Finally, ten years after my first treatise on grand operations, appeared the important work of the Arch Duke Charles, which united the two kinds, didactic and historic ; this prince having at first given a small volume of strategic maxims, then four volumes of critical history on the campaigns of 1796 and 1799, for developing their practical application. This work, which does as much honor to the illustrious prince as the battles which he has gained, put the complement to the basis of the strategic science, of which Lloyd and Bulow had first raised the veil, and of which I had indicated the first principles in 1805, in a chapter upon lines of operations, and in 1807, in a chapter upon the fundamental principles of the art of war, printed by itself at Glogau in Silesia.

The fall of Napoleon, by giving up many studious officers to the leisures of peace, became the signal for the apparition of a host of military writings of all kinds. General Rogniat gave matter for controversy in wishing to bring back the system of the legions, or of the divisions of the republic, and in attacking the somewhat adventurous system of Napoleon. Germany was especially fertile in dogmatic works; Xilander in Bavaria, Theobald and Muller of Wurtemberg, Wagner, Decker, Hoyer and Valintini in Prussia, published different books, which presented substantially but the repetition of the maxims of the Arch Duke Charles and mine, with other developments of application.

Although several of these authors have combatted my chapter on central lines of operations with more subtlety than real success, and others have been, at times, too precise in their calculations, we could not refuse to their writings the testimonials of esteem which they merit, for they all contain more or less of excellent views.

In Russia, General Okounief treated of the important article of the combined or partial employment of the three arms, which makes the basis of the theory of combats, and rendered thereby a real service to young officers.

In France, Gay-Vernon, Jacquinot de Presle and Roquancourt, published courses which were not wanting in merit.

Under these circumstances, I was assured by my own experience, that there was wanting, to my first treatise, a collection of maxims like that which preceded the work of the Arch Duke; which induced me to publish, in 1829, the first sketch of this analytical compend, adding to it two interesting articles upon the military policy of States.

I profited of this occasion to defend the principles of my chapter on lines of operations, which several writers had badly comprehended, and this polemic brought about at least more rational definitions, at the same time maintaining the real advantages of central operations.

A year after the publication of this analytical table, the Prussian General Clausewitz died, leaving to his widow the care of publishing posthumous works which were presented as unfinished sketches. This work made a great sensation in Germany, and for my part I regret that it was written before the author was acquainted with my summary of the Art of War, persuaded that he would have rendered to it some justice.

One cannot deny to General Clausewitz great learning and a facile pen; but this pen, at times a little vagrant, is above all too pretentious for a didactic discussion, the simplicity and clearness of which ought to be its first merit. Besides that, the author shows himself by far too skeptical in point of military science ; his first volume is but a declamation against all theory of war, whilst the two succeeding volumes, full of theoretic maxims, proves that the author believes in the efficacy of his own doctrines, if he does not believe in those of others.

As for myself, I own that I have been able to find in this learned labyrinth but a small number of luminous ideas and remarkable articles ; and far from having shared the skepticism of the author, no work would have contributed more than his to make me feel the necessity and utility of good theories, if I had ever been able to call them in question ; it is important simply to agree well as to the limits which ought to be assigned them in order not to fall into a pedantry worse than ignorance ;* it is necessary above all to distinguish the difference which exists between *a theory of principles* and *a theory of systems.*

It will be objected perhaps that, in the greater part of the articles of this summary, I myself acknowledge that there are few absolute rules to give on the divers subjects of which they treat ; I agree in good faith to this truth, but is that saying there is no theory ? If, out of forty-five articles, some have ten positive maxims, others one or two only, are not a 150 or 200 rules sufficient to form a respectable body of strategic or tactical doctrines ? And if to those you add the multitude of precepts which suffer more or less exceptions, will you not have more dogmas than necessary for fixing your opinions upon all the operations of war ?

At the same epoch when Clausewitz seemed thus to apply himself to sapping the basis of the science, a work of a totally opposite nature appeared in France, that of the Marquis de Ternay, a French *émigré* in the service of England. This book is without contradiction, the most complete that exists on the tactics of battles, and if it falls sometimes into an excess contrary to that of the Prussian general, by prescribing, in doctrines details of execution often impracticable in war, he cannot be denied a truly remarkable merit, and one of the first grades among tacticians.

I have made mention in this sketch only of general treatises, and not of particular works on the special arms. The books of Montalembert, of Saint-Paul, Bousmard, of Carnot, of Aster, and of Blesson, have caused progress to be made in the art of sieges and of fortification. The writings of Laroche-Aymon, Muller and Bismark, have also thrown light upon many questions regarding the cavalry. In a journal with which, unfortu-

---

* An ignorant man, endowed with a natural genius, can do great things ; but the same man stuffed with false doctrines studied at school, and crammed with pedantic systems, will do nothing good unless he forget what he had learned.

nately, I was not acquainted until six years after its publication, the latter has believed it his duty to attack me and my works, because I had said, on the faith of an illustrious general, that the Prussians had reproached him with having copied, in his last pamphlet, the unpublished instructions of the government to its generals of cavalry. In censuring my works, General Bismark has availed himself of his rights, not only in virtue of his claim to reprisals, but because every book is made to be judged and controverted. Meanwhile, instead of replying to the reproach, and of giving utterance to a single grievance, he has found it more simple to retaliate by injuries, to which a military man will never reply in books, which should have another object than collecting personalities. Those who shall compare the present notice with the ridiculous pretensions which General B——— imputes to me, will judge between us.

It is extraordinary enough to accuse me of having said that the art of war did not exist before me, when in the chapter of Principles, published in 1807, of which I have before spoken, and which had a certain success in the military, world, the first phrase commenced with these words: "*the art of war has existed from time immemorial.*" * * * What I have said is, that there were no books which proclaimed the existence of general principles, and made the application of them through strategy to all the combinations of the theatre of war: I have said that I was the first to attempt that demonstration, which others improved ten years after me, without, however, it being yet complete. Those who would deny this truth would not be candid.

As for the rest, I have never soiled my pen by attacking personally studious men who devote themselves to science, and if I have not shared their dogmas, I have expressed as much with moderation and impartiality: it were to be desired that it should ever be thus. Let us return to our subject.

The artillery, since Gribeauval and d'Urtubie has had its Aide-Memoire, and a mass of particular works, in the number of which are distinguished those of Decker, Paixhans, Dedon, Hoyer, Ravichio and Bouvroy. The discussions of several authors, among others those of the Marquis de Chambray and of General Okounieff upon the fire of infantry. Finally, the dissertations of a host of officers, recorded in the interesting military journals of Vienna, of Berlin, of Munich, of Stutgard and of Paris, have contributed also to the successive progress of the parts which they have discussed.

Some essays have been attempted towards a history of the art, from the ancients down to our time   Tranchant Laverne has done so with spirit and sagacity, but incompletely. Cario Nisas, too verbose with regard to the ancients, mediocre for the epoch from the revival to that of the Seven Years War, has completely failed on the modern system. Roquancourt has treated the same subjects with more success. The Prussian Major Ciriaci and his continator have done still better. Finally, Captain Blanch, a Neapolitan officer, has made an interesting analysis of the different periods of the art as written and practised.

After this long list of modern writers, it will be judged that Marshal de Saxe, if he were to return among us, would be much surprised at the present wealth of our military literature, and would no longer complain of the darkness which shrouds the science. Henceforth good books will not be wanting to those who shall wish to study, for at this day we have principles, whereas, they had in the 18th century only methods and systems.

Meanwhile, it must be owned, to render theory as complete as possible, there is an important work wanting, which, according to all appearances, will be wanting yet a long time; it is a thoroughly profound examination of the four different systems followed within a century past: that of the Seven Years War; that of the first campaigns of the Revolution; that of the grand invasions of Napoleon; finally, that of Wellington. From this investigation it would be necessary to deduce a mixed system, proper for regular wars, which should participate of the methods of Frederick and of those of Napoleon; or, more properly speaking, it would be necessary to develop a double system for ordinary wars of power against power, and for grand invasions. I have sketched a view of this important labor, in article 24, chapter III: but as the subject would require whole volumes, I have been obliged to limit myself to indicating the task to him who should have the courage and the leisure to accomplish it well, and who should at the same time be fortunate enough to find the justification of those mixed doctrines, in new events which should serve him as tests.

In the meantime, I will terminate this rapid sketch by a profession of faith upon the polemics of which this compend and my first treatise have been the subject. In weighing all that has been said for or against, in comparing the immense progress made in the science for the last thirty years, with the incredulity of M. Clausewitz, I believe I am correct in concluding that the ensemble of my principles and of the maxims which are derived from them, has been badly comprehended by several writers; that some have made the most erroneous application of them; that others have drawn from them exaggerated consequences which have never been able to enter my head, for a general officer, after having assisted in a dozen campaigns, *ought to know that war is a great drama, in which a thousand*

*physical or moral causes operate more or less powerfully, and which cannot
be reduced to mathematical calculations.*

But, I ought equally to avow without circumlocution, that twenty
years of experience have but fortified me in the following convictions:

" There exists a small number of fundamental principles of war, which
could not be deviated from without danger, and the application of which,
on the contrary, has been in almost all time crowned with success.

" The maxims of application which are derived from those principles
are also small in number, and if they are found sometimes modified according to circumstances, they can nevertheless serve in general as a compass to the chief of an army to guide him in the task, always difficult
and complicated, of conducting grand operations in the midst of the
noise and tumult of combats.

" Natural genius will doubtless know how, by happy inspirations, to
apply principles as well as the best studied theory could do it; but a
simple theory, disengaged from all pedantry, ascending to causes without
giving absolute systems, based in a word upon a few fundamental maxims, will often supply genius, and will even serve to extend its development by augmenting its confidence in its own inspirations.

" Of all theories on the art of war, the only reasonable one is that
which, founded upon the study of military history, admits a certain number of regulating principles, but leaves to natural genius the greatest part
in the general conduct of a war without trammeling it with exclusive
rules.

" On the contrary, nothing is better calculated to kill natural genius
and to cause error to triumph, than those pedantic theories, based upon
the false idea that war is a positive science, all the operations of which
can be reduced to infallible calculations.

" Finally, the metaphysical and skeptical works of a few writers will
not succeed, either, in causing it to be believed that there exists no rule for
war, for their writings prove absolutely nothing against maxims supported
upon the most brilliant modern feats of arms, and justified by the reasoning even of those who believe they are combatting them."

I hope, that after these avowals, I could not be accused of wishing to
make of this art a mechanism of determined wheelworks, nor of pretending on the contrary that the reading of a single chapter of principles is
able to give, all at once, the talent of conducting an army. In all the
arts, as in all the situations of life, *knowledge* and *skill* are two altogether
different things, and if one often succeed through the latter alone, it is

never but the union of the two that constitutes a superior man and assures complete success. Meanwhile, in order not to be accused of pedantry, I hasten to avow that, by *knowledge*, I do not mean a vast erudition; it is not the question to *know a great deal* but to *know well;* to know especially what relates to the mission appointed us.

I pray that my readers, well penetrated with these truths, may receive with kindness this new summary, which may now, I believe, be offered as the book most suitable for the instruction of a prince or a statesman.

———

I have not thought it my duty to make mention, in the above notice, of the military historical works which have signalized our epoch, because they do not in reality enter into the subject which I have to treat. However, as those of our epoch have also contributed to the progress of the science, in seeking to explain causes of success, I shall be permitted to say a few words on them.

Purely military history is of a thankless and difficult kind, for, in order to be useful to men of the art, it requires details not less dry than minute, but necessary in order to cause positions and movements to be judged accurately. Therefore, until the imperfect sketch of the Seven Years War which Lloyd has given, none of the military writers had come out of the beaten track of official narratives or of panegyrics more or less fatiguing.

The military historians of the 18th century who had held the first rank were, Dumont, Quincy, Bourcet, Pezay, Grimoard, Retzow and Tempelhoff; the latter especially had made of it a kind of school, although his work is a little overcharged with the details of marches and encampments : details very good, without doubt, for fields of combat, but very useless in the history of a whole war, since they are represented almost every day under the same form.

Purely military history has furnished, in France as in Germany, writings so numerous since 1792, that their nomenclature alone would form a pamphlet. I shall, nevertheless, signalize here the first campaigns of the Revolution by Grimoard; those of General Gravert; the memoirs of Suchet and of Saint-Cyr; the fragments of Gourgaud and of Montholon; the great enterprise of victories and conquests under the direction of General Beauvais; the valuable collection of battles by Colonel Wagner and that of Major Kaussler; the Spanish War by Napier; that of

Egypt by Reynier; the campaigns of Suwaroff by Laverne; the partial narratives of Stutterhein and of Labaume.*

History at once political and military offers more attractions, but is also much more difficult to treat and does not accord easily with the didactic species; for, in order not to destroy its narration, one should suppress precisely all those details which make the merit of a military narrative.

Until the fall of Napoleon, politico-military history had had for many centuries but a single remarkable work; that of Frederick the Great, entitled *History of my time.*† This species, which demands at the same time an elegant style and a vast and profound knowledge of history and politics, requires also a military genius sufficient for judging events accurately. It would be necessary to describe the relations or the interests of states like Ancillon, and recount battles like Napoleon or Frederick, to produce a *chef-d'œuvre* of this kind. If we still await this *chef-d'œuvre*, it must be owned that some good works have appeared within the last thirty years; in this number we must put the war in Spain of Foy; the summary of military events of Mathieu H. Dumas, and the manuscripts of Fain; although the second is wanting in firm points of view, and the last sins through too much partiality. Afterwards come the works of M. Ségur the younger, a writer full of genius and of wise views, who has proved to us, by the history of Charles VIII, that with a little more nature in his style he might bear away from his predecessors the historic palm of the great age which yet awaits its Polybus. In the third rank we shall place the histories of Toulongeon and of Servan.‡

Finally, there is a third kind, that of critical history, applied to the principles of the art, and more especially designed to develop the relations of events with those principles. Feuquières and Lloyd had indicated the road without having had many imitators until the Revolution. This last species, less brilliant in its forms, is for that perhaps only the more useful in its results, especially where criticism is not pushed to that rigor which would often render it false and unjust.

---

* We might cite yet the interesting narratives of Saintine, of Mortonval. of Lapenne Lenoble. Lafaille, as well as those of the Prussian Major Spahl upon Catalonia, of Baron Volderndorf on the campaigns of the Bavarians, and a host of other writings of the same nature.

† Several political historians, like Ancillon, Ségur the elder, Karamsin, Guichardin, Archenholz. Schiller Daru, Michaud and Salvandy. have recounted also with talent many operations of war, but they cannot be counted in the number of military writers.

‡ I do not speak of the political and military life of Napoleon recounted by himself because it has been said that I was the author of it; with regard to those of Norvins and of Tibaudeau, they are not military.

Within the last twenty years, this half didactic, half critical history has made more progress than the others, or at least it has been cultivated with more success, and has produced incontestable results. The campaigns published by the Arch-Duke Charles, those anonymous ones of General Muffling, the partial relations of Generals Pelet, Boutourlin, Clausewitz,* Okounieff, Valentini, Ruhle; those of Messrs. de Laborde, Koch, de Chambrai, Napier; finally, the fragments published by Messrs. Wagner and Scheel, in the interesting journals of Berlin and Vienna, have all more or less assisted in the development of the science of war. Perhaps I may be permitted also to claim a small part in this result in favor of my long critical and military history of the wars of the Revolution, and of the other historical works which I have published, for, written especially to prove the permanent triumph of the application of principles, those works have never failed to bring all the facts to this dominant point of view, and in this respect at least, they have had some success; I invoke in support of this assertion, the *piquante* critical analysis of the war of the Spanish Succession, given by Captain Dumesnil.

Thanks to this concurrence of didactic works and of critical history, the teaching of the science is no longer so difficult, and the professors who would be embarrassed at this day, in making good courses with a thousand examples to support them, would be sad professors. It must not be concluded, however, that the art has arrived at that point that it cannot make another step towards perfection. There is nothing perfect under the sun!!! And if a committee were assembled under the presidency of the Arch Duke Charles or Wellington, composed of all the strategic and tactical notabilities of the age, together with the most skillful generals of engineers and artillery, this committee could not yet succeed in making a perfect, absolute and immutable theory on all the branches of war, especially on tactics!

---

* The works of Clausewitz have been incontestably useful. although it is often less by the ideas of the author. than by the contrary ideas to which he gives birth. They would have been more useful still. if a pretentious and pedantic style did not frequently render them unintelligible. But if. as a didactic author. he has raised more doubts than he has discovered truths, as a critical historian. he has been an unscrupulous plaigerist. pillaging his predecessors. copying their reflections, and saying evil afterwards of their works, after having travestied them under other forms. Those who shall have read my campaign of 1799. published ten years before his, will not deny my assertion, for there is not one of my reflections which he has not repeated.

SUMMARY OF THE ART OF WAR.

DEFINITION OF THE ART OF WAR.

THE art of war, as is generally conceived, is divided into five purely military branches : *strategy, grand tactics, logistics, (la logistique,) the art of the engineer and elementary tactics (la tactique de détail) ;* but there is an essential part of this science which has, until now, been improperly excluded from it, it is *the policy of war.** Although this belongs more especially to the science of the statesman, than to that of the warrior, since we have imagined to separate the gown from the sword, it cannot be denied, however, that if it be useful to a subaltern general, it is indispensable to every general-in-chief of an army : it enters into all the combinations which can determine a war, and into those of the operations which may be undertaken; hence it belongs necessarily to the science of which we treat.

From these considerations, it seems that the art of war is, in reality, composed of six very distinct parts.

The 1st is the policy of war.

The 2d is strategy, or the art of properly directing masses upon the the-

---

* There exists, to my knowledge, but a very few works upon this matter ; the only one even which bears the title, is the *Policy of War*, by Hay du Chatelet, (1769.) It is there found that an army, wishing to pass a stone bridge, should cause it to be visited by carpenters and architects, and that Darius would not have been conquered if, instead of opposing all his forces to Alexander, he had fought him with but the half ! Astonishing maxim of military policy. Maizeroy has had some ideas quite as vague, in what he calls the dialetics of war. Lloyd has gone fartherest into the question ; but how much his work leaves to be desired, and how much it has been belied by the events from 1792 to 1815 !

atre of war, whether for the invasion of a country, or for the defence of one's own.

The 3d is the grand tactics of battles and combats.

The 4th is logistics, or the practical application of the art of moving armies.*

The 5th is the art of the engineer, the attack and defence of places.

The 6th is elementary tactics.

We might even add to these the philosophy, or moral part of war; but it appears more suitable to unite it in the same section with the policy.

We now propose to analyze the principal combinations of the first four branches; our object not being to treat on elementary tactics, nor the art of the engineer, which makes a science by itself.

In order to be a good infantry, cavalry and artillery officer, it is useful to know all those branches equally well; but to become a general, or a distinguished staff officer, this knowledge is indispensable. Fortunate are those who possess it, and the governments which know how to put them in their place!

---

* I shall explain in article 41, the motives which had determined me to speak first of *la logistique* under a more secondary point of view; I shall be thanked, I hope, for the new relations under which I have considered it.

CHAPTER I.

THE POLICY OF WAR.

We shall give this title to the combinations by which a statesman should judge when a war is suitable, opportune, or even indispensable, and to determine the divers operations which it will necessitate in order to attain its end.

A state is led to war:

To claim rights or to defend them ;

To satisfy great public interests, such as those of commerce, of industry, and of all that concerns the prosperity of nations;

To sustain neighbors whose existence is necessary to the security of the state, or to the maintainance of the political equilibrium ;

To fulfil stipulations of alliances, offensive and defensive ;

To propagate doctrines, to suppress or defend them ;

To extend its influence or its power by acquisitions necessary to the safety of the state ;

To save menaced national independence ;

To avenge outraged honor;

Through a mania for conquests, and through a spirit of invasion

It is presumed that these different kinds of war have some influence on the nature of the operations which they will require, in order to arrive at the end proposed, upon the magnitude of the efforts which it will be necessary to make to that effect, and upon the extent of the enterprises which we shall be at liberty to form.

Without doubt each of those wars can be offensive or defensive; even he who should be the aggressor will, perhaps, be anticipated, and reduced to defend himself, and the attacked will be able to take immediately the initiative if he has known how to prepare himself for it. But there will yet be other complications arising from the respective situation of the parties.

1. War may be made singly against another power.

2. It may be made singly against several states allied to each other.

3. It may be made with a powerful ally against a single enemy.

4. A party may be the principal in the war, or only an auxiliary.

5. In this latter case, it may intervene from the commencement of the war, or in the midst of a struggle already more or less engaged.

6. The theatre of war may be transported into the enemy's country, into an ally's territory, or into one's own territory.

7. If a war of invasion be made, it may be neighboring or remote, wise and well considered, or extravagant.

8. A war may be national, either against us, or against the enemy.

9. Finally, there exist civil and religious wars equally dangerous and deplorable.

War once decided upon, without doubt it should be made according to the principles of the art, but it will be admitted, however, that there may be a great difference in the nature of the operations that shall be undertaken, according to the divers chances to be run. For example, two hundred thousand French wishing to subject Spain, aroused against them as one man, would not manœuvre like two hundred thousand French wishing to march upon Vienna, or any other capital, there to dictate peace (1809) ; and they would not do the guerillas of Mina the honor to combat them in the same manner that they fought at Borodino.* Without going so far for examples, could it be said that the two hundred thousand French of whom we have just spoken, ought equally to march upon Vienna, whatever should be the moral condition of the governments, and of the population between the Rhine and the Inn, and between the Danube and the Elbe? It is conceived that a regiment ought always to fight very nearly the same, but it is not so with generals-in-chief.

To these different combinations, which belong more or less to diplomatic policy, may be added others, which have relation only to the conduct of armies. We shall give to the latter the name of *military policy*, or the *philosophy of war*, for they belong exclusively neither to diplomacy, nor to strategy, and are none the less for that of the highest impor-

---

* This, in reply to Major Proketsch, who, despite his well known erudition, believed himself able to sustain that the policy of war could have no influence upon its operations and that war should always be made in the same manner.

tance in the plans of the cabinet, as well as in those of a general of an army. Let us commence by analyzing the combinations which relate to diplomacy.

ARTICLE I.

OFFENSIVE WARS FOR CLAIMING RIGHTS.

When a state has rights over a neighboring country, it is not always a reason for claiming them by main force. The convenience of the public interest must be consulted before determining thereto.

The most just war will be that which, founded upon incontestable rights, shall yet offer to the state positive advantages, proportionate to the sacrifices and the chances to which it is exposed. But there present themselves unfortunately, in our day, so many rights contestable and contested, that the greater part of wars, although founded in appearance upon heritages, testaments and marriages, are in reality no more than wars of convenience. The question of the Spanish succession under Louis XIV, was the most natural in right, since it reposed on a solemn testament supported by family ties, and by the general wish of the Spanish nation; nevertheless it was one of the most contested by all Europe; it produced a general coalition against the legitimate legatee.

Frederick II, profiting by a war of Austria against France, evokes old parchments, enters Silesia by main force, and seizes upon that rich province, which doubles the strength of the Prussian monarchy. The success and importance of this resolution made it a master stroke; for, if Frederick had not succeeded, it would have been unjust however to blame him for it: the magnitude of the enterprise and its opportuneness could excuse such an irruption, as far as an inroad is excusable.

In such a war, there are no rules to give; *to know how to wait and to profit is everything.* Offensive operations ought to be proportioned to the end proposed. The first is naturally that of occupying the provinces claimed; the offensive can afterwards be pushed according to circumstances and the respective forces, to the end of obtaining the cession desired, by menacing the adversary at home ; all depends upon the alliances which one will have been able to secure, and upon the military means of the two parties. The essential in such an offensive, is to have a scrupulous care not to awaken the jealousy of a third party, who might come to the succor of the power which it is proposed to attack. It is for policy to forsee this case, and to parry an intervention, by giving all the guaranties necessary to one's neighbors.

ARTICLE II.

WARS DEFENSIVE IN POLICY AND OFFENSIVE MILITARILY.

A state attacked by its neighbor, who claims old rights upon a province, rarely decides to yield it without combat, and through pure conviction of those rights, it prefers to defend the territory demanded of it, which is always more honorable and more natural. But, instead of remaining passively on the frontier, awaiting its aggressor, it may suit it to take the initiative or offensive ; all depends then on the reciprocal military positions.

There is often an advantage in making a war of invasion ; there is often one also in awaiting the enemy at home. A power, strongly constituted within itself, which has no cause for divisions, nor fear from a third aggression upon its own territory, will always find a real advantage in carrying hostilities upon the enemy's soil. In the first place, it will avoid the ravaging of its provinces, then it will carry on the war at the expense of its adversary, finally it will put all the moral chances on its side, by exciting the ardor of its people, and striking the enemy on the contrary with stupor, from the commencement of the war. Meanwhile, under the purely military point of view, it is certain that an army operating in its own country, upon an *échiquier* of which all the natural or artificial obstacles are in its favor or in its power, where all its manœuvres are free and seconded by the country, by its inhabitants and its authorities, may expect great advantages.

These truths, which seem incontestable, are susceptible of being applied to every kind of war ; but if the principles of strategy are immutable, it is not the same with the truths of the policy of war, which undergo modifications through the moral condition of the people, the localities, and the men who are at the head of armies and of states. These are the divers shades which have given credit to the gross error that there are no fixed rules in war. We hope to prove that the military science has principles that could not be violated without defeat, when a skillful enemy has to be dealt with ; it is the political and moral part of war alone which offers differences that cannot be subjected to any positive calculation, but which are nevertheless susceptible of being subjected to the calculations of probabilities. It is necessary then to modify plans of operations according to circumstances, although in order to execute those plans it is necessary to remain faithful to the principles of the art. It will be admitted, for example, that a war against France, Austria or Russia, could not be combined like a war against the Turks, or any Oriental nation, whose brave but undisciplined hordes, are susceptible of no order, no rational manœuvre, nor of any steadiness under reverses.

ARTICLE III.

WARS OF CONVENIENCE.

The invasion of Silesia by Frederick II, was a war of convenience; that of the Spanish succession equally so.

There are two kinds of wars of convenience : those which a powerful state may undertake to give itself natural limits, to obtain an extremely important political or commercial advantage ; those which it may make for diminishing the power of a dangerous rival, or for hindering its increase. These latter enter, it is true, into wars of intervention ; it is not probable that a state will attack singly a dangerous rival ; it will do it scarcely but by coalition, in the course of conflicts arising from relations with a third.

All these combinations being within the domain of policy rather than of war, and the military operations entering into the categories which we shall treat, we shall pass over in silence the little that might be said on this subject.

ARTICLE IV.

WARS WITH OR WITHOUT ALLIES.

It is natural that every war with an ally should be preferable to a war without allies, supposing besides, all the other chances equal. Doubtless a great State will be more sure of succeeding, than two weaker States which should ally themselves against it ; but yet is it better to have the reinforcement of a neighbor than to struggle alone ; not only do you find yourself reinforced by the contingent which he furnishes you, but the enemy is enfeebled in a still greater proportion, for he will not have need merely of a considerable corps to oppose to that contingent, he will be obliged still to watch portions of his territory which otherwise would have been secure from insult. It will be seen, in the following paragraph, that there are no allies so insignificant as to be disdained with impunity by a never so formidable State ; a truth which, for the rest, could not be called in question without denying all the teachings of history.

ARTICLE V.

WARS OF INTERVENTION.*

Of all wars that a State can undertake, the most suitable, the most advantageous for it, is certainly the war of intervention in a struggle already engaged. The cause for it will easily be comprehended : a State which thus intervenes, puts in the balance all the weight of its power, in common with the power in favor of which it interferes ; it enters therein when it wishes, and when the moment is most opportune for giving decisive action to the means it brings.

---

* This article was written in 1829.

There are two kinds of. intervention : the first is that which a State seeks to introduce in the interior affairs of its neighbors, the second is to intervene seasonably in its exterior relations.

Publicists have never been agreed as to the right of internal intervention ; we shall not dispute with them upon the point of right, but we will say that the fact has often happened. The Romans owed a part of their grandeur to those interventions, and the empire of the English Company in India is no otherwise explained. *Interior* interventions do not always succeed ; Russia owes in part the development of her greatness to that which her sovereigns knew how to bring into the affairs of Poland ; Austria, on the contrary, came near being ruined for having attempted to interfere in the affairs of the French revolution. These kinds of combinations are not in our province.

Intervention in the *external relations* of one's neighbors, is more legitimate, more natural and more advantageous perhaps. In fact, doubtful as it is, that a State has the right to meddle with what passes within the interior jurisdiction of its neighbors, equally certain is it that it will be accorded the right to oppose whatever of trouble and disorder the latter may carry outside, which could reach it.

Three motives may engage us to intervene in the exterior wars of our neighbors. The first is a treaty of alliance offensive and defensive, which engages us to sustain an ally. The second, is the maintainance of what is termed the political equilibrium : a combination of modern ages, as admirable as it appears simple, and which was, nevertheless, too often forgotten by those even who should have been its most fervent apostles.* The third motive, is to profit by a war engaged, not only with the object of preventing bad consequences from it, but also for causing the advantages of it to turn to the profit of him who intervenes.

History offers a thousand examples of powers which have decayed for having forgotten these truths : " that a State declines when it suffers the immoderate aggrandizement of a rival State, and that a State, though it even be of the second order, can become the arbiter of the political balance, when it knows how seasonably to put a weight in that balance."

---

* To believe in the possibility of a perfect equilibrium. would be absurd. It can be but a question of a relative and approximate balance. The principle of the maintainance of the equilibrium ought to be the basis of policy. as the art of putting in action the most possible forces on the decisive point. is the regulating principle of war. Of course, the maritime equilibrium is an essential portion of the European political balance.

This is enough to demonstrate the advantage of wars of intervention under an elevated political point of view.

With regard to the military point of view, it is plain that an army, appearing as a third party in a struggle already established, becomes preponderant. Its influence will be all the more decisive, in proportion as its geographical situation shall have importance relatively to the positions of the two armies already at war. Let us cite an example. In the winter of 1807, Napoleon crossed the Vistula, and ventured under the walls of Königsberg, having Austria in his rear, and the whole mass of the Russian empire before him. If Austria had caused a hundred thousand men to debouch from Bohemia upon the Oder, it would have been finished, in all probability, with the omnipotence of Napoleon; his army would have been too fortunate in opening itself a way to regain the Rhine, and everything leads to the belief that it would not have succeeded. Austria preferred waiting to have its army increased to four hundred thousand men; it took then the offensive with this formidable mass two years after and was conquered; whilst that with a hundred thousand men engaged at the proper moment, she would have decided more surely and more easily the fate of Europe.

If interventions are of different natures, the wars which result from them are also of several kinds.

1. You intervene as an auxiliary, in consequence of anterior treaties, and by means of secondary corps, the strength of which is determined.

2. You intervene as a principal party, to sustain a more feeble neighbor, whose States you go to defend, which carries the theatre of war far from your frontiers.

3. You intervene also as principal party, when you are in the neighborhood of the theatre of war, which supposes a coalition of several great powers against one.

4. You intervene in a struggle already begun, or before the declaration of war.

When you intervene only with a moderate contingent, in consequence of stipulated treaties, you are but an accessory, and the operations are directed by the principal power. When you intervene by coalition and with an imposing army, the case is different.

The military chances of those wars are various. The Russian army, in the Seven Years War, was, in reality, an auxiliary of Austria and France; it was, however, a principal party in the north, until the occupation of

Old Prussia by its troops; but when Generals Fermor and Soltikoff conducted the army into Brandenburg, then it no longer acted but in the Austrian interest; those troops, thrown far from their base, were at the mercy of a good or bad manœuvre of their allies.

Such remote excursions expose to dangers, and are ordinarily very delicate for the general of an army. The campaign of 1799, and of 1805, furnished sad proofs of this, which we shall recall in treating of those expeditions under the military aspect, (art. 30.)

It results from these examples, that those remote interventions often compromise the armies which are charged with them; but on the other hand, one has the advantage that his own country at least could not be so easily invaded, since the theatre of war is carried far from his frontiers; what makes the misfortune of a general, is here a benefit for the State.

In wars of this nature, the essential thing is, *to select a chief who is at once a politician and a military man; to stipulate well with your allies the part which each is to take in the operations; finally to determine an objective point which shall be in harmony with the common interests;* it is by the neglect of these precautions that the greater part of coalitions have failed, or struggled with difficulty against a power less strong as a whole, but more united.

The third kind of war of intervention, or of seasonableness, indicated above, that in a word which consists in intervening with all one's power, and in proximity with his frontiers, is more favorable than the others. It is the situation in which Austria would have been found in 1807, had she known how to profit from her position; it is also that in which she was found in 1813. Adjacent to Saxony, where Napoleon had just united his forces, taking in reverse, even the front of the French operations on the Elbe, she put two hundred thousand men in the balance, with almost a certainty of success; the empire of Italy and her influence over Germany, lost through fifteen years of reverses, were re-conquered in two months. Austria had, in this intervention, not only the political chances, but moreover the military chances in her favor: a double result, which indicates the highest degree of advantages to which the chiefs of a State can aspire.

The cabinet of Vienna succeeded all the more surely, as its intervention was not merely of the nature of those mentioned in article 3, that is to say, sufficiently contiguous to her frontiers to permit the greatest possible development of her strength, but because still she intervened in a struggle already commenced, in which she entered with all the weight of her means, and at the instant which suited her.

This double advantage is so decisive that we have seen, not only the great monarchies, but even very small States, become preponderant, by knowing how to seize this fitness of time. Two examples will suffice to prove this. In 1552, the Elector Maurice, of Saxony, dared to declare himself openly against Charles Fifth, master of Spain, of Italy, and of the Germanic empire; against Charles, victorious over Francis First, and pressing France in his firm grasp. This movement, which transported the war to the heart of the Tyrol, arrested the great man who menaced to swallow up everything. In 1706, the Duke of Savoy, Victor Amedius, declaring against Louis XIV, changes the face of affairs in Italy, and brings back the French army upon the banks of the Adige, to the walls of Turin, where it experienced the bloody catastrophe which immortalized the Prince Eugene. How insignificant statesmen will appear to those who have meditated upon these two events, and upon the great questions to which they apply!

We have said enough upon the advantages of these opportune interventions; the number of examples could be multiplied to infinity, but that could add nothing to the conviction of our readers.

ARTICLE VI.

WARS OF INVASION THROUGH A SPIRIT OF CONQUEST OR OTHER CAUSES.

It is important before all, to remark that there are two very different kinds of invasions: those which attack neighboring powers, and those which are carried to a distance, traversing vast countries, the population of which might be more or less neutral, doubtful or hostile.

Wars of invasion, made through a spirit of conquest, are not unfortunately always the most disadvantageous; Alexander, Cæsar, and Napoleon, in the half of his career, have only too well proved this. However, those advantages have limits fixed by nature even, and which it is necessary to guard against crossing, because one falls then into disastrous extremes.

Cambyses in Nubia, Darius among the Scythians, Crassus and the Emperor Julian among the Parthians, finally, Napoleon in Russia, furnish bloody testimony to those truths. It must be owned, nevertheless, the mania for conquest was not always the only motive of the conduct of the latter; his personal position, and his struggle with England urged him to enterprises, the evident object of which was to come out victorious in this struggle; love of war and its hazards was manifest in him, but he was still drawn on by necessity to bend under England or to triumph in his efforts. One might say that he was sent into this world to teach gen erals of armies and statesmen all that which they ought to avoid; his vic tories are lessons of skill, activity and audacity; his disasters are moderating examples imposed by prudence.

A war of invasion without plausible motives, is an outrage against humanity, like those of Zingis Khan; but when it can be justified by a great interest and a laudable motive, it is susceptible of excuses, if not even of approbation.

The invasion of Spain, executed in 1808, and that which had place in 1823, differ certainly as much in their object as in their results; the first, dictated by a spirit of invasion, and conducted with cunning, menaced the existence of the Spanish Nation, and was fatal to its author; the second, combatting only dangerous doctrines, and looking to general interests, succeeded all the better that it found a decisive point of support in the majority of the people whose territory it for a moment violated. We shall not undertake to judge them according to natural right; such questions belong to the political right of intervention. Far from discussing them, we merely present them here as proofs that an invasion is not always of the Zingis Khan species. The first which we have just cited, contributed to the ruin of Napoleon; the other replaced France in the relative situation to Spain which she ought never to have lost.

Let us entreat Heaven to render those invasions as rare as possible; but let us acknowledge that a State does better in invading its neighbors than in allowing itself to be attacked. Let us acknowledge also that the most sure means against fostering the spirit of conquest and usurpation, is to know how to intervene at the proper moment for placing barriers to it.

Supposing then, a war of invasion resolved upon and justified. not upon an immoderate desire of conquest, but upon sound State reasons, it is important to measure this invasion by the object proposed and by the obstacles which may be encountered in it, either from the country itself, or from its allies.

An invasion against a people exasperated and ready for all sacrifices, who can expect to be sustained in men and money by a powerful neighbor, is a hazardous enterprise; the war of Napoleon in Spain, plainly proves this; the wars of the French Revolution in 1792, 1793 and 1794, demonstrate it still better; for if this last power was taken, less unprovided than Spain, neither had it a great alliance for assisting in its defence; it was assailed by all Europe, both by land and by sea.

In view of such examples, of what interest could dry maxims be? It is from the history of those great events that it is necessary to draw rules of conduct.

The invasions of the Russians in Turkey, presented, in some respects, the same symptoms of national resistance; meanwhile it must be owned that the conditions were different; the religious hatred of the Ottomans might make them fly to arms; but settled in the midst of a Greek population twice as numerous as themselves, the Turks did not find, in a general insurrection, that support which they would have found if all the empire had been mussulman, or if they had mingled the interests of the Greeks with those of the conquerors, as France knew how to do with the people of Alsace, the best Frenchmen of the kingdom: in this case they would have been stronger; but there would have been no longer any religious fanaticism.

The war of 1828, has proved that the Turks were respectable only on their frontiers, where were found united their most warlike militia, whilst the interior is falling into ruins.

When an invasion has nothing to fear from the people, and when it is applied to a bordering State, then there are strategic laws which decide in regard to it and which must above all be consulted; this is what rendered the invasions of Italy, of Austria, and of Prussia, so prompt. Those military chances will be treated of in Article 30.

But when on the contrary, an invasion is remote and is to traverse vast countries to arrive at its end, it is policy much more than strategy to which it is necessary to have recourse in order to prepare for its success. In fact, the first condition of this success will always be the sincere and devoted alliance of a power in the neighborhood of that it is wished to attack, since there will be found in its frank and interested concurrence, not only an increase of strength, but yet a solid base for establishing your depôts beforehand, and for basing your operations, and finally, an assured refuge in case of need. Now, in order to expect such an alliance, it is necessary that the power upon which you would count, have the same interest as yourself in the success of the enterprise.

If policy is especially decisive in remote expeditions, that is not saying that it is without influence even upon contiguous invasions, for a hostile intervention may arrest the most brilliant career of success. The invasions of Austria in 1805 and 1809, would probably have taken another turn if Prussia had intervened in them ; that of the north of Germany in 1807, depended equally as much upon the cabinet of Vienna. Finally, that of Romelia in 1829, assured by measures of a wise and moderate policy, could have had fatal results if care had not been taken to remove every chance of an intervention by those negociations.

ARTICLE VII.

WARS OF OPINION.

Although wars of opinion, national struggles and civil wars are sometimes confounded in the same conflict, they differ meanwhile sufficiently from each other to make it our duty to treat of them separately.

Wars of opinion present themselves under three aspects : they are limited to an intestine struggle, that is to say, to civil war, or they are at the same time interior and exterior ; it may happen also, but rarely, that they be confined to a conflict with the foreigner.

Wars of opinion or doctrine between two States,* belong also to the class of wars of intervention, for they will always result either from doctrines which a party would impose upon its neighbors through propagandism, or from doctrines which it will be wished to combat and to put down, which leads in every case to intervention.

These wars, whether they arise from religious dogmas or from political dogmas, are not for that the less deplorable, for, as well as national wars,

---

* I speak here of wars between two powers and not of intestine wars, which make a separate article.

they always excite violent passions which render them hateful, cruel and terrible.

The wars of Islamism, those of the Crusades, the Thirty Years War, those of the League, all offer, with more or less force, the symptoms of their species. Doubtless, religion was sometimes a political pretext or means, rather than an affair of dogmas. It is probable that the successors of Mahomet troubled themselves more with extending their empire than with preaching the Koran, and it was doubtless not for making the church of Rome triumph, that Philip II sustained the League of France. We agree even with M. Ancelot, that Louis IX, when he made his crusade to Egypt, thought more of the commerce of India than of conquering the Holy Sepulcher.

When it is thus, the dogma is not merely the pretext, it is also sometimes a powerful means, for it fulfills the double object of exciting the ardor of one's own people, and of creating for himself a party. For example, the Swedes, in the Thirty Years War, and Philip II in France, had in the country an auxiliary more powerful than their own armies, But it happens also that the dogma which is combatted for has none but enemies, and then the struggle is terrible. This was the case with the struggles of Islamism and the Crusades.

Wars of political opinions present nearly the same categories. It is true that in 1792, extravagant societies were seen who really thought to spread the famous declaration of the rights of man over all Europe, and governments, justly alarmed, took up arms doubtless with the only idea of rolling back the lava of this volcano into its crater and of stifling it therein.

But the means were not happy, for war and aggression are bad measures for arresting an evil which lies entirely in passions excited by a momentary paroxysm, all the less durable for being the most violent. Time is the true remedy against all bad passions, and against anarchical doctrines. An enlightened nation may submit an instant to the yoke of an exasperated and factious multitude, but those storms pass away and reason returns. Attempting to arrest such a multitude by a foreign force is very like attempting to stay a mine at the moment when the match has just reached the powder and caused its explosion. Is it not wiser to allow the mine to spring and to fill the funnel afterwards than to be exposed to being blown up with it?

A profound study of the French Revolution has convinced me that if the Girondins and the National Assembly had not been menaced by armaments, they never would have dared to lay a sacrilegious hand upon the feeble but venerable Louis XVI. The Gironde would never have been crushed by the Mountain but for the reverses of Dumouriez and the menaces of invasion. And if the parties had been left to jostle each other at their ease, it is probable that the National Assembly, instead of giving place to the terrible convention, would have returned by degrees to the restoration of good monarchical doctrines tempered according to the wants and immemorial usages of France.

Considered under the military relation, those wars are terrible, for the invading army attacks not only the military forces of the enemy, but his exasperated masses. It may be objected, it is true, that the violence of a party will procure of itself a support by the creation of a contrary party; it is incontestable that this result is more certain still than in religious struggles; but if the exasperated party hold all the resources of the public strength, the armies, the places, the arsenals, and if it support itself upon masses the most numerous, what can the support of a party destitute of all those means effect? What were a hundred thousand Vendéans and a hundred thousand federalists able to do for the coalition of 1793?

History offers but a single example of a struggle like that of the French revolution, and it seems to demonstrate all the danger of attacking an excited nation. Meanwhile, the bad conduct of the military operations could have contributed also to this result, and in order to be able to deduce certain maxims from this war, it would be necessary to know what would have happened if, after the flight of Dumouriez, the allies, instead of destroying the fortresses with cannon shots, and of taking possession of them in their name, had written to the commandants of those fortresses, that they wanted neither France, nor its places, nor its brave army, and had marched with two hundred thousand men upon Paris. Perhaps, they would there have restored the monarchy, but perhaps also they would not have returned, unless an equal force had protected their retreat upon the Rhine. This is what would be difficult to decide, since the trial was never made, and everything would have depended in this case upon the course which the French army would have taken.

The problem then presents two equally grave hypotheses; the campaign of 1793 has resolved it but in one sense: it would be difficult to resolve it in the other; it is to experience alone that like solutions belong. With regard to the military rules to be given for these wars, they are nearly the same as those for national struggles; they differ, however, in one capital point; it is that in the latter, the country ought to be occupied and subjected, the places besieged and reduced, the armies destroyed, all the provinces subjugated; whereas, in affairs of opinion, it is not so much the object to subdue the country, and to occupy one's self with accessories; there are necessary sufficient means for moving directly to the end, without halting at any consideration of detail, and endeavoring, above all things, to shun whatever could alarm the nation as to its independence and the integrity of its territory.

The war made in Spain in 1823, and of which we have spoken in the preceding article, is an example to cite in favor of those truths, and in opposition to that of the French Revolution. Doubtless the conditions were somewhat different, for the French army of 1792, was composed of elements more solid than that of the radicals of the island of Leon. The war of the Revolution was at once a war of opinion, a national and civil war, whilst, if the first war with Spain, in 1808, was altogether national, that of 1823 was a partial struggle of opinions without nationality : hence the enormous difference in the results.

The expedition of the Duke d'Angoulême was, moreover, well conducted in regard to execution.* Far from amusing himself with taking places, his army acted conformably to the maxims above mentioned ; after having pushed briskly to the Ebro, it was divided here to cut off at their sources, all the elements of the hostile strength, because it well knew that, seconded by a majority of the inhabitants of the country, it could be divided without danger. If it had followed the instructions of the ministry, who prescribed to it to subdue methodically all the country and places situated between the Pyrenées and the Ebro, in order to base itself militarily, it would, perhaps, have failed in its object, or at least, rendered the struggle long and bloody, by rousing the national pride with the idea of an occupation like that of 1807. But, emboldened by the good reception of all the population, it comprehended that it was an operation more political than military, and that it was a question of leading on rapidly to the end. Its conduct, very different from that of the allies in 1793, merits the reflection of all those who should have like expeditions to direct. It was, therefore, in less than three months under the walls of Cadiz.

If what is passing at this day in the Peninsula, attests that policy knew not how to profit from its success, and to found a suitable and solid

---

* There were some faults committed under the triple relation, political, military and administrative but they were, it is said, the work of coteries which are never wanting at every general head quarters. For the rest, the ensemble of the operations did honor to General Guilleminot, who directed them under the prince, and who, according to the Spaniards, could claim the principal part of the success.

order of things, the fault was neither in the army nor its chiefs, but in the Spanish government, which delivered up to violent reactionary counsels, was not equal to its mission. Arbiter between two hostile interests, Ferdinand blindly threw himself into the arms of that one of the parties which affected a great veneration for the throne, but which counted to make the most of the royal authority for its own profit, without troubling itself about future consequences. Society remained divided into two hostile camps, which it would not have been impossible to calm and to bring together in course of time. Those camps have come anew to blows, as I had predicted at Verona in 1823 ; a great lesson, from which it appears for the rest, that no person is disposed to profit in this beautiful and too unhappy country, although history is not wanting in examples to attest that violent reactions are, no more than revolutions, proper elements for constructing and consolidating. God grant that there may result from this frightful conflict, a throne strong and respected, equally free of all factions, and supported upon a disciplined army as well as the general interests of the country : a throne, finally, capable of rallying this incomprehensible Spanish nation which, from qualities not less extraordinary than its defects, was ever a problem for those even whom we should have thought in the best condition to judge it.

ARTICLE VIII.

NATIONAL WARS.

National wars, of which we have already been forced to say a few words in speaking of those of invasion, are the most formidable of all ; this name can be given only to those which are made against a whole population, or at least against the majority of that population, animated by a noble fire for its independence; then every step is disputed by a combat; the army which enters into such a country holds in it only the field where it encamps ; its supplies can only be obtained at the point of the sword, its convoys are every where menaced or carried away.

This spectacle of the spontaneous movement of a whole nation is rarely seen, and if it presents something grand and generous which commands admiration, the consequences of it are so terrible that, for the sake of humanity, we should desire never to witness it.*

Such a movement may be produced by the most opposite causes: a serf people can be raised in mass at the voice of its government, and its masters even set the example by putting themselves at its head, when they are animated by a noble love for their sovereign and for their country; in the same manner a fanatic people arm themselves at the voice of their monks, and a people excited by political opinions, or by the sacred love they bear for their institutions, precipitate themselves to meet the enemy in order to defend what they hold most dear.

The command of the sea enters for much in the results of a national invasion; if the people aroused has a great extent of coast, and is master of the sea, or in alliance with a power which commands it, then its resistance is centupled, not only through the facility had for feeding the fire of insurrection, of alarming the enemy on all points of the country which he occupies, but still by the difficulties which will be interposed to its supplies by the maritime route.

The nature of the country contributes also a great deal to the facility of a national defense; mountainous countries are always those in which a people is most formidable. After those come countries cut up by vast forests.

The struggle of the Swiss against Austria and against the Duke of Burgundy; those of the Catalans in 1712 and in 1809; the difficulties which the Russians experience in subduing the people of Caucasus; finally, the reiterated efforts of the Tyroleans, demonstrated sufficiently that mountain people have always resisted longer than those of the plains, as much through their character and manners, as from the nature of those countries. Defiles and great forests favor, as well as cliffs, this kind of partial defense; and the Bocage of La Vendée, become so justly celebrated, proves that every difficult country, even though it be but intersected with hedges, ditches and canals, produces a like result when it is bravely defended.†

---

* It will be seen farther on that this general rising must not be compounded with the national defense prescribed by institutions and regulated by governments.

† The hedges and ditches which separate properties in La Vendée are so large that they make of each farm a veritable redoubt, the obstacles of which the inhabitants of the country alone are practiced in overcoming. Ordinary hedges and ditches, although useful, could not have the same importance.

The obstacles which a regular army encounters, in wars of opinion as well as in national wars, are immense and render very difficult the mission of the General charged with conducting it. The events which we have just cited, as also the struggle of the Low Countries against Philip II, and that of the Americans against the English, furnish evident proofs of this : but the much more extraordinary struggle of La Vendée against the victorious Republic ; those of Spain, Portugal and the Tyrol against Napoleon ; finally those, so desperate of the Morea against the Turks, and of Navarre against the forces of Queen Christine, are examples more striking still.

It is especially when the hostile populations are supported by a considerable nucleus of disciplined troops, that such a war offers immense difficulties.* You have but an army, your adversaries have an army and a whole people raised in mass or at least in good part ; a people turning every thing into arms, of which each individual conspires for your ruin, of which all the members, even the non-combattants have an interest in your perdition, and favor it by every means in their power. You occupy little but the soil upon which you encamp ; beyond the limits of this camp, every thing becomes hostile to you, and multiplies by a thousand means the difficulties which beset you at every step.

Those difficulties become especially exaggerated when the country is much cut up by natural accidents : each armed inhabitant knows the smallest footpaths and their terminations ; he finds every where a parent, a brother, a friend, who seconds him : the chiefs are acquainted in the same manner with the country, and learning instantly the least of your movements, can take the most efficacious measures for defeating your projects, whilst that, deprived of all information, out of condition to risk detachments of scouts for obtaining it, having no other support than your bayonets, nor security but in the concentration of your columns, you act like blind men ; each of your combinations becomes an illusion, and when, after the best concerted movements, the most rapid and fatiguing marches, you think you have reached the goal of your efforts and are about to strike in a clap of thunder, you find no other traces of the enemy than the smoke of his bivouacs. Very like Don Quixot, you tilt thus

---

* Without the assistance of regular disciplined armies, popular risings would always be easily put down ; they could procrastinate, like the remnants of La Vendée, but could never prevent invasion or conquest.

against wind-mills, whilst your adversary is throwing himself upon your communications, breaking up the detachments left to guard them, surprising your convoys, your depôts, and making upon you a disastrous war in which you must necessarily succumb in the end.

I myself have had, in the war with Spain, two terrible examples of this nature. When Ney's Corps replaced that of Soult at Corunna I had cantoned the companies of the artillery train between Betanzos and Corunna, in the midst of four brigades which were distant from them two to three leagues; no Spanish troops showed themselves within twenty leagues around; Soult still occupied Santiago de Compostella, Maurice Mathieu's division was at Ferrol and at Lugo; that of Marchand at Corunna and Betanzos; meanwhile one fine night those companies of the train disappeared, men and horses, without our ever being able even to learn what had become of them; a single wounded Corporal escaped, and assured us that peasants, conducted by priests or monks, had massacred them.

Four months afterwards, Marshal Ney marched, with a single division to the conquest of the Asturias, and descended by the valley of the Navia, whilst Kellerman debouched from Leon by the route of Oviedo. A part of the corps of Romana, which guarded the Asturias, defiled by the slopes of the heights which enclosed the valley of the Navia, at a league at most from our columns, without the Marshal knowing a word of it; at the moment when the latter reached Gijon, the army of Romana fell in the midst of the isolated division of Marchand, which, dispersed to guard all Galicia, came near being taken separately, and only escaped by the prompt return of the Marshal to Lugo. The war with Spain offered a thousand scenes as lively as this. All the gold of Mexico would not have sufficed for procuring the French any information, and all that was given them was but a lure to make them fall the more easily into snares.

No army, however inured to war it may be, could struggle with success against such a system applied to a great people, unless it were by forces so formidable that it could occupy strongly all the important points of the country, cover its own communications, and still furnish active corps sufficiently large for beating the enemy wherever he should present himself. But when this enemy himself has a tolerably respectable regular army for serving as a nucleus to the resistance of the population, what forces would not be necessary in order to be at once superior every where, and to assure remote communications against numerous corps?

It is particularly important to study well the war in the Spanish Peninsula, in order to appreciate all the obstacles which a general and brave troops may encounter in the conquest or the occupation of a country thus roused. What efforts of patience, of courage and of resignation were not necessary to the phalanxes of Napoleon, of Masséna, of Soult, of Ney, and of Suchet, in order to hold out for six whole years against three or four hundred thousand armed Spaniards and Portuguese, seconded by the regular armies of the Wellingtons, the Beresfords, the Blakes, the Romanas, Cuestas, Castagnos, Redings and Balesteros !

The means of succeeding in such a war are difficult enough ; to display in the first place a mass of forces proportionate to the resistance and to the obstacles which are to be encountered ; to calm the popular passions by all the means possible ; to use them now and then ; to display a great mixture of policy, of mildness and severity, and above all great justice ; such are the first elements of success. The examples of Henry IV in the wars of the League, of Marshal Berwick in Catalonia, of Suchet in Aragon and in Valencia, of Hoche in Vendee, are models of different kinds, but which may be employed according to circumstances with the same success. The admirable order and discipline, maintained by the armies of Generals Diebitsch and Paskévitch in the late war, are also models to cite, and contributed not a little to the success of their enterprises.

The extraordinary obstacles which a national struggle presents to an army wishing to invade a country, have led some speculative minds to desire that there might never be any other wars, because then they would become more rare, and conquest becoming thus more difficult, would offer less attractions to ambitious chiefs.

This reasoning is more specious than just, for, in order to admit its consequences, it would be necessary to be able always to inspire populations with the disposition for flying to arms ; afterwards it would be necessary to be certain that henceforth there would be no wars but those of conquest, and that all those legitimate, but secondary wars, which have for object only the maintainance of the political equilibrium, or the defense of public interests, should be banished for ever. Otherwise, what means would there exist of knowing when and how it would be suitable to excite a national war ? For example, if a hundred thousand Germans passed the Rhine, and penetrated into France with the primitive object of opposing the conquest of Belgium by this power, but with no other project of ambition against it, would it be necessary to raise en masse, all the population of Alsace, of Lorraine, of Champagne, of Burgundy, men, women and children, to make a Saragassa of every little walled town, and thus to bring about through reprisals the murder, pillage, and burning of the whole country ? If this be not done, and th-

German army occupy those provinces at the end of certain successes, who will answer that it do not then seek to appropriate a part of them, although in the beginning it had no such intention?

The difficulty of answering these two questions thus proposed, would seem to militate in favor of national wars; but are there no means of repelling such an aggression without recourse to risings in mass, and a war of extermination? Does there not exist a medium between those struggles of populations, and the ancient regular wars, made only by permanent armies? Does it not suffice, in order to defend a country well, to organize a militia or *landwehr* which, clad in uniform, and called by government to intervene in the struggle, would regulate thus the part which the populations were to take in the controversy, would not put them entirely out of the pale of the laws of nations, and would place just limits to a war of extermination?

For my part, I shall answer affirmatively, and in applying this mixed system to the questions above propounded, I would guarantee that fifty thousand French regular troops, supported by the national guards of the East, would have an easy affair with that German army which should have crossed the Vosges; for, reduced to fifty thousand men by a host of detachments, it would have, on arriving near the Meuse, or in the Argonne, more than a hundred thousand men on its back. It is precisely in order to succeed in this *juste milieu*, that we have presented as an invariable maxim, the necessity of preparing for the army good national reserves; a system which offers the advantage of diminishing the expenses in time of peace, and of assuring the defense of the country in case of war. This system is nothing else than that employed by France in 1792, imitated by Austria in 1809, and by all Germany in 1813. In view of this I should not have expected the misplaced attacks of which it has been the subject.

I shall resume this discussion by affirming that without being an Utopian philanthropist or a *condottieri*, one can wish that wars of extermination might be banished from the code of nations, and that the national defences, through a regulated militia, could suffice henceforth, with good political alliances, for assuring the independence of States.

As a military man, preferring loyal and chivalric war to organized assassination, I own, that if it were necessary to choose, I should ever prefer the good time when the French and English guards politely invited each other to fire first, as was the case at Fontenoy, to the frightful epoch when the curates, the women and the children organized over the whole soil of Spain, the murder of isolated soldiers.

If, in the eyes of General R * * *, this opinion is yet a blasphemy, I shall console myself without difficulty, at the same time acknowledging that there is a mean term between these two extremes, which answers all wants, and which is precisely the system which has cost me so many unjust criticisms.

— •

-

ARTICLE IX.

———

CIVIL AND RELIGIOUS WARS.

———

Intestine wars, when they are not connected with a foreign quarrel, are ordinarily the result of a struggle of opinions, of political or religious party spirit. In the middle ages, they were oftener the shocks of feudal coteries. The most deplorable wars are, without doubt, those of religion. It is comprehended that a State may combat its own children, to prevent political factions which enfeeble the authority of the throne and the national strength ; but that it should slaughter its subjects in order to force them to pray in Latin or in French, and to acknowledge the supremacy of a foreign pontiff, is what reason can hardly conceive. Of all kings, the most to be pitied was, without contradiction, Louis XIV, driving away a million of industrious protestants, who had put his grandfather upon the throne, a protestant like them. Wars of fanaticism are horrible when mingled with external wars ; they are frightful, even when they are only family quarrels. The history of France in the time of the League, will be a lasting lesson for nations and kings ; it is difficult to believe that this people, yet so noble and chivalric under Francis First, should have fallen in twenty years into an excess of brutality so deplorable.

To give maxims for these kinds of wars would be absurd ; there is but one upon which sensible men are agreed, this is to unite the two sects, or the two parties, in order to drive away the foreigner who should wish to meddle in the quarrel, then to explain to each other with moderation, to the end of mingling the rights of the two parties into a pact of reconcili-

ation.   In fact, the intervention of a third power in a religious dispute,
could never be other than an act of ambition.*

It is conceived that governments intervene in good faith against a political phrenzy, the dogmas of which may menace the social order ; although ordinarily those fears are exaggerated and serve often as a pretext
it is possible for a State to believe itself truly so menaced at home.   But
in the matter of theological disputes, it is never the case, and the intervention of Philip II in the affairs of the League, could have no other object than the division or subjection of France to his influence, to the end
of dismembering her by degrees.

ARTICLE X.

DOUBLE WARS, AND THE DANGER OF UNDERTAKING
TWO WARS AT ONCE

The celebrated maxim of the Romans, never to undertake two great
wars at a time, is too well known and too well appreciated to require any
demonstration of its wisdom.

A state may be constrained to make war against two neighboring peoples ; but circumstances must be very inauspicious, when it does not find
in this case, an ally which comes to its succor for its own preservation,
and the maintainance of the political equilibrium.   It is rare also, that
those two peoples leagued against it, have the same interest in the war,
and engage therein all their means ; now, if one of them be only an auxiliary, it will already be but an ordinary war.

---

* Colonel Wagner, in translating the first edition of my Compend, has found my assertion too absolute, basing himself upon the support given by Gustavus Adolphus to the
Protestants of Germany, and by Elizabeth to those of France ; a support dictated according to him by a wise policy. Perhaps he is right, for the pretention of Rome and its
church to universal dominion, was flagrant enough to give fear to the Swedes, and even to
the English ; but this was not the case with Philip II ; besides, ambition can well have
entered into the calculations of Gustavus and Elizabeth

Louis XIV, Frederick the Great, the Emperor Alexander and Napoleon, sustained gigantic struggles against coalesced Europe. When such struggles arise from voluntary aggressions which could be avoided, they indicate a capital fault on the part of him who engages in them, but if they arise from imperious and inevitable circumstances, they must at least be remedied, by seeking to oppose means or alliances capable of establishing a certain ponderation of the respective forces.

The great coalition against Louis XIV, caused, as we have said, by his projects upon Spain, took, nevertheless, its origin in the preceding aggressions which had alarmed all his neighbors. He could oppose to leagued Europe only the faithful alliance of the Elector of Bavaria, and the more equivocal one of the Duke of Savoy, who himself was not slow to increase the number of the coalitionists. Frederick sustained war against the three most powerful monarchies on the continent, with the support alone of subsidies from England, and of fifty thousand auxiliaries from six different small States; but the division and feebleness of his adversaries were his best allies.

Those two wars, like that sustained by the Emperor Alexander in 1812, were almost impossible to avoid.

France had all Europe on her hands in 1793, in consequence of the extravagant provocations of the Jacobins, of the exaltation of the two parties, and of the Utopias of the Girondins who braved, they said, all the kings of the earth in counting on the support of the English squadrons! The result of those absurd calculations was a frightful disorder, from which France extricated herself as by a miracle.

Napoleon is then in a manner the only one of modern sovereigns who has voluntarily undertaken two, and even three frightful wars at once, those with Spain, with England and with Russia; but yet did he support himself in the latter, with the concurrence of Austria and of Prussia, without speaking even of Turkey and of Sweden, upon which he counted with too much confidence, so that this enterprise was not so adventurous on his part as has generally been believed, judged according to the turn of affairs.

It is seen from what precedes, that there is a great distinction to be made between a war undertaken against a single State, in which a third should come to take a part by means of an auxiliary corps, and two wars conducted simultaneously at the most opposite extremities of a country, against two powerful nations which should engage all their resources to overwhelm him who should have menaced them. For instance, the double

hand to hand struggle of Napoleon in 1809, with Austria and Spain, sus
tained by England, was much more grave for him, than if he had had to do
only with Austria, assisted by any auxiliary corps whatever, fixed by
known treaties. Struggles of this last kind enter in the category of ordinary wars.

It must be concluded then in general, that double wars should be avoided
as much as possible; and that when the case happens, it is even better to
dissemble the wrongs of one of our neighbors until the opportune moment
arrives for requiring the redress of the just grievances of which we might
have to complain. However, this rule could not be absolute; the
respective forces, the localities, the possibility of finding allies also on our
side for re-establishing a sort of equilibrium between the parties, are so
many circumstances which will have an influence on the resolutions of a
State which should be menaced with a like war. We shall have accomplished our task, by pointing out at once the danger and the remedies
which can be opposed to it.

CHAPTER II.

MILITARY POLICY, OR THE PHILOSOPHY
OF WAR.

Wᴇ have already explained what is understood under this denomination. They are all the moral combinations which relate to the operations of armies. If the political combinations of which we have just spoken are also moral causes which have an influence upon the conduct of a war, there are others which, without belonging to diplomacy, are none the more combinations of strategy or of tactics. We could then give them no denomination more rational than that of military policy or philosophy of war.[*]

We shall stop at the first, for, although the true acceptation of the word philosophy may be applied to war as well as to the speculations of metaphysics, so vague an extent has been given to this acceptation, that we experience a kind of embarrassment in uniting those two words. It will be recollected then that by *policy of war*, I understand all the relations of diplomacy with war, whilst that *military policy* designates only the military combinations of a State or of a general.

Military policy may embrace all the combinations of a project of war,

---

[*] Lloyd has well treated this subject in the 2d and 3d parts of his Memoirs; his chapters on the General and on the Passions are remarkable; the 4th part is also interesting; but it wants completeness, and his points of view are not always just. The Marquis de Cham bray has also treated this subject, and not without some success, although he has found opponents; moreover, he has only walked in the footsteps of M. Tranchant de Laverne

other than those of diplomatic policy and strategy; as the number of them is pretty large, we could not devote a special article to each, without going beyond the limits of this compend, and without deviating from our object, which is not to give a complete treatise of those matters, but merely to point out their relations with military operations.

In fact, we may range in this category the passions of the people against whom we are going to combat; their military system; the means of first line and of reserve; the resources of their finances; the attachment they bear to their government, or to their institutions. Besides that, the character of the chief of the State; that of the chiefs of the army, and their military talents; the influence which the cabinet or the councils of war exercise upon the operations, from the distance of the capitol; the system of war which controls in the hostile staff; the difference in the constitutive force of the armies, and in their armament; the geography and the military statistics of the country where one is to penetrate; finally, the resources and the obstacles of every nature which may there be encountered, are so many important points to consider, and which are, nevertheless, neither of diplomacy nor of strategy.

There are no fixed rules to give on such matters, unless it be that a government should neglect nothing to arrive at a knowledge of these details, and that it is indispensable to take them into consideration in the plans of operations which it shall propose to itself. We are about to sketch, however, the principal points which ought to guide in these kinds of combinations.

ARTICLE XI.

MILITARY STATISTICS AND GEOGRAPHY.

By the first of these sciences is understood as perfect a knowledge as possible, of all the elements of power, and all the means of war of the enemy we are called upon to combat; the second consists in the topographical and strategical description of the theatre of war, with all the obstacles which art and nature may offer to enterprises ; the examination of the permanent decisive points which a frontier or even the whole extent of a country presents. Not only the public ministry, but the chief of the army and of the staff should be initiated into this knowledge, under pain of finding cruel mistakes in their calculations, as often happens, even in our day, notwithstanding the immense progress which civilized nations have made in all the sciences, statistical, political, geographical and topographical. I will cite two examples of them of which I was a witness ; in 1796, the army of Moreau, penetrating into the Black Forest, expected to find terrible mountains, defiles and forests, which the ancient Hercinius called to memory with frightful circumstances ; we were surprised after having climbed the cliffs of that vast plateau, which look upon the Rhine, to see that those steeps and their counterforts form the only mountains, and that the country, from the sources of the Danube to Donauwerth, presents plains as rich as fertile.

The second example, still more recent, dates in 1813 ; the whole army of Napoleon, and that great captain himself, regarded the interior of Bohemia as a country cut up with mountains, whereas, there exists scarcely one more flat in Europe, as soon as you have crossed the belt of secondary mountains with which it is surrounded, which is the affair of a march.

All the European military men had nearly the same erroneous opinions upon the Balkan, and upon the real force of the Ottomans in the interior. It seems that general orders were given from Constantinople to cause this enclosure to be regarded as almost impregnable, and as the palladium of the empire, an error which, in my quality of inhabitant of the Alps, I have never shared. Prejudices, not less deeply rooted, led to the belief, that a people, all the individuals of which went unceasingly armed, would form a redoubtable militia, and would defend themselves to the last extremity. Experience has proved, that the ancient institutions which placed the *elite* of the Janizaries in the frontier cities of the Danube, had rendered the population of those cities more warlike than the inhabitants of the interior, who make war against the unarmed rayahs ; this phantasmagoria has been appreciated at its just value ; it was but an imposing curtain which nothing sustained, and the first enclosure forced, the prestige has disappeared. In truth, the projects of reform of the Sultan Mahmoud had exacted the overthrow of the ancient system without giving time to substitute a new one for it, so that the empire found itself taken unprepared ; experience has proved, however, that a multitude of brave men, armed to the teeth, does not still constitute a good army, nor a national defense.

Let us return to the necessity of being well acquainted with the geography and military statistics of an empire. Those sciences are wanting, it is true, in elementary treatise, and remain yet to be developed. Lloyd, who has made on them an essay in the fifth part of his Memoirs, in describing the frontiers of the great states of Europe has not been happy in his sayings and his predictions ; he sees obstacles everywhere ; he presents, among others, as impregnable, the frontiers of Austria upon the Inn, between the Tyrol and Passau, where we have seen Moreau and Napoleon manœuvre, and triumph with armies of a hundred and fifty thousand men in 1800, 1805 and 1809. The greater part of those reasonings are open to the same criticism ; he has seen things too materially.

But if these sciences are not publicly taught, the archives of the European staffs must be rich with valuable documents for teaching them, at least in the special schools of this corps.

In waiting for some studious officer to profit from those documents, published or unpublished, for giving the public a good military and strategical geography, it may, thanks to the immense progress which topography has made in our day, be supplied in part, by means of the excellent maps published within the last twenty years in all countries. At the epoch of the commencement of the French revolution, topography was yet in its infancy ; excepting the semi-topographical map of Cassi, there was scarcely any but the works of Bakenberg, which would have merited that name. The Austrian and Prussian staffs had, meanwhile, good schools already, which from time to time, have borne their fruits ; the maps recently published at Vienna, Berlin, Munich, Stuttgard, Paris, as well as those of the interesting institute of Herder, at Friburg in Brisgau, assure to future generals immense resources, unknown to their predecessors.

Military statistics is scarcely better known than geography ; there are only a few vague and superficial tables, in which are thrown at hazard the number of armed men and vessels which a State possesses, as well as the revenues that it is supposed to have, which is far from constituting entirely a science necessary for combining operations. Our aim is not to examine here thoroughly those important matters, but to indicate them as means of success in those enterprises which it should be desired to form.

ARTICLE XII.

DIVERS OTHER CAUSES WHICH HAVE AN INFLUENCE UPON THE SUCCESS OF A WAR.

If the excited passions of the people which we are to combat are a great enemy to conquer, a general and a government ought to employ all their efforts to calm those passions. We could add nothing to what we have said on this subject in speaking of national wars.

On the other hand, a general ought to do every thing to electrify his soldiers, and to give them that same transport which it is important to allay in his adversaries. All armies are susceptible of the same enthusiasm, the motives and the means only differ according to the spirit of the nations. Military eloquence has made the subject of more than one work ; we will only indicate it as a means. The proclamations of Napoleon ; those of General Paskevitsch ; the addresses of the ancients to their soldiers ; those of Suwarof to men still more simple, are models of different kinds. The eloquence of the juntas of Spain, and the mira-racles of the Madôna del Pilar, have led to the same results by very op♦ posite roads. In general, a cherished cause, and a chief who inspires confidence by past victories, are great means for electrifying an army and facilitating its successes.

Some military men have contested the advantages of enthusiasm, and preferred to it imperturbable sang-froid in combats. Both have advantages and inconveniences which it is impossible to mistake ; enthusiasm leads to the greatest actions, the difficulty is to sustain it constantly ; and when an excited troop is discouraged, disorder is introduced into it more rapidly.

The greater or less activity and audacity in the chiefs of the respective armies is an element of success or of reverse which could not be subjected to rules.

A cabinet and a general-in-chief ought to take into consideration the intrinsic value of their troops, and their constitutive force compared with that of the enemy. A Russian general, commanding troops the most solidly constituted in Europe, may undertake every thing in open field against undisciplined and disordered masses, however brave elsewhere may be the individuals who compose them. Concert gives strength, order procures concert, discipline leads to order ; without discipline and without order no success is possible.*

The same Russian general, with the same troops, will not be able to dare every thing against European armies, having the same instruction, and nearly the same discipline as his own. Finally, one can venture before a Mack what he would not venture before a Napoleon.

The action of the cabinet upon the armies has an influence also upon the audacity of their enterprises. A general whose genius and arm are chained by an aulic council at four hundred leagues from the theatre of war, will struggle with disadvantage against him who shall have all liberty of action.

With regard to the superiority as to skill in the generals, it will not be contested that it is one of the most certain pledges of victory, especially when all other chances shall be supposed equal. Doubtless great captains have many times been seen beaten by mediocre men ; but an exception does not make a rule. An order badly comprehended, a fortuitous event, may cause to pass into the camp of the enemy all the chances of success, which a skillful general should have prepared by his manœuvres ; it is one of those hazards which one can neither foresee nor avoid. Would it be just, for that reason, to deny the influence of principles or of science, under ordinary circumstances? Undoubtedly not, for this hazard even produces the finest triumph of principles, since they will be found applied by the army against which it was wished to employ them, and it will conquer through their ascendancy. But in yielding to the evidence of those reasons, it will be inferred from them, perhaps, that they militate against science. That would not be better founded, since the science consists in putting on one's side all the chances possible to foresee, and it cannot be extended to the caprices of destiny. Now, for a hundred battles gained by skillful manœuvres, there are two or three gained by fortuitous accidents.

If the skill of the general-in-chief is one of the surest elements of vic-

---

* If irregular troops are nothing when they compose the whole army, and if they do not know how to gain battles, it must be owned that, supported by good troops they are an auxiliary of the highest importance ; when they are numerous, they reduce the enemy to despair, by destroying his convoys, intercepting all his communications, and holding him as it were invested in his camps ; they render above all retreats disastrous, as the French experienced in 1812. (See article 45.)

tory, it will easily be judged that the choice of generals is one of the most delicate points of the science of governments, and one of the most essential parts of the military policy of a State; unfortunately, this choice is subjected to so many petty passions, that chance, seniority, favor, spirit of coterie, jealousy, will often have as much part in it as the public interest and justice. This object is, moreover, so important, that we shall consecrate to it a special article.

ARTICLE XIII.

MILITARY INSTITUTIONS.

One of the most important points of the military policy of a State, is that which concerns the institutions that govern its army. An excellent army, commanded by a mediocre man, may effect great things : a bad army, commanded by a great captain, will do, perhaps, as much ; but it would do much more still, if it joined the good quality of the troops to the talents of their chief.

Twelve essential conditions concur in the perfection of an army :

The first, is to have a good system of recruiting ;

The second, a good formation ;

The third, a system of well organized national reserves ;

The fourth, troops and officers well instructed in the manœuvres, and in the interior and field service ;

The fifth, a discipline strict, without being humiliating ;

The sixth, a system of recompense and of emulation well combined ;

The seventh, special arms, (engineers and artillery) having a satisfactory instruction ;

The eight, an armament well contrived, and superior, if it be possible, to that of the enemy ; applying this not only to offensive but to defensive arms ;

The ninth, a general staff, capable of turning to good account all those elements, and the good organization of which responds to the classical instruction of its officers ;

The tenth, will be a good system for the supplies, the hospitals, and the administration in general.*

The eleventh, is a good system for organizing the command of armies and the high direction of operations;

The twelfth, consists in the excitation of the military spirit.

It must be said none of these conditions could be neglected without grave inconveniences.

A fine army well manœuvred, well disciplined, but without skillful conductors, and without national resources, allowed Prussia to fall in fifteen days under the blows of Napoleon. On the other hand, it has been seen, in very many circumstances, how much a State ought to congratulate itself for having a good army; it was the care and the skill of Philip and Alexander in forming and instructing their phalanxes, which rendered those masses so movable, and so fit to execute the most rapid manœuvres, and which permitted the Macedonians to subjugate Persia and India with that handful of choice soldiers. It was the excessive love of the father of Frederick for soldiers, which procured this great king an army capable of executing all his enterprises.

A government which neglects its army under any pretext whatever, is then a government guilty in the eyes of posterity, since it prepares humiliations for its colors and its country, instead of preparing them for successes by following a contrary course. Far from us the thought that a government ought to sacrifice every thing for the army! This would be an absurdity. But it ought to make it the object of its constant cares, and if the prince have not himself a military education, it is difficult to attain that end. In this case, which, unfortunately, happens but too often, it must be supplied by wise and provident institutions, at the head of which will be placed, without doubt, a good staff system, a good system of recruiting, and a good system of national reserves. It is, especially in times of protracted peace, that it is important to watch over the preservation of armies, for it is then that they can more easily degenerate, and that it is important to maintain in them a proper spirit, and to exercise

---

* To these different conditions may be added a good system of clothing and equipment, for, if these articles have a less direct influence in the operations of the field of battle than the armament, they contribute, nevertheless, to the preservation of the troops; now, in the long run, an army which shall take the best care of its old soldiers, may hope for a notable superiority over young levies incessantly renewed. The English army has been cited as a model in this kind; but it is easy with the treasures of England to provide well for small armies of fifty or sixty thousand men, the thing is more difficult for continental powers with their great armies.

them in great manœuvres, very incomplete semblances, doubtless, of effective wars, but which incontestably prepare troops for them. It is not less important to prevent them from falling into effeminacy, by employing them in labors useful for the defense of the country.

The isolation of troops by reigments in garrisons, is one of the worst systems that can be followed, and the Russian and Prussian formation by permanent divisions and corps d'armée, seems much preferable. In general, the Russian army might at this day be offered as a model in a great many respects, and if, in many points, what is practiced therein, would become useless and impracticable elsewhere, we must acknowledge that in general, we could borrow from it many good institutions.

With regard to recompenses and advancement, it is essential to protect seniority of service, at the same time opening a door to merit; three quarters of the promotions ought to be according to the order of the register, and the other quarter reserved to men who should make themselves remarkable by their merit and their zeal. In time of war, the order of the register ought on the contrary to be suspended, or reduced at least to a third of the promotions, leaving the other two-thirds to actions of eclat, and to well established services.

Superiority of armament may augment the chances of success in war; it does not of itself gain battles, but it contributes to it. Every one recollects how the great inferiority of the French in artillery came near becoming fatal to them at Eylau, and at Marengo. It is recollected also, what the French heavy cavalry have gained in adopting the cuirass, which it had so long repulsed; each one knows finally, of what advantage is the lance; doubtless lancers as foragers are no better than hussars; but charging in line is a very different affair; how many thousands of brave horsemen have been victims of the prejudice they had against the lance, because it constrains a little more in carrying than the sabre!

The armament of armies is still susceptible of many improvements, and that one who shall take the initiative in these ameliorations, will assure to itself great advantages. The artillery leaves little to be desired, but the offensive and defensive arms of the infantry and the cavalry, merit the attention of a provident government.

The new inventions which have had place within the last twenty years, seem to menace us with a great revolution in the organization, the armament, and even the tactics of armies. Strategy alone will remain with its principles, which were the same under the Scipios and the Cæsars as under Frederick, Peter the Great and Napoleon, for they are independent of the nature of arms, or the organization of troops.

The means of destruction are being perfected with a frightful progression; the congreve rockets, of which the Austrians have succeeded, it is said, in regulating the effect and the direction; the schrapnell shells, which launch floods of grape to the range of the ball; steam guns of Perkins, which vomit as many balls as a battalion, are going to centuple perhaps the chances of carnage, as if the hecatombs of the species of Eylau, of Borodino, of Leipzig, and of Waterloo, were not sufficient for desolating the European populations.

If sovereigns do not unite in congress to proscribe those inventions of death and destruction, there will remain no other course to take than to compose the half of armies of cuirassed cavalry, to be able to capture with the greatest rapidity all the machines; and the infantry even will be compelled to retake its iron armour of the middle ages, without which a battalion could be struck down before approaching the enemy. We may then see again the famous gendarmerie, men and horses, all barbed with iron.

In awaiting these circumstances, yet consigned to scarcely probable eventualities, it is certain that the artillery, and every kind of murderous pyrotechny, have made advances which ought to lead us to think of the modification of the deep order, which Napoleon abused. We shall return to this subject in the chapter on tactics.

Let us resume then, finally, in a few words the essential bases of the military policy which a wise government ought to adopt.

1. Is to give to the prince an education at the same time political and military; he will find in his councils rather good administrators than statesmen and soldiers; he ought then to seek to be one himself.

2. If the prince does not conduct his armies in person, the most important of his duties and the dearest of his interests will be that of causing himself to be well replaced; that is to say, to confide the glory of his reign and the security of his States, to the general the most capable of directing his armies.

3. The permanent army ought not only always to be found on a respectable footing; it must be in condition to be doubled at need by reserves wisely prepared. Its instruction and its discipline should be in accordance with its good organization: finally, the system of armament should be equal at least, if not superior, to its neighbors.

4. The *materiel* should equally be upon the best footing, and to have the necessary reserves.

5. It is important that the study of the military sciences be protected

and recompensed, as well as courage and zeal. The corps to which those sciences are necessary ought to be esteemed and honored. It is the only means of calling into them from all parts men of merit and genius.

6. The general staff should be employed in time of peace in labors preparatory to all possible eventualities of war. Its archives ought to be found provided with numerous historical details of the past, and with all the documents statistical, geographical, topographical and strategical of the present and the future. It is essential then that the chief of this corps and a part of its officers be permanently in the Capitol in time of peace, and that the depôt of war be nothing else than the depôt of the general staff, with the exception of a secret section to be given to it for documents which should be concealed from the subaltern officers of the corps.

7. Nothing should be neglected to have the military geography and statistics of neighboring States, to the end of knowing their material and moral means of attack and defense, as well as the strategical chances of the two parties; there should be employed in those scientific labors, distinguished officers, and they should be recompensed when they acquit themselves of them in a remarkable manner.

8. War once decided upon, it is necessary to resolve upon, if not an entire plan of operations, which is always impossible, at least a system of operations in which there shall be proposed an object, and a base shall be assured, as well as the material means necessary for guaranteeing the success of the enterprise.

9. The system of operations ought to be in unison with the object of the war, with the kind of enemies we will have to fight, with the nature and resources of the country, with the character of the nations and that of the chiefs who conduct them, either with the army or in the interior of the State. It ought to be calculated upon the natural and moral means of attack or defense which the enemies may have to oppose to us; finally, we ought to take into consideration the probable alliances which may supervene for or against the two parties in the course of the war, and which would complicate the chances of it.

10. The state of the finances of a nation should not be omitted in the list of the chances of war which we are called upon to weigh. Nevertheless it would be dangerous to accord to it all the importance which Frederick the Great seems to attach to it in the history of his time. This great King may have been right at a time when armies were recruited in most part by voluntary enlistment; then the last crown gave

the last soldier; but if national levies are well organized, money will have no longer the same influence, at least for one or two campaigns. If England has proved that money procured soldiers and auxiliaries, France has proved that love of country and honor equally gave soldiers, and that at need war supported war. Doubtless France found in the richness of its soil and in the exaltation of its chiefs, sources of transient power which could not be admitted as the general base of a system; but the results of its efforts were not less striking. Each year the numerous echos of the cabinet of London, and M. D'Yvernois especially, announced that France was about to succumb for the want of money, whilst that Napoleon was keeping up two millions of savings in the Tuileries, at the same time cancelling regularly the expenses of the State and the pay of his armies.*

A power which should abound in gold could badly defend itself; history attests that the richest people are not the strongest nor the happiest. Iron weighs as much at least as gold in the scales of military force. Meanwhile let us hasten to acknowledge the happy union of wise military institutions, of patriotism, of order in the finances, of internal riches and public credit, will constitute the strongest nation, and the one most capable of sustaining a long war.

A volume would be necessary to discuss all the circumstances in which a nation may develop more or less of power, whether through gold or through iron, and to determine the case in which war may be supported by war. This result obtains only in directing your armies abroad, and all countries are not equally of a nature to furnish resources to an assailant.

We should go beyond our limits by treating thoroughly these matters; it will suffice, for the object which we propose, to indicate the relations which they have to a project of war; it is for the statesman to grasp the modifications which circumstances and localities may bring into those relations.

Before passing to the chapter on strategy, we shall terminate this sketch of the military policy of States, by a few observations upon the choice of generals-in-chief, upon the superior direction of the operations of war, and upon the military spirit to be impressed upon armies.

---

* There was a deficit at his fall, but there was none in 1811; it was the result of his disasters, and of the extraordinary efforts which he was required to make.

ARTICLE XIV

COMMAND OF ARMIES, AND THE SUPERIOR DIRECTION
OF MILITARY OPERATIONS.

There has been a great deal of argument as to the advantage and the inconveniences which would result to a State whose monarch should march in person at the head of his armies. Whatever may be thought of it, it is certain, that if the prince feels within himself the capacity and the genius of a Frederick, of a Peter the Great, or of a Napoleon, he will take good care not to leave to his generals the honor of doing great things which he could do himself, for this would be wanting to his own glory, as well as to the good of the country.

Not having the mission to debate whether warrior kings are better for the people than pacific ones, a philanthropic question, foreign to our subject, we must limit ourselves to acknowledging, that with equality of merit and of chances, a sovereign will always have the advantage over a general who shall not himself be the chief of the State. Without taking into the account that he is responsible only to himself for the bold enterprises which he might form, he will be able still to do a great deal through the certainty he will have of the disposition of all the public resources for arriving at the object which he shall propose to himself. He will have, moreover, the powerful vehicle of favors, of recompenses and of punishments ; he will have the utmost devotion at his command for the greatest good of his enterprises ; no jealousy will be able to trouble the execution of his projects, or, at least, it will be very rare, and will happen only far from his presence on secondary points.

These are doubtless motives sufficient for deciding a prince to put himself at the head of his armies, whenever he shall have a decided vocation to that effect, and the struggle shall be worthy of him. But if, far from having the genius for war, he is of a feeble character, and easy to circumvent, then his presence in the army, instead of producing any good, would open the way for every intrigue : each one would offer him his projects, and as he would not have the necessary experience to judge of the best, he would abandon himself to the counsels of his familiars. The general who should command under him, constrained and thwarted in all his enterprises, would be out of condition for doing anything good, though even he should have all the talent necessary for conducting a war. It will be objected that the prince could well be present with the army, without constraining the generalissimo, by placing on the contrary all confidence in him alone, and aiding him with his sovereign power. In this case, that presence might produce some good, but it would often cause great embarrassment; if the army were ever turned, cut off from its communications, and obliged to open itself a way sword in hand, what sad results would not this position of the monarch at the head quarters produce?

When the prince shall feel the necessity of placing himself at the head of his armies, but without possessing yet the confidence in himself necessary for directing every thing according to his own will, the best system which he can adopt, will be to imitate precisely what the Prussian government did with Blucher; that is to say, to call to his assistance two generals the most famed for their capacity, the one taken from among men of acknowledged executive qualities, the other taken from among the best instructed chiefs of the staff. This trinity, if it agree well, can give excellent results, as had place in the army of Silesia in 1813.

The same system would be suitable also in the case where the monarch should judge it proper to confide the command to a prince of his house, as has frequently been seen since the time of Louis XIV. The prince was often decorated only with the titular command, whilst a counselor was imposed upon him who commanded in reality. This was the case with the Duke of Orleans and Marsin, at the famous battle of Turin, then with the Duke of Burgundy and Vendome, at the battle of Oudenard. I believe even that it was so at Ulm, between the Arch-Duke Ferdinand and Mack.

This last mode is deplorable, for then, in fact, no person is responsible. Every one knows that at Turin, the Duke of Orleans judged with more sagacity than Marshal Marsin, and the exhibition of full secret powers from the king was necessary, to cause the battle to be lost against the advice of the prince who commanded. In the same manner at Ulm, the Arch-Duke Ferdinand displayed more courage and skill than Mack, who was to serve him as mentor.

If the prince have the genius and experience of an Arch-Duke Charles, he should be given the command with carte-blanche, and with the choice of his instruments. If he have not yet required the same titles, he may be surrounded like Blucher, with an instructed chief of staff, and with a counselor taken from among men of tried execution. But in no case would it be wise to give those counselors other power than a consultative voice.

We have said above, that if the prince does not himself conduct his armies, the most important of his duties will be that of causing himself to be well replaced, and this, unfortunately, is what scarcely ever happens. Without going back to the times of antiquity, it suffices to recall the more recent examples which the ages of Louis XIV and Louis XV have furnished us. The merit of Prince Eugène, measured by his ill shaped figure, carried the greatest captain of his time into the hostile ranks; and after the death of Louvois, they saw the Tallards, the Marsins, the Villerois, succeed the Turennes, the Condés, and the Luxumbourgs; later were seen the Soubises and the Clermonts succeed the Marshal Saxe. From the perfumed selections, made in the boudoirs of the Pompadours and the Dubarrys, down to the love of Napoleon for *Sabreurs*, there are, doubtless, many states of divers natures to pass over, and the margin is sufficiently great for offering to the least enlightened government, all the means of arriving at a rational result; but, in all times, human frailties will show their influence in one manner or another, and cunning or suppleness will often gain the day, over the modest merit which shall wait until it be known how to employ it.

Setting aside even all the chances taken in the nature of the human heart, it is just to acknowledge how difficult such selections are, even for chiefs of the government the most ardent in their desires for the public welfare. In the first place, to choose a skillful general, one must be a military man himself, and in condition to judge, or else refer to the judgments of others, which involves necessarily the inconvenience of coteries. The embarrassment is, doubtless, not so great, when there is at command a general already illustrious from many victories; but, besides that every general is not a great captain for having gained a battle, (witness Jourdan, Scherer, and many others,) it does not always happen that a State has a victorious general at its disposition. After long intervals of peace, it might chance that no European general should have commanded-in-chief. In this case, it would be difficult to know by what title one general should be preferred to another; those who, by long peace services, shall be at the head of the list, and shall have the grade requisite for commanding the army, will they be the most capable of doing it?

Moreover, the communications of chiefs of the State with their subordinates, are so rare and so transient, that there is no occasion for astonishment at the difficulty of putting men in their place. The faith of the prince, seduced by appearances, will then sometimes be surprised, and with sentiments the most elevated, he can be deceived in his selections, without being liable to be reproached for it.

One of the surest means for avoiding this misfortune, would seem to be to realize the fine fiction of Fénélon in Telemachus, and to seek the faithful Philocles, sincere and generous, who placed between the prince and all aspirants to the command, would be able, by his more direct relations with the public, to enlighten the monarch as to the choice of individuals, the best recommended by their talents, as well as by their character. But will this faithful friend himself never yield to personal affections? Will he know how to divest himself of prepossessions? Was not Suwaroff repulsed by Potemkin because of his personal appearance, and was not all the skill of Catharine needed to cause a regiment to be given to a man who afterwards shed so much lustre upon her arms?

It has been thought that public opinion would be the best guide; nothing is more hazardous. Has not public opinion mode a Cæsar of Dumouriez, who understood nothing of great warfare? Would it have placed Bonaparte, at the head of the army in Italy, when he was known but by two directors? Meanwhile it must be acknowledged that this opinion, if it be not always infallible, is none the more to be disdained, especially, when it survives great crises and the experience of events.

The qualities most essential for a general-in-chief will ever be: *A great character, or moral courage which leads to great resolutions; then sang-froid or physical courage which predominates over dangers.* Knowledge appears but in the third rank; it were blindness not to acknowledge that it will be a powerful auxiliary. Moreover, as I have already said elsewhere, we must not understand thereby a vast erudition; it is not necessary to know a great deal, but to understand well, and above all to be deeply penetrated with regulating principles. At the end of all these qualities will come personal character; a man brave, just, firm, equitable, knowing how to esteem the merit of others instead of being jealous of it, and skillful in making it serve to his own glory, will ever be a good general, and may even pass for a great man. Unfortunately this eagerness to render justice to merit is not the most common quality, mediocre minds are always jealous, and inclined to surround themselves badly, fearing to pass in the world for being led, and not knowing how to comprehend that the man nominally placed at the head of armies has always nearly the entire glory of their successes, even though he should have the least part therein.

The question has often been agitated whether the command should be given in preference to the general habituated from long experience to the conduct of troops, or to generals of the staff or scientific arms, little habituated, themselves to managing troops. It is incontestable that grand warfare is a science altogether separate, and that one may very well combine operations without having himself led a regiment to the enemy; Peter the Great, Condé, Frederick and Napoleon are in point to prove it. It cannot be denied then that a man come from the staff may become a great captain as well as any other; but it will not be for having grown old in the functions of quarter-master that he will have the capacity for supreme command, it will be because he possesses in himself the natural genius for war and the requisite character. In the same manner, a general from the ranks of the infantry or of the cavalry, will be as fit as a learned tactician to command an army.

The question seems then difficult to resolve in an absolute manner, and here still individualities will be everything. In order to arrive at a rational solution, it is necessary to take a middle course and recognize:

That a general of the staff, the artillery or engineers, who shall also have conducted a division or a corps d'armee, will have, with equal chances, a real superiority over him who shall only be acquainted with the service of one arm or of a special corps;

That a general of troops who shall have studied war will be equally proper for command;

That great character precedes all the qualities requisite for a general-in-chief;

Finally that the union of wise theory with a great character will constitute the great captain.

The difficulty of assuring constantly a good choice, has give rise to the idea of supplying it by a good staff, which, placed as advisers of the generals, would have a real influence over the operations. Undoubtedly a superior staff corps, in which should be perpetuated good traditions, will always be one of the most useful and happy of institutions; but it will be necessary to watch that false doctrines are not introduced therein, for then this institution would become fatal. Frederick the Great, in founding his military academy at Potsdam, scarcely expected that it would terminate in the *rechte schulter vor* of General Ruchel,[*] and in presenting the oblique order as the infallible talisman, which causes the gain of battles: so true is it that from the sublime to the ridiculous there is often but a step.

---

[*] This General believed, at the battle of Gena, that he could save the army by commanding his soldiers to advance the right shoulder in order to form an oblique line!

Besides that, it would be necessary to avoid with great care exciting a conflict between the generalissimo and his chief of staff; and if the latter ought to be taken from amongst the best recognized notabilities of this corps, still it will be necessary to leave to the generals the choice of the individuals with whom he will best sympathise.   To impose a chief of staff on the generalissimo would be to lead to a confusion of powers; to allow him to take a man who is a cypher among his clients would be more dangerous still, for if he is himself a mediocre man, placed by favor or chance, his choice will be felt.   The mean term for avoiding these evils, will be to give to the general-in-chief, the choice amongst many generals of an incontestable capacity, who will be designated for him, but leaving him to take the one who shall suit him.

It has been thought also, in almost all armies successively, that more solemnity and weight would be given to the direction of military operations, by assembling often councils of war to aid the generalissimo with their advice.   Undoubtedly, if the chief of the army is a Soubise, a Clermont, or a Mack, a mediocre man in a word, he could often find in the council of war better opinions than his own; the majority even could make better decisions than he; but what success could be expected from operations conducted by others than those who have planned and combined them?   What will the execution of a project lead to, which the general-in-chief only half comprehends, since it will not be his own thought?

I have had myself a terrible experience of this pitiful part of prompter at head quarters, and no one perhaps can better than myself appreciate it at its just value.   It is especially in the midst of a council of war that this part must be absurd, and the more numerous the council, and the higher the military dignitaries of which it shall be composed, the more difficult it will be to cause truth and reason to triumph in it if there be ever so little dissidence.

What would a council of war have done in which Napoleon, in quality of counselor, should have proposed the movement of Arcola, the plan of Rivoli, the march by the St. Bernard, the movement of Ulm, and that upon Gera and Jena?   The timid would have found those operations rash even to folly; others would have seen a thousand difficulties of execution; all would have rejected them.   If, on the contrary, the council should have accepted them, and another than Napoleon should have conducted them, would they not certainly have failed?

Therefore, in my opinion, councils of war are a deplorable resource; it can only have one favorable side, which is when the council is of the same opinion as the general-in-chief. It may then give to the latter more confidence in his own resolutions, and he will have, moreover, the conviction that each of his lieutenants, penetrated with the same idea as himself, will do his best to assure its execution. This is the only good which a council of war can produce, which, besides, ought always to be a council purely consultative and nothing more. But if, in place of this perfect accord, there be dissidence, then such a council can have only unfortunate results.

From what precedes, I think it may be concluded, that the best manner of organizing the command of an army, when we shall not have a great captain, who has already given numerous proofs, will be :

1. To confide this command to a man of tried bravery, bold in combat, immoveable in danger ;

2. To give him for a chief of staff, a man of high capacity, of a frank and loyal character, with whom the generalissimo may live in good harmony ; the glory is sufficiently great to yield a part of it to a friend who should have concurred in preparing successes. It was thus that Blucher, assisted by the Gneisenaus and Mufflings, covered himself with a glory which probably he never would have acquired all alone. Without doubt, this kind of double command would never equal that of a Frederick, of a Napoleon, or of a Suwarof, but, in default of this unity of a great captain, it is certainly the preferable mode.

Before finishing upon these important matters, is remains for me yet to say a few words upon another manner of influencing military operations : it is that of councils of war established in the capitol near the government.

Louvois, directed a long time from Paris, the armies of Louis XIV, and did it with success. Carnot directed also from Paris the armies of the Republic ; in 1793 he did very well, and saved France ; in 1794 he did at first very badly, then repaired his faults by chance ; in 1796 he did decidedly very badly. But Louvois and Carnot directed alone the operations without assembling a council.

The Aulic council of war, established at Vienna, had often the mission of directing the operations of the armies ; there has never been but one voice in Europe upon the fatal effects which have resulted from it ; is it wrong or right ? Austrian generals can alone decide.

As far as I am concerned, I think that the only attribute which such a council should have, is reduced to the adoption of a general plan of operations. It is already known that I do not understand by that, a plan which would trace out a whole campaign, would constrain generals and can them to be beaten inevitably; but I understand the plan which should determine the aim of the campaign, the offensive or defensive nature of the operations, then the material means which it would be necessary to prepare beforehand for the first enterprises, then for the reserves, then for possible levies in case of invasion. It cannot be denied that all these things may and even must be discussed, in a government council, composed of generals and ministers; but there, ought to be limited the action of such a council, for if it has the pretention to tell the generalissimo not only to march to Vienna or to Paris, but still to indicate to him the manner in which he must manœuvre in order to arrive there, then the poor general will be certainly beaten, and all the responsibility of his reverses will weigh upon those who, at two hundred leagues from the enemy, pretend to direct an army, which it is already so difficult to direct well when one is upon the ground.

ARTICLE XV.

MILITARY SPIRIT OF NATIONS, AND THE MORAL OF ARMIES.

A government would adopt in vain the best regulations for organizing an army, if it did not apply itself also to exciting a military spirit in the country. If, in the city of London, they prefer the title of richest cashier to military decoration, that may do with an insular country, protected by its innumerable squadrons; but a continental nation, which should adopt the manners of the city of London, or of the bourse of Paris, would sooner or later be the prey of its neighbors. It was to the assemblage of civic virtues and military spirit passed from institutions into manners that the Romans were indebted for their greatness; when they lost those virtues, and when, ceasing to regard the military service an honor as well as a duty, they abandoned it to the mercenary Goths, Heruli and Gauls, the loss of the empire became inevitable. Without doubt, nothing of that which may augment the prosperity of a country ought to be forgotten or despised ; it is necessary even to honor skillful men and traders who are the first instruments of this prosperity, but it is necessary that this be subordinate to the great institutions which make the strength of States, by encouraging the masculine and heroic virtues. Policy and justice will be agreed in that, for, whatever Boileau may say of it, it will always be more glorious *to brave death in the steps of the Cæsars,* than to fatten on the public miseries, by playing upon the vicissitudes of the credit of the State. Woe to those countries where the luxury of the contractor and the stockholder insatiable of gold, shall be placed above the uniform of the brave man who shall have sacrificed his life, his health or his fortune, in the defence of the country.

The first means of encouraging the military spirit is to surround the army with all consideration, public and social. The second, is to assure to the services rendered to the State, the preference in all the administrative employments which should chance to be vacant, or to require even a given time of military service for certain employments. It would be a subject worthy of the most serious consideration, that of comparing the ancient military institutions of Rome with those of Russia and Prussia, and of drawing afterwards the parallel between them and the doctrines of modern Utopists who, declaiming against all participation of the officers of the army in the other public functions, no longer wish any but rhetoricians in the great offices.*

Without doubt, there are many employments which require special studies ; but would it not be possible for the military man to devote himself, in the numerous leisures of peace, to the study of the career which he should wish to embrace, after having paid his debt to his country in that of arms ? And if administrative places were given by preference to officers retired from service with the grade of captain at least, would it not be a great stimulant for them to seek to arrive at this grade ? Would it not also be a stimulant for officers to think, in their garrisons, of seeking their recreations elsewhere than in the theatres and public cafés.

Perhaps it will be found that this facility of passing from the military service to places of civil administration, would be rather injurious than favorable to the military spirit, and that, in order to strengthen the latter, it would be suitable on the contrary to place the condition of soldier altogether beyond other careers. The Janizaries and the Mamelukes had their origin in this principle. These soldiers were bought at the age of seven

* For example, in France, in place of excluding the military from elections, the right of elector ought to be given to all colonels, and that of eligibility to all generals ; the most venal of the deputies will not be the military men.

or eight years, and they were reared in the idea that they must die under their colors. The English even, those men so proud of their rights, on becoming soldiers, contract the obligation for life ; and the Russian soldier must serve for twenty-five years, which is almost equivalent to a life enlistment like that of the English.

With such armies, as well as in those which are recruited by voluntary enlistment, perhaps it wouln be in fact, more suitable not to admit a fusion between the posts of military officers and civil places. But, whenever the military service shall be a temporary duty imposed on the population, the case seems different, and the Roman institutions which required a service of ten years in the legions, before being able to aspire to the various public functions, appears rather in effect the best means of preserving the martial spirit, especially at an epoch when the general tendency to material well-being, seems to become the dominant passion of societies.

However that may be, I think, that under all possible regimes, the constant aim of a wise government will be to elevate the military service to the end of nourishing the love of glory and all the warlike virtues, under penalty of incurring the blame of posterity, and of experiencing the fate of the Roman empire.

It will not be all to inspire the military spirit in the populations ; it will be necessary still to encourage it in the army. What, in fact, would be gained, though the uniform should be honored in the city and imposed as a civic duty, if men did not carry under their colors all the warlike virtues ? We should have a militia numerous, but without valor.

The moral exaltation of an army and military spirit are two very different things which we must take care not to confound, and which produce nevertheless, the same effect. The first is, as has been said, produced by passions more or less transient, such as political or religious opinions, and a great love of country ; whilst that military spirit being inspired by the skill of a chief or by wise institutions, depends less on circumstances and ought to be the work of a far seeing government.*

Let courage be recompensed and honored, let the grades be respected, and let discipline be in sentiment and in conviction still more than in form.

Let the body of officers and the ranks in general be convinced that resignation, bravery and the sentiment of duty, are virtues without which no

---

* It is important especially that this spirit should animate the lists of officers and non-commissioned officers ; soldiers always go well when those lists are good and the nation is brave.

army is respectable, no glory possible ; let all know well that firmness in reverses is more honorable than enthusiasm in successes, for there is only courage necessary for taking a position, whilst heroism is required for making a difficult retreat before a victorious and enterprising enemy, without being disconcerted, and opposing to it a bold front. It is the duty of the prince to recompense a handsome retreat as highly as the finest victory.

To harden the armies to labor and fatigue ; not to allow them to be idle in the effeminacy of garrisons in times of peace ; to inculcate in them the sentiment of their superiority over the enemy ; without, however, lowering the latter too much ; to inspire the love of great actions ; in a word, to excite enthusiasm by inspirations in harmony with the spirit which governs the masses ; to decorate valor and punish weakness ; and finally to brand cowardice ; these are the means of forming a good military spirit.

It was effeminacy above all which was the ruin of the Roman legions ; those formidable soldiers who carried casque, buckler and cuirass under the burning sky of Africa in the days of the Scipios, found them too heavy under the cold sky of Gaul and Germany ; then the empire was lost.

I have said that it is necessary never to inspire too much contempt for the enemy, because that where you should find an obstinate resistance, the *moral* of the soldier might be shaken by it. Napoleon, addressing himself at Jena to the corps of Lannes, praised the Prussian cavalry, but promised that it could do nothing against the bayonets of his Egyptians !

It is necessary also to forewarn the officers, and through them the soldiers, against those sudden turns which often seize the bravest armies when they are not restrained by the curb of discipline, and by the conviction that order in a troop is the pledge of its safety. It was not for the want of courage that a hundred thousand Turks were beaten at Peterwaradin by the Prince Eugene, and at Kagoul by Roumanzof ; it was because that once repulsed in their disorderly charges, each one found himself delivered to his personal inspirations, all fighting individually without any order in the masses. A troop seized with panic finds itself in the same state of demoralization, for disorder being once introduced, all concert and all ensemble in the individual wills becomes impossible ; the voice of the chiefs can no longer make itself heard ; every manœuvre for reestablishing the combat becomes impossible of execution, and then there remains safety only in a shameful flight.

The peoples of lively and ardent imagination are more subject than others to these panics, and those of the south are almost all in this category. The remedy is in strong institutions and skillful chiefs alone. The French even, whose military virtues have never been questioned when they have been well conducted, have often witnessed those alarms which it is permitted to call rediculous. Who does not recall the inconceivable panic terror with which the infantry of Marshal Villars was seized after having gained the battle of Friedlingen (1704)? The same thing had place in the infantry of Napoleon after the victory of Wagram, when the enemy was in full retreat. And, what is more extraordinary still, is the rout of the 97th demi-brigade at the seige of Genoa, where fifteen hundred men fled before a platoon of hussars, whilst that those same men took two days after the Diamond Fort by one of the most vigorous coups-de-main of modern history.

It would seem, nevertheless, very easy to convince brave soldiers that death strikes more quickly and more surely men flying in disorder, than those who remian united to present a bold front to the enemy, or rally promptly if they happen to be momentarily forced. The Russian army in this respect, may serve as a model for all those of Europe, and the steadiness which it has displayed in all its retreats, belong as much to the national character as to the national instinct of the soldiers and to the establishment of a rigid discipline. It is not indeed always the vivacity of imagination of troops which introduces disorder among them, the want of habits of order has much to do with it, and the want of precautions in the chiefs to assure the maintainance of them, contributes still more to it. I have been often astonished at the indifference of the greater part of generals on this subject; not only did they disdain to take the least logistic precaution for assuring the direction of small detachments and isolated men, they adopted no rallying signals in order to facilitate, in the different corps of an army, the reunion of the fractions which might be scattered in consequence of a sudden terror, or even an irresistible charge of the enemy; but they were even offended that any one should think of proposing to them such precautions. In the meantime the most incontestable courage, and the severest discipline would be often impotent for remedying a great disorder, which the good habit of division rallying signals would much more easily obviate. Without doubt there are cases where all human resources would be insufficient for the maintainance of order; such, for example, is that where the physical sufferings to which the troops should find themselves a prey, should have succeeded in rendering them deaf to all kinds of appeal, and where the chiefs themselves should be unable to do anything to reorganize them; this is what happened in 1812. But beyond these exceptionable cases, good habits of order, good logistic precautions, and a good discipline will succeed the most often, if not in preventing all panic. at least in carrying a prompt remedy thereto.

It is time to quit those matters of which I have desired only to trace a sketch, and to pass on to the examination of the purely military combinations.

CHAPTER III.

STRATEGY.

DEFINITION AND FUNDAMENTAL PRINCIPLE.

THE art of war, independently of the parts which we have just succinctly explained, is composed yet, as has been seen above, of five principal branches : strategy, grand tactics, logistics, (*la logistique*) elementary tactics, (*la tactique de detail*,) and the art of the engineer. We shall treat only of the first three, for reasons already indicated; it is necessary then to commence by defining them.

In order to do so more surely, we shall follow the order in which the combinations which an army may have to make, present themselves to its chiefs at the moment when war is declared; commencing naturally with the most important, which constitute in some sort the plan of operations, and proceeding thus the reverse of tactics, which should begin with small details in order to arrive at the formation and the employment of a great army.*

We will suppose then the army about to take the field; the first care of its chief will be to settle with the government upon the nature of the

---

* To learn tactics it is necessary to study first the school of the platoon, then that of the battalion, finally the evolutions of the line ; then you pass to the small operations of the campaign, then to castrametation, afterwards marches, finally the formation of armies. But in strategy we begin at the top, that is to say, with the plan of campaign.

war which it shall make; afterwards it will be his duty to study well the theatre of its enterprises; then he will choose, in concert with the chief of the State, the most suitable base of operations, according as its frontiers and those of its allies shall favor thereto.

The choice of this base, and still more the end which it shall be proposed to attain, will contribute to determine the zone of operations that will be adopted. The generalissimo will take a first objective point for his enterprises; he will choose the line of operations which would lead to this point, whether as a temporary line, or as a definitive line.

The army marching upon this line of operations, will have a front of operations or a strategic front; behind this front it will do well to have a line of defense, to serve as a support in case of need. The transient positions which its army corps will take on the front of operations, or upon the line of defense, will be strategic positions.

When the army shall arrive near its first objective point, and the enemy shall commence to oppose its enterprises, it will attack him, or manœuvre to constrain him to a retreat; it will adopt to this effect one or two strategic lines of manœuvres, which being temporary, may deviate to a certain point from the general line of operations, with which they must not be confounded.

To connect the front of operations with the base, one will form as he advances, his staple line and lines of supply, depôts, &c.

If the line of operations be somewhat lengthened in depth, and there be hostile corps in reach of disturbing it, choice will have to be made between the attack and expulsion of those corps, and the pursuit of the enterprise against the hostile army, paying no attention to them, or merely observing them; if this latter course be resolved upon, there will result from it a double front of operations and great detachments.

The army being near obtaining its objective point, and the enemy wishing to oppose this, there will be a battle; when this shock shall be indecisive, it will be resolved to recommence the struggle; if a victory be gained, our enterprises will be carried on for attaining or passing beyond the first objective point and adopting a second.

When the aim of this first objective shall be the taking of an important place of arms, the siege will commence. If the army is not sufficiently numerous for continuing its march, leaving a siege corps behind it, it will take a strategic position for covering it; thus, in 1796, the army of Italy, not numbering fifty thousand combattants, was not able to pass Mantua, in order to penetrate to the heart of Austria, leaving twenty-five thousand men before the place, and having besides forty thousand men in front, upon the double line of the Tyrol and the Frioul.

In the case, on the contrary, where the army should have sufficient forces to obtain greater advantages from its victory, or rather where it should have no siege to make, it would march to a second objective point more important still. If this point be found at a certain distance, it will be necessary to procure an intermediate point of support; an eventual base will then be formed by means of one or two cities secure from insult, which will doubtless have been occupied; in the contrary case, a small strategic reserve will be formed, which will cover the rear and protect the grand depôt by field works. When the army shall pass considerable rivers, *têtes de ponts* will be hastily constructed there, and if the bridges are in cities enclosed by walls, a few intrenchments will be raised to augment the defense of those posts, and to double thus the solidity of the eventual base, or of the strategic reserve which should there be placed.

If, on the contrary, the battle has been lost, there will be a retreat to the end of approaching the base, and of drawing therefrom new forces, as well from the detachments which would be drawn in, as from the places and intrenched camps, which would arrest the enemy or oblige him to divide his means.

When winter approaches, there will be winter cantonments, or else operations will be continued by that one of the two armies which, having obtained a decided superiority, and finding no serious obstacles in the hostile line of defense, should wish to profit from its ascendancy; there would then be a winter campaign; this resolution, which, in all cases, becomes equally painful for both armies, presents no special combinations; unless it be the necessity for a redoubled activity in the enterprises, in order to obtain the most prompt *dénoûment*.

Such is the ordinary movement of a war; such will also be that which we shall follow, in order to proceed to the examination of the different combinations which those operations lead to.

All those which embrace the ensemble of the theatre of war, are in the domain of strategy, which will thus comprehend:

1. The definition of this theatre and of the different combinations which it might offer;

2. The choice and the establishment of the fixed base, and of the zone of operations;

3. The determination of the objective point to be attained, whether it be offensive or defensive;

4. The determination of the decisive points of the theatre of war ;

5. The fronts of operations and lines of defense ;

6. The choice of the lines of operations which lead from the aforesaid base to the objective points, or to the front of operations ;

7. That of the best strategic lines to take for a given operation ; the different manœuvres for embracing those lines in their divers combinations ;

8. The bases of eventual operations, and strategic reserves ;

9. The marches of armies considered as manœuvres ;

10. The magazines considered in their relations with the marches of armies.

11. Fortresses regarded as strategical means ; as refuges for an army, or as obstacles to its march ; the sieges to make and to cover ;

12. Intrenched camps, *têtes de ponts*, &c. ;

13. Diversions and great detachments.

Independently of those combinations which enter principally in the projection of the general plan for the first enterprises of the campaign, there are other mixed operations, which participate of strategy for the direction to be given them, and of tactics for their execution ; as the passage of rivers and streams, retreats, winter quarters, surprises, descents, great convoys, &c.

The 2d branch is tactics, that is to say, the manœuvres of an army on the field of battle, or of combat, and the different formations for leading troops to the attack.

The 3d branch is logistics, (*la logistique*) or the practical art of moving armies, the material details of marches and of formations, the situation of non-intrenched camps and cantonments, in a word, the execution of the combinations of strategy and of tactics.

Several futile controversies have had place for determining, in an absolute manner, the line of demarkation which separates those divers branches of the science. I have said that strategy is the art of making war upon the map, the art of embracing the whole of a theatre of war ; tactics is the art of combatting on the ground, of placing thereon one's forces according to the localities, and of putting them in action on the different points of the field of battle, that is to say, within a space of four or five leagues, in such a manner that all the acting corps may receive orders and execute them in the course even of the action ; finally, *la logistique* is in substance only the science of preparing the application of the other twọ. My definition has been criticised without a better one being given ; it is certain that many battles have been decided by strategical movements, and have been even but a series of such movements ; but that has never been the case except against dispersed armies, which is an exception ; now the general definition, being applicable only to pitched battles, is none the less exact.*

Thus, independently of the measures of local execution which are within its province, grand tactics, in my view, will comprehend the following objects :

1. The choice of positions and of defensive lines of battle ;

2. The offensive defense in combat ;

3. The different orders of battle, or grand manœuvres for attacking a hostile line ;

4. The meeting of two armies in march and unexpected battles ;

5. The surprise of armies ;†

6. The dispositions for conducting troops to the combat ;

7. The attack of positions and intrenched camps ;

8. *Coups de main.*

All the other operations of war enter into the details of *petite guerre*, such as convoys, foraging, the partial combats of advanced and rear guards, the attack even of small posts, in a word, all that which must be executed by an isolated division or detachment.

FUNDAMENTAL PRINCIPLE OF WAR.

The essential object of this work is to demonstrate that there excists a fundamental principle of all the operations of war, a principle which

---

* It may be said that tactics is the combat, and that strategy is all the war before and after the combat, sieges alone excepted, even they belong to strategy so far as the deciding upon those necessary to be made. and how they must be covered. Strategy decides where we should act, *la logistique* conducts and places the troops there ; tactics decides their employment and the mode of execution.

† The surprise of armies in open field is here meant, and not the surprise of winter quarters.

ought to preside over all the combinations in order that they be good. , It consists :

1. In carrying by strategic combinations the mass of the forces of an army successively upon the decisive points of a theatre of war, and as much as possible upon the communications of the enemy, without endangering its own ;

2. In manœuvering in such a manner as to engage this mass of the forces with fractions only of the hostile army ;.

3. In directing equally, on the day of battle, by tactical manœuvres, the mass of one's forces upon the decisive point of the field of battle, or upon that of the hostile line which it would be important to overwhelm ;

4. In managing so that those masses be not merely present upon the decisive point, but that they be put in action there with energy and concert, in a manner to produce a simultaneous effort.

This general principle has been found so simple that it has not lacked criticisms.*

It has been objected that it were very easy to recommend the carrying one's principal force upon the decisive points, and to know how to engage them thereon ; but that the art consists precisely in recognizing these points.

Far from contesting so *naïve* a truth, I own that it would be at least ridiculous to utter a like general principle, without accompanying it with all the developments necessary for causing its different chances of application to be comprehended ; I have, therefore, neglected nothing for putting every studious officer in condition to determine easily the decisive points of a strategical or tactical field (*un échiquier stratégique ou tactique.*) There will be found in article 19, the definition of those different points, and there will be recognized in all articles from the 18th to the 22d, those which apply to the divers combinations of a war. Military men who, after having meditated upon them attentively, should still believe that the determination of those decisive points is an insoluble problem, ought to despair of ever comprehending any thing of strategy.

In fact, a theatre of operations never presents but three zones, one to the right, one to the left, and one at the centre. In the same manner each zone, each front of operations, each strategical position and line of

---

*To meet these criticisms, I ought, perhaps, to place here the entire chapter of the general principles of the art of war, which terminates my Treatise on Grand Operations, (chap. XXXV. of the 3d edition) ; but powerful motives have prevented me from despoiling my first work of the chapter which makes its principal merit, and which my censors ought at least to read.

defense, as well as each tactical line of battle, has never but those same subdivisions, that is to say, two extremeties and a centre. Now, there will always be one of those three directions which it will be proper to follow, in order to reach the important object desired, one of the other two will be more or less removed from it, and the third will be altogether opposed to it. Hence, in combining hostile positions with geographical points, and with the projects which should be formed, it seems that every question of strategic movement, as well as of tactical manœuvre, would always be reduced to knowing whether we ought to manœuvre to the right, to the left, or directly to the front; the choice between three alternatives so simple, could not be an enigma worthy of a new sphinx.

I am far from pretending, nevertheless, that the whole art of war consists merely in the choice of a good direction to be given to masses, but it could not be denied that it is at least the fundamental point of strategy. It will be for talent of execution, skill, energy, and *coup d'œil*, to complete what good combinations will have been able to propose.

We are about to apply then the principle indicated, to the different combinations of strategy and tactics, then to prove, by the history of twenty celebrated campaigns, that all their successes or reverses were the result of the application, or of the neglect of this principle.*

STRATEGICAL COMBINATIONS.

ARTICLE XVI.

SYSTEM OF OFFENSIVE OR DEFENSIVE OPERATIONS.

War once resolved upon, the first thing to be decided, is to know whether it is to be offensive or defensive. First of all, it is proper to define well what is understood by these words :

---

* The account of those twenty campaigns, together with fifty plans of battles, will be found in my history of the Seven Years War, in that of the wars of the Revolution, and in the political and military life of Napoleon.

The offensive presents itself under several aspects; if it be directed against a great State, which it embraces entirely, it is then *an invasion ;* if it be applied only to the attack of a province, or of a line of defense more or less limited, it is no longer an invasion, but an ordinary offensive ; finally, if it be but an attack upon any position whatever of the hostile army, and limited to a single operation, it is called *the initiative of movements.* As we have said in the preceding chapter, the offensive considered morally and politically, is almost always advantageous, because it carries the war upon foreign soil, spares your own country, diminishes the resources of the enemy, and augments yours ; it elevates the *moral* of the army, and often imposes dread upon the adversary ; meanwhile it happens also that it excites his ardor, when it makes him feel that the question is to save his menaced country.

Under the military relation, the offensive has its good and its bad side ; in strategy, if it be pushed to an invasion, it gives lines of operations *lengthened in depth,* which are always dangerous in an enemy's country. All the theatre of operations, the mountains, the rivers, the defiles, the fortifications, being obstacles favorable to the defense, are thus against the offensive ; the inhabitants and the authorities of the country will be hostile to it, instead of being instruments in its favor. But if it obtain a success, it strikes the hostile power to the heart, deprives it of the means of war, and may bring about a prompt *dénoument* to the struggle.

Applied to a mere transient operation, that is to say, considered as the initiative of movements, the offensive is always advantageous, especially in strategy. In fact, if the art of war consist in directing one's forces upon the decisive point, it is comprehended that the first means of applying this principle will be to take the initiative of movements. He who has taken this initiative knows beforehand what he is doing and what he wishes ; he arrives with his masses at the point where it is convenient for him to strike. He who waits is anticipated every where ; the enemy falls upon fractions of his army ; he neither knows where his adversary means to direct his efforts, nor the means which he ought to oppose to him.

In tactics, the offensive has also its advantages ; but they are less positive, because the operations not being upon so large a sphere, he who has the initiative cannot conceal them from the enemy, who, discovering this instantly, can, by the aid of good reserves, remedy it upon the spot. Besides that, he who marches upon the enemy has against him all the disadvantages resulting from the obstacles of the ground which he will be obliged to overcome in order to approach the line of his adversary, which leads to the belief, that in tactics especially, the chances of the two systems are pretty nearly balanced.. For the rest, whatever advantages could be expected from the offensive strategically and politically, it is obvious that this system could not be adopted exclusively for a whole war, for it is not even certain that a campaign commenced offensively may not finish with the defensive.

Defensive war, as we have already said, has also its advantages when it is wisely combined. It is of two kinds : the inert or passive defense, and the active defense with offensive returns. The first is always pernicious ; 'the second may procure great success. The aim of a defensive war being to cover, as long as possible, the portion of the territory menaced by the enemy, it is evident that all the operations should have for object the retarding of his progress, the thwarting of his enterprises, by multiplying the difficulties of his march, without, meanwhile, allowing the army to be seriously broken. He who decides upon invasion, does it always in consequence of any ascendancy whatever, he should aim then at as prompt a *dénoument* as possible ; the defender, on the contrary, ought to put it off until his adversary is weakened by detachments, marches, fatigues, &c.

An army is scarcely reduced to a positive defense but in consequence of reverses or a notable inferiority. In this case it seeks, by the support of its places, and by favor of natural or artificial barriers, the means of re-establishing the equilibrium of chances, by multiplying the obstacles which it can oppose to the enemy.

This sytem, when it is not pushed too far, presents also happy chances ; but it is in the case only when the general who believes himself compelled to resort to it, has the good sense not to be reduced to an inert defense ; that is to say, when he shall take care not to await passively, in fixed posts, all the blows which the enemy should be pleased to deliver him. He must apply himself on the contrary, to redouble the activity of his operations, and to seize every occasion which presents, of falling upon the feeble points of the enemy, by taking the initiative of movements.

This kind of warfare, which I have heretofore named the offensive-defensive,* may be advantageous in strategy as well as in tactics. In acting thus, you have the advantages of the two systems, for you have that of the initiative, and you are better able to seize the moment when it is suitable to strike, when you find yourself in the midst of a theatre which has been prepared beforehand, at the centre of the resources and supports of your country.

---

* Others have named it the active defensive, which is not correct, since the defense could be very active without being offensive. We may, nevertheless, adopt the term, which is more grammatical.

In the first three campaigns of the Seven Years War, Frederick the Great was the aggressor ; but in the last four he gave the true model of an offensive defense. It must be confessed also, that he was marvelously seconded by his adversaries, who emulously gave him all the leisure and the occasions for taking the initiative with success.

Wellington also played this part in the greater portion of his career in Portugal, in Spain and in Belgium, and, in fact, it was the only one which suited his position. It is always easy to play the Fabius, when one does it on an ally's territory, when he has not to trouble himself about the fate of the capital, or of the provinces menaced ; in a word, when he is at liberty to consult military convenience only.

Definitively, it appears incontestable, that one of the greatest of a general's talents, is to know how to employ by turns these two systems, and especially, to know how to retake the initiative in the midst even of a defensive struggle.

ARTICLE XVII.

OF THE THEATRE OF OPERATIONS.

The theatre of a war embraces all the countries in which two powers may attack, whether by their own territory, or by that of their allies, or of the secondary powers which they will draw into the vortex through fear or through interest. When a war is complicated with maritime operations, then its theatre is not restrained to the frontiers of a State, but may embrace the two hemispheres, as has happened in the struggles between France and England, from Louis XIV down to our day.

Thus, the general theatre of a war is a thing so vague, and so dependent upon incidents, that it must not be confounded with the theatre of operations which each army may embrace, independently of all complications.

The theatre of a continental war between France and Austria, may embrace Italy alone, or Germany and Italy, if the German princes take part in it.

It may happen that the operations are combined, or that each army is destined to act separately. In the first case, the general theatre of opertions ought to be considered only as the same *échiquier*, upon which strategy should cause the armies to move with the common object which shall have been resolved upon. In the second case, each army will have its special theatre of operations, independent of the other.

The theatre of operations of an army comprehends all the ground which it should seek to invade, as well as that which it may have to defend. If it is to operate by itself, this theatre forms its whole *échiquier*, out of which it might indeed seek an issue in the case where it should find itself invested therein on three sides, but out of which it ought never to combine any manœuvre, since nothing would be provided for a common action with the secondary army.

If, on the contrary, the operations are concerted, then the theatre of operations of each army, taken separately, becomes, in some sort, but one of the zones of operations of the general *échiquier* where the belligerents are to operate with the same object.

Independently of the topographical accidents with which it is strewn, each theatre or *échiquier*, which is to be operated upon by one or several armies, is composed for both parties :

1. Of a fixed base (or basis) of operations ;

2. Of an objective aim ;

3. Of fronts of operations and lines of defense ;

4. Of zones and lines of operations ;

5. Of strategic lines and lines of communications ;

6. Of natural or artificial obstacles to conquer or to oppose to the enemy ;

7. Of important geographical strategic points to occupy in the offensive, or to cover defensively ;

8. Of accidental bases of operations intermediate between the objective aim and the positive base.

9. Of points of refuge in case of reverses.

To render the demonstration more intelligible, I will suppose France, wishing to invade Austria with two or three armies, destined to be united under one chief, and departing from Mayence, from the Upper Rhine, from Savoy, or from the maritime Alps. Each country, which one or the other of these armies would have to pass over, will be, in some sort, a zone of operations of the general *échiquier*. But if the army of Italy is to act only as far as the Adige, without concerting any thing with the army of the Rhine, then what was considered only as a zone of operations in the general plan, becomes the sole *échiquier* of that army and its theatre of operations.

Hence each *échiquier* should have its special base, its objective point, its zones and lines of operations which lead from the base to the objective aim in the offensive, or from the objective aim to the base in the defensive.

With regard to the material or topographical points, with which a theatre of operations is found more or less furrowed in every direction, the art is not wanting in works which have discussed their different strategical or tactical properties ; the routes, the rivers, the mountains, the forests, the cities offering resources, or secure from a *coup de main*, the strong holds, have been the object of many debates, in which the most erudite have not always been the most luminous.

Some have given to names strange significations ; it has been published and taught, that rivers were lines of operations *par excellence!* Now, as such a line could not exist without having two or three roads for moving the army within the sphere of its enterprises, and at least one line of retreat, those modern Moseses pretended thus to transform rivers into lines of retreat, and even into lines of manœuvre ! It would appear much more natural and correct to say that rivers are excellent lines of supply, powerful auxiliaries for the establishment of a good line of operations, but are never this line itself.

It is not with less astonishment that we have seen it affirmed by a grave writer, that, *if a country were to be created to make of it a good theatre of war, it would be necessary to avoid constructing converging routes therein, because they facilitate invasion !* As if a country could exist without a capital, without rich and industrious cities, and as if the routes did not per force converge towards those points where the interests of a whole country are naturally and irresistably concentrated. ' Even though a steppe were made of all Germany, in order to reconstruct in it a theatre of war to the liking of the author, commercial cities would rise again, chief towns would be re-established, and all the roads would converge anew towards those vivificating arteries. Besides, did not the Arch-Duke Charles owe to these converging routes the facility with which he beat Jourdan in 1796 ? And, in fact, do not those routes favor the defense as much as the attack, since two masses, falling back on two converging rays, can unite quicker than the two masses which should follow, and thus beat them separately.

Other authors have insisted that mountainous countries are full of strategic points, and the antagonists of this opinion have affirmed that strategical points were, on the contrary, more rare in the Alps than in the plains, but that, on the other hand, if they were less numerous, they were for that reason all the more important and decisive.

Some writers have presented also high mountains as so many Chinese Walls, inaccessible for every thing; whereas, Napoleon, in speaking of the Rhetian Alps, said, " *that an army ought to pass wherever a man could plant his foot.*"

Generals, experienced also in mountain warfare, have acknowledged, in the same manner, the great difficulty of conducting therein a defensive war, except by uniting the advantages of a rising in mass of the populations to those of a reuglar army, the first for guarding the summits and harrassing the enemy, the latter for delivering him battle upon the decisive points at the junction of the great valleys.

In animadverting upon these contradictions, we do not yield to a futile spirit of criticism, but merely to the desire of demonstrating to our readers that, far from having carried the art to its utmost limits, there still exist a multitude of points to discuss :

We shall not undertake to demonstrate here the strategical value of the divers topographical or artificial accidents which compose a theatre of war, for the most important will be examined in the different articles of this chapter, to which they belong; but, it may be said in general, that this value depends much upon the skill of the chiefs, and upon the spirit with which they are animated; the great captain who had crossed the St. Bernard, and ordered the passage of the Splugen, was far from believing in the *impregnability* of those chains, and he little suspected that a miserable, muddy stream, and a walled enclosure were to change his destinies at Waterloo.

ARTICLE XVIII.

BASES OF OPERATIONS.

The first point in a plan of operations is to be assured of a good base; this name is applied to the extent of the frontiers of a State from whence an army will draw its resources and reinforcements; that from whence it will have to depart for an offensive expedition, and where it will find a refuge in time of need; that, in fine, upon which it will have to support itself, if it covers its country defensively. In this last case, the line of the frontiers will become the first line of defense, and the army will then have to provide itself with a base in second line, either in the direction of the centre of the State, or in a direction nearly parallel to the frontier, according to what will be explained in article 38, upon so styled excentric retreats.

Although the base of operations is also ordinarily that of resources, meanwhile, every line by which a part of those resources should come, would not for that be a line of operations, but a line of supply.

Each army may have several successive bases. A French army operating in Germany, has for a first base the Rhine; but if it be withdrawn behind that river, it has a new base upon the Moselle; it may have a third upon Seine, and a fourth upon the Loire.

When an army is repulsed upon its first base, this becomes then a line of defense, especially if it be fortified; in this case, the army must have a new base in second line.

A base, supported upon a large and impetuous river, the banks of which should be held by good fortresses, situated in command of this river, would be, without contradiction, the most favorable that could be desired.

The larger the base, the less easy it is to cover, but the less easy will it be also to cut off the army from it.

A State, the capital or centre of power of which, is too near the first frontier, offers less advantages for basing its defenders, than a State whose capital is more removed.

Every base, to be perfect, should offer two or three places, of a capacity sufficient for establishing thereon magazines, depôts, &c. It should have at least one intrenched *tête de pont*, upon each of the unfordable rivers found upon it.

Until now, there has generally been sufficient accord upon all the requisites we have just enumerated; but there are other points upon which opinions have been more divided. Several writers have insisted that, to be perfect, a base should be parallel with that of the adversary; whereas, on the contrary, I have uttered the opinion that bases, perpendicular to those of the enemy, are the most advantageous, particularly those which, presenting two faces nearly perpendicular, the one to the other, and forming a reentrant angle. would assure a double base at need, would control two sides of the strategic field (*échiquier stratégique,*) would procure two lines of retreat very distant from each other, and finally, would facilitate every change of the line of operations which the unexpected turn of the chances of war could render necessary.

I demonstrated nearly thirty years ago, in my treatise on grand military operations, the influence which the direction of frontiers ought to exercise upon that of the base and of the lines of operations. It is recollected that, in applying those truths to the different theatres of war, I compared the latter to an *échiquier,* bounded on one side or the other by a sea, or by a great neutral power, which would form equally an insurmountable obstacle. See how I expressed myself :

" The general configuration of the theatre of war may have also a great influence upon the direction to be given to lines of operations, (and consequently to the bases.)

" In fact, if the whole theatre of war form a field, or figure, presenting four faces, more or less regular, it may happen that one of the armies, at the commencement of the campaign, occupies a single one of those faces, as it is possible that it may hold two of them, whilst the enemy should occupy but one only, and that the fourth should form an insurmountable obstacle. The manner in which this theatre of war would be embraced, would present then very different combinations in each of those hypotheses.

" In order better to make this comprehended, I will cite the theatre of war of the French armies in Westphalia, from 1757 to 1762, and that of Napoleon in 1806." (See Fig. 1.)

FIGURE I.

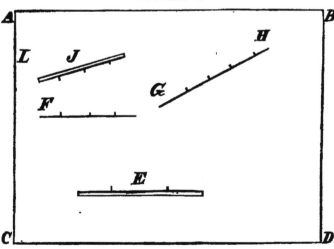

"In the first of these theatres of war, the side AB was formed by the North Sea, the side BD by the line of the Weser, base of the army of the Duke Ferdinand ; the line of the Main formed the side CD, base of the French army, and the face AC was formed by the line of the Rhine, equally guarded by the armies of Louis XV.

"It is seen, then, that the French armies, operating offensively, and holding two faces, had in their favor the North Sea, forming the third side, and that consequently they had only to gain the side BD by manœuvres, in order to be masters of the four faces, that is to say, the base and all the communications of the enemy, as the above figure shows.

"The French army E, departing from the base CD, to gain the front of operations FGH, cut off the allied army J, from the side BD, which formed its base ; this latter would then have been thrown back upon the angle L, A, M, formed near Emden, by the lines of the Rhine, the Ems and the North Sea ; whilst the French army, E, could always communicate with its bases of the Main and Rhine.

The manœuvre of Napoleon upon the Saale in 1806, was combined absolutely in the same manner ; he occupied at Jena and at Naumburg the line FGH, and marched afterwards by Halle and Dessau, in order to throw back the Prussian army J, upon the side AB, formed by the sea. The result is sufficiently well known.

"The great art of directing properly one's lines of operations consists then in combining his marches in such a manner as to seize the hostile communication, without losing his own ; it is easily seen that the line FGH, in consequence of its prolonged position, and the crotchet left upon the extremity of the enemy, preserves always one's communications with the base CD ; it is the exact application of the manœuvres at Marengo, Ulm, and Jena.

"When the theatre of war shall not be adjacent to the sea, it will always be limited by a great neutral power, which will guard its frontiers and close one of the sides of the square ; doubtless it will not be a barrier as insurmountable as the sea ; but, in general thesis it can always be considered an obstacle upon which it would be dangerous to fall back after a defeat, and advantageous for the same reason to crowd an enemy upon. The territory of a power which should have a hundred and fifty or two hundred thousand men, is not violated with impunity, and if a beaten army took this course, it would be none the less cut off from its base.

"If it were a small power which limited the theatre of war, it is proba-

ble that it would soon be united with it, and the face of the square would
be found merely a little more retired, to the frontiers of a great power or
to a sea.

"To be assured of the correctness of these ideas, it is sufficient to cast
an eye over the theatre of the campaign of 1806 and 1807. The Baltic
Sea, and the frontiers of Austrian Gallicia, formed the two faces AB and
CD of the square. I think that it was very important to both the parties,
not to allow themselves, to be thrown upon either of those obstacles.

"The configuration of the frontiers will sometimes modify the form of the
faces of the square, or, more correctly speaking, the faces of the *échiquier*.
It may have the form of a trapezoid, as in the following figure.

FIGURE II.

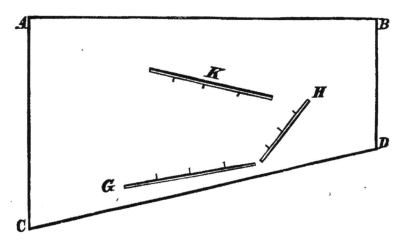

"In this latter case, the army GH, which should be master of the faces
AC and CD, would have still greater advantages, since the base of its adversary narrowing towards BD, the latter would have many more difficulties
in regaining his communications; the front of this base offering less development, would present also less resources for manœuvering, and it
would give, on the contrary, to the army GH, the means of operating
with more success, since the direction of its line CD, would naturally lead
it upon the communications of its adversary, and the space which it would
have to occupy, in order to cut them off, would be less extended, consequently more easy to take up.

"The theatre of war in Prussia and Poland, of which we have just spoken, was actually similar to this, for the frontiers of Gallicia, prolonged to the Narew, formed, with the line of the Vistula, the contracted side BD. The manner in which Napoleon manœuvred before the battle of Eylau, was absolutely the same as that which is found traced; a fortuitous incident prevented him from obtaining from it all the success which he expected, but his manœuvre was none the less wise for that. Meanwhile, this operation offered also its unfavorable chances, because of political antecedents; the first was founded upon the small confidence which could be accorded to the Austrian neutrality; the second upon the great remoteness of the base of the French army which put its communications with the Elbe at the mercy of the cabinet of Vienna; it depended only upon the latter, from this epoch, to put an end to those immoderate invasions; the manœuvre of the French general might be strategically good, whilst the operations of the statesman was nothing else than audacious."

The base in Bohemia in 1813, proves, as well as all that precedes, in favor of my opinion; for it was by the perpendicular direction of that base to that of the French army, that the Allies succeeded in paralyzing the immense advantages which the line of the Elbe would, but for that, have procured for Napoleon; a circumstance which made all the chances of the campaign turn in their favor. In the same manner, in 1812, it was, by basing themselves perpendicularly upon the Oka and Kalouga, that the Russians were able to execute their flank march upon Wiazma and Krasnoï.

Moreover, to be convinced of this, it is sufficient to reflect, that the front of operations of an army, the base of which should be perpendicular to that of the enemy, would be found established parallelly to the line of operations of its adversaries, and that it would thus become very easy to operate upon their communications and their line of retreat.

I have already said that perpendicular bases would be especially favorable when they should present a double frontier, as will be seen in the above-mentioned figures; now, the critics will not fail to object that this does not accord with what I have said in favor of frontiers salient to the side of the enemy, and against double lines of operations with an equality of forces.

The objection would be more specious than just, for the greatest advantage of a perpendicular base results precisely in that it forms a salient which takes in reverse a part of the theatre of operations. Again, the possession of a base with two faces by no means implies the necessity of occupying both in force; it suffices on the contrary, to have upon one of them, a few fortified points, with a small corps of observation, whilst the weight of one's forces would be carried on the other face, as had place in the campaigns of 1800 and 1806. The nearly right angle, formed by the Rhine, from Constance to Basle, and from thence to Kehl, offered to Gen. Moreau one base parallel, and another perpendicular to that of his antagonist. He pushed two divisions by his left upon the first of those bases, towards Kehl, in order to draw the attention of the enemy in that direction, whilst he filed with nine divisions upon the extremity of the perpendicular face to the side of Schaffhausen, which brought him, in a few marches, to the gates of Augsburg, after the two detached divisions had already rejoined him.

Napoleon, in 1806, had also the double base of the Main and the Rhine; forming almost a right reentrant angle ; he contented himself with leaving Mortier upon the parallel face, that is to say, upon that of the Rhine, whilst that with all the mass of his forces, he gained the extremity of the perpendicular face, and thus anticipated the Prussians at Gera and at Naumburg, on their line of retreat.

Here are, I trust, sufficient proofs to demonstrate the necessity of suspecting somewhat, that strategy, which is treated too geometrically, and to convince one that if this science has made great progress, it can still be improved by modifying the *geometrical systems*, by those founded upon the principles and the experience of war, which counsel a slight deviation from the first.

Another not less important question, as to the best direction to be given to bases of operations, is that which has respect to bases established upon the sea shore, and which has also given rise to grave errors ; for, as favorable as they are for some, equally formidable would they be for others, as may be seen from all that precedes. After having pointed out the danger there would be for a continental army to be thrown back upon the sea, it should appear astonishing that any one could have vaunted the advantages of bases established upon its shores, and that they could suit any but an insular army. In fact, Wellington, coming with his fleet to the succor of Portugal and of Spain, could adopt no better base than that of Lisbon, or, more properly speaking, the *presqu 'île* of Torres-Vedras, which covers the only avenues to that capital on the land side. Here the banks of the Tagus, and those of the sea, covered not only his two flanks, but they yet assured his line of retreat, which could have place only upon his vessels.

Seduced by the advantages which this famous intrenched camp of Torres-Vedras had procured the English general, and only judging from effects, without going back to causes, many generals, very learned in other respects, would no longer acknowledge as good bases, any but those which, situated on the sea shore, would procure the army easy supplies, and places of refuge, with flanks secure from insult. This blindness was pushed to such a degree, that General Pfuhl sustained, in 1812, that the natural base of the Russians was at Riga, a strategical blasphemy, which was also uttered in my presence, by one of the most renowned of the French generals.

Fascinated by similar ideas, Colonel Carion-Nizas, dared even to publish, that in 1813, Napoleon ought to have placed half of his army in Bohemia, and to have thrown a hundred and fifty thousand men *at the mouths of the Elbe,* near Hamburg! Forgetting that the first rule of all bases of a continental army, is that they rest upon the front the most opposite to the sea; that is to say, upon that which would place the army at the centre of all the elements of its military power, and if its population, from which it would be found separated and. cut off, if it committed the grave fault of resting upon the sea.

An insular power, acting upon the continent, ought naturally to make the diametrically opposite calculation, to the end, nevertheless, of applying the same axiom, which prescribes to each, *to seek his base upon the points where he can be sustained by all his means of war, and find, at the same time, a certain refuge.*

A power, strong both upon sea and land, and whose numerous squadrons command a sea adjacent to the theatre of operations, might, indeed, be able still to base a small army of forty or fifty thousand men upon its shore, by assuring it a well protected refuge, and supplies of every kind; but to give such a base to continental masses of a hundred and fifty thousand men, engaged with forces disciplined and nearly equal in numbers, would ever be an act of folly.

Meanwhile, as every maxim has its exceptions, there is a case in which it might be proper to deviate from what we have just said, and to carry ones operations to the sea side; it is when we should have to do with an adversary little to be dreaded in the field, and when being decided masters of that sea, we could supply ourselves easily from that quarter, whilst it would be difficult to do so in the interior of the country. Although it is very rare to see those three conditions united, it was, nevertheless, what happened in the war with Turkey, in 1828 and 1829. All attention was fixed upon Warna and Bourgas, merely observing Shoomla, a system which would not have been maintained in front of an European army, even though the sea had been held, without exposure to a probable ruin.

Notwithstanding all that has been said by the idlers who decide upon the fate of empires, this war was well conducted, saving a few faults ; the army took care to cover itself by making sure of the fortresses of Brailof, Warna and Silistria, then by preparing itself a depôt at Sizipoli. As soon as it was sufficiently based, it pushed directly upon Adrianople, which previously would have been a folly. If it had not come from so far in 1828, or had had two months more of good weather, all would have been terminated in this first campaign.

Besides the permanent bases, which are ordinarily found established on one's own frontiers, or at least in the country of an ally that can be counted upon, there are also eventual or temporary ones, which depend upon operations undertaken in a hostile country ; but as these are rather transient points of support we shall say a few words of them in a special article, to the end of avoiding the confusion which might result from a similitude of denomination. (See article 23.)

ARTICLE XIX.

STRATEGICAL POINTS AND LINES, DECISIVE POINTS OF A THEATRE OF WAR, AND OBJECTIVES OF OPERATIONS.

There are strategic points and lines of divers natures. Some receive this name from the fact alone of their situation, from which results all their importance on the field of operations ; they are then permanent geographical strategic points. Others acquire their value from the relations which they have with the position of the hostile forces, and with the enterprises which it should be designed to form against them ; *these, then, are strategic points of manœuvre*, and altogether eventual. Finally, there are strategic points and lines which have but a secondary importance, and others the importance of which is at once immense and incessant ; these last I have named *decisive strategic points*.

I am about to endeavor to explain those relations as clearly as I myself conceive them, which is not always so easy as is believed in such matters.

Every point of the theatre of war which should have a military importance, either from its situation at the centre of communications, or from military establishments and fortified works of whatever description, which would have an influence over the strategic field, will be, in reality, a territorial or geographical strategic point.

An illustrious general affirms, on the contrary, that every point which might unite the above-mentioned conditions, would not be for that a strategic point, if it were not found in a suitable direction relatively to the operation which should be had in view. I shall be pardoned for declaring a different opinion, for a strategical point is always such from its nature, and that one even which should be the farthest removed from the theatre of first enterprises, could be drawn into it by the unexpected turn of events, and thus acquire all the importance of which it would be susceptible. It had been more exact then, in my opinion, to say that all strategic points were not decisive points.

Strategic lines are equally either geographical or relative only to temporary manœuvres ; the first may be subdivided into two classes, namely, the geographical lines which from their permanent importance, belong to the decisive points of the theatre of war,* and those which have value only because they connect two strategical points together.

For fear of confounding these different subjects, we shall treat separately of the strategic lines which relate to a combined manœuvre, in order to limit ourselves here to what concerns *the decisive and objective points* of the zone of operations upon which the enterprises will be directed.

Although there exist intimate relations between these two kinds of points, seeing that every objective must necessarily be one of the decisive points of the theatre of war, there is, meanwhile, a distinction to be made, for all decisive points could not be at the same time the objective aim of operations. Let us occupy ourselves, then, in the first place, in defining the former, which will conduct more easily to the good choice of the second.

I think the name *decisive strategic point*, may be given to all those

---

*I shall be reproached yet, perhaps, for a barbarism. because I give the name decisive or objective point to lines, and that a point could not be a line. It is useless to observe to my readers, that objective points are not geometrical points, but a grammatical formula, expressing the object which an army proposes to itself. And if the word *decisive* be objected to, seeing that a point by itself is rarely decisive, the word *important*. may be substituted for it, although it does not express so strongly the idea which I attach to it.

which are susceptible of exercising a notable influence, whether upon the whole of the campaign, or upon a single enterprise. All points, the geographical situation and artificial advantages of which would favor the attack or defense of a front of operations, or of a line of defense, are of this number, and the great well situated places of arms hold the first rank among them.

The decisive points of a theatre of war are then of several kinds. The first are the geographical points, or lines, the importance of which is permanent, and is derived from the configuration even of the *échiquier*. Let us take, for example, the theatre of war of the French in Belgium; it is quite plain that the one of the two parties which shall be master of the course of the Meuse, will be master of the country; for its adversary, outflanked and shut up between the Meuse and the North Sea, could not receive battle parallelly to this sea, without running the risk of a total loss. In the same manner, the valley of the Danube presents a series of important points, which have caused it to be regarded as the key to South ern Germany.

Geographical decisive points are also those which would control the junction of several valleys, and the centre of the great communications which intersect a country. For example, Lyons is an important strategic point, because it commands the two valleys of the Rhone and the Saône, and is found at the centre of the communications of France with Italy, and of the south with the east; but it would be decisive only so far as there should be found there a strong place, or intrenched camp with *têtes de ponts*.

Leipzig is incontestably a strategic point, because it is found at the junction of all the communications of the north of Germany. If this city were fortified, and situated on the two banks of a large river, it would be almost the key of the country, (if a country has a key, and this figurative expression means any thing else than a decisive point.)

All capitals, being at the centre of the routes of a country, would thus be decisive strategic points, not only for that reason, but through other motives which add to this importance.

Besides those points, there exist, in mountainous countries, defiles which are the only practicable issues for an army; these geographical points may be decisive in an enterprise upon the country; it is known what importance the defile of Bard, covered by a little fort, had in 1800.

The second kind of decisive points is that of eventual points of manœuvre, which are relative, and result from the situation of the troops of the two parties ; for example, Mack, being found concentrated in 1805, near Ulm, and awaiting the Russian army by Moravia, the decisive point for attacking him was Donauwerth, or the Lower-Lech, for, in gaining it before him, one cut off his line of retreat upon Austria, and upon the army destined to second him. On the contrary, in 1800, Kray, finding himself in the same position at Ulm, did not wait for the concurrence of any army from the side of Bohemia, but rather from the Tyrol and the victorious army of Melas in Italy ; hence the decisive point for attacking him was no longer Donauwerth, but the side opposite in preference, that is to say, by Schaffhausen, since it was the means of taking in reverse his front of operations, of cutting off his retreat, and of isolating him from the secondary army, as well as from his base, by throwing him back upon the Maine. In the same campaign of 1800, the first objective point of Bonaparte, was to fall upon the right of Melas by the St. Bernard, in order to seize his communications ; it is judged that the St. Bernard and Aosta were not decisive geographical points, but rather those of manœuvre, since their importance depended upon the march of Melas on Nice.

It may be laid down as a general principle, that the decisive points of manœuvre, are upon that one of the extremities of the enemy from whence he could be the more easily separated from his base and from his secondary armies, without exposing one's self to running the same risk. The extremity opposite to the sea ought always to be preferred, because it is as advantageous to drive the enemy upon the sea, as it is dangerous to expose yourself to a like chance ; unless you have to do with an insular and inferior army, in which case you may seek to cut it off from its vessels.

If the hostile army be scattered, or extended over a very long line, then the decisive point will be the centre ; for, by penetrating there, the division of the hostile forces will be augmented, that is to say, their weakness will be doubled, and these troops overwhelmed in detail, will doubtless be ruined.

The decisive point of a field of battle is determined :

1. From the configuration of the ground ;

2. From the combination of the localities with the strategic aim of an army.

3. From the positions of the respective forces.

But, in order not to anticipate the combinations of tactics, we shall treat of those points in the chapter on battles.

OBJECTIVE POINTS.

It is with these points as with the preceding, that is to say, there are objective points of manœuvre, and others which are geographical, such as an important fortress, the line of a river, a front of operations which would offer good lines of defense, or good points of support for ulterior enterprises.

In strategy, the object of a campaign determines the objective point. If this object be offensive, the point will be the occupation of the hostile capital, or that of a military province, the loss of which could determine the enemy to peace. In a war of invasion, the capital is ordinarily the objective point which the assailant proposes to himself. However, the geographical situation of that capital, the political relations of the belligerent powers with neighboring powers, their reciprocal resources, whether positive or federative, form as many combinations, foreign in reality to the science of combat, but very intimately connected, nevertheless, with plans of operations, and which may decide whether an army should desire or fear to push to the hostile capital.

In default of this capital, the objective point will be any front of operations whatever, which should serve as first base to the enemy, and where should be found certain important places, the possession of which would secure to the army that of the territory occupied; for example, in a war against Austria, if France invaded Italy, its first objective would be to attain the line of the Ticino and of the Pô; the second objective would be Mantua and the line of the Adige; the third would be the Noric Alps, &c.

In the defensive, the objective point, instead of being that which we should wish to conquer, would be that which we should seek to cover. The capital being looked upon as the focus of a power, becomes the principal objective point in the defensive; but there may be points nearer, as, for example, the defense of the first front and the first base of operations; thus, a French army, being reduced to the defensive behind the Rhine, will have for a first objective point the preventing the passage of the river; it will seek to succor the places of Alsace, if the enemy succeed in effecting his passage and in besieging them; the second objective will be to cover the first base of operations, which shall be found on the Meuse, or the Moselle.

With regard to objective points of *manœuvre*, their whole importance will be judged by what we have already said above of decisive points of the same kind. It is, in some sort, in the good choice of those points of manœuvre, that consists the most valuable talent of a general, and the surest pledge of great successes. It is certain, at least, that it was the the most incontestable merit of Napoleon.

Rejecting the old routine, which looked only to the capture of one or two places, or to the occupation of a petty adjacent province, he appeared convinced that the first means of doing great things, was to strive, above all, to dislocate and to ruin the hostile army; certain that States and provinces fall of themselves, when they have no longer organized forces for covering them.* To measure, with a sure *coup d'œil*, the chances which the different zones of a theatre of war would offer; to direct your masses concentrically upon that one of your zones which should evidently be the most advantageous; to neglect nothing for instructing yourself as to the approximate position of the hostile masses; then to burst, with the rapidity of lightning, upon the centre of this army, if it be divided, or upon that one of the two extremities which should conduct the most directly upon its communications, to outflank it, to cut it off, to break it up; to pursue it to the utmost, forcing it in divergent directions; finally, quitting it only after having annihilated or dispersed it—this is what all the first campaigns of Napoleon indicate as one of the best systems, or at least, as the basis of that which he preferred.

Applied later to the immense distances, and to the inhospitable countries of Russia, those manœuvres had not, in truth, the same success as in Germany; however, it must be acknowledged, that if this kind of warfare is not suited to all capacities, nor to all countries, nor to all circumstances, its chances are none the less vast, and are really founded on the application of principles; the excessive abuse which Napoleon made of this system, could not destroy the real advantages which might be expected from it, when one knows how to impose a limit to his successes, and to put his enterprises in harmony with the respective condition of the armies and the nations adjacent.

The maxims which could be given upon these important strategical operations, are almost wholly contained in what we have just said upon decisive points, and in what we shall explain further on, in speaking of the choice of lines of operations. (Art. 21.)

As for what concerns the choice of objective points of manœuvre, all will depend ordinarily upon the object of the war, upon the character

---

* The war in Spain, and all national wars, may be cited as exceptions; meanwhile, without the succor of an organised army, either foreign or national, every partial struggle of populations will succumb in the long run.

which circumstances or the will of cabinets should impress upon it ; finally, upon the reciprocal means of war. In many instances, objective points will be principally geographical, for there will then be had in view only the taking of a few cities, or the obtaining the evacuation of petty adjacent provinces ; in others it will be, as with Napoleon, the destruction of the hostile army that must be aimed at. The manœuvres at Ulm and Jena could not be advised to an army which should march merely to besiege Antwerp. For far different motives it would not have been prudent, to counsel them to the French army beyond the Niemen, five hundred leagues from its frontiers.

There is yet a particular kind of objective points which could not be passed over in silence ; they are those which, having for object any military point whatever, relate, nevertheless, to the combinations of policy, much more than to those of strategy; in coalitions, especially, it is rare that they do not play a very great part, by the influence they have upon the operations and combinations of cabinets ; they might be named then, *political objective points*, without the charge of technological mania.

In fact, besides the intimate relations which exist between policy and war for the preparation of the latter, there are, in almost all campaigns, military enterprises, formed for satisfying political views, often very important, but frequently very unreasonable, and which, strategically speaking, would be grave faults, rather than useful operations. We shall limit ourselves to citing two examples of them : the expedition of the Duke of York to Dunkirk, in 1793, suggested to the English, by ancient maritime and commercial views, gave to the operations of the Allies a divergent direction which caused their failure, and this objective point was good neither in strategy nor in tactics.

The expedition of the same prince to Holland, in 1799, equally dictated by the same views of the cabinet of London, strengthened by the mental reservations of Austria upon Belgium, was not less fatal, in causing the march of the Arch-Duke Charles from Zurich upon Manheim, an operation quite contrary to the manifest interests of the Allies at the epoch in which it was resolved upon.

These truths prove that the choice of political objective points ought to be subordinate to those of strategy, at least, so far as great military questions may be decided by arms.

For the rest, this subject is so vast and so complicated that it would be absurd to attempt to subject it to rules ; the only one that can be proposed is that which we have just indicated : to put it in practice it is necessary, either that the political objective points adopted in the course of a campaign, be in accordance with the principles of strategy, or, in the contrary case, that they be adjourned until after a decisive victory.

By applying this maxim to the two events above cited, it will be acknowledged that it was at Cambrai, or in the heart of France, that it was necessary to conquer Dunkirk in 1793, and to deliver Holland in 1799; that is to say, by uniting the efforts of the coalition upon a decisive point of the frontiers, and by striking there a heavy blow. For the rest, expeditions of this nature enter almost always into the class of great diversions, to which we shall devote a special article.

ARTICLE XX.

FRONTS OF OPERATIONS, LINES OF DEFENSE, AND STRATEGICAL POSITIONS.*

There are certain points in the military science which have so much affinity to each other, that we are tempted to take them for one and the same thing, although they are substantially different.

Of this number are fronts of operations, lines of defense, and strategical positions. One will be assured by the following observations, of the intimate relations, and of the difference which exist between them, and will appreciate the motives which have decided us to unite them in the same article.

LINES OF DEFENSE.

Lines of defense are of several natures; they are strategical and tac-

---

* This article ought strictly to be placed after that on lines of operations, especially in a methodical instruction; meanwhile, as in the latter, fronts of operations are frequently in question, I thought I might leave things as they are

tical. In the first, there are those which are permanent, and relate to the system of defense of the State, as fortified frontier lines, &c.; others which are only eventual, and have reference merely to the transient position where an army is found.

The lines of frontiers are the permanent lines of defense, when they present a mixture of natural and artificial obstacles, such as chains of mountains, great rivers and fortresses, forming between each other a well connected system. Thus, the chain of the Alps between Piedmont and France, is a line of defense, since the practicable passages are garnished with forts which would interpose great obstacles to the enterprises of an army, and at the outlets of the gorges, great places of arms cover the different valleys of Piedmont. In the same manner the Rhine, the Oder and the Elbe may, in some respects, also be considered as permanent lines of defense, because of the important places which cover them.

All those combinations relating rather to a system of places than to the operations of a campaign, we shall treat of them in the article on fortresses, (Art. 26.)

With regard to *eventual lines of defense*, it may be said that every considerable river, every chain of mountains, and every great defile, having upon its accessible points a few temporary intrenchments, may be regarded as a line of defense at once strategical and tactical, since it serves to suspend, for some days, the march of the enemy, and compels him often to deviate from his direct route to seek a less difficult passage; in this case it procures an evident strategic advantage; but if the enemy attack it in front, it has, unquestionably, a tactical advantage, since it is always more difficult to force an army behind a river, or in a post strong by nature and art, than to attack it in an open plain.

However, this tactical advantage must not be exaggerated, lest we should fall into the system of positions (*starke positionen*,) which has caused the ruin of so many armies; for, whatever may be the difficulties at first of a defensive camp, it is certain that he who waits in it passively will end by succumbing.* Besides, every position which is very strong by nature, being of difficult access,† is as difficult of egress as of ingress, and the enemy will be able, with a few troops, to hold and block up, as it were, the issues of the army in position, with forces inferior to its defenders; this is what happened to the Saxons in the camp of Pirna, and to Wurmser at Mantua.

---

* It must be observed that it is not a question here of fortified camps, which make a great difference, and will be treated of in Art. 36.

† Positions of encampments are here referred to, and not fields of battle.

FRONTS OF OPERATIONS.

A front of operations is the extent of a line which an army occupies in advance of its base, and in the sphere of which it acts momentarily, whether in an enemy's country, or in its own.

The front of operations seems, then, to be, in reality, only what is also called a transient line of defense; however, they are two things which it is useful to distinguish.

In general, the line of defense implies with it a defensive idea, for an army which invades a country rarely occupies itself with choosing therein a line of defense, unless it be constrained to it by the unexpected turn of events; but, although it should not look to this precaution, that would not prevent its having a front of operations, even though it should move forward from success to success.

In my view, the term general front of operations ought to be applied to the whole front which an army presents to the enemy, within the extent of the zone adopted, and which can also be named the strategic front; whilst the line of defense will oftener be but a part of this front, where the army will have assembled its principal forces when it shall await the enemy in its positions; from whence it may be concluded: 1st, that the front of operations is a whole of which the line of defense forms but a part; 2dly, that the latter is ordinarily found in rear, or as a second line of the former; 3dly, that the one is applied especially to an army on the defensive, whilst the other is applicable equally to all acting armies.

For example, at the time of the commencement of hostilities, at the end of 1813, the general front of operations of Napoleon extended first from Hamburg to Wittenburg, from whence it ran along the line of the Allies to near Glogau and Breslau, since his right was at Lowenberg; finally, he fell back in rear upon the frontier of Bohemia to Dresden. His forces were distributed upon this great front in four masses, the strategic positions of which were interior or central. Withdrawn later behind the Elbe, his real line of defense then extended only from Wittenberg to Dresden, with a crotchet in rear on Marienberg; for Hamburg and Magdeberg even, were found already outside of his strategic field, and he would have been lost if he had thought of carrying his operations in that direction.

As another example, I will cite his position around Mantua in 1796. His front of operations extended, in reality, from the mountains of Bergamo to the Adriatic Sea, whilst that in need his true line of defense was upon the Adige, between Lake Garda and Legnano, afterwards on the Mincio, between Peschiera and Mantua.

In a first edition of this chapter, I cited for examples, the lines of the Lech, of the Iser, and of the Inn, as fronts of operations for a French army acting in Bavaria, from whence it will be concluded, perhaps, that I confounded here the lines of defense with the front of operations. But I spoke thus, regarding Bavaria only as an isolated *échiquier*, which it might be the question to cover; in reality, if we attach to the operations of that French army an idea more general, and based upon the lessons of history, it is certain that those rivers would be veritable lines of defense; whilst that in consequence of the combinations of the Austrians, the front of operations would embrace, perhaps, the two banks of the Danube, and the part of the Tyrol the most adjacent to the theatre of war, that is to say, the northern Tyrol to the Brenner; not that it would be necessary that all this space should be at the same time the theatre of simultaneous manœuvres, but from the fact alone, that at any moment the presence of the enemy at a given point thereon, might be discovered, and the carrying there of considerable forces rendered necessary.

As fronts of operations and lines of defense are determined by circumstances and localities, there are few axioms to give relative thereto. For the one as for the other, it is important to have sure communications with the different points of the line of operations; it is advantageous also to have upon the flanks, the same as upon the front, great natural or artificial obstacles which may serve as points of support. The points of support which a front of operations should offer, are also called *pivots of operations*, these are partial bases for a given time, and must not be confounded with the pivots of a manœuvre. For example, in the campaign of 1796, Verona was an excellent pivot of operations for all the enterprises which Napoleon undertook around Mantua during eight whole months. Dresden was in like manner in 1813, the pivot of all his movements. Those points are temporary or eventual places of arms.

The pivots of manœuvre are the moveable corps that are left upon a point, the occupation of which is essential, whilst the bulk of the army marches to great enterprises; thus the corps of Ney was the pivot of the manœuvre which Napoleon made by Donauwerth and Augsburg, to cut off Mack from his line of retreat; this corps increased to five divisions, masked Ulm, and held the left bank of the Danube. The manœuvre finished, the pivot ceased to exist, whereas, a pivot of operations is a material point, advantageous under the double strategical and tactical relation, and serves as a support for an entire period of the campaign.

With regard to the line of defense, the most desirable quality, in my view, is that this line be as little extended as possible, for the more contracted it shall be, the more easily will the army cover it, if it be thrown back upon the defensive. For the front of operations it is not altogether the same, because if this front were too contracted, it would be difficult for an offensive army to make strategic manœuvres which might lead to great results, seeing that this contracted front would offer to the defensive army the means of covering it more easily. However, a too great front of operations is none the more suitable to the successes of offensive strategic operations; for a too immense extent would give to the enemy, if not a good line of defense, at least spaces vast enough for escaping the results of a well combined strategic manœuvre. Thus, the splendid operations of Marengo, Ulm and Jena, could not have had such results upon a theatre as extended as that of the war with Russia in 1812, because the army, cut off from its principal line of retreat, could have found another by throwing itself upon a different zone from that which it had primitively adopted.

The direction which is given to a front of operations may have a notable influence upon the strategical movements of an army, and merits under this relation a particular attention. In general thesis, it seems that this front ought to be parallel to the primitive base, and to traverse the line of operations in a manner to extend beyond its two sides to the end of better covering it; there are, nevertheless, circumstances in which it would be very advantageous, on the contrary, to present to the enemy a front of operations perpendicular to the general base and parallel to the principal line of operations. This direction might form thus a kind of new temporary or eventual base, which would place the army in a situation almost as favorable as that traced in the figure on page 90, for the army FG, since it would procure the possession of two sides of the strategic *échiquier*. The front of operations which Napoleon adopted in his march upon Eylau presented all these peculiarities: his pivots of operations were at Warsaw and at Thorn, which made of the Vistula a sort of temporary base; the front of operations was parallel to the Narew, from whence Napoleon departed, supporting himself on Sierock, Pultusk and Ostrolenka, to the end of manœuvreing by his right, to throw the Russians upon Elbing and the Baltic Sea. In such cases the front of operations, if it should find the least point of support in its new direction, would produce the same advantage that we have pointed out in Article 18 for bases of operations perpendicular to those of the enemy. It is merely necessary to keep in view that, for a like operation, an army must be sure of being able at need, to regain its temporary base; that is to say, it is indispensable that this base be prolonged far behind the strate-

gic front and be found covered by it : Napoleon marching from the Narew by Allenstein upon Eylau, had behind his left the place of Thorn,
and, farther still from the front of the army, the *tête de pont* of Praga
and Warsaw ; so that his communications were perfectly secure, whilst
that Benningsen, forced to face him and to take his line of combat parallelly to the Baltic, might be cut off from his base and rolled back upon
the mouths of the Vistula.

A strategical front may be given a like direction perpendicular to the
base, either by a temporary movement of conversion, executed for an
operation of a few days merely, or by adopting it for an indefinite time,
with the object of profiting from the advantages which certain localities
might offer for procuring the army a good line of defense, and good pivots
of operations which are equivalent almost to a real base.

It happens often that an army is compelled to have double fronts of
operations, either from the configuration of certain theatres of war, or
because that every line of offensive operations somewhat extended in depth,
requires to be well secured on its flanks.   In the first case, the frontier of
Turkey and that of Spain might be cited as an example.   Armies which
should wish to cross the Balkan or the Ebro would be forced to have a
double front of operations: the first for facing the valley of the Danube,
the other for showing front to forces coming from Saragossa or from
Leon.

All considerably vast countries present more or less that same necessity ;
for example, a French army marching in the valley of the Danube will
always have, either on the side of Bohemia, or on the side of the Tyrol,
need of a double strategical front, as soon as the Austrians should have
thrown into these provinces corps sufficiently numerous to give it serious
uneasiness.   Those countries alone, whose frontiers should be very narrow on the side of the enemy, would be exceptions, because the corps
which should be left thereon, in retiring to menace the flanks of the
enemy, would themselves be easily cut off and taken.

This necessity of double fronts of operations is one of the gravest of
inconveniences for an offensive army, since it compels great detachments,
always injurious, as we shall see farther on (Art. 28.)

Before quitting subjects which are often confounded with each other in
the same combinations, I ought to say a few words more upon strategical
lines of defense.   It is incontestable that each of these lines should have
also, upon its development, a particular point upon which to rally for its
tactical defense when it shall be the object seriously to combat the enemy
who might have succeeded in crossing the front of the strategical position.

For example, every army guarding a considerable portion of the course of a river, not being able to hold in force the whole extent of this line, should have, a little in rear of the centre, a field of battle well chosen beforehand for gathering there its divisions of observation, and for opposing thus all its concentrated forces to the enemy. I shall make no observations upon those positions of combat which, entering into the domain of tactics, will be treated of in Article 31, and I am to speak here only of strategic lines of defense ; that is to say, those which make in some sort a part of the front of operations of an acting army.

A single remark remains for us to make upon these last, which is, that an offensive army, entering a country with the intention of subduing it, or even merely for occupying it temporarily, will always act with prudence, however great may have been its anterior successes, by preparing itself a good line of defense for serving it at need, as a refuge in the case of a reverse of fortune coming to change the face of affairs. These lines entering for the rest into the combination of the temporary or eventual bases of which we shall speak in Article 23, we shall limit ourselves to indicating them here in order to complete the sketch which we offer. In a science where everything is so closely connected, these repetitions are an inevitable inconvenience.

STRATEGICAL POSITIONS.

There is a certain disposition of armies to which may be given the name strategical position, to distinguish it from tactical positions, or those of combat. The first are those which are taken for a given time, to the end of embracing the front of operations on a larger scale than could have place for combat. All positions taken behind a river, or on a line of defense, the divisions of which should be at a certain distance asunder, count in this number ; those which the armies of Napoleon had at Rivoli, Verona and Legnano, to watch the Adige, those which he had in 1813 in Saxony and in Silesia in advance of his line of defense, were strategical positions, as well as those of the Anglo-Prussian armies on the frontier of Belgium before the battle of Ligny (1815), and that of Massséna upon the Albis, along the Limmat and the Aar in 1799. Even win ter quarters when they are very compact and placed in front of the enemy without being guarantied by an armistice, are nothing else than strategic positions ; such were those of Napoleon on the Passarge in the winter of 1807.

It is seen then that this denomination may be equally applicable to all the situations in which an army might be found, either for covering several points at the same time, or forming any line of observation whatever ; finally, for every position of expectation. Thus the positions extended over a line of defense, a double front of operations, the corps covering a a siege whilst the army is operating on another side; in a word, almost all the great detachments composed of considerable fractions of an army are equally to be ranged in this category, or, more properly speaking, constitute the different parts of a strategical position.

The essential conditions for every such position are, that it be more concentrated than the hostile forces to which it should be opposed, and that all the parts of the army have easy and sure communications, in order to be able to unite without the enemy being in condition to offer opposition thereto ; thus with nearly equal forces, all central or interior positions would be preferable to exterior positions, since the latter would necessarily embrace a much more extended front, and would occasion a scattering of forces, always dangerous. The great mobility of the parts which compose a strategic position can also contribute to their security, or even to their superiority, by the alternate employment of the forces upon all the important points of the *échiquier*. Finally, an army could not occupy surely a strategic position, without taking the precaution to have one or two tactical positions fixed upon beforehand, with the view to uniting thereon, to receive the enemy and to combat him with all the disposable forces, when his projects should be well unmasked: it was thus that Napoleon had prepared his battle fields of Rivoli and of Austerlitz — Wellington, that of Waterloo, and the Arch-Duke Charles, that of Wagram.

In the strategic positions which an army takes in the course of a campaign, whether in march, whether for remaining in observation, or for awaiting the occasion for retaking the offensive, it will occupy also compact cantonments: these kinds of positions require on the part of the general, a practised calculation, for judging all that he may have to fear from the enemy. The army ought to embrace a space sufficient for finding therein means of existence, and meanwhile it must remain as much as possible in condition to receive the enemy, should he present himself ; two conditions difficult enough to reconcile. There is no better means than that of employing its divisions upon a space nearly square, that is to say, as extended in depth as in breadth, in such a manner, that in case of necessity the army may be united upon any point of the *échiquier* where the enemy should chance to disturb it. Nine divisions, placed thus at half a march from each other, may in twelve hours be united upon that of the centre. There should be practised for the rest in such a case, all that is recommended for winter quarters.

For the rest, as those strategical positions are connected with nearly all the combinations of a war, they will be represented in the greater part of the articles which treat of those divers combinations, and we could add nothing striking upon this subject without falling into repetitions.

From what precedes, one could be convinced that the front of operations is the space embraced by the enterprises of an army, on the side where the enemy is found; that the line of defense is the part of that front where the bulk of the forces should be united when reduced to the defensive; finally, that strategic positions designate the provisory distribution of the forces of an army, whether upon the line of defense, or upon the front of operations. It will be concluded from thence, in accordance with my views, that those three combinations, which seem to be confounded with each other, so much analogy is there between them, are distinct objects, but that the same rules may apply equally to all three; at least, in what concerns the manner in which the troops should be distributed and put in action.

ARTICLE XXI.

ZONES AND LINES OF OPERATIONS.

By zone of operations, there should be understood a certain fraction of the general theatre of war, which should be passed over by an army with a determinate aim, and principally when this aim should be combined with that of a secondary army. For example, in the ensemble of the campaign of 1796, Italy was the zone of operations of the right; Bavaria was that of the army of the centre (Rhine and Moselle); finally, Franconia was the zone of the army of the left (Sambre and Meuse).

A zone of operations may sometimes present but a single line of operations, as much from the configuration itself of the country, as from the small number of routes practicable for an army which should be found therein. But this case is rare, and the zone will ordinarily present several lines of operations, the number of which will depend in part upon the projects of the general, and in part upon the number of great communications which the theatre should offer for his enterprises.

It ought not to be concluded from this, however, that each road is in itself a line of operations; doubtless, according to the turn which the events of the war might take, each good route at first unoccupied could become momentarily a line of operations; but so long as it should be followed only by detachments of scouts, or should be found in a direction out of the sphere of the principal enterprises, it would be absurd to confound it with the real line of operations. Besides that, three or four practicable roads which should be found at one or two marches only from each other, and should conduct to the same front of operations, would not form three lines of operations.

In fact, this name could only be given to a space sufficient for the centre and the two wings of an army to be able to move thereon in the sphere of one or two marches from each of those wings or extremities,* which supposes the existence of at least three or four roads leading to the front of operations.

It may here be inferred that, if the words zone and lines of operations have been until now confounded and employed often the one for the other, it has been the same in regard to lines of operations, strategic lines, and roads of eventual communication.

I think, then, that the term *zones of operations* ought to be employed to designate a great fraction of the general theatre of war; that of *lines of operations* will designate the part of that grand fraction which an army will embrace in its enterprises, whether it follow several routes, or whether it follow but one; the term *strategical lines* would designate, then, the important lines which connect the different decisive points of the theatre of war, whether with each other, or with the front of operations of the army; finally, for the same reason, this name would be given also to the lines which an army would follow in order to attain those points, or to march to a decisive manœuvre, and by deviating an instant from the

---

* This paragraph is rather obscure. It should read, perhaps, this name could be given only to a space sufficient to allow an army to move in a sphere such that its wings may be separated by one or two marches from the centre. *Translators.*

general line of operations. Finally, the term *lines of communications* will be suitable for designating the different practicable routes which should be found in the extent of the zone of operations.*

Let us yet cite an example in order to render these ideas more clear. In 1813, after Austria had acceded to the great coalition against Napoleon, three allied armies were to invade Saxony, another Bavaria, and another Italy; thus Saxony, or more properly speaking, the country situated between Dresden, Magdeburg and Breslau, formed, then, the *zone of operations* of the principal mass. This zone had three *lines of operations* conducting to the objective point, Leipzig: the first was that of the army of Bohemia, leading from the mountains of Erzgebirge by Dresden and Chemnitz upon Leipzig; the second was the line of operations of the army of Silesia, going from Breslau by Dresden or by Wittemberg upon Leipzig; finally, the third was the line of operations of the Prince of Sweden's army, departing from Berlin to go by Dessau to the same objective point. Each of those armies marched upon two or three routes parallel and little distant from one another, meanwhile it could not be said that it had three lines of operations.

This example will suffice, I trust, to demonstrate that this designation could not be applicable to every road that might be found upon the theatre of war, but rather to the portion of this theatre which the projects of the general will have embraced, and where he will have directed all his means of war, his active columns, his staple lines, his parks and depôts.

This distinction being well established, it remains for us to define what should be understood by *manœuvre-lines*. In my first treatise, I had thought that I might give this name to all the combinations of a general-in-chief which relate to the choice of territorial lines of operations, that is to say, to the direction the most suitable to give to his forces in order to apply the general principles of war. This figurative expression has been judged of variously, because it has been taken literally, without the pains necessary to penetrate its meaning. It is true that the same word has frequently been used to designate the divers strategic lines temporarily adopted for any enterprise whatever, and which are nevertheless not to be confounded with the general line of operations. To the end of distinguishing them, the first might be designated by the name strategical combinations of lines of operations, and the others could be called eventual

---

* This definition, which differs a little from that which I had at first given, seems to me to satisfy all exigences; I shall have occasion to develop it successively in the present article and in the one which follows.

strategical lines of manœuvre :* we shall treat of the latter in a special article.

If the choice of zones of operations offers few combinations, and depends more frequently upon the topography of the theatre of war, it is not always the same with the choice of lines of operations ; for the latter relating especially to the position and the employment of the hostile forces, will necessarily offer complications more varied and susceptible of being subjected to rules.   Those different combinations constitute as many different manœuvres, and forming one of the essential branches of strategy, they require a definition as exact as possible.

COMBINATIONS OF LINES OF OPERATIONS CON-SIDERED AS STRATEGICAL MANŒUVRES.

The relation of these lines with those which nature has traced, with the positions of the enemy and the views of a general-in-chief, form as many different classes which receive a name from the character of those relations themselves.

The *general line of operations* of an army is that which the bulk of its forces will follow, and upon which will be found in echelons its depôts, its means of transportation and its store-houses ; the line of retreat will also ordinarily be the same, but in urgent cases the army may be forced to take a different line of retreat ; a resolution always painful, and which could not be taken without submitting to great sacrifices.

We shall call *simple lines of operations*, those of an army acting in the same direction from a frontier, without forming great corps independent of each other.

---

* I will give an example of these two combinations. In 1796, the armies of Moreau and Jourdan formed two exterior lines of operations against the Arch-Duke Charles, who operated on two interior or central lines, united under the same command. These are combinations of lines of manœuvre-operations.

In the same year, Wurmser, debouching from the Tyrol to the succor of Mantua, had at first only the simple line of operations of the Adige, but arrived at Roveredo he formed three columns separated by great obstacles ; he operated then upon *three momentary stra* *tegical lines.* which were not general lines of operations.

By *double lines of operations*, I understand those which two armies independent of each other would form upon the same frontier, or those also of two masses nearly equal in forces and obeying nevertheless the same chief, but acting separately at great distances asunder and for a long period of time.*

Interior lines of operations are those which an army would form to oppose several hostile masses, but to which would be given a direction such that the different corps could be drawn towards each other and their movements connected, before the enemy could possibly oppose to them a greater mass.†

Exterior lines present the opposite result ; they are those which an army will form at the same time upon the two extremities of one or several hostile lines.

Concentric lines of operations are several lines which depart from distant points to arrive on the same point, in front or in rear of their base.

By *divergent lines* is understood those which a single mass will take departing from a given point, and dividing in order to move upon several divergent points.

Deep lines are those which, departing from their base, pass over a great extent of ground to arrive at their end.

---

* This definition has been criticised, and as it in fact has given rise to mistakes I think it my duty to explain it.

In the first place it must not be forgotten that manœuvre-lines are referred to, that is to say those of combination, and not highways. Then it must be admitted also that an army marching by two or three routes but little distant from each other in a manner to unite in forty-eight hours, has not for that reason three lines of manœuvre-operations. When Moreau and Jourdan entered Germany with two masses of seventy thousand men independent of each other, they formed indeed a double line, but a French army from which a single detachment should depart from the Lower Rhine to march upon the Maine, whilst five or six other corps should march from the Upper Rhine upon Ulm, would not for that form a double line of operations in the sense which I give to that term for designating a manœuvre. In the same manner Napoleon uniting seven corps to march by Bam·berg upon Gera.whilst Mortier with one corps only marched upon Cassel to occupy the Hesse and to flank the principal enterprise, formed but a general line of operations with an accessory detachment. The territorial line was composed of two rays, but the operation was not double.

† Some German writers have said that I confounded central positions (*central-stellungen*), with lines of operations. In this they are wrong ; an army may have a central position in presence of two hostile corps, and not have interior lines of operations. these are two very different things. Others have pretended that I could have employed the term ray$_s$ of operations to designate what I mean by double lines, &c.; with regard to these, their reasoning is more specious, especially if one would figure to himself the theatre of operations by a circle, but as every radius is a line, I think it a dispute of words.

I shall employ the term *secondary lines* to designate the relations between two armies, when they act upon the same development of frontiers ; thus the army of the Sambre and Meuse was, in 1796, a secondary line of the army of the Rhine ; in 1812, the army of Bagration was secondary to the army of Barclay.

Accidental lines are those brought about by events which change the primitive plan of campaign and give a new direction to the operations. These last are rare and of great importance ; they are ordinarily comprehended only by a vast and active genius.

Finally we might add to this nomenclature *provisory lines of operations* and *definitive lines :* the first would designate those which an army follows to march to a first decisive enterprise, without prejudice to adopting a more solid or more direct one after first successes ; but they seem to belong as much to the class of eventual strategic lines, as to that of lines of operations.

These definitions sufficiently prove how much my ideas differ from those of the authors who have preceded me. Indeed those lines have been considered under their material relations only : Lloyd and Bulow gave them but a relative value to the magazines and the depôts of armies; the latter has even asserted, *that there were no longer any lines of operations when an army encamped near its magazines.* The following example will suffice to destroy this paradox. I will suppose two armies encamped, the first upon the upper Rhine, the second in advance of Dusseldorff or any other point of that frontier. I will admit that their grand depôts are immediately beyond the river, which is without contradiction the most sure, the most advantageous and the nearest approached position which it is possible to suppose them. Those armies will have an offensive or defensive aim ; hence they will incontestably have territorial lines and lines of manœuvre.

1. Their defensive territorial line departing from the point where they are found, will go to that of the second line which they are to cover ; now, they would both be cut off from it if the enemy chanced to establish himself in the interval which separates them from it. Melas could have had for a year munitions in Alexandria, though he would have been none the less cut off from his base of the Mincio, as soon as the victorious enemy occupied the line of the Po.*

---

* It has been thought that this might be subject to contestation ; I do not think so : Melas deprived of recruits. shut up between the Bormida, the Tanaro and the Po, being scarcely able to receive emissaries or couriers, must have ended by opening himself a way, or by capitulating, if not succored.

2. Their line of manœuvre would be double against a simple, if the enemy concentrated his forces to overwhelm successively those armies; it would be double exterior against double interior, if the enemy also made two corps, but gave them a direction such that he could unite them more promptly.

It is seen then that Bulow has started from an inexact basis; his work must necessarily be affected by it and contain maxims at times erroneous. We shall endeavor to trace some which seem to us more conformed to the general principles of war, and to support them by a series of proofs which will leave nothing to be desired; we shall reproduce here the analysis already presented of the lines of operations followed in the last wars of the 18th century, limiting ourselves however to those of the French revolution (those of the Seven Years War can be referred to in Chap. 14 of the treatise on grand military operations). This ensemble will complete what we have to say here upon the important article which forms, in my opinion, the basis of the first strategical combinations.

OBSERVATIONS UPON THE LINES OF OPERATIONS
OF THE FRENCH REVOLUTIONARY WARS.

At the commencement of this terrible struggle, which had chances so various, Prussia and Austria were the only open enemies of France, and the theatre of war extended to Italy only for observing each other reciprocally, because this country was too far removed from the object. The development of the field of operations, comprehending the space which extends from Huninguen to Dunkirk, presented three principal zones: that of the right contained the line of the Rhine, from Huninguen to Landau, and from thence to the Moselle; that of the centre was formed of the interval between the Moselle and the Mense; that of the left comprehended the extent of from Givet to Dunkirk.

When France declared war, in the month of April 1792, her intention was to anticipate the union of her enemies; she had then a hundred thousand men upon the extent of the three zones of which we have just spoken, and the Austrians had not over thirty-five thousand in Belgium. It is impossible then to penetrate the motive which prevented the French from conquering that province, where nothing could have resisted them. Four months elapsed from the declaration of war until the assembling the Allied forces. Was it not probable nevertheless, that the invasion of Belgium would have prevented that of Champagne by giving to the Prussian King the measure of the forces of France, and deciding him not to sacrifice his armies for the secondary interest of imposing upon her a form of government? And if this invasion of Champagne had not the consequences which everybody expected from it, to what was it due that it did not change the face of Europe?

When the Prussians arrived towards the end of July at Coblentz, it is certain that the French could no longer make a war of invasion, and that this part was destined for the Allied armies : it is known how they acquitted themselves of it.

The French forces on the development of the frontiers of which we have just spoken, amounted then to about a hundred and fifteen thousand men. Spread over a front of a hundred and forty leagues, divided into five army corps, it was impossible that those forces could present a very efficacious resistance ; for in order to prevent them from acting, it was sufficient to operate on their centre to oppose their junction. To this military reason were united every State reason ; the object proposed was entirely political ; it could be attained only by rapid and vigorous operations : the territorial line situated between the Moselle and Meuse, which was that of the centre, less fortified than the rest of this frontier, presented besides the excellent place of Luxembourg for a base ; it was chosen then with discernment ; we are about to see that the execution did not respond to the plan.

The court of Vienna had the greatest interest in this war, on account of its family relations and the dangers to which its provinces would have been exposed in case of reverse. By a political speculation of which it would be difficult to give an account, the principal part was nevertheless abandoned to the Prussians ; the house of Austria co-operated in the invasion with but thirty battalions ; forty-five thousand men remained in observation in the Brisgaw, on the Rhine and in Flanders. Where then were concealed those imposing forces which that power subsequently displayed? What better destination could have been assigned them than that of protecting the flanks of the army of invasion? This astonishing system, for which moreover Austria paid very dearly, might explain the resolution of the Prussians, of leaving later the scene, which they unfortunately quitted at the very instant when they should have entered upon it.

If I have allowed myself to be drawn into this observation foreign to the art, it is because of its close connection with the existence of a corps which should have covered, not the Brisgaw, but the flank of the Prussians, by fronting the Moselle and holding Luckner in the camp of Metz. It must be owned, however, that the Prussian army did not give to its operations all the activity necessary for assuring their success; it remained eight days in its camp of Kons to no effect; if it had anticipated Dumouriez at the Islettes, or had attempted more seriously to drive him from thence, it would have had still all the advantage of a mass concentrated against several isolated divisions, in order to overthrow them successively, and render their union impossible. I think that Frederick, in such a case, would have justified the words of Dumouriez, (the latter said at Grandpré that, if he had had to do with the great king, he would have found himself already repulsed far behind Châlons.)

The Austrians proved, in this campaign, that they were then still imbued with the false system of Daun and Lacy, of covering all to hold all. The idea of having twenty thousand men in the Brisgaw, whilst the Moselle and the Sarre remained disgarnished, demonstrated that they were afraid of losing a village, and that this system compelled them to form those great detachments which ruin armies. Forgetting that heavy battalions are always in the right, they believed it necessary to occupy the whole development of the frontiers, in order that they should not be invaded, whilst it is a means of rendering them accessible on all points.

I will not enlarge further here upon that campaign. I shall merely observe that Dumouriez abandoned without cause the pursuit of the Allied army, in order to transfer the theatre of war from the centre to the extreme left of the general échiquier; moreover, he did not know how to give to this movement a great object, and went to attack in front the army of the Duke de Saxe-Teschen, near Mons, whilst that by descending the Meuse upon Namur, with his mass, he would have been able to roll it back upon the North Sea, near Nieuport or Ostend, and to annihilate it entirely, by a battle more fortunate than that of Jemmapes.

The campaign of 1793 offers a new example of the influence of a bad direction of operations. The Austrians gained victories, and retook Belgium, because Dumouriez extended unskillfully his front of operations to the gates of Rotterdam. Until then, the Allies were deserving of all eulogies; the desire of reconquering those rich countries justified that enterprise, wisely directed against the extreme right of the great front of Dumouriez. But when they had repulsed the French army under the cannon of Valenciennes; when the latter, disorganized, delivered up to all the ravages of the anarchy which desolated the interior, found itself in no condition to resist, why remain six months before a few places, and leave the committee of public safety time to form new armies? When the deplorable situation of France, and the destitute condition of the army of Dampierre is recalled, can any thing be comprehended of the parades of the Allies before the places of Flanders?

A war of invasion is especially advantageous, when the empire which is attacked is wholly in the capital. Under the government of a great prince, and in ordinary wars, the chief place of the empire is at the general head-quarters; but under a feeble prince, in a republican State, and still more in a war of opinions, the capital is ordinarily the centre of national power.*

If this truth could have been called in question, it would have been justified on this occasion. So much in Paris was France, that two-thirds of the nation raised the standard against the government which oppressed it. If, after having beaten the French army at Famars, the Dutch and Hanoverians had been left in observation before its remnants, whilst the English and the great Austrian army should have directed their operations upon the Meuse, the Sarre and the Moselle, in concert with the Prussian army, and a part of the useless army of the Upper Rhine, it is certain that a mass of a hundred and twenty thousand men would have been able to act with two flanking corps for covering its line of invasion. I think even that, without changing the direction of the war, or running great risks, the Hanoverians and Dutch might have been left the care of masking Maubeuge and Valenciennes, to the end of pursuing with the bulk of the army the remnants of that of Dampierre. *But, after several victories, two hundred thousand men were occupied in laying sieges, without gaining an inch of ground.* At the moment when they menaced to invade France, they established fifteen or sixteen corps in defensive positions to cover their own frontier! When Valenciennes and Mayence had succumbed, instead of attacking with all their forces the camp of Cambrai, they ran excentrically to Dunkirk on one side, and to Landau on the other.

It is not less astonishing that, after having made, at the commencement of the campaign, the greatest efforts upon the right of the general *échiquier,*

---

* The taking of Paris by the Allies decided the fate of Napoleon, but this circumstance does not destroy my assertion. Napoleon, without an army, had all Europe upon his back, and the nation itself had separated its cause from his. If he had had fifty thousand more old soldiers, it would indeed have been seen that his capital was truly at general head-quarters.

they should direct them afterwards upon the left; thus, whilst the Allies acted in Flanders, the imposing forces which were upon the Rhine did not second them, and when those forces operated offensively in their turn, the Allies remained inactive upon the Sambre. Do not these false combinations resemble those of Soubise and of Broglie in 1761, as well as all the lines of the Seven Years War?

In 1794, the scene is wholly changed. The French pass from a painful defensive to a brilliant offensive. The combinations of that campaign were, doubtless, well established; but they have been exaggerated in presenting them as a new system of war. To be assured of the justice of my assertion, let us cast a glance over the respective positions of the armies in this campaign, and in that of 1757; we see that they were nearly the same, and that the direction of the operations resemble each other absolutely. The French had four corps, which united into two great armies; as the king of Prussia had four divisions, which formed two armies at the debouches of the mountains. The two great corps took in their turn a concentric direction in 1794, upon Brussels, as Frederick and Schwérin had done in 1757, on Prague. The single difference which exists between these two plans, is that the Austrian troops, less disseminated, had in Flanders a position less extended than that of Braun in Bohemia, but this difference was certainly not in favor of the plan of 1794. This last had, moreover, against it the position of the North Sea; in order to outflank the right of the Austrians, it was ventured to send Pichegru between the shores of that sea and the mass of the hostile forces; the most dangerous and faulty direction that could be given to great operations. This movement was precisely the same as that of Benningsen upon the Vistula base, which was near compromising the Russian army in 1807. The fate of the Prussian army, thrown back upon the Baltic, after having been cut off from its communications, is another proof of this truth.

If the Prince of Coburg had operated as has been done in our day, he would easily have made Pichegru repent of having executed that audacious manœuvre a month before Jourdan was in condition to second him. The Austrian grand army, destined for the offensive, was at the centre, before Landrecies; it was composed of a hundred and six battalions, and a hundred and fifty squadrons; it had on its right flank, the corps of Clairfayt to cover Flanders, and on its left the corps of the Prince de Kaunitz to cover Charleroi. The gain of the battle under the walls of Landrecies caused it to open its gates, there was found upon General Chapuis the plan of the diversion in Flanders, and he was sent *twelve battalions!* A long time after, and when the successes of the French were known, the corps of the Duke of York marched to his succor. But what did the remainder of the army before Landrecies, since the departure of those forces obliged it to retard its invasion? Did not the Prince of Coburg lose all the advantages of his central position, allowing all his heavy detachments to be beaten in detail, enabling the French to consolidate in Belgium? Finally, the army was put in motion, after having sent a part of its forces to the Prince de Kaunitz, at Charleroi, and left a division at Cateau. If, instead of scattering this great army, it had been directed at once upon Turcoing, there could have been united in it a hundred battalions and a hundred and forty squadrons. What would have been the result then of the famous diversion of Pichegru, cut off from his frontiers, and shut up between the North Sea and two hostile fortresses?

The plan of invasion of the French, had not only the radical defect of all exterior lines, it was faulty also in execution; the diversion on Courtrai took place the 26th of April, and Jourdan only arrived at Charleroi the 3d of June, more than a month afterwards. What a fine occasion for the Austrians to profit from their central position! I think, that had the Prussian army manœuvered by its right, and the Austrian army by its left, that is to say, both upon the Meuse, affairs would have taken a very different turn; in fact, establishing themselves upon the centre of a disseminated line, their mass would certainly have prevented the union of its several parts. It may be dangerous to attack, in a pitched battle, the centre of an army in continuous line, which has the facility of being sustained simultaneously by its wings and all its reserves; but it is quite otherwise with a line of a hundred and thirty leagues.

In 1795, Prussia and Spain retired from the coalition; the theatre of war upon the Rhine was contracted, and Italy opened to the French armies a new field of glory. Their lines of operations in this campaign were still double; it was wished to operate by Dusseldorff and Manheim; Clairfayt, wiser than his predecessors, carried alternately, his mass upon those two points, and gained victories so decisive at Manheim and in the lines of Mayence, that they forced the army of the Sambre-and-Meuse to repass the Rhine to cover the Moselle, and brought Pichegru back under Landau.

In 1796, the lines of operation are traced upon those of 1757, and upon those of 1794; but obtain, as in the preceding year, a very different result. The armies of the Rhine and of the Sambre-and-Meuse, start from the two extremities of their base, to take a concentric direction upon the Danube. They formed, as in 1794, two exterior lines. The Arch-

Duke Charles, more skillful than the Prince de Coburg, profits from the interior direction of his own, to give them a point of concentration more approached; he then seizes the instant when the Danube covers Latour, for stealing a few marches upon Moreau, and for throwing all his forces upon the right of Jourdan, whom he overwhelms; the battle of Wurz- burg decides the fate of Germany, and constrains the army of Moreau, extended upon an immense line, to make its retreat. .

Bonaparte, in Italy, commences his extraordinary career. His system is to isolate the Piedmontese and Austrian armies; he succeeds, by the battle of Millesimo, in making them take two exterior strategic lines, and beats them afterwards in detail, at Mondovi and at Lodi. A for- midable army is assembled at the Tyrol, for saving Mantua, which he be- sieges; it commits the imprudence of marching there in two corps, *sepa- rated by a lake*. The lightning is less prompt than the French general; he raises the siege, abandoning every thing, directs himself, with the better part of his forces, upon the first column which debouches by Brescia, beats it and throws it back into the mountains. The second column ar- rived upon the same ground, is there beaten in its turn, and forced to re- tire into the Tyrol, in order to communicate with its right. Wurmser, upon whom these lessons are lost, wishes to cover the two lines of Roveredo and Vicenza; Bonaparte, after having overthrown and repulsed the first upon the Lavis, changes direction then to the right, debouches by the gorges of the Brenta upon the line of the left, (Austrian) and forces the remnant of that fine army to save themselves in Mantua, where they are finally constrained to capitulate.

In 1799, hostilities recommence; the French, punished for having formed two exterior lines in 1796, have, nevertheless, three upon the Rhine and the Danube. An army of the left observes the Lower Rhine, that of the centre marches upon the Danube; Switzerland, which flanks Italy and Suabia, is occupied by a third army as strong as the other two. *The three corps could be united only in the valley of the Inn, forty leagues from their base of operations!* The Arch-Duke has equal forces, but unites them on the centre, which he overthrows at Stockach, and the Hel- vetic army is forced to evacuate the Grisons and eastern Switzerland.

The Allies commit in their turn the same fault as their adversaries, and instead of pursuing the conquest of this central bulwark, which cost them so dearly afterwards, they form a double line in Switzerland and the Lower Rhine. Their army in Switzerland is overthrown at Zurich, whilst that of the Lower Rhine is amusing itself at Manheim.

In Italy the French form the double enterprise of Naples, where thirty- two thousand men are uselessly occupied, whilst on the Adige, where the greatest blows ought to be struck, the too feeble army sustains overwhelming reverses. When that army of Naples returns to the North, it again commits the fault of taking a strategical direction opposite to that of Moreau; Suwaroff profits skillfully from the central position left him, marches upon the first of those armies, and defeats it at some leagues from the other.

In 1800, all is changed; Bonaparte has returned from Egypt, and this campaign presents a new combination of lines of operations; a hundred and fifty thousand men defile by the two flanks of Switzerland, debouch on the one side upon the Danube, and on the other upon the Po; this wise movement assured the conquest of immense countries; modern history had offered until then no similar combination; the French armies form two interior lines which reciprocally sustain each other; the Austrians, on the contrary, are forced to take an exterior direction, which deprives them of communicating with each other. By the skillful combination of its march, the army of reserve cuts off the enemy from his line of operations, and preserves itself all its relations with its own frontiers and with the army of the Rhine, which forms its secondary line.

The analysis of the memorable events of which we have just sketched the outline, will suffice to convince us of the importance of choosing good manœuvre-lines in military operations. In fact, it may repair the disasters of a lost battle, render an invasion vain, extend the advantages of a victory, and assure the conquest of a country.

In comparing the combinations and the results of the most celebrated campaigns, it will be seen also that all lines of operations which have succeeded, adhere to the fundamental principle which we have at divers times presented; *for simple lines and interior lines have for object the putting in action, on the most important point, and by means of strategic movements, a greater number of divisions, and consequently a stronger mass than the enemy.* It will be equally obvious that all those which have failed, contained the vices opposed to these principles, since all multiplied lines tend to present feeble and isolated parties, to the mass which is to overwhelm them.

MAXIMS ON LINES OF OPERATIONS.

From all the events analyzed above, and still more from those which followed closely the first publication of this chapter in 1805, I believe that the following maxims may be deduced.

1. If the art of war consists in putting into action the most forces possible on the decisive point of the theatre of operations, the choice of the line of operations being the first means of succeeding, may be considered the fundamental basis of a good plan of campaign.* Napoleon proved this by the direction which he knew how to assign to his masses in 1805, on.Donauwerth, and in 1806 on Gera; skillful manœuvres, which military men could not study too much.

2. The direction which it is suitable to give to that line, depends not only upon the geographical situation of the theatre of operations, as we shall demonstrate further on, but still upon the position of the hostile forces upon that strategic field. *However, it could only be given upon the centre, or upon one of the extremities; in the case only where we should have infinitely superior forces, it would be possible to act upon the front and extremities at the same time; in every other supposition this would be a capital fault.*†

In general it can be laid down as a principle, that the best direction of a *manœuvre-line* will be upon the centre of the enemy, if the latter commit the fault of dividing his forces upon a too extended front; but that in every other hypothesis, this direction ought to be given upon one of the extremities, and from thence upon the rear of the hostile line of defense or front of operations.

The advantage of this direction does not arise merely from the circumstance that in attacking an extremity, but a part of the hostile army is combatted; there is derived from it a still greater in that his line of defense is menaced and taken in reverse. It was thus that the army of the Rhine, having gained in 1800 the extreme left of the line of defense of the Black Forest, caused it to fall almost without a combat, and delivered upon the right bank of the Danube two battles which, although not very decisive

---

* I believe it my duty to repeat that I have never admitted the possibility of tracing beforehand the plan of a whole campaign. That could only extend to the primitive project which indicates the objective point that is proposed to be attained, the general system that will be followed for arriving at it, and the first enterprise that will be formed to that effect; the rest depends naturally on the result of this first operation, and on the new chances which it will.bring about.

† The inferiority of an army is not calculated upon the exact figure of the number of its soldiers; the talents of the chief, the *moral* of the troops, their constitutive qualities, count also in the balance, and the superiority will even be relative, although numerical proportions enter therein for much.

in themselves, had for result the invasion Suabia and Bavaria, on account of the good direction of the line of operations. The consequences of the march which carried the army of reserve by the St. Bernard and Milan upon the extreme right, and afterwards upon the rear of Melas, were much more brilliant still; they are sufficiently well known to dispense with our recalling them here.

This manœuvre, entirely similar to that which we have traced upon the map of the Alps, is found, it is true, in flagrant opposition to certain rather too exclusive systems, which require bases parallel to those of the enemy, and double lines of operations forming a right angle, the summit of which should be directed upon the centre of the strategic front of the adversary. But we have already said enough of those systems to demonstrate that our's is preferable. However, when it shall be the question to operate upon the centre of the enemy, nothing would oppose the adoption of the right-angled system of Bulow, provided that no account is held of the exaggerated conditions with which its commentators have loaded it, and that the double lines which it renders necessary should be interior, as will be seen hereafter.

3. It must not be believed, nevertheless, that it is sufficient to gain the extremity of a hostile front of operations, in order to be able to throw one's self with impunity upon the rear; for there are cases where, in acting thus, he will find himself cut off from his own communications.

In order to avoid this danger, it is important to give to your line of operations a geographical and strategic direction, such, that the army preserve behind it a sure line of retreat, or that, at need, it may find one on another side where it could throw itself, in order to regain its base by one of those changes of lines of operations of which we shall speak hereafter. (See 12th maxim.)

The choice of such a direction is so important, that it characterizes of itself alone one of the greatest qualities of a general-in-chief, and I shall be permitted to cite two examples of it, to make myself better understood.

For example, if Napoleon, in 1800, after having passed the St. Bernard, had marched direct by Turin upon Asti or Alexandria, and had received battle at Marengo, without being assured previously of Lombardy and the left bank of the Po, he would have been cut off from his line of retreat more completely than Melas was from his, whilst that having at need the two secondary points of Casal and Pavia on the side of the St. Bernard, and those of Savona and Zendi on the side of the Appenines, he had, in case of reverse, all the means of regaining the Var or the Valais.

In the same manner in the campaign of 1806, if he had marched from Gera straight to Leipzig, and had there awaited the Prussian army returning from Weimar, he would have been cut off from his base of the Rhine, as well as the Duke of Brunswick from that of the Elbe ; whereas by moving from Gera to the west in the direction of Weimar, he placed his front of operations in advance of the three routes of Saalfield, Schleiz and Hof, which served him as lines of communication, and which he covered thus perfectly. And even if the Prussians had imagined they could cut him off from his lines of retreat by throwing themselves between Gera and Bareith, then they would have opened to him his most natural line, the fine highway from Leipzig to Frankfort, besides the ten roads which lead from Saxony through Cassel to Coblentz, Cologne, and even Wesel. Here is enough to prove the importance of those kinds of combinations ; let us return to the series of maxims announced.

4. To manœuvre wisely, it is necessary to avoid forming two independent armies upon the same frontier ; such a system could scarcely be suitable except in cases of great coalitions, or when there should be immense forces which could not be made to act upon the same zone of operations without being exposed to an incumbrance more dangerous than useful. Still, even in this case would it not always be better to subject these two armies to one chief, who would have his head-quarters with the principal army ?

5. In consequence of the principle we have just announced, it is certain that with equal forces, a simple line of operations on the same frontier will have the advantage over a double line of operations.

6. It may happen nevertheless, that a double line becomes necessary, 1st, from the configuration of the theatre of war, afterwards, because the enemy will have formed one himself, and it will be necessary to oppose a part of the army to each of the two or three masses which he will have formed.

7. In this case, the interior or central line will be preferable to the exterior line, since the army which shall have the interior line will be able to make each of its fractions co-operate in a plan combined between them, and can thus assemble the mass of its forces before the enemy, for deciding upon the success of the campaign.

An army whose lines of operations should offer such advantages would then be in condition, by a strategical movement, well combined, to overthrow successively the fractions of the adversary which should offer themselves alternately to its blows. To assure the success of this movement, a corps of observation would be left before the part of the hostile army which it should be desired merely to hold in check, prescribing to it not to accept a serious engagement, but to content itself with suspending the march of the enemy by favor of the accidents of the ground, and in falling back upon the principal army.

8. A double line may be suitable also when you have a numerical superiority so decided, that you can manœuvre in two directions without being liable to see one of your corps overthrown by the enemy. In this hypothesis it would be a fault to accumulate your forces on a single point, and thus to deprive yourself of the advantages of your superiority, by rendering it impracticable for a part of your forces to act. Nevertheless, in forming a double line, it will always be prudent to reinforce suitably the part of the army which, by the nature of the theatre of war and the respective situations of the two parties, would be called upon to play the most important part.

9. The principal events of the late wars prove the correctness of two other maxims. The first is, that two interior lines, sustaining each other reciprocally, and showing front, at a certain distance, to two masses superior in numbers, ought not to allow themselves to be compressed by the enemy in a too contracted space, where they might end by being simultaneously overthrown, as happened to Napoleon in the celebrated battle of Leipzig. The second is that interior lines ought not to go either into the contrary excess, by extending to a too great distance, for fear of allowing the enemy time to gain decisive successes against the secondary corps left in observation. It could be done, nevertheless, when the principal object in view should be so decisive that the whole fate of the war might depend upon it; in this case, one could look with indifference upon what might happen at secondary points.

10. For the same reason, two concentric lines are preferable to two divergent lines; the first, more conformed to the principles of strategy, procure moreover the advantage of covering the lines of communications and of supply; but in order that they be exempt from danger, they should be combined in such a manner that the two armies which pass over them, may not meet separately the united forces of the enemy, before being themselves in condition to operate their junction.

11. Divergent lines may nevertheless be suitable, either after a battle gained, or after a strategic operation by which you will have succeeded in dividing the forces of your adversary by breaking his centre. Then it becomes natural to give your masses excentric directions in order to finish the dispersion of the vanquished; but, although acting upon diver-

gent lines, those masses will nevertheless find themselves on interior lines, that is to say, more approached to each other, and more easy to reunite than those of the enemy.

12. It happens at times that an army sees itself forced to change its line of operations in the midst of a campaign, which we have designated under the name of accidental lines. It is one of the most delicate and important of manœuvres, which may give great results, but may lead also to great reverses, when it is not combined with sagacity, for it is scarcely used but for extricating an army from an embarrassing situation. We have given, in Chapter X. of the Treatise on grand operations, an example of such a change, executed by Frederick in the course of the raising of the siege of Olmutz.

Napoleon projected several of them, for he was accustomed, in his adventurous invasions, to have such a project ready for parrying unexpected events. At the epoch of the battle of Austerlitz, he had resolved, in case of check, to take his line of operations through Bohemia upon Passau or Ratisbon, which offered to him a country, new and full of resources, instead of retaking that by Vienna, which offered nothing but ruins, and on which the Arch-Duke Charles might be able to anticipate him.

In 1814, he commenced the execution of a manœuvre more bold, but favored at least by localities, and which consisted in basing himself upon the belt of fortresses of Alsace and Lorraine, opening to the allies the road to Paris. It is certain that had Mortier and Marmont been able to join him, and he had had fifty thousand men more, this project would have been followed by the most decisive results, and put the seal to his brilliant military career.

13. As we have said above (maxim 2), the configuration of frontiers and the geographical nature of the theatre of operations, may exercise a great influence upon the direction itself to be given to these lines, as well as upon the advantages to be derived from them. Those central positions which form a salient angle towards the enemy, like Bohemia and Switzerland, are the most advantageous, because they naturally lead to the adoption of interior lines and facilitate the means of taking the enemy in reverse. The sides of this salient angle are so important there that it is necessary to join all the resources of the art to those of nature to render them unattackable.

In default of those central positions, they might be supplied by the relative direction of manœuvre lines as the following figure shows.

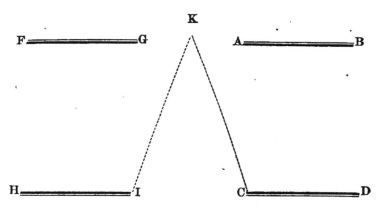

C D manœuvering upon the right flank of the army A B; and H I directing itself upon the left flank of F G, will form two interior lines, C K and I K, upon an extremity of each of the exterior lines A B, F G, which they will be able to overthrow one after the other by carrying alternately against them the mass of their forces. This combination presents the results of the lines of operations of 1796, of 1800 and 1809.

14. The general configuration of the bases may also have a great influence upon the direction to be given to the lines of operations, which must naturally be subordinate to the situation of their respective bases, as will be obvious by recalling what we have said before upon this article. Indeed, by a simple examination of the figure annexed to said article, page 90, it will be seen that the greatest advantage which would result from the conformation of frontiers and bases, would consist in prolonging the latter perpendicularly to the base of the enemy, that is to say parallelly to his line of communications, which would give the facility of seizing this line, and of separating thus the enemy from his base.

But if, instead of directing your own operations so as to effect this, you choose badly the direction of your line, all the advantage of the perpendicular base will become null. It is evident that the army E, which should possess the double base A C and C D, if it marched by the left towards the point F, instead of prolonging itself by its right towards G H, would lose all the strategical advantages of its base, C D. (See page 90.)

The great art of directing our lines properly consists, then, as we have just seen, in combining their relations with the bases and with the movements of the army, in such a manner as to be able to seize upon the com·

munications of the enemy without being liable to lose our own ; a strategical problem the most important as it is the most difficult to resolve.

15. Independently of the cases before cited, there is yet one which exercises a manifest influence upon the direction to be given to lines of operations ; it is that in which the principal enterprise of the campaign should consist in effecting the passage of a great river in the presence of a large and intact hostile army. In this case, it is sensibly felt that the choice of the line of operations could not depend merely upon the will of the general-in-chief, or upon the advantage which he would find in attacking a certain part of the hostile line ; for the first thing to be considered, is to know the point where the passage could be effected most surely, and that upon which would be found the material means necessary to that effect. The passage of the Rhine by Jourdan, in 1795, was executed near Dusseldorff, for the same reason which decided that of the Vistula by Marshal Paskievitch near Ossick, 1831 ; that is to say, because the army not having in its train a sufficient bridge equipage, it was necessary to send up large commercial ships bought in, Holland by the French army, the same as the Russian army had purchased theirs at Thorn and Dantzic. The neutral territory of Prussia furnished, in these two circumstances, the facility of sending those vessels up the river, without the enemy being able to interpose any obstacle thereto. This facility, of an incalculable advantage in appearance, forced the French nevertheless to the double invasions of 1795 and of 1796, which failed precisely because the double line of operations resulting therefrom gave the means of partially defeating them. Paskievitch, better advised, caused the Upper Vistula to be passed only by a secondary detachment, and after the principal army had already arrived at Lowicz.

When there are military positions in sufficiency, there are less vicissitudes to be undergone in the passage. Meanwhile, it is necessary still to choose the point which offers the most chances of success in consequence of the localities and the position of the hostile forces. The discussion between Napoleon and Moreau about the passage of the Rhine in 1800, which I have reported in the 13th volume of the History of the wars of the Revolution, is one of the most curious examples of the different combinations which this at once strategical and tactical question presents.

The position chosen for the passage exercises the same influence upon the direction suitable to give to the first marches after it is effected, in view of the necessity of covering the bridges against the enemy, at least until after a victory ; this choice may nevertheless, in every state of things, present a just application of principles for it will definitively be limited always to the single alternative of a passage upon the centre or upon one of the extremities.

An army united, which should force the passage upon one of the points of the centre, against a somewhat extended cordon, could divide itself afterwards into two divergent lines to the end of dispersing the parts of the hostile cordon which, being found thus out of condition to unite, will scarcely think of troubling the bridges.

If the line of the river be sufficiently short to allow the hostile army to remain concentrated, and if the means be had of taking after the passage a front of operations perpendicular to the river, then it would be best perhaps to pass it upon one of the extremities, to the end of throwing back all the hostile forces out of the direction of the bridges. For the rest we shall treat of this subject in Article 37, on the passage of rivers.

16. There is still a combination of lines of operations, which ought not to be passed over in silence. It is the notable appearance which exists between the chances of a line of operations established in one's own country and that established in a hostile country. The nature of these hostile countries will have an influence also upon those chances. An army crosses the Alps or the Rhine to carry war into Italy or Germany; it finds at first, States of the second order; supposing even that their chiefs are allied to each other, there will be nevertheless in the real interest of those small States, as well as in their populations, rivalries which would prevent the same unity of impulsion and of force which would be met with in a great State. On the contrary, a German army, which shall pass the Rhine or the Alps to penetrate into France, will have a line of operations much more hazardous and more exposed than those French who should penetrate into Italy, for the first would have to encounter the whole mass of the forces of France united in action and will.*

An army on the defensive, which has its lines of operations on its own soil, has resources in everything; the inhabitants of the country, the authorities, the productions, the places, the public and even the private magazines, the arsenals, all favor it; it is not the same abroad, at least not ordinarily; one does not always find banners arrayed against the national standard, and even in that case he will still have against him all the advantages which the adversary will find in the elements of the public force.

---

* It will be comprehended that I speak here of the ordinary chances of a war between two powers merely, in a calm state within themselves. The chances of wars of party make exceptions.

I have said that the nature of countries influence also the chances of lines of operations; in fact, besides the modifications which we have just explained, it is certain that the establishment of lines of operations in countries rich, fertile and industrial, offer to the assailants many more advantages than those in countries more barren and desert, especially when whole populations are to be contended with. There will be found indeed in those fertile, industrial and populous countries, a thousand things necessary to every army, whereas in the others nothing will be met with but huts and straw, the horses will merely find pasturage there, but as for everything else, it will be necessary to carry it along, so that the embarrassments of the war will thereby be increased without end and brisk and bold operations will be more rare and hazardous. The French armies, so accustomed to the comforts of Suabia and rich Lombardy, came near perishing in 1806 in the mud of Pultusk, and did perish in 1812 in the marshy forests of Lithuania.

17. There is yet a rule relative to lines of operations to which several writers have attached a great importance, that seems very just when reduced to geometrical formula, but which, in its application, might be ranged in the class of Utopias. According to this rule, it would be necessary that the countries lateral to each line of operations should be disembarrassed of every enemy, to a distance which would equal the depth of that line, because, otherwise, those enemies could menace the line of retreat; an idea which has been translated geometrically, as follows : " There can be no security for an operation until the enemy is driven out- " side of a semi-circle, the centre of which is the most central subject "(*Mittelstes Subject*), and the radius of which (*Halbmesser*) is equal to the " length of the line of operations."

Then, in order to prove this somewhat obscure axiom, it is demonstrated that the peripheric angles of a circle, which have the diameter for opposite side, form right angles, and that in consequence the angle of ninety degrees required by Bulow for lines of operations, that famous strategical *caput-porci*, is the only rational system : from which it is afterwards charitably concluded, that those who do not choose to make war trigonometrically are ignoramuses.

This maxim sustained with so much warmth and so specious on paper, is found nevertheless belied by the events of war : the nature of the country, the lines of rivers and mountains, the moral state of the two armies, the spirit of the people, the capacity and energy of the chiefs, are not measured by angles, diameters, and peripheries. Doubtless considerable corps could not be tolerated upon the flanks of a line of retreat, in a manner to seriously disturb it ; but to push too far the maxims so much vaunted, would be to deprive one of every means of making a movement into the enemy's country ; now, it would be all the more natural to free one's self of it, as there is not a campaign of the last wars and of those of Prince Eugene and of Marlborough that does not test the nullity of these pretended mathematical rules. Did not General Moreau find himself at the gates of Vienna in 1800, whilst Fussen, Sharnitz and all the Tyrol, were yet in the power of the Austrians? Did not Napoleon find himself at Placentia when Turin, Genoa and the Coldi Tendi were occupied by the army of Melas? I shall ask finally what geometrical figure did the army of Prince Eugene of Savoy form when it marched by Stradella and Asti to the succor of Turin, leaving the French on the Mincis at a few leagues only from his base?

Those three events would suffice, in my opinion, to prove that the compass of the geometrician will ever wane, not only before such geniuses as Napoleon and Frederick, but before great characters such as the Suwaroffs, the Massenas, &c.

God forbid, nevertheless, that I should think of depreciating the merit of officers, versed in those sciences which have taught us to calculate even the courses of the stars. I have for them, on the contrary, a kind of veneration ; but my own experience authorizes me to think that if their science is necessary for constructing or attacking places and intrenched camps, as well as for drafting plans and projecting maps, if it gives besides real advantages in all calculations of practical application, it is but a feeble succor in the combinations of strategy and grand tactics where the moral impulsions, seconded by the laws of statics, play the principal part.* Those even of these respectable disciples of Euclid, who might be capable of commanding an army well, must to do it with glory and success, forget a little of their trigonometry ; it is at least the course that Napoleon had taken, whose most brilliant operations seem to belong much more to the domain of poetry than to that of the exact sciences ; the cause of this is simple, *it is that war is an impassioned drama* and by no means a mathematical operation.

---

* It will be objected that strategy especially is combined by means of lines ; that is true, but to know whether one of those lines leads to a suitable point or to a gulf, and to calculate the shortest distance from the point where we are to that which we wish to attain. there is no need of geometry, for a post map would be more useful for that than a compass. I have known a general almost the rival of Laplace, whom I have never been able to make comprehend why such a strategical line would be preferable to such another. nor how that of the Meuse was the key of the low countries, when they are defended especially by a continental army.

I shall be pardoned this digression ; I have been attacked by vain formulas, it is natural that I should defend myself, and the only favor which I ask of my critics, is to be as equitable towards me as I am towards them. They want war too methodical, too measured, I would make it brisk, bold and impetuous, perhaps even sometimes audacious. * * * * *Suum cuique.*

Far from me, however, the thought of repelling all the precautions which may flow from the principle even of those measured rules, for they could never be neglected entirely; but to be reduced to making war geometrically, would be to impose fetters on the genius of the greatest captains, and to submit to the yoke of an exaggerated pedantry. For my part, I shall ever protest against such theories, as well as against the apology of ignorance.

OBSERVATIONS ON INTERIOR LINES, AND THE ATTACKS OF WHICH THEY HAVE BEEN THE OBJECT.

I ask pardon of my readers if I divert their attention for a moment, in order to add here a few words upon the controversies of which this article has been the subject. I have hesitated if I should defer these observations to the end of the volume, but as they contain useful elucidations of the doctrines which precede, I have thought I might place them here.

The critics have been very little agreed in their reproaches; some have disputed upon the meaning of certain words and definitions; others have censured certain points of view which they had badly comprehended; the latter finally have taken occasion from a few important events, to deny my fundamental dogmas, without troubling themselves whether the conditions which modify those dogmas, were indeed the same as those which they supposed (which I formally deny,) and without reflecting that in admitting even their applications as exact, a fortuitous exception could not destroy a rule consecrated by the experience of centuries, and founded upon principles.

Several of those military writers, willing to contest my maxims upon interior or central lines of operations, have opposed to them the famous march of the Allies upon Leipzig, which succeeded by a contrary system.* This memorable event seems, at first sight, calculated to shake the faith of those who believe in principles; but, besides presenting one of those exceptional cases rare in the history of all ages, it is evident that nothing could be concluded against rules supported by thousands of other examples; and it will be easy for us to demonstrate that, far from being able to draw from these facts the least argument against the dogmas which we have presented, they prove on the contrary, all their solidity. In fact, my critics had forgotten that in case of a considerable numerical superiority, I recommended, for the superior army, double lines of operations as the most advantageous; especially when they were concentric, and directed in a manner to operate a common effort against the enemy so soon as the moment for the decisive shock should have arrived.† Now, in this march of the armies of Schwartzenberg, Blucher, the Prince of Sweden and Benningsen, we find again precisely that case of numerical superiority which was to militate in favor of the system adopted. With regard to the inferior army, in order that it should conform to the principles set forth in this chapter, it would be necessary that it should direct its efforts upon an extremity of its adversaries, and not upon their centre, so that the events opposed to me prove doubly in favor of my maxims.

Moreover, if the central position of Napoleon between Dresden and the Oder became fatal to him, it must be attributed to the disasters of Culm, of the Katzbach, of Dennewitz, in a word, to faults of execution wholly foreign in reality to the system. *That which I propose consists in acting offensively upon the most important point with the major part of your forces, remaining at secondary points on the defensive, in strong positions or behind a river, until the decisive blow being struck, and the operation terminated by the total defeat of an essential part of the hostile army, you find yourself at liberty to direct your efforts upon one of the other menaced points.* So soon as secondary armies are exposed to a decisive shock du-

---

* It is thirty-three years since I presented these maxims for the first time; the quite recent events which have transpired in Navarre, prove how just they are. and how much the principles so simple upon which they repose are frequently misconceived. The troops of Don Carlos, attacked by three great corps at considerable distances asunder. have gained a complete victory by favor of their central position put to good profit. The ignoramuses cry treason, when immutable principles alone have caused the loss of Evans. If the generals who have succeeded each other for ten years past in Spain. had ever thought of the application of principles. such a rout could never have happened; but to read and to meditate are things too vulgar for men who unceasingly proclaim themselves invincible.

† See chapter 12 of the treatise on grand military operations. vol 2. page 158.

ring the absence of the bulk of the army, the system is badly comprehended, and this was precisely what happened in 1813.

In fact, if Napoleon, victorious at Dresden, had pursued the army of the Sovereigns into Bohemia, far from sustaining the disaster of Culm, he would have presented himself menacingly before Prague, and would perhaps have dissolved the coalition. He committed the fault of not troubling seriously their retreat ; and to this fault was added another not less grave, that of engaging decisive battles upon points where he was not found in person with the weight of his forces. It is true that at the Katzbach his instructions were not followed ; for they prescribed the waiting for Blucher, and the falling upon him when he should furnish occasion for it by hazardous movements, whilst Macdonald on the contrary, ran to meet the Allies, crossing, by isolated corps, torrents which the rains were swelling every hour.

Supposing that Macdonald had done what was prescribed to him, and that Napoleon had followed up his victory at Dresden, we shall be forced to own that his plan of operations, based upon interior strategic lines, and upon a line of operations with double concentric rays, would have been crowned with the most brilliant success. It is sufficient to glance at his campaigns in Italy in 1796, and in France in 1814, to be satisfied that he knew how to operate by the application of this system.

To these different considerations must be added a circumstance not less important, in order to demonstrate that it would be unjust to judge of central lines by the fate which those of Napoleon experienced in Saxony : *it is that his front of operations was found outflanked upon the right, and taken in reverse by the geographical position of the frontiers of Bohemia,* a case which rarely presents itself. Now, a central position which has such defects, could not be compared with one which has not. When Napoleon applied this system in Italy, in Poland, in Prussia, and in France, he was not thus exposed to the blows of an enemy established on his flanks and rear ; Austria could have menaced him at a distance in 1807 ; but she was in a state of peace with him, and disarmed.

In order to judge of a system of operations, it is necessary to admit that the reciprocal chances are equal, and this was not the case in 1813, neither in respect to geographical positions, nor in regard to the condition of the respective forces. Independently of this fact, which is evidence of the shallowness of my Aristarchuses, it seems absurd to cite the reverses of the Katzbach and of Dennewitz, sustained by the lieutenants of Napoleon, as proofs capable of destroying a principle, the most simple application of which would have exacted that those lieutenants should not accept of a serious engagement, instead of seeking a battle as they did.   In fact, what advantage could one flatter himself with obtaining from the system of central lines, if the parts of the army which he should have enfeebled in order to carry his efforts upon other points, committed the fault of hurrying themselves, to meet a disastrous struggle, instead of being contented with the part of a corps of observation.*   It would then be the enemy who would be found to have applied the principle, and not he who might have taken the interior line.   Moreover, the campaign which followed that of Leipzig, soon came to demonstrate the correctness of the contested maxims ; Napoleon's defensive in Champagne, from the battle of Brienne to that of Paris, proved to a demonstration all that I could have said in favor of central masses.

However, the experience of those two celebrated campaigns has given birth to a strategical problem, which it would be difficult to resolve by simple assertions founded on theories; it is to know whether the system of central masses loses of its advantages when the masses which it is the question to put in action are very large.   Persuaded, like Montesquieu, that the greatest enterprises perish through the magnitude even of the preparations that are made to assure their success, I should be much inclined to pronounce for the affirmative.   It appears to me incontestable that a mass of a hundred thousand men, occupying a central zone against three isolated armies of thirty to thirty-five thousand men each, would be more sure of overwhelming them separately, than it were possible for a mass of four hundred thousand combattants against three armies of a hundred and thirty-five thousand men, and for several important reasons.

1.   Because, with an army of a hundred and thirty to a hundred and forty thousand combattants, you can resist easily a more considerable force, in view of the difficulty of finding the ground and the time necessary for putting such great forces in action on the day of battle ;

2.   Because, even if you are repulsed from the field of battle, you have still at least a hundred thousand men to secure a good system of retreat, without allowing yourself to be too much broken up, whilst awaiting a junction with one of the other two secondary armies ;

3.   Because a central mass of four hundred thousand men requires such a quantity of provisions, munitions, horses, and *materiel* of every kind, that

---

* I well know that one cannot always refuse combat without risking greater dangers than that of a check; Macdonald would also have been able to accept a battle with Blucher, if he had better comprehended the instructions of Napoleon, instead of doing quite the contrary. (See Political and Military Life of Napoleon, vol. 4. in the *pieces justificatives.*)

it will have much less mobility and facility for transporting its efforts from one part of the zone of operations to another ; without taking into the account yet the impossibility of obtaining provisions from a country naturally too circumscribed for feeding such masses.

4. Finally, it appears certain that the two fractions of an army which the central mass ought to oppose to the two exterior hostile lines, with the instruction to limit themselves to holding them in check, would always require armies of eighty or ninety thousand men, since it is the object to hold a hundred and thirty-five thousand in check ; so that if the armies of observation committed the folly of engaging in serious combats, they might sustain reverses, the consequences of which would be so deplorable that they would surpass much the advantages obtained by the principal army.

Notwithstanding all those doubts and all those mitigating reasons, if ever I had to dispose of an army, I should not hesitate to give it an interior direction in all the cases where I have recommended them as being the most favorable; or else I should assign to it in every other hypothesis, a direction upon the extremity of the front of operations of the enemy, according to the maxims above explained ; leaving to my adversaries the pleasure of manœuvering according to the opposite systems. Until this experiment can have place they will permit me to remain firm in my belief, justified by the campaigns of Eugéne of Savoy, of Marlborough, of Frederick the Great, and Napoleon.

Since I have undertaken to defend principles which seem incontestable, I will seize this occasion to reply to objections, still less founded, which distinguished, but often passionate and unjust writers, have raised against the above mentioned article.

The first are from the Bavarian Colonel Xilander, who, in his course of strategy, has often misconceived the principles which have served me as a basis. This writer, otherwise full of erudition, has acknowledged in a pamphlet and a more recent periodical journal, that he had been unjust and bitter in his manner of judging my work. He confesses even that he had not awaited the publication of my reply for acknowledging his wrong, although he has repeated it in a second edition.

This avowal, full of *naiveté*, which does him honor, dispenses with my returning to what he has said on the subject, but as his work is of the number of those which seduce through the orthodox forms of the positive sciences, I ought, nevertheless, for the sake of the art, to maintain what I have said relatively to the reproach which he made me *of having raised with difficulty the scaffolding of an excentric system, in order to return finally to an opposite system.*

I repeat, this contradiction which he so gratuitously imputed to me, and which would be at least an inconsistency, does not exist. I have presented exclusively neither the concentric system, nor the excentric system; my whole work tends to prove the lasting influence of principles, and to demonstrate that operations, to be skillful and happy, must produce the application of those fundamental principles. Now, excentric or divergent operations, as well as the concentric, may be either very good or very bad; all depends upon the respective situation of the forces.

The excentric, for example, are good when they are applied to a mass departing from a given centre, and acting in a divergent direction, to divide and annihilate separately two hostile fractions which should be found to form two exterior lines; such was the manœuvre of Frederick, which produced, at the end of the campaign of 1767, the splendid battles of Rosbach and Leuthen; such were also almost all the operations of Napoleon, whose favorite manœuvre consisted in uniting, by well calculated marches, imposing masses on the centre, to divide them afterwards excentrically in pursuit of the enemy, after having pierced or turned his front of operations; this manœuvre had for object to finish thus the dispersion of the vanquished.*

On the other hand, concentric operations are good in two hypotheses: 1. When they tend to concentrate a divided army, on a point where it would be sure to arrive before the enemy; 2. When they tend to make act, towards a common end, two armies which could not be anticipated and overthrown separately by any more concentrated enemy.

But let us reverse the question; then we shall have quite the opposite consequence; then we shall be assured how immutable principles are, and how much we should be on our guard against confounding them with systems. In fact, those same concentric operations, so advantageous in the two hypotheses above mentioned, may become the most pernicious when they are found applied to a different position of the respective forces. For example, if two masses start from points removed from each other, to march concentrically upon an enemy whose forces should be on lines interior and more approached to each other, there would result that this

---

* M. Xilander will find it less astonishing that one could by turns approve of manœuvres concentric and divergent, when he shall reflect that among the most splendid operations of Napoleon, there are several where the two systems are alternately employed in 24 hours, as for example, the affairs around Ratisbon in 1809.

march would produce the union of the hostile forces before their own, and would expose the latter to inevitable defeat. This is what happened to Moreau and Jourdan before the Arch-Duke Charles, in 1796. Departing even from one point only, or from two points much less removed from each other than Dusseldorf and Strassburg, this risk may be run. What was the fate experienced by the concentric columns of Wurmser and Quasdanovich, wishing to direct themselves upon the Mincio by the two shores of Lake Garda? Will the catastrophe which was the result of the march of Napoleon and Grouchy upon Brussels have been forgotten? Both having started from Sombref, they wished to move concentrically upon that city, the one by Quatre-Bras, and the other by Wavre ; Blucher and Wellington, taking an interior strategic line, united before them, and the terrible disaster of Waterloo attested to the world that the immutable principles of war are not violated with impunity.

Such events prove better than all the reasoning in the world, that no system of operations is good but when it offers the application of principles. I have not the pretention to believe that I have created those principles, since they have existed in all time; that Cæsar, Scipio and the Consul Nero* have applied them as well as Marlborough and Eugene, not to say better. But I believe that I am the first to have demonstrated them, with all the chances of their application, in a work in which the precepts emanate from the proofs themselves, and where the application is constantly found in the reach of military readers. The dogmatic form would have suited the professors better, I own ; but I doubt whether it would have been as clear and as strongly demonstrative for young officers, as the historical form adopted in my treatise on grand military operations.

Some of my critics have gone so far as to censure the term lines of operations, which I give to surfaces, and to sustain that the true lines of operations were rivers; an assertion which, to say the least of it, is strange. No person would take it into his head to say that the Danube or the Rhine are lines of operations, upon which an army can act. Those rivers would be at the most lines of supply for facilitating arrivals, but not for manœuvering an army, unless its chief had the miraculous power of making an army march in the midst of the waters. My critic will say, perhaps, that he meant to speak of valleys and not of rivers ; I would have him observe then, that a valley and a river are meanwhile, very different things, and that a valley is also a surface, and not a line.

---

* The splendid strategical movement of this Consul, which gave the death-blow to the power of Hannibal in Italy, is not surpassed by the finest exploits of modern wars.

Thus, in the physical sense, as in the didactic sense, the definition is doubly inexact, but supposing it even tolerable, still it would be necessary that a river, in order to be used as a line of operations for an army, should always flow in the direction in which this army should march; and it is almost always the contrary. The greater part of rivers are rather defensive barriers or *fronts of operations,* which they could not be, and considered at the same time as lines of operations. The Rhine is a barrier for France as for Germany; the lower Danube is a barrier for Turkey and Russia; the Ebro is a barrier for Spain, the Rhone is a barrier against an army which should come from Italy to attack France; the Elbe, the Oder, the Vistula, are barriers against armies marching from west to east, or from east to west.

With regard to routes, the assertion is not more just, for it could not be said that the hundred traveled roads through Suabia are a hundred lines of operations. There are, doubtless, no lines of operations without roads; but a road in itself could not be a line of operations.

I have enlarged somewhat upon this article upon lines of operations, because I regard it as the corner-stone of strategical movements, and that it is important for the art not to allow sophisms to be accredited. The public will decide upon these controversies; as for myself, I have the innate consciousness of having sought in good faith to advance the science, and without being accused of self-love, I think I may flatter myself with having contributed thereto.

ARTICLE XXII.

STRATEGICAL LINES.

We have made mention, in Articles 19 and 21, of strategical lines of manœuvre, which differ essentially from lines of operations; it will not be useless to define them, for many military men frequently confound them.

Strategical lines are of several kinds, as has been seen in Article 19. We have not occupied ourselves with those which have a general and permanent importance from their situation, and from their relations with the configuration of the country, such as the lines of the Danube, or of the Meuse, the chains of the Alps and the Balkan. As the latter figure in the number of the decisive points of the theatre of war, or in that of the lines of defense of which we have already spoken, and as they are traced by nature, we shall have nothing to say of them, for they could be subjected to no other investigation than the detailed and profound study of the military geography of Europe, and to a description, the immense scope of which, it may well be supposed, does not accord with that of this summary ; the Arch-Duke Charles has given an excellent model of this study in his description of Southern Germany.

But we name strategic lines also, all the communications which lead by the most direct or the most advantageous way from one important point to another, as well as from the front of operations of the army to all the objective points which it may have the project to attain.

It is comprehended, therefore, that the whole theatre of war is found furrowed with such lines, but that those which it should be wished to pass over with any object whatever, are alone of any real importance, at least for a given period. This fact will suffice to make comprehended the great difference which exists between a general line of operations adopted for a whole campaign, and those eventual strategical lines, changeable as the operations of armies themselves.

Finally, independently of material or territorial strategical lines, we have already said that there existed a kind of combination, in the disposition and the choice of those lines, which constitutes as many different manœuvres, and we have named them *strategical lines of manœuvre.*

An army which should have Germany for a general *échequier*, would take for zone of operations the space between the Alps and the Danube, or else that between the Danube and the Main, finally, that between the mountains of Franconia and the sea. It would have upon the zone adopted, a simple line of operations, or at most, two concentric lines of operations, it would have those lines interior and central, or else exterior ; whilst it would embrace perhaps twenty strategical lines, one after another in proportion as its enterprises should be developed ; it would have at first one, for each of its wings, which would terminate in the general line of operations ; then, if it operate upon the zone between the Danube and the Alps, it might adopt according to events sometimes the strategical line which should lead from Ulm upon Donanwerth and Ratisbon, sometimes that which should lead from Ulm towards the Tyrol ; finally, that which should conduct from Ulm upon Nuremberg or upon Mayence, and all according as the turn of events should render necessary.

It may be affirmed, then, without incurring the blame of creating a confusion of words, that all the definitions given in the preceding article for lines of operations, are necessarily reproduced for strategical lines, and also the maxims which are derived from them. Those lines must be *concentric* when the object is to prepare for a decisive shock, then *excentric* after the victory; strategical lines are rarely simple, for an army will scarcely march upon a single road, but when they shall be double, triple, quadruple even, they must also be interior if the forces of the armies are equal, or exterior for those which should have a great numerical superiority. We could, it is true, deviate at times from the too strict application of this maxim, by throwing an isolated corps in an exterior direction, even in case of an equality of forces, when it shall be the question to obtain a great result without running great risks, but this is already entering again into the category of detachments, which we shall treat separately, and could not be applicable to principal masses. Of course strategical lines could not be interior in the case when our efforts should be directed against an extremity of the hostile front of operations.

Departing from thence, it will seem that all the maxims which we have presented upon lines of operations, would be the only ones which we could reproduce, and our readers will not blame us for sparing them their repetition ; they can easily of themselves make the application of them.

There is, meanwhile, one which it is our duty to point out: it is that in general, in the choice of momentary strategical lines, it is important to avoid wholly uncovering the line of operations and exposing it to the enemy. This may be tolerated when it is the question to extricate one's self from a great danger or to seek great results ; but it is necessary at least, even in this case, to prepare the means of escape by one of those sudden changes of lines of operations which we have before indicated, and it is important that the operation be not of long duration.

Let us apply those divers combinations to the lessons of history, it is the best means of comprehending them ; and let us take for first example the campaign of Waterloo. The Prussian army had the Rhine for a base ; its line of operations ran from Cologne and from Coblentz upon Luxemburg and Namur ; Wellington had Antwerp for a base, and for a line of operations, the short route to Brussels. The sudden attack of Napoleon on Fleurus decided Blucher to receive battle parallelly to the English base, and not to his own, for which he did not appear to trouble himself. This was pardonable, because strictly he could always hope to regain

Wesel or at least Nimeguen, and in the last extremity he would have been able even to seek a refuge in Antwerp. But if a Prussian army, deprived of its powerful maritime allies, had committed such a fault, it would have been annihilated.

Beaten at Ligny, and a refugee at Gembloux, then at Wavre, Blucher had but three strategical lines to choose, that which led direct to Maestricht, that which went farther to the north towards Venloo, or else that which led to the English army near *Mont Saint-Jean*. He audaciously took the latter, and triumphed by the application of interior strategic lines, which Napoleon had neglected for the first time, perhaps, in his life. It will be admitted that the line followed, from Gembloux by Wavre, upon *Mont Saint-Jean*, was neither the line of operations of the Prussian army, nor a line of battle, but rather a strategic line of manœuvre: a central or interior line, audaciously chosen, in that the natural line of operations was left uncovered in order to seek safety in the important junction of the two combined armies, which in reality rendered this resolution conformable to the principles of war.

An example less happy was that of Ney at Dennewitz; debouching from Wittemberg upon the direction to Berlin, he prolonged himself to the right in order to gain the extreme left of the Allies; but by this movement he left his primitive line of retreat exposed to all the blows of an enemy superior in numbers and in veteran troops. It is true that he had the mission of putting himself in connection with Napoleon, whose project was to join him by Herzberg or Luckau; but then the Marshal should at least have taken, from his first movement, all the logistical and tactical measures for assuring this change of strategical line, and to have informed his army of it. He did nothing of the kind, whether through neglect, or from a feeling of aversion to every supposition of a retreat; the cruel losses which he sustained at Dennewitz were the sad result of this imprudence.

One of the operations which best retraces the different combinations of strategic lines is that of Napoleon through the gorges of the Brenta in 1796. His general line of operations, departing from the Appenines, led to Verona, where it stopped. When he had repulsed Wurmser upon Roveredo and had resolved to penetrate into Tyrol in his pursuit, he pushed into the valley of the Adige to Trent and the Lavis, where he learned that Wurmser had thrown himself by the Brenta upon the Frioul, without doubt to take him in reverse. There were but three courses to choose: to remain in the narrow valley of the Adige at the risk of being compromised there; to retrograde by Verona to meet Wurmser; or else, what was grand, but rash, to throw himself after Wurmser in that valley of the Brenta enclosed by rocky mountains, and the issues of which could be barred by the Austrians.

Napoleon was not a man to hesitate between three such alternatives; he left Vaubois upon the Lavis to cover Trent, and threw himself with the remainder of his forces upon Bassano; the brilliant results of this bold movement are known.   Surely the route from Trent to Bassano was not the line of operations of the French army, but a strategic line more audacious still than that of Blucher upon Wavre.   However, it was a question only of three or four days operation, at the end of which Napoleon would either be conqueror or vanquished at Bassano; in the first case he opened his communication direct with Verona and with his line of operations, in the contrary case he regained Trent in all haste, where, rallied upon Vaubois, he would equally fall back upon Verona, or Peschiera.   The difficulties of the country which rendered this march audacious under one aspect, favored it also under another; for Wurmser, though even he had triumphed at Bassano, could in no wise disturb the return upon Trent, no road permitting him to anticipate Napoleon in that direction.   There would have been only the case in which Davidovich, left upon the Lavis, should have driven Vaubois from Trent, which would have somewhat embarrassed Napoleon; but that Austrian general, beaten anteriorly at Roveredo, ignorant for several days of what the French army was doing, and believing that he had it all upon his back, would scarcely have thought of retaking the offensive when Napoleon, repulsed at Bassano, would already have returned.   Even though Davidovich had advanced to Roveredo, facing Vaubois, he would there have been surrounded in that gulf of the Adige between the two French masses which would have made him undergo the fate of Vandamme at Culm.

I have enlarged upon this incident to show that the calculation of time and distances, joined to a great activity, can cause to succeed enterprises in appearance altogether imprudent.   I conclude from thence, that it is sometimes permitted to throw an army momentarily on a direction which would uncover its lines of operations, but that all measures should be taken that the enemy do not profit from it, as much by the rapidity of its execution, as by demonstrations which might deceive him, and leave him in ignorance of what is passing.   Meanwhile, it is one of the most hazardous of manœuvres, and one which should never be resolved upon but in urgent cases.

We think we have sufficiently demonstrated the divers combinations which those strategic lines of manœuvre present, in order that each of our readers may be able to appreciate their different species and the maxims which should preside over their choice.

ARTICLE XXIII.

MEANS OF ASSURING LINES OF OPERATIONS BY TRANSIENT BASES OR STRATEGICAL RESERVES.

When you penetrate offensively into a country, you may, and you ought even, to form *eventual bases* which, without being either as strong or as sure as those of your own frontiers, can nevertheless be considered as temporary bases ; a line of river with *têtes de ponts*, with one or two large cities secure from a *coup de main* for covering the grand depôts of the army, and to serve for the union of the troops of reserve, may form an excellent base of this kind.

Such a line, however, could not of course serve as a transient base, if a hostile force were found in proximity with the line of operations which should conduct from this supposed base to the real base of the frontiers. Thus Napoleon would have had a good real base on the Elbe, in 1813, if Austria had remained neutral : but this power having declared against him, the line of the Elbe being taken in reverse, was no longer but a very good pivot of operations for favoring a momentary enterprise, but dangerous in the end, if one chanced to sustain there a notable check.

Now as every army beaten in a hostile country may always be exposed to his adversary manœuvering in a manner to cut it off from its frontiers if it persisted in remaining in the country, it must indeed be acknowledged that those remote temporary bases will be rather momentary points of support than real bases, and that they enter in some sort into the category of eventual lines of defense.

However this may be, we cannot either flatter ourselves with always finding, in an invaded country, posts secure from insult, fit to offer as points of support suitable for forming even a temporary base. In this case we might supply it by the establishment of a strategic reserve, an invention altogether peculiar to the modern system, and the advantages, as well as the inconveniences of which deserve to be examined.

STRATEGICAL RESERVES.

Reserves play a great part in modern wars; scarcely was there an idea of them formerly. From the government which prepares the national. reserves, down to the chief of a platoon of skirmishers, each at this day wishes to have his reserve.

Besides the national reserves, of which we have spoken in the chapter on military policy, and which are only raised in urgent cases, a wise government takes care to assure good reserves for completing the active armies; it is, then, for the General to know how to dispose of them when they are in the circumference of his command. A State will have its reserves, the army will have its own, each army corps, and even each division or detachment will not fail either to assure itself one.

The reserves of an army are of two kinds : those which are in the line of battle, ready for combat, those which are destined to keep the army full, and which, whilst organizing, may occupy an important point of the theatre of war, and serve even as strategical reserves. Doubtless many campaigns have been undertaken and brought to a successful close without such reserves being thought of; their establishment also depends, not only upon the extent of the means that can be disposed of, but still more upon the nature of the frontiers, and the distance which separates the front of operations, or the objective aim from the base.

However, so soon as the invasion of a country is decided upon, it is natural to think of the possibility of being thrown back upon the defensive. Now, the establishment of a reserve intermediate between the base and the front of operations, offers the same advantage as the reserve of an active army will procure on the day of battle; for it can fly to the important points which the enemy should menace, without enfeebling the acting army for that purpose. In truth, the formation of such a reserve will require a certain number of regiments which must be drawn from the active army ; meanwhile it cannot be denied that a rather large army has always reinforcements to expect from the interior, recruits to instruct, moveable militia to exercise, regimental depôts and convalescents to turn to account ; in organizing then a system of central depôts for laboratories of munitions and equipment, by causing to be united to those depôts 'l the detachments going to and returning from the army, joining thereto merely a few battalions of good troops, to give a little more consistency, a reserve would thus be formed from which eminent services might be drawn.

In all his campaigns, Napoleon never failed to organize them; even in 1797, in his audacious march upon the Noric Alps, he had at first the corps of Joubert on the Adige, afterwards that of Victor, returning from the Roman States to the environs of Verona. In 1805, the corps of Ney and Augerau alternately played this part in Tyrol and in Bavaria, as well as Mortier and Marmont around Vienna.

Napoleon, marching to the war of 1806, formed such reserves on the Rhine; Mortier used them for subjecting Hesse. At the same time second reserves were formed at Mayence under Kellerman, and came, as fast as they were formed, to occupy the country between the Rhine and the Elbe, whilst Mortier was called into Pomerania. When Napoleon decided to push upon the Vestula at the end of the same year, he ordered, with a great deal of ostentation, the union of an army of the Elbe; its force was to be sixty thousand men, its object, to cover Hamburg against the English, and to impose upon Austria, whose dispositions were as manifest as her interest.

The Prussians had formed a similar one at Halle in 1806; but it was badly placed; if it had been established upon the Elbe, at Wittenberg or Dessau, and had done its duty, it would, perhaps, have saved the army, by giving to the Prince of Hohenlohe and Blucher time to gain Berlin, or Stettin at least.

Those reserves will be especially useful in countries which should present a double front of operations; they can then fulfill the double destination of observing the second front, and of being able at need to concur in the operations of the principal army, if the enemy chance to menace its flanks, or if a reverse forced it to approach the reserve. It is useless to add, that it is necessary, nevertheless, to avoid falling into dangerous detachments, and whenever those reserves can be dispensed with, it will be necessary to risk it, or at least to employ them only at the depôt. It is scarcely but in remote invasions, or in the interior of one's own country, when it is menaced with invasion, that they seem useful, for if war be made at five or six marches only from the frontier, in order to dispute an adjacent province, those reserves would be an altogether superfluous detachment. In your own country you can most frequently dispense with them; it will only be in the case of serious invasion, when you will order new levies, that such a reserve, in an intrenched camp, under the protection of a place serving as a grand depôt, will be indispensable. It is for the talent of the general to judge of the opportuneness of the reserves, according to the state of the country, the depth of the line of operations, the nature of the fortified points which should be held therein ; finally, according to the proximity of any hostile province. He will also decide upon their position, and the means of turning to account detachments which would enfeeble the active army less, than if drawn from choice divisions.

I shall be excused from demonstrating that those reserves ought to occupy the most interesting strategic points which should be found between the real base of the frontiers and the front of operations, or between the objective point and this same base ; they will guard the strong-holds if there be any already subjected ; they will observe or invest those which shall not be so ; and if none are possessed to serve as points of support, they can labor in tracing at least a few intrenched camps or *têtes-de-ponts*, to protect the grand depôts of the army, and to double the strength of their own position.

For the rest, all that we have said in Article 20 upon lines of defense relative to pivots of operations, may also be applied to transient bases, as well as to strategic reserves, which shall be doubly advantageous when they shall posses such pivots well situated.

ARTICLE XXIV.

OF THE ANCIENT SYSTEM OF WARS OF POSITION, AND

THE PRESENT SYSTEM OF MARCHES.

We understand by the ancient system of positions, that ancient manner of making war with armies encamped in tents, living by their magazines and their bakeries, reciprocally watching each other, the one for besieging a place, the other for covering it ; the one coveting a small province, the other opposing its designs by self-styled impregnable positions ; a system which was generally in practice from the middle ages down to the French revolution.

In the course of this revolution great changes supervened; but there were at first divers systems, and they were not all improvements in the art. In 1792, war was commenced as it had been finished in 1762 ; the French armies encamped under their places, and the Allies encamped for besieging them. It was not until 1793, when it saw itself assailed within and without, that the republic threw a million of men and fourteen armies upon its enemies ; of necessity other methods were to be taken; those armies having neither tents, nor pay, nor magazines, marched, bivouacked or cantoned ; their mobility was increased by it, and became an instrument of success. Their tactics changed also; their chiefs held them in columns, because they are more easy to manage than deployed lines, and by favor of the broken country of Flanders and the Vosges, where they fought, they threw out a part of their forces as skirmishers to cover their columns.

This system, which was born thus of circumstances, succeeded at first beyond all expectation ; it disconcerted the methodical troops of Prussia and of Austria, as well as their chiefs : Mack, among others, to whom the successes of the Prince of Coburg were attributed, augmented his reputation by publishing instructions for extending lines to the end of opposing a thinner order to those skirmishers ! The poor man had not perceived that the skirmishers made the noise, but that the columns carried the positions.

The first generals of the republic were fighting men, and nothing more ; the principal direction came from Carnot and the Committee of Public Safety ; it was sometimes good, but also frequently bad. It must be owned, nevertheless, one of the best strategical movements of this war came from him ; it was he who directed, at the end of 1793, a choice reserve successively to the succor of Dunkirk, Maubeuge and of Landau ; so that this small mass, transported by post, and seconded by the troops already assembled on those places, succeeded in causing the French territory to be evacuated.

The campaign of 1794 began badly, as has already been said ; it was the force of circumstances which led to the strategical movement of the army of the Moselle upon the Sambre, and not a premeditated plan ; for the rest this movement decided the success at Fleurus and the conquest of Belgium. In 1795, the French committed such great faults, that they were imputed to treason ; the Austrians, on the contrary, better directed, by Clairfayt, Charteler and Schmidt, than by Mack and the Prince of Coburg, proved that they had some conception of strategy.

Every one knows that the Arch-Duke triumphed in 1796, over Jourdan and Moreau, by a single march, which was the application of interior lines.

Until then the French armies had embraced great fronts, either more easily to obtain provisions, or that their generals imagined they were doing well in putting all their divisions in line, leaving to their chiefs the care of disposing of them for combat as they could, and keeping in reserve but slender detachments incapable of repairing any thing, if the enemy chanced to overthrow a single one of those divisions.

Such was the state of things when Napoleon made his debut in Italy; the rapidity of those marches routed the Austrians and Piedmontese from the commencement of his operations; for, disengaged of all useless material, he surpassed the mobility of all modern armies; he conquered the Peninsula by a series of strategical marches and combats.

His movement upon Vienna in 1797, was a rash operation, but legitimated perhaps by the necessity of conquering the Arch-Duke Charles before the arrival of the reinforcements coming from the Rhine.

The campaign of 1800, more characteristic still, signalised a new era in the projection of plans of war, and in the directions of lines of operations; from thence date those bold objective points, which have in veiw nothing less than the capture or destruction of armies, and of which we have spoken in Article 19. Orders of battle were equally less extended, the organization of armies into corps of two or three divisions, became more rational. The system of modern strategy was from that time carried to its zenith, for the campaigns of 1805 and 1806 were only corollaries of the great problem resolved in 1800.

With regard to tactics, that of columns and of skermishers, which Napoleon found quite established, suited too well the broken country of Italy not to be adopted.

At this day there presents itself a grave and capital question, it is to decide whether the system of Napoleon is suitable to all capacities, to all epochs, and to all armies; or if, on the contrary, it were possible that governments and generals could return to the methodical system of wars of position, after having meditated upon the events of 1800 and 1809. Let us compare, in fact, the marches and encampments of the Seven Years War, with those of the seven weeks war, (an epithet which Napoleon gave to the campaign of 1806,) or with the three months which elapsed from the departure from the camp of Boulogne in 1805, to the arrival upon the plains of Moravia, and let us decide then whether the system of Napoleon is preferable to the ancient one.

This system of the French Emperor was *to make ten leagues a day, to combat, and to canton afterwards in repose.* He has himself told me that he recognized no other kind of war than this.

It will be objected that the adventurous character of this great captain was joined to his personal position, and to the situation of minds in France, to excite him to do what no other chief would have dared to do in his place, whether he were born upon a throne, or whether he were a simple general under the orders of his government. If this is incontestable, it appears to me true also, that between the system of immoderate invasions and that of positions, there is a medium, so that, without imitating his impetuous audacity, it will be possible to follow the routes which he has trodden, and that the system of wars of position will probably be proscribed for a long time, or at least considerably modified and improved.

Doubtless, if the art is found enlarged by the adoption of the system of marches, humanity will lose thereby more than it will gain, for those rapid incursions, and those bivouacs of considerable masses, feeding from day to day upon the same countries which they invade, do not badly recall the devastations of the peoples which overran Europe from the 4th to the 13th century. However, it is little probable that they will be renounced so soon, for a great truth has been at least demonstrated by the wars of Napoleon, it is that distances could no longer secure a country from invasion, and that States which wish to secure themselves from it, ought to have a good system of fortresses and lines of defense, a good system of reserves and military institutions, finally, a good system of policy. Therefore, the populations organize themselves every where into militia, to serve as reserves to the active armies, which will maintain their force upon a footing more and more formidable; now, the greater armies are the more necessary the system of rapid operations and prompt denouements becomes.

If, in the sequel, social order recovers a calmer tone, if nations, instead of combatting for their existence, fight no longer except for relative interests, to round their frontiers, or to maintain the European equilibrium; then a new law of nations may be adopted; and it will perhaps be possible to put armies upon a less exaggerated footing. Then also, in a war of power against power, armies of eighty or a hundred thousand men may be seen to return to a mixed system of war, which would hold the middle ground between the volcanic incursions of Napoleon, and the impossible system of the *Starke Positionen* of the last century. Until then we must admit this system of marches which has produced so great events, for the first who should dare to renounce it in presence of a capable and enterprising enemy, would probably become its victim.

By the science of marches, we do not understand at the present day, simply those minute details of logistics which consist in well combining the order of troops in column, the time of their departure and arrival, the precautions necessary in their journey, the means of communication, either between themselves, or with the point which is assigned them, these are all things which make an essential branch of the functions of the staff. But, besides these very material details, there exists a combination of marches which belong to the grand operations of strategy. For example, the march of Napoleon by the St. Bernard, to fall upon the communications of Melas ; those which he made in 1805 by Donauwert, to cut off Mack, and 1806 by Gera, to turn the Prussians ; the march of Suwaroff to fly from Turin upon Trebbia to meet Macdonald; that of the Russian army upon Taroutin, then upon Krasnoi, were decisive operations, not from their relations with *la logistique*, but from their relations with strategy.

However, properly considered, those skillful marches are never but means of putting in practice. the various applications of the principle which we have indicated, and which we shall yet develope ; to make a fine march, is then nothing else than carrying the mass of one's forces upon the decisive point ; now, the whole science will consist in determining well that point after the manner we have essayed to demonstrate in Article 19. In fact, what was the march by the St. Bernard, if not a line of operations directed against an extremity of the strategic front of the enemy, and from thence upon his line of retreat? What were the marches to Ulm and Jena but the same manœuvre? What was the march of Blucher to Waterloo, but the application of the interior strategical lines recommended in Article 22 ?

Hence it may be concluded, that all strategical movements which tend to direct the masses of an army successively upon the different points of the hostile front of operations, will be skillful marches, since they will apply the general principle indicated, page 81 , by putting in action the mass of forces upon fractions merely of the hostile army. The operations of the French at the end of 1793, fron Dunkirk to Landau, those of Napoleon in 1796, in 1809 and in 1814, may be cited as models of this kind. It would be useless to enlarge upon those combinations, since they enter by their applications in the series of maxims already presented.

We shall observe, nevertheless, that there exists a species of marches which have been designated under the name of flank marches, and which we could not pass over in silence. In all times they have been presented as hazardous manœuvres, without any thing satisfactory having ever been written on this subject. If we understand thereby tactical manœuvres made in view of the hostile line of battle, doubtless such a flank movement is a very delicate operation, although it succeeds at times; but if ordinary strategical marches are meant, I can see nothing dangerous in a flank march, unless the most common logistical precautions have been neglected. In a strategical movement, the two hostile main bodies ought always to be separated by an interval of about two marches, (counting the distance which separates the respective advanced guards, from the enemy and from their own columns.) In such a case there could exist no real danger in the strategical journey from one position to another.

There are two cases, nevertheless, where a flank march seems altogether inadmissible : the first is·that where the system of the line of operations, of the strategical lines and front of operations, should all present the flank to the enemy in the whole course of an enterprise. Such was the famous project of marching upon Leipzig, without being disquieted about Dresden and the two hundred and fifty thousand men of Napoleon, a project which, resolved upon at Trachenberg in the month of August, 1813, would probably have been fatal to the allied armies, if my soliditations made at Jungferteinitz, had not caused it to be modified. The second case is when we should have a remote or deep line of operations, like that of Napoleon at Borodino ; especially if this line of operations offered still but a single suitable line of retreat ; then every flank movement which should leave it exposed, would be a grave fault.

In countries where good secondary communications should be numerous, flank movements would be less dangerous, because at need one could have recourse to a change of line of operations if he were repulsed. The physical and moral state of armies, the more or less energetic character of the chiefs and of the troops, could also have an influence upon the opportuneness of·such movements.

In fact, the often cited marches of Jena and of Ulm were veritable flank manœuvres, quite like that upon Milan after the passage of the Chiusella, and like that of Marshal Paskiewics for crossing the Vistula at Ossiek ; every one knows how they succeeded.

It is otherwise with tactical movements, made by flank in presence of the enemy. Ney was punished for this at Dennewitz ; Marmont at Salamanca, and Frederick the Great at Kollin. •

Meanwhile, the manœuvre of Frederick the Great at Leuthen, become so celebrated in the annals of the art, was a veritable movement of this kind, (see chapter VI, Treatise on Grand Operations ;) but skillfully covered by a mass of cavalry, concealed by the heights, and operated against

an army which remained immovable in its camp, it had an immense success, because, at the moment of the shock, it was really the army of Daun
which lent the flank, and not that of the king. Moreover, it must be
owned also, that with the old system of moving by lines at platoon distance, in order to form, without deployment, by a right or left into line of
battle, the movements parallel to the hostile line are not flank marches,
since then the flank of columns is, in reality, nothing else than the line
of battle.

The famous march of Prince Eugene in sight of the French camp, for
turning the lines of Turin, was much more extraordinary still than that
of Leuthen, and was not less successful.

In these different battles, I repeat, they were tactical and not strategical
movements; the march of Prince Eugene, from Mantua upon Turin, was
one of the greatest strategical operations of the age; but the movement
here alluded to was that made on the eve of the battle for turning the
French camp. For the rest, the difference of results which those five
days present, is an additional proof that in this point also tactics is
variable.

With regard to the logistical part of marches, although it forms but
one of the secondary branches of the military art, it is so closely connected with great operations, that it may be regarded as the executive
part of them; hence I believe it my duty to say a few words of it, uniting
it in Article 41, with some ideas upon *la logistique* in general.

ARTICLE XXV.

MAGAZINES AND THEIR RELATIONS TO MARCHES.

The combinations which are most nearly connected with the system of
marches, are those of magazines, for, in order to march quickly and for a
long time, provisions are necessary; now the art of subsisting a numerous
army, in a hostile country especially, is one of the most difficult. The science of a commissary general of subsistence has its special treatises, to

which we shall refer our readers, limiting ourselves to indicating what it has in common with strategy.*

The system of supply of the ancients has never been well known, for, all that Vegetius says of the administration of the Romans, does not suffice to discover to us the machinery of a subject so complicated. A phenomenon which will ever be difficult to conceive, is that Darius and Xerxes were able to subsist immense armies in Thrace, (Romelia,) whilst, in our day, one would have difficulty to subsist there thirty thousand men. In the middle ages, the Greek emperors, the barbarians, and still later, the crusaders fed there also considerable masses of men.

Cæsar has said that war ought to nourish war, and it is hence generally concluded that he always lived at the expense of the country which he passed over.

The middle ages were remarkable for their great migrations of all kinds, it would be very interesting to know exactly the number of Huns, Vandals, Goths and Mongols, which successively traversed Europe, and how they lived on their marches.

In the earlier times of modern history, it is to be believed that the armies of Francis First, crossing the Alps to enter fertile Italy, did not carry great magazines in their trains ; for they were only forty or fifty thousand men strong, and such an army is not embarrassed with living in the rich valleys of the Ticino, and of the Pô.

Under Louis XIV and Frederick II, more considerable armies, fighting on their own frontiers, lived regularly by the magazines and bakeries which followed them ; which constrained much their operations, by precluding· them from moving from their depôts beyond a space proportioned to the means of transportation, to the quantity of rations which they carry, and to the number of days which was necessary for the vehicles to go and return from the camp.

In the Revolution, necessity caused these magazines to be despised ; large armies, invading Belgium and Germany without provisions, lived sometimes among the inhabitants, sometimes by forced requisitions upon the country, finally, by marauding and pillage. To march cantoning among the inhabitants is very possible in Belgium, in Italy, in Suabia, upon the rich banks of the Rhine and of the Danube, especially if the army, marching by several columns, does not exceed a hundred or a hundred and twenty thousand men ; but it becomes very difficult in other coun-

---

* The work of Count Cancrin, formerly *Intendant-General* of the Russian armies could not be too highly recommended ; there exist few as satisfactory on the art of administering the subsistence department.

tries, and impossible in Russia, Sweden, Poland, and in Turkey. It is conceived with how much more velocity and impetuosity an army acts, when it has no other calculation to make than that of the vigor of the limbs of its soldiers. This system gave great advantages to Napoleon;- but he abused it, by extending it upon a large scale, and in countries where it was impracticable.

The general of an army ought to know how to make all the existing resources of the country he invades concur in his enterprises ; he must employ the authorities, when they remain therein, to levy uniform and legal requisitions, which he will cause to be paid for when he has the means of so doing ; when the authorities do not remain, he should establish provisory ones, composed of the notables, and clad with extraordinary powers. He will cause those provisions required to be collected upon points the most favorable to the movements of the army, according to the principles of lines of operations. To the end of husbanding the supplies, he will cause to be cantoned in the cities and villages the greatest possible numbers of troops, securing an indemnity to the inhabitants for the surcharge which will result therefrom. The army, besides its provisions and forage, will have parks of auxiliary carriages furnished by the country, in order that the provisions may reach it wherever it should remain stationary.

It is as difficult to establish rules as to what it would be prudent to undertake, without forming magazines in advance, as to trace the exact demarcation between the possible and impossible. The countries, the seasons, the force of the armies, the spirit of the population, all vary in these combinations ; but we may establish as general maxims :

1. That in fertile and populous countries, the inhabitants of which should be hostile, an army of a hundred or a hundered and twenty thousand men moving towards the enemy, but yet sufficiently distant to embrace without danger, a certain extent of country, may march during the whole time that a given operation may require, drawing its resources from the country. Now, as a first operation never requires more than a month for the bulk of its masses to be in motion, it will suffice to provide, by reserve supplies, for the eventual necessitfes of the army, and especially for those of the forces which should be obliged to remain stationary at the same point. For example, the army of Napoleon, half'united around Ulm, to blockade Mack therein, might have need of biscuit until the surrender of the city, and if it were wanting the operation might fail.

2. During this time, it would be necessary to apply one's self to collecting, with all possible activity, the resources which the country offers, in

order to form magazines of reserve, and to relieve the wants which the army should experience after the success of the operation, whether for concentrating in positions of repose, or for departing from thence, and marching to new enterprises.

3. The magazines which should have been collected by purchase, or requisitions upon the country, ought to be disposed as much as possible in echelons, on three different rays of communications, which will facilitate on one side the supply of each of the wings of the army, and on the other the greatest possible extension of the sphere of successive requisitions ; finally, the means of better covering, if not the whole, at least a good part of the line of depôts. With this last aim it would not be useless that the depôts of the two wings should be established on rays converging towards the principal line of operation, which will ordinarily be found to be that of the centre. By this precaution two real advantages will be obtained, the first, of placing the magazines in greater security from the insults of the enemy, by augmenting the distance which separates them from him ; the second would be to facilitate the concentric movements in rear, which the army might execute, in order to unite on a single point of the line of operation, with the object of falling in its turn upon the enemy, and of wresting from him, by seizing again the initiative of attack, the momentary ascendancy which he should have acquired.

4. In countries where the population is too sparse, and the soil little fertile, an army will lack the most essential resources ; hence it will be prudent not to remove it too far from its magazines, and to carry along supplies of reserve sufficient to give it time, at need, to fall back upon the base of its grand depôts.

5. In national wars, and in countries where the whole population flies and destroys every thing, as has happened in Spain, Portugal, Russia and Turkey, it is impossible to move without being followed by regular magazines, and without having a sure base of supplies in proximity with the front of operations, which renders a war of invasion much more difficult, not to say impossible.

6. It does not suffice to assemble immense provisions, there is yet necessary the means of causing them to follow the army, and it is in this that consists the greatest difficulty, especially when it is wished to march to brisk and rapid enterprises. In order to facilitate the march of the magazines it is necessary, in the first place, to compose them of the most portable provisions, such as biscuit, rice, &c. ; then it will be necessary to have military carriages which unite lightness and solidity, to the end of being able to pass over all kinds of roads. It is important, also, as we

have said, to collect the greatest number possible of the vehicles of the country, taking care that the proprietors or conductors be well treated and protected by the troops ; parks of them will be formed in echelons in order not to remove them too far from their homes, and to have successive resources husbanded. Finally, it will be necessary to habituate the sol dier to carry for a few days biscuit, rice, or even flour, in default of other provisions.

7. The neighborhood of the sea offers very great facilities for the sup-plying of an army ; that one which is master of the sea, it seems ought never to want for anything. However, this advantage is not without its inconvenience for a great continental army, for with the object of remain-ing in sure relations with its magazines, it will allow itself to be drawn into carrying its operations upon the shore, which would expose it to cruel disasters, if the enemy acted with the mass of his forces upon the extremity opposite to the sea.* If it remove too far from the shore, it may then be exposed to see its communications menaced or even inter-cepted, and the material means of every kind must of necessity be aug-mented in proportion as it shall so remove itself.

8. The continental army, which shall employ the sea to facilitate its arrivals, must not neglect to have its principal base of operations by land with a reserve of supplies, independent of maritime means, and a line of retreat upon the extremity of its strategical front opposite the sea.

9. The rivers or navigable streams, whose course should be nearly par-allel with the routes which should serve as a line of operations to an army, would furnish, as well as canals, great facilities for the transportation of provisions ; and although these means are not comparable to those which great navigation procures, they would, notwithstanding, be very valuable. It is concluded thence with reason that lines of operations parallel to a river are the most favorable, especially in that they render arrivals more easy, and permit a great diminution of the embarrassment of carriages ; but so far from the river being within itself the true line of operations, as has been pretended, it would be necessary always to have care that the greater part of the troops should be able to keep removed from it, to the end of preventing the enemy, coming to attack them in force on the ex-tremity opposite to the river, from placing them in a position quite as fatal as if they were hemmed in upon the sea.

---

* It is seen that I mean to speak here only of wars between European nations which know how to manœuvre ; one might deviate from these rules against Asiatic and Turkish hordes, little to be feared in the field ; they have neither instruction nor troops capable of punishing the faults which should be committed before them

It must be observed, however, that in a hostile country it is very rare to be able to profit by a river for the arrival of provisions, either because of the destruction of its vessels, or because light corps might disturb its navigation. In order to render it sure it would be necessary to direct corps upon the two banks, which is not without danger, as Mortier experienced at Dirnstein. In a friendly or allied country the case is different, and the advantages of rivers are more real.

10. In default of bread or biscuit, flesh upon the foot has often sufficed for the immediate wants of an army; and in populous countries, beasts are always sufficiently abundant to provide it for some time. But these resources are soon exhausted, and they drive troops to marauding; it is important, then, to regulate by all means possible the requisitions for beasts, to pay for them if practicable, and especially to cause the columns to be followed by bullocks bought out of the sphere of the marches of the army.

I could not terminate this article without citing a saying of Napoleon, which will appear strange, but which, however, has its good side. I have heard him say that, in his first campaigns, the hostile army was always so well provided that, when he found himself embarrassed to feed his own, he had only to throw it upon the rear of the enemy, where he was certain to find every thing in abundance. A maxim which it would doubtless be absurd to lay down as a system, but which explains perhaps the success of more than one rash enterprise, and which demonstrates how much veritable war differs from too measured calculations.

ARTICLE XXVI.

FRONTIERS, AND THEIR DEFENSE BY FORTRESSES OR INTRENCHED LINES. WAR OF SIEGES.

Fortresses have two capital destinations to fulfill, the first, is to cover the frontiers; the second, to favor the operations of an army in the field.

The defense of the frontiers of a State by places is in general a somewhat vague thing; doubtless, as we have said in the article on lines of defense, there are some countries, the approaches of which, covered by great natural obstacles, offer very few accessible points which it would be possible still to cover by works of art; but in open countries the thing is more difficult. The chains of the Alps, of the Pyrannees, those less elevated of the Crapacks, of the Riesengebirg, of the Erz Gebirg, of the Rohmerwald, of the Black Forest, of the Vosges and of the Jura, are all more or less susceptible of being covered by a good system of places. (I do not speak of the Caucasus, as elevated as the great Alps, because it will never probably be the theatre of great strategical operations.)

Of all those frontiers, that between France and Piedmont was the best covered; the valleys of the Stura and Suza, the passes of the Argentaro, of Mount Genevre, of Mount Cenis, alone reputed practicable, were covered with forts in masonry, then considerable places were found in the outlets of the valleys into the plains of Piedmont; nothing appeared more difficult to overcome.

However, it must be owned, those fine defenses of art never wholly prevented an army from passing, first, because the little forts that may be constructed in the gorges are susceptible of being carried, then because some road, judged impracticable, is always found where an audacious enemy succeeds, by force of labor, in opening himself an issue. The passage of the Alps by Francis I., so well described by Gaillard, that of the St. Bernard by Napoleon; finally, the expedition by the Splugen, so well described by Mathiew Dumas, prove for the rest this truth; *an army*, said Napoleon, *passes wherever a man can plant his foot!* a maxim, perhaps, a little exaggerated, but which characterizes that great captain, and which he himself has applied with so much success! We shall say, farther on, a few words upon this mountain warfare.

Other countries are covered by great rivers, if not immediately in first line, at least in second. It is astonishing, meanwhile, that those lines, which seem so well calculated to separate nations, without interrupting their commercial relations and neighborhood, form no part of the real line of frontiers; for it could not be said that the line of the Danube separated Bessarabia from the Ottoman Empire so long as the Turks had footing in Moldavia. In the same manner, the Rhine was never a real frontier between France and Germany, since the French had for a long time places on the right bank, whilst the Germans had Mayence, Luxembourg, and the *têtes de ponts* of Manheim and Wesel upon the left bank.

However, if the Danube, the Rhine, the Rhone, the Ebro, the Oder, the Vistula, the Pô and the Adige are no part of the lines of first frontier, that does not prevent fortifying them as permanent lines of defense, upon all the points where they can offer a satisfactory system of defense, for covering the front of operations.

One of the lines of this kind, which may be cited for an example, is that of the Inn, which separated Bavaria from Austria ; flanked on the south by the Tyrolean Alps, on the north by the mountains of Bohemia and by the Danube, its front, which is not extensive, is found covered by the places of Passau, Braunau and Salsburg. Lloyd compares, somewhat poetically, this frontier to two impregnable bastions, the curtain of which, formed by three fine places, has for ditch one of the most impetuous of rivers ; but he has exaggerated a little those material advantages, for the epithet impregnable, with which he decorates them, has received three cruel denials in the campaigns of 1800, 1805 and 1809.

The greater part of European States, far from having frontiers as formidable as those of the Alps and of the Inn, present countries with open plains, or mountains accessible upon a considerable number of points ; our project not being to offer the military geography of Europe, we shall limit ourselves to presenting the general maxims which may be applied to all countries indiscriminately.

When a frontier is found in open country, it is necessary to renounce the idea of making of it a formal and complete line of defense by multiplying therein too many places, which require armies to garnish their ramparts, and never definitively prevent an entrance into the country. It will be wiser to content one's self with establishing a few good places, skilfully chosen, not merely for preventing the enemy from penetrating, but for augmenting the obstacles to his march, at the same time protecting and favoring, on the contrary, the movements of the active army charged with repulsing him.

Fortresses have then a manifest influence upon military operations, but the art of constructing them, of attacking and defending them, belonging to the special arm of the engineers, it would be foreign to our object to treat of those matters, and we will limit ourselves to examining the points in which they pertain to strategy.

The first is the choice of the site where it is suitable to construct one. The second is the determination of the cases in which we may neglect places to pass beyond, and those in which we are forced to besiege them. The third consists in the relations existing between the siege of the place and the active army which is to cover it.

As much as a well situated place favors operations, to the same degree those established out of important directions are fatal ; they are a scourge for the army which must be enfeebled for guarding them, and a scourge for the State which expends soldiers and money in pure loss.

I venture to affirm that many places in Europe are in this category.

It is true that a place is rarely of itself an absolute obstacle to the march of a hostile army, it is incontestible that it constrains it, that it forces it to detachments, to detours in its march ; on the other side, it favors the army which possesses it by giving to it all the opposite advantages ; it will assure its marches, will favor the debouch of its columns, if it be on a river ; will cover its magazines, its flanks and its movements ; finally, it will give it a refuge at need.

The idea of girding all the frontiers of a State with strong places very near each other, is a calamity ; this system has been falsely imputed to Vauban, who, far from approving it, disputed with Louvois upon the great number of useless points which that minister wished to fortify. The maxims of this part of the art may be reduced to the following principles :

1. A State ought to have places disposed in *echelon* upon three lines from the frontier towards the capitol.* Three places in the first line, as many in the second, and a grand place of arms in the third line, near the centre of the power, form a system nearly complete for each part of the frontiers of a State. If there be four such fronts, that will make from twenty-four to thirty places.

It will be objected, perhaps, that this number is already very considerable, and that Austria even has not so many. But it is necessary to consider that France has more than forty upon a third only of her frontier, (from Besançon to Dunkirk), without there yet being sufficient in third line, at the centre of its power. A committee assembled, some years since, to determine upon those fortresses, concluded that it was necessary to add still more. That does not prove that there are not already too many, but that rather there are some wanting upon important points, whilst that those of the first line, too much accumulated, ought to be maintained because they exist. Considering that France has two fronts, from Dunkirk to Basle, one from Basle to Savoy, one from Savoy to Nice, besides the altogether separate line of the Pyrannees, and the maritime line of the coasts, there results that it has six fronts to cover, which would require from forty to

---

* The memorable campaign of 1829 has still proved these truths. If the Porte had had good forts in masonry in the defiles of the Balkan, and a fine place near Faki, we should not have arrived at Adrianople, and events might have been complicated.

fifty places. Every military man will agree that these are as many as are necessary; for the front of Switzerland and the coasts of the ocean require less than those of the north-east. The essential thing in order that they attain their object, is to establish them according to a well combined system. If Austria had a less considerable number of places, it is because she was surrounded by the small States of the Germanic Empire, which, far from menacing her, put their own fortresses at her disposition.

Moreover, the number indicated expresses only that which appears necessary for a power presenting four fronts nearly equal in development. The Prussian monarchy, forming an immense front from Konigsberg to the gates of Metz, could not be fortified upon the same system as France, Spain or Austria. Thus the geographical dispositions, or the extreme extent of certain States, may cause this number to be diminished or augmented, especially when there are maritime places to add thereto.

2. Fortresses ought always to be constructed upon the important strategical points designated in Article XIX. Under the tactical relation, we ought to endeavor to place them in preference on a site which is not commanded, and which, facilitating the debouch, would render its blockade more difficult.

3. Places which unite the greatest advantages, either for their own defense, or favoring the operations of the active armies, are incontestibly those which are found so placed on great rivers as to command both banks; Mayence, Coblentz, Strasbourg, comprehending Kehl, are true models of this kind.

This truth admitted, it must be acknowledged also, that places established at the confluence of two great rivers have the advantage of commanding three different fronts of operations, which augments their importance; (the place of Modlin is a case in point.) Mayence, when it yet had the fort of Gustavsburg on the left bank of the Maine, and Cassel on the right, was the most formidable place of arms in Europe; but as it would require a garrison of twenty-five thousand men, a State could not have many of that extent.

4. The great places surrounding commercial and populous cities, offer resources for an army; they are much preferable to the small, especially when the aid of the citizens can yet be counted upon to second the garrison: Metz arrested all the power of Charles V.; Lisle suspended for a whole year the operations of Eugene and Marlborough; Strasbourg was many times the bulwark of the French armies. In the late wars those places were passed by because all the masses of Europe precipitated

themselves in arms upon France; but could an army of one hundred and fifty thousand Germans, which should have before it a hundred thousand French, penetrate with impunity to the Seine, neglecting such well furnished places? This is what I should be careful not to affirm.

5. Formerly war was made by places, camps and positions; in latter times, on the contrary, it has been made only with organized forces, without being troubled either by material obstacles or those of art. To follow exclusively the one or the other of those systems would equally be an abuse. The true science of war consists in taking a *juste milieu* between these two extremes.

Doubtless the most important thing will be always to aim first at completely defeating and dissolving the organized masses of the enemy which should hold the field; to attain this decisive end fortresses may be passed by; but if only a partial success were obtained, then it would become imprudent to pursue an excessive invasion. For the rest, all depends upon the situation and the respective strength of the armies, as well as the spirit of the populations.

Austria, warring alone against France, could not repeat the operations of the grand alliance of 1814. Moreover, it is probable that we shall not soon see fifty thousand French risking themselves beyond the Noric Alps, in the heart of the Austrian monarchy, as Napoleon did in 1797.* Such events depend upon a concurrence of circumstances which form an exception to common rules.

6. It will be concluded from what precedes, that places are an essential support, but that the abuse of them would be injurious, since instead of adding to the forces of the active army, it weakens by dividing them; that an army, seeking with reason to destroy the hostile forces in the field, may without danger glide between several places in order to attain this end, having care however to cause them to be observed; that it could not in the meanwhile invade a hostile country by crossing a great river, like the Danube, the Rhine and the Elbe, without reducing, at least one of the places situated upon that river, to the end of having an assured line of retreat; master of one such place, the army can then continue the offensive, at the same time employing its siege material to the successive reduction of the other fortresses; for the farther the acting army shall

---

* I do not blame Napoleon for having taken the offensive in the Friant; he had before him thirty-five thousand Austrians, which were awaiting twenty thousand more coming from the Rhine; the French general attacked the Arch-Duke before the arrival of those reinforcements, and pushed his successes briskly because there was nothing before him which could compromise his point. He operated within the rules, on account of the antecedents and the respective positions of the two parties,

advance, the more able will the siege corps be to flatter itself with terminating the enterprise without being obstructed.

7. If great places are much more advantageous than small, when the population is friendly, it must be admitted also, that the latter may have meanwhile their degree of importance, not for arresting the enemy, who might easily mask them, but for favoring the operations of an army in the field : the fort of Koenigstein was as useful to the French in 1813, as the vast place of Dresden, because it procured the *tête de pont* upon the Elbe. In mountainous countries, small forts well situated are worth as much as places, for the question is only to close passages, and not to serve as a refuge to an army ; the small fort of Bard came near arresting the army of Bonaparte in the valley of Aosta in 1800.

8. It must be deduced hence that each part of the frontiers of a State ought to be interspersed with one or two great places of refuge, with secondary places, and even with small posts proper for facilitating the operations of the acting armies. Cities surrounded by walls with a shallow ditch, may even be very useful in the interior of the country, for placing therein depôts, storehouses, magazines, hospitals, &c., secure from the light corps which should scour the country ; especially if the care of them were confided to the moveable militia, in order not to weaken the army.

9. Great places situated out of strategical directions are a real misfortune for the State and the army.

10. Those which are on the banks of the sea can have importance only in the maritime combinations of war, or for magazines ; they may become disastrous for a continental army, in offering to it the deceitful prospect of a support. Benningsen came near compromising the Russian armies in basing himself in 1807, upon Konigsberg, because of the facility which that city gave for supplying himself. If the Russian army, instead of concentrating, in 1812, upon Smolensk, had chosen to support itself upon Dunabourg and Riga, it would have run the risk of being thrown back upon the sea, cut off from all its bases of power, and annihilated.

With regard to the relations which exist between sieges and the operations of active armies, they are of two kinds.

If the army of invasion can dispense with attacking the places which it passes by, it cannot dispense with blockading them, or at least with observing them ; in the case in which it should have several of them upon a small space, it will be necessary to leave a whole corps under the same chief who shall invest or observe them according to circumstances

When the army of invasion decides to attack a place, a sufficient corps is charged specially with laying siege to it according to rules; the remainder of the army may either continue its offensive march or take position for covering the siege.

Formerly the false system prevailed of investing a place by a whole army, which buried itself in lines of circumvallation and countervallation, requiring as much expense and trouble as the siege itself. The famous affair of the lines of Turin, 1706, where the Prince Eugene of Savoy forced, with forty thousand men, a French army of seventy-eight thousand, well intrenched, but which, having six leagues of fortifications to guard, found itself everywhere inferior, suffices to destroy this ridiculous system.

Therefore, notwithstanding the just admonition which is experienced at the recital of the marvellous works executed by Cæsar for investing Alisum, and in spite of all that Guichard has said of it, no general of our day would take it into his head to imitate that example.* However, whilst censuring lines of circumvallation, it is necessary to acknowledge the necessity for an investing corps, to double the force of its positions by detached works, which should command the issues by which the garrison or succoring troops could disturb it, as Napoleon did at Mantua, and the Russians at Varna. Be that as it may, experience has demonstrated that the best means of covering a siege is to defeat and pursue as far as possible the corps of hostile troops which should cover it. It is that which should be adopted, unless the numerical inferiority of the forces be opposed to it. In this case it is necessary to take a strategic position which covers the avenues by which the succoring army could arrive, and as soon as it approaches, it is proper to unite as much as possible of the siege corps with the army of observation, in order to fall upon the first, and to decide, by a vigorous blow, whether the siege can be continued or not. Bonaparte, before Mantua, in 1796, has given the model of the wisest and most skilful operations which an army of observation may undertake; we refer our readers then to what we have said of it in the history of the wars of the Revolution.

---

* Continuous lines are referred to here; we should not neglect to fortify a position of investment by detached works.

INTRENCHED LINES.

Besides lines of circumvallation and countervallation, of which we have spoken above, there exists another kind, which, more vast and extensive still, belong in some sort to permanent fortification, since they are to cover a part of the portion of a State

The system of such intrenched lines is as absurd, as a fortress or intrenched camp constructed to serve as a momentary refuge to an army, is advantageous.

It is conceived that the question here is not of a line of intrenchments of little extent, which would close a narrow gorge; this enters into the system of forts, like that of Fussen or of Charnitz, of which we have spoken; but the question is of lines extended over several leagues and destined to close the whole of a section of frontier, as for example those of Wisesmburg; covered by the Lautern which runs before the front, supported on the Rhine at the right and the Vosges at the left, those lines seemed to fulfill all the conditions necessary for being secure from attack, and yet they were forced as often as they were assailed.

The lines of Stollhofen, which played upon the right of the Rhine the same part as those of Wissemburg upon the left, was not more fortunate. Those of the Queich and of the Kinzig had the same fate.

The lines of Turin, (1706) and those of Mayence (1795), though destined to serve for circumvallation, offer a complete analogy, to all possible lines, if not by their strength, at least by their extent, and by the fate which they experienced.

However well supported these lines may be by natural obstacles, it is certain that independently of their great extent, which paralyses their defenders, they will almost always be susceptible of being turned. To be buried thus in intrenchments where we could be outflanked, enveloped and compromised, and where we are always forced in front even though we should be secure against being turned, is then a manifest folly, which it is to be hoped will never occur again.

Be that as it may, we shall give, in the chapter on tactics (Art. 36), some notions upon the manner of attacking or defending them.

Meanwhile it will not be useless to add here, that as ridiculous as it would seem at this day to bury ourselves in continuous lines, equally absurd would it be to neglect the use of detached works for augmenting the strength of a siege corps, the security of a position, or the defense of a defile which enters, for the rest, into the categories of which we shall treat further on.

ARTICLE XXVII.

RELATIONS OF INTRENCHED CAMPS AND TETES DE PONTS WITH STRATEGY.

It would be misplaced to give here details upon the situation of ordinary camps, upon the disposition and formation of advanced guards, as well as upon the resources which field fortifications offers for the defending of posts. Intrenched camps alone belong to the combinations of grand tactics, and even of strategy, by the support which they lend momentarily to an army.

It will be seen, by the example of the camp of Buntzelwitz, which saved Frederick in 1761, by those of Kehl and of Dusseldorf in 1796, that such a refuge may have a great importance. In 1800, the intrenched camp of Ulm gave Kray the means of arresting for a whole month the army of Moreau upon the Danube. It is known how many advantages Wellington derived from that of Torres-Vedras, and those which Shoomla procured the Turks, for defending the country between the Danube and the Balkan.

The regulating principle to be given upon this matter, is that camps be established upon a point at once strategical and tactical; if that of Drissa was useless to the Russians in 1812, it is because it was placed out of the true direction of their defensive system, which was to pivot upon Smolensk and Moscow; it was therefore necessary to abandon it at the end of a few days.

The maxims which we have given for determining great decisive points in strategy, may be applied to all intrenched camps, for it is upon such points merely that it is proper to place them. The destination of these camps varies; they may serve equally as points of departure for an offensive operation, as *têtes de ponts* for debouching beyond a great river, as supports for winter cantonments, finally as places of refuge for a beaten army.

Meanwhile, however good may be the site of an intrenched camp, we may be assured, unless it be, like that of Torres-Vedras, on a peninsula, backed against the sea, and destined to protect the re-embarkation of an insular army, it is very difficult to find a strategical point secure from being turned by the enemy. So soon as such a point can be turned either by the right or by the left, the army which occupies it will be forced to abandon it, or run the risk of being invested therein; the intrenched camp of Dresden offered in 1813 an important support to Napoleon for two months; as soon as he was outflanked by the Allies, it had not even the advantages which an ordinary place would have procured, for its extent caused to be sacrificed to it two *corps d'armée* which were lost in a few days, for want of provisions.

In spite of these truths, it must be owned that intrenched camps, being seldom destined but to procure a temporary point of support for a defensive army, they may always accomplish their object, though even the enemy might be able to pass beyond them strategically; the essential thing is that they be not liable to be assailed in reverse, that is to say that all its faces be equally secure from a sudden attack, and besides that they be in proximity with a fortress, either for securing the magazines therein, or for covering the front of the camp most adjacent to the line of retreat.

In general such a camp, situated upon a river, with a vast *tête de pont* on the other side to command the two banks, and placed near a great fortified city offering resources, like Mayence or Strasburg, will assure to an army incontestable advantages; but it will never be more than a temporary refuge, a means of gaining time and of assembling reinforcements; when it shall be the question to drive away the enemy, it will ever be necessary to have recourse to open field operations.

The second maxim which may be given upon these camps, is that they are especially favorable for an army at home, or near its base of operations. If a French army threw itself in an intrenched camp on the Elbe, it would none the less be ruined for it, so soon as the space between the Rhine and the Elbe should be occupied by the enemy. But if it were found even momentarily invested in an intrenched camp under Strassburg, it could with the least succor retake its superiority and hold the field : the hostile army which should be invested, itself placed in the middle of France, between the succoring corps and that of the intrenched camp, would have much to do to repass the Rhine.

Thus far we have considered these camps under the exclusively strategical point of view. Meanwhile several German generals have pretended that intrenched camps were calculated to cover places and to prevent their siege, which appears to me a little sophistical. Doubtless a place will be less easy to besiege so long as the army shall remain encamped upon its glacis, and it may be said that those camps and places lend each other a mutual support. But in my opinion the true and principal design of in-

trenched camps will always be to give at need a temporary refuge to an
army, or will be an offensive means for debouching upon a decisive point
and beyond a great river.   To bury an army under a place, to expose it to
be outflanked and cut off, merely to retard a siege, appears to me an act
of folly.   They will cite the example of Wurmser who, they say, prolonged for several months the resistance of Mantua : but did not his army perish therein ?   Was this sacrifice in reality useful ?   I do not think so, for
the place having been once delivered and re-victualed, and the siege park
having fallen into the power of the Austrians, the attack was obliged to
be changed to a blockade : now, as the place could only be taken by famine, Wurmser ought rather to have hastened its surrender than retard-
ed it.

The intrenched camps which the Austrians had established before Mayence in 1795 would have prevented, it is true, the siege of that city if the
French had had the means of making it, at least as long as the Rhine
should not have been crossed.   But so soon as Jourdan, in contempt of
that camp, showed himself on the Lahn, and Moreau in the Black Forest,
it was necessary to raise it and to abandon the place to its own defense.
There would be then only the case where a fortress were found situated
upon a point so extraordinary that it became impossible to pass beyond
without taking it, that we could construct an intrenched camp with the
special destination of preventing its attack.   What place in Europe can
flatter itself with occupying such a site ?

Far then from sharing the idea of those German authors, it appears to
me on the contrary that a question of considerable importance in regard
to the establishment of those intrenched camps in transient fortification,
under places in reach of a river, would be to decide, whether it were better that the camp be situated upon the same bank as the place, or rather
if the latter should not be found on the opposite bank.   In the case where
it should be indispensable to choose between these two propositions, in
default of being able to situate the place in a manner to embrace the two
banks at the same time, I should not hesitate to pronounce for the latter
course.

In fact, in order to serve as a refuge or to favor a debouch, it is very
necessary that the camp be beyond the river on the side of the enemy : in
this case the principal danger to be feared would be that ,the enemy should
take the camp in reverse by passing the river some leagues farther off :
now if the place were found on the same side as the camp, it would be of
no use to him, whereas if it were found constructed on the opposite bank
in front of the camp, it would be almost impossible to take it in reverse.

Thus the Russian army, which could not hold the camp of Drissa twenty-four hours (in 1812), would have been able to brave the enemy therein for a long time, if a place had existed on the right bank of the Dvina in order to put the rear of the camp under shelter. Thus Moreau braved for three whole months all the efforts of the Arch-Duke Charles at Kehl, whereas if Strassburg had not been on the opposite bank, the camp could easily have been turned by a passage of the Rhine.

In truth it would be desirable that the camp should have also its protection upon the same bank, and under this aspect a place holding both banks would well fulfill the double destination. That of Coblentz, recently constructed seems to mark the epoch of a new system: that which the Prussians have adopted at this place, and which participates at the same time of intrenched camps and permanent places, would merit a profound examination; but if this vast establishment offers some defects, it may be affirmed nevertheless that it would also offer immense advantages to an army destined to operate on the Rhine.

In fact, the inconvenience of temporary intrenched camps established on great rivers, is that they are scarcely useful except when they are found beyond the river, as we have said. Now in this case, they are exposed to all the dangers resulting from a capture of the bridges, which might place the army in the same position as that of Napoleon at Essling, and would leave it exposed to a total want of provisions or munitions, as well as to the perils of an attack by storm from which field works would not always be secure. The system of detached forts in permanent fortifications, such as has been applied at Coblentz, offers the advantage of averting these dangers, by putting the magazines under shelter of the city—situated upon the same bank as the army, and by guaranteeing the latter against an attack, at least until the establishment of the bridges. If the city were on the right bank of the Rhine, and there existed only an intrenched camp of field works on the left of the river, there would be on the contrary no positive security, either for the magazines or for the army.

In the same manner if Coblintz were a good ordinary fortress, without detached forts, a considerable army would not find therein an asylum so easily, and especially would it have much less facility for debouching therefrom in presence of an enemy. However if Coblentz is a formidable establishment the fortress of Ehrenbreitstein, which is to protect the right bank, is defective in being of so difficult access that the blockade of it would be all the more easy as the debouch for a considerable army could be effectively disputed.

The new system employed by the Arch-Duke Maximilian for fortifying the intrenched camp of Linz by means of towers in masonry has been much spoken of for some time past. As I am only acquainted with it by hearsay I could not reason upon it particularly. I only know that the system of towers which I have seen employed at Genoa by the skillful Colonel Andreas, has appeared to me susceptible of being turned to account and improved. I have been assured that the towers constructed at Linz sunk in the ditches and covered by the glacis, had the advantage of giving a razant and cross fire, and of being concealed from the direct shots of the enemy's cannon. Such towers well flanked and connected by a parapet, may make a very advantageous camp but always subject nevertheless to the inconvenience of closed lines. If the towers are isolated and covered with care in the intervals by field works which could be thrown up in time of war, they will be better doubtless than a camp covered merely by *flèches* and ordinary redoubts, but they do not seem to offer as many advantages as the great detached forts of Coblentz. These towers are forty in number, armed each with six pieces which can be concentrated on whichever side may be desired; their fire may be crossed; they are connected by a palisaded covered way, and by a broad ditch. There are besides a fort or cidatel and three great towers on the left bank of the Danube. Whatever defect may be found in such an establishment, there is no doubt that it would have exercised a great influence upon the events of 1805 and 1809 if it had existed at that epoch, for the strategic point is the best chosen, as well as all those of the other establishments which Austria has made since 1814.*

For the rest localities enter for much in the choice of the different systems, and the essential problem to resolve, for such establishments " is to give with the least possible expense a temporary shelter to an army, with every security for one's depôts and every facility for debouching offensively, when the opportune moment shall have arrived." Now a system may fulfill this object whatever otherwise may be its defects against a regular attack.

TÊTES DE PONTS.

Of all the works of field fortification there are none as important as *têtes-de-ponts*. The difficulties which the passage of rivers and especially

---

* See note at the end of the volume.

of great rivers offer when they have place in front of an enemy, suffice to demonstrate the immense utility of tètes-de-ponts; we can indeed do much better without intrenched camps than without these works, for in putting your bridges secure from insult you secure yourself against all the disastrous chances which could result from the forced retreat upon the banks of a river.

When those tétes-de-ponts serve as a redoubt to a large intrenched camp they are then doubly advantageous; they will be triply so if they embrace likewise the bank opposite to that where the camp should be seated, since then these two establishments will lend each other a mutual support, and will equally assure the two banks. It would be useless to add that those works are especially important in a hostile country, and upon all fronts where there should not exist a permanent place which could dispense with them. I shall observe still that the principal difference between the system of intrenched camps and that of tétes-de-ponts, is that the first are preferable when they are composed of detached and closed works, whilst that tétes-de-ponts will oftener be contiguous enclosed works: but if they are composed of detached works a feeble corps would suffice to secure them from insult.

As for the rest those intrenchments enter into the same class as those of camps, and as their attack or defense belongs more particularly to tactics, we shall speak of them in Chapter IV, Article 36; it suffices to have pointed out here their strategical importance.

ARTICLE XXVIII.

DIVERSIONS AND GREAT DETACHMENTS.*

The detachments which an army may be called upon to make in the

---

* Colonel Wagner, in his translation already cited, has been pleased to make upon this article observations, the justness of which I have appreciated, and which have decided me to re-write it entirely. If we still differ in the manner of looking at some points, I am pleased to think that they will be of little importance

I have hesitated whether to place this article in the chapter of strategy or in that of mixed operations (Chap. 8) but it appears to me to belong definitively more particularly to strategic operatieus.

course of a campaign, are so closely connected with the success of all its enterprises, that they should be regarded as one of the most important, but also one of the most delicate branches of war.

In faqt if nothing is more useful than a great detachment when it is seasonably made and well combined, nothing is more dangerous when it is made in an inconsiderate manner. Frederick the Great even counted in the number of the most essential qualities of a General that of knowing how to induce his adversary to detachments, either in order to carry them off, or to attack the army during their absence.

The mania of detachments has been so much abused that, by a contrary excess, many have believed in the possibility of doing without them. Doubtless it would be much more sure and agreeable to keep an army united in a single mass; but as it is a thing entirely impracticable, it is very necessary to be resigned to make detachments when it becomes indispensable to the success of the enterprise which it should be wished to form. The essential thing is to make as few of them as possible.

There are several kinds of them:

1. The great corps thrown outside of the zone of operations, in order to effect divisions upon points more or less essential;

2. The great detachments made in the zone of operations to cover the important points of that zone, to form a siege, to guard a secondary base, and to protect the line of operations if it be menaced;

3. The great detachments made upon fronts of operations, in face of the enemy, to concur directly in a concerted enterprise;

4. The small detachments thrown at a distance to attempt *coups-de-main* upon posts the taking of which might act favorably.

I understand by diversions, those secondary enterprises formed far from the principal zone of operations, at the extremities of a theatre of war, and upon the concurrence of which the success of a campaign should be foolishly calculated. Such diversions are only useful in two cases, that where the corps employed in making it should be out of condition, from its distance, to be put in action elsewhere; or else when it should be thrown upon a point where it would find a great support among the population, which enters in the domain of political combinations more than in those of the military art. A few examples will not be out of place to illustrate this.

The fatal results which the expedition to Holland by the Anglo-Russians, and that of the Arch-Duke Charles, had had upon the affairs of the Allies at the end of 1799, and which we have pointed out in Article 19, are yet present to the memory of every body.

In 1805, Napoleon occupied Naples and Hanover; the Allies thought to send the Anglo-Russian corps to drive him out of Italy, and the Anglo-Russian and Sweedish corps to repel him from Hanover; nearly sixty thousand men are destined for these two centrifugal expeditions. But whilst their troops were assembling at the two extremities of Europe, Napoleon has ordered the evacuation of Naples and Hanover; St. Cyr comes to join Massena in the Frioul, and Bernadotte, quitting Hanover, comes to take an active part in the events of Ulm and Austerlitz: after those astonishing successes, Naples and Hanover were easily retaken. These are proofs against diversions: let us cite an example of the circumstances where they would be suitable.

In the civil wars of 1793, if the Allies had detached from their armies twenty thousand veteran troops to disembark them in Vendée, they would have produced a much greater effect than by augmenting the masses which warred without success at Toulon, on the Rhine and in Belgium. Here is a case where a diversion might have been not only very useful, but decisive

We have said that independently of remote diversions and of light corps, great detachments were frequently employed within the zone of the operations of an army.

If the abuse of these great detached corps for objects more or less secondary, presents still, more dangers than the abuse of diversions, it is nevertheless but just to acknowledge that they are often advantageous, at times even indispensable.

Those detachments are of two principal kinds: the first consists in the permanent corps which we are obliged sometimes to establish in a direction opposed to that on which we are operating, and which are to manœuvre thereon during the whole campaign; the others are corps detached temporarily to exercise a salutary influence upon any enterprise whatever.

In the number of the first ought to be placed, before all, the fractions detached armies, whether for forming the strategic reserve of which we have spoken, or for covering lines of operations and of retreat, when the configuration of the theatre of war may leave them exposed to the blows of the enemy. For example, a Russian army, wishing to cross the Balkan, is forced to leave a part of its forces to observe Shoomla, Ruschuk and the valley of the Danube, the direction of which is such that it chances to fall perpendicularly upon the line of operations: whatever success be obtained, it will always be necessary to leave a respectable force either near Giurgewo, or near Craiova and even to the right of the river near Ruschuk.

This single example suffices to prove that there are cases where a double front of operations could not be dispensed with, which from that time will require considerable corps to be detached to show front to a portion of the hostile army which might be left in rear. We could cite other localities and other circumstances where this measure would not be less necessary; the one is the double front of operations of the Tyrol and the Frioul for a French army which passes the Adige; on whatever side it wishes to direct its principal effort, it could not do it without leaving upon the other front, a corps proportioned to the hostile forces which might there be found, otherwise it would abandon all its communications. The third example is the frontier of Spain, which presents also to the Spaniards the facility of presenting a double front of operations, the one covering the direct road to Madrid, the other being based either upon Saragossa, or upon Galicia; on whatever side it is wished to act, a detachment proportioned to the enemy must be left near the other.   •

All that can be said upon this matter, is that it is advantageous to enlarge as much as possible the field of operations, and to render moveable those forces left in observation, whenever it can be done, and that it will be the object to strike decisive blows. One of the most remarkable proofs of this truth was given by Napoleon in the campaign of 1797. Obliged to leave a corps of fifteen thousand men in the valley of the Adige, to hold the Tyrol whilst directing himself on the Noric Alps, he preferred to draw in this corps at the risk of compromising for a moment his line of retreat, rather than leave the two fractions of his army disunited and exposed to be overthrown in detail. Persuaded that he should conquer with his army if he united it, he judged that the momentary presence of a few hostile detachments upon his communications would not then be dangerous.

Great moveable and temporary detachments are made for the following motives :

1. To constrain the enemy to a retreat by menacing his line of operations, or to cover your own ;

2. To march to meet a hostile corps, and to prevent its junction, or to facilitate the junction of an expected reinforcement ;

3. To observe and to hold in check a great fraction of the hostile army, whilst you project striking a blow at the other portion of that army ;

4. To seize a considerable convoy of provisions or of munitions upon which would depend the continuation of a siege, or the success of a strategical enterprise; to protect the arrival of a convoy which you yourself may expect;

5. To operate a demonstration with a view to drawing the enemy in a direction where you desire him to march, in order to facilitate an operation undertaken on another side;

6. To mask and even to invest one or several great places for a given time, whether you may wish to attack them, or whether you desire merely to shut up the garrison in its ramparts;

7. To carry an important point upon the communications of an enemy already in retreat.

However seductive it may appear to obtain the divers objects indicated in this nomenclature, it must be owned, nevertheless, that these are always objects more or less secondary, and that the essential thing being to triumph on decisive points, you must guard against yielding to the attractions of multiplied detachments, for many armies have been seen to succumb for not having known how to remain concentrated.

We shall recall here several of those enterprises to prove that their success or their loss depends, sometimes upon seasonableness, sometimes upon the genius of him who directs them; oftener still upon faults of execution. Every one knows how Peter the Great preceded the destruction of Charles XII, by causing to be captured, by a considerable corps, the famous convoy which Lowenhaupt conducted. It is generally recollected how Villars completely defeated at Denain the great detachment which Prince Eugene had made under Albemarle.

The destruction of the great convoy which Laudon took from Frederick during the siege of Olmutz, obliged the king to evacuate Moravia. The fate of the two detachments of Fouquet at Landshut, in 1760, and of Fink at Maxen, in 1795, equally attests how difficult it is to avoid the necessity of making detachments and the danger which results therefrom.

Later still, the disaster of Vandamme at Culm, was a cruel lesson for corps advanced too audaciously; however, it must be admitted that in this last occasion the manœuvre was skillfully meditated, and that the fault was less having pushed the detachment than in not having sustained it as could easily have been done. That of Fink was destroyed at Maxen almost upon the same ground and for the same reason.

With regard to demonstrative divisions made in the same sphere with the army, they have a positive advantage, when they are combined with the object of making the enemy arrive upon a point where it is convenient to fix his attention, whilst the weight of the forces are assembled upon a quite opposite point where it is desired to strike an important blow. It is necessary then not only to avoid engaging the corps which is employed in this demonstration, but to recall it promptly upon the main body; we shall cite two examples, which will prove the opportuneness of this precaution.

In 1800, Moreau, wishing to deceive Kray upon the true direction of his march, caused his left wing to be carried from Kehl towards Rastadt, whilst he filed with his army upon Stockach; his left, after simply showing itself, fell back then towards his centre by Friburg in Brisgau.

In 1805, Napoleon, master of Vienna, threw the corps of Bernadotte upon Iglau, to scatter terror in Bohemia, and to paralyse the Arch-Duke Ferdinand, who was assembling a corps; he launches on the other side Davoust upon Presburg to impose upon Hungary; but he changed them immediately upon Brunn, in order that they should come and take part in the events which were to decide the whole campaign, and a signal victory became the result of these wise manœuvres. Those kinds of operations, far from being contrary to principles, are necessary to favor their application.

It will easily be conceived, from all that precedes, that absolute maxims could not be given upon operations so varied, and the success of which depends upon so many particulars thus difficult to seize. It will be for the talents and the *coup d'œil* of generals to judge when they should risk those detachments; the only admissable precepts we have already presented; they are to make as few of them as possible, and to draw them in as soon as they have accomplished their mission.

For the rest their inconvenience can be remedied in part, by giving good instructions to those who command them; it is in this that consists the greatest talent of a general of the staff.

Since we have cited the small detachments destined for *coups de main*, in the number of those which may be useful, we shall indicate a few of this nature, which will enable us to form a judgment thereon. We recollect the one which the Russians executed at the end of 1828, for seizing Sizepoli, on the Gulf of Burgas. The taking of this feebly intrenched post, which was hastily put under cover, procured, in case of success, an essential point of support beyond the Balkan, for establishing therein beforehand the depôts of the army which was to cross those mountains; in case of non-success it would compromise nothing, not even the little corps which had an assured retreat upon its vessels.

In the same manner, in the campaign in 1796, the *coup de main* attempted by the Austrians upon Kehl, and for destroying its bridge whilst Moreau was returning from Bavaria, could have had important results if it had not failed.

In these kinds of enterprises we risk little for gaining a great deal, and as they could not compromise in any manner the mass of the army, they cannot but be approved.

Light corps thrown in the midst of the hostile zone of operations, are to be classed in the same category; some hundreds of horsemen thus hazarded are never a grave loss, and may often cause considerable detriment to the enemy. The light detachments made by the Russians in 1807, 1812 and 1813, seriously disturbed the operations of Napoleon, and at times caused them to fail by intercepting his orders and all his communications.

We employ in preference for those kinds of expeditions, officers at once dexterous and bold, known under the name of partisans; veritable *enfants perdu*, they are to do all the evil they can to the enemy without too much compromising themselves; doubtless, when the occasion presents itself for striking an important blow, they ought also to know how to dash headlong upon the enemy; but in general, address and presence of mind in avoiding all useless danger, are, still more than systematic audacity, the true qualities necessary to a partisan. I refer for the rest to what I have said of them in Chapter XXXV, of the treatise on grand operations, and to Article 45 farther on, upon light cavalry.

ARTICLE XXIX.

STRATEGICAL OPERATIONS IN MOUNTAINS.

We should not have presented strategy under all of its aspects, had we not traced a sketch of the part it may have in the operations of a mountain warfare. We do not pretend to analyse those local intricacies of posts reputed almost impregnable, which form the romantic part of the tactics of combats; we shall seek to indicate merely the relations of a mountainous country with the different articles which make the subject of this chapter.

A mountainous country presents itself under four entirely different points of view in the combinations of a war; it may be the complete theatre of this war, or form but a zone of it; it is possible also that its whole surface may be mountainous, or that it will form but a belt of mountains, issuing from which, an army would debouch into vast and rich plains.

If we except Switzerland, the Tyrol, the Noric provinces, (I comprehend in this denomination Carinthia, Styria, Carniola and Illyria,) a few provinces of Turkey and Hungary, Catalonia and Portugal, all the other countries of Europe seldom present but those mountainous belts.* Then it is but a defile painful to pass, a temporary obstacle which, once overcome, presents an advantage to the army which has succeeded in seizing it, rather than being perilous to it. Indeed, the obstacle once surmounted, and the war transported into the plains, the chain thus crossed may be considered, so to speak, as a kind of eventual base, upon which one could fall back and find a temporary refuge. The only thing essential to be observed in such an occurrence, is never to allow yourself to be anticipated thereon by the enemy in case you should be forced to retreat.

The Alps even make no exception to this rule in the part which separates France from Italy; the Pyrennées, the least elevated chain of which is however as extended in depth, are equally in the same category; in Catalonia alone they reign over the whole surface of the country as far as the Ebro, and if the war be limited to this province, the whole *échiquier* being mountainous leads necessarily to other combinations than where there exists only a belt.

Hungary differs little in this respect from Lombardy and Castile, for if even the Krapaks present in their eastern and northern part a belt as strong as the Pyrennées, it must be owned meanwhile that it is but a temporary obstacle, and that the army which should cross it, debouching, either into the basins of the Waag, of the Neytra or of the Theiss, or into the fields of Mongatsch, would have to decide the great questions in the vast plains between the Danube and the Theiss. The only difference is in

---

* I do not make mention here of the Caucasus, because this country, the constant theatre of petty warfare, has not been thoroughly explored, it has always been regarded as a secondary affair in the great conflicts for empire, and it will never be the theatre of a great strategical operation.

the routes, which, rare but superb in the Alps and the Pyrennées, are wanting in Hungary, or are scarcely practicable.*

In the northern part this chain, less elevated perhaps, but more extended in depth, would seem indeed to belong in some sort to the class of *echiquiers* wholly mountainous; meanwhile, as it forms but a part of the general *échiquier*, and as its evacuation might be rendered necessary by the decisive operations which should be carried on in the valleys of the Theiss, or of the Waag, it may be ranged in the number of transient barriers. For the rest, it could not be dissembled that the attack and the defense of this country would be one of the most interesting double strategical studies.

The chains of Bohemia, of the Vosges, of the Black Forest, although much less important, are also placed in the category of mountainous belts.

When an entirely mountainous country, like the Tyrol and Switzerland, forms only a zone of the theatre of operations, then the importance of its mountains is but relative, and we can limit ourselves more or less to masking them like a fortress, in order to move to the decision of great questions in the valleys. It is quite otherwise if this country forms the principal *échiquier*.

It has long been doubted whether possession of the mountains controlled the valleys, or whether possession of the valleys controlled the mountains. The Arch-Duke Charles, that judge so enlightened and so competent, has inclined to the last assertion, and demonstrated that the valley of the Danube was the key of Southern Germany. Meanwhile, it must be admitted, every thing must depend in these kinds of questions upon the relative forces and upon the dispositions of the country. If sixty thousand French advanced into Bavaria, having in presence an Austrian army equal in forces, which should throw thirty thousand men into the Tyrol, with the hope of replacing them by reinforcements at its arrival upon the Inn, it would be sufficiently difficult for the French to push as far as that line, leaving upon their flank such a force master of the debouches of Scharnitz, of Fussen, of Kufstein and of Lofers. But if this French army had as many as one hundred and twenty thousand combattants, and should have gained sufficient successes to be assured of their superiority over the army which should be before it, then it could always form a detachment suffi-

---

* I speak of the condition of the country in 1810. I am ignorant whether it has participated subsequently in the great movement which has had place in all the Austrian monarchy for the amelioration of routes, and the opening of great strategical communications.

cient for masking the debouches of the Tyrol and push its march to Linz, as Moreau did in 1800.

Thus far we have considered mountainous countries as accessory zones. If we consider them as the principal *échiquier* of the whole war, questions change their face somewhat, and strategical combinations seem to become more complicated. The campaign of 1799 and that of 1800, are equally rich in interesting lessons on this branch of the art. In the relation which I have published of them, I endeavored to cause them to be comprehended by the historical exposition itself of the events ; I could not do better than refer my readers to it.

If we recall the dissertation which I have made upon the results of the imprudent invasion of Switzerland by the French Directory, and upon the fatal influence which it exercised in doubling the extent of the theatre of operations, and in making a single *échiquier* from the Texel to Naples, we cannot too much applaud the genius which inspired the cabinets of Vienna and Paris in the transactions which, for three centuries, had guaranteed the neutrality of Switzerland. Every one will be convinced of this truth, by reading with some attention the interesting campaigns of the Arch-Duke, of Suwaroff and of Masséna in 1799, as well as those of Napoleon and of Moreau in 1800. The first is a model of operations on an *échiquier* entirely mountainous ; the second is one for wars where the fate of mountainous countries is to be decided upon plains.

I shall endeavor to recapitulate here some of the truths which have appeared to me to result from this examination.

When a country, cut up with mountains, over its whole surface becomes the principal *échiquier* of the operations of the two armies, the combinations of strategey cannot be calculated entirely upon the maxims applicable to open countries.

In fact, the transversal manœuvres for gaining the extremities of the front of operations of the enemy, then become of a more difficult execution, and are often even impossible ; in such a country one can operate with a considerable army only in a small number of valleys, where the enemy shall have had care to place sufficient advanced guards, to the end of suspending the march as long as would be necessary to take into consideration the means of defeating the enterprise ; and as in the counterforts which separate those valleys there ordinarily exist only foot-paths insufficient for the movements of armies, no transversal march could have place thereon but for light divisions.

The important strategical points, marked by nature at the confluence of the principal valleys, or, if it be preferred, at the confluence of the rivers which they enclose, are so clearly traced, that it were to be blind to mistake them; now, as they are small in number, the defensive army occupying them with the mass of its troops, the aggressor will oftener be reduced, in order to dislodge it therefrom, to have recourse to direct attacks or main force.

However, if great strategical movements are more rare and more difficult on such a theatre, it is not saying that they are on that account the less important; on the contrary, if you succeed in seizing upon one of these knots of communication of great valleys, on the line of retreat of the enemy, his loss is still more certain than in open countries, because by occupying on this line one or two defiles of difficult access, it would often suffice for causing the ruin of a whole army.

But if the attacking party have difficulties to overcome, it must be owned also that the defensive army has no less of them, from the necessity which it thinks there is of covering all the issues by which one might arrive in mass upon those decisive points. In order to make better comprehended what I have just said upon transversal marches, and upon the difficulty of directing them in mountains as easily as in plains, I shall be permitted to recall the one which Napoleon made in 1805, to cut off Mack from Ulm; if it were facilitated by the hundred roads which furrow Suabia in all directions; if it had been impracticable in a mountainous country, for want of transversal routes for making the long tour from Donanwerth by Augsburg upon Memmingen, it must be admitted also that, by favor of those hundred roads, Mack would equally have been able to make his retreat more easily than if he had been surrounded in one of those valleys of Switzerland and of the Tyrol from whence one could only issue by a single road.

On the other hand, the general who is reduced to the defensive may, in an open country, preserve a very great part of his forces united, for if the enemy divide in order to occupy all the roads which that general would be at liberty to take in his retreat, it will be easy for him to cut his way through this multitude of isolated divisions; but in a very mountainous country, where an army has ordinarily but one or two principal issues, into which several other valleys chance to terminate in the same direction occupied by the enemy, the concentration of forces is more difficult, seeing that, if a single one of those valleys be neglected, there might result grave inconveniences.

Nothing, in fact, could better demonstrate the difficulty of the strategic defense of mountains than the embarrassment in which one finds himself when he wishes to give, not rules, but even advice to generals charged with such a task. If the only question were the defense of a definite point of operations, of small extent, formed by four or five valleys or convergent rays terminating at the central knot of those valleys, at two or three small marches from the summits of the chain, no doubt the thing would be more easy. It would suffice then to recommend the construction of a good fort upon each of those rays, at the point of the defile which is narrowest and the most easy to turn ; then to place, under the protection of those forts, some brigades of infantry to dispute the passage, whilst that a reserve of the half of the army, placed at this central knot of the union of the valleys, would be in condition either to sustain those advanced guards most seriously menaced, or to fall in mass upon the enemy when he should attempt to debouch, and when we would have united all the columns to receive him. By adding, to those dispositions, good instructions to the generals of those advanced guards, whether for assigning them the best rallying point as soon as the fatal cordon should be pierced, or for prescribing to them to continue to act in the mountains upon the flanks of the enemy, then one might believe himself invincible, by favor of the thousand difficulties which the localities present to the assailant. But when, by the side of such a front of operations, there is found still another nearly like it upon the right, then a third upon the left; when it is required to defend at the same time all those fronts, under penalty of seeing fall, at the first approach of the enemy, that one which should be neglected, then the question is changed, the embarrassment of the defender is redoubled in proportion to the extent of the line of defense, and the system of cordons appears with all its dangers, without it being easy to adopt any other.

We could not be better convinced of those truths, than by retracing the position of Masséna in Switzerland in 1799. After the loss of the battle of Stockach by Jourdan, he held the line from Basle by Schaffhausen and Rheineck to the St. Gothard, and from thence by the Furca to Mt. Blanc. He had enemies in front of Basle, he had them at Waldshut, at Schaffhausen, at Feldkirch and at Coire ; the corps of Bellegarde menaced the St. Gothard, and the army of Italy had designs upon the Simplon and the St. Bernard. How was the periphery of such a circle to be defended ? How leave one of the great valleys uncovered. at the risk of losing every thing ? From Rheinfeld to the Jura towards Soleure, there are but two light marches, and there was the gorge of the Mouse-trap in which the French army found itself engaged. There then was the pivot of the defense ; but was Schaffhausen to be left uncovered how were Rheineck and the St. Gothard to be abandoned, how open Valais and the access to Berne, without giving up all Helvetia to the coalition? And if it were wished to cover all even by simple brigades, where would be the army when it should be required to deliver a decisive battle to any hostile mass which might present itself? To concentrate one's forces in the plain is a natural system, but in regions of difficult gorges it is to deliver up the keys of the country to the enemy, and then it is no longer known upon what point it would be possible to unite an inferior army without compromising it.

In the situation where Massena was found after the forced evacuation of the line of the Rhine and Zurich, it seemed that the only strategical point for him to defend, was the line of the Jura; he had the temerity to hold firm on that of the Albis, shorter than that of the Rhine, but which left him yet exposed, upon an immense line, to the blows which the Austrians might deliver him. And if, instead of pushing Bellegarde upon Lombardy by the Valteline, the Aulic Council had made him march upon Berne, or unite with the Arch-Duke, all would have been over with Massena. Those events seem then to prove that, if countries with high mountains are favorable to a tactical defense, it is not the same for a strategical defense, which, obliged to be disseminated, must seek a remedy for this inconvenience by augmenting its mobility, and by passing often to the offensive.

General Clausewitz, whose logic is frequently at fault, pretends on the contrary, that, motion being the difficult part of mountain warfare, the defender ought to avoid the least movement, under the penalty of losing the advantage of local defenses. Meanwhile he finishes by demonstrating, himself, that the passive defense must succumb, sooner or later, under an active attack, which tends to prove that the initiative is not less favorable in the mountains than in the plains. If it could be doubted, the campaign of Massena would for the rest prove it, for if he maintained himself in Switzerland, it was by attacking the enemy whenever he found occasion for so doing, although it were necessary to seek him upon the Grimsel and the St. Gothard. Napoleon had done as much in the Tyrol in 1796, against Wurmser and Alvinzi.

With regard to strategical manœuvres of detail, we shall be able to form an idea of them by reading the inconceivable events which accompanied the expedition of Suwarof by the St. Gothard upon the Muttenthal. In applauding the manœuvres prescribed by the Russian marshal for taking Lecourbe in the valley of the Reuss, we shall admire the presence of mind, the activity and immovable firmness which saved this general and his division ; we shall then see Suwarof, in the Schachenthal and the Muttenthal, placed in the same situation as Lecourbe, and to extricate himself from it with the same skill.　Not less extraordinary will appear the fine ten days campaign of General Molitor, who, surrounded with four thousand men in the canton of Glaris by more than thirty thousand allies, succeeded in sustaining himself behind the Linth after four admirable combats.　It is in the study of these facts that we may recognise *all the vanity of theories of detail,* and be assured that a strong and heroic will can do, in mountain warfare especially, more than all the precepts in the world.　After such lessons might I venture to say that one of the regulating principles of this warfare is not to risk ourselves in the valleys without being secure of the heights ?　A maxim somewhat trite, of which no captain of voltigeurs should be ignorant.　Might I not say also, that in this warfare, more than every where else, it is necessary to seek to make it on the communications of the enemy ; finally, that in those difficult countries, good temporary bases or lines of defense established at the centre of great confluents, and covered by strategical reserves, will be, with a great mobility and frequent offensive returns, the best means for defending the country.

I could not, however, terminate this article, without causing to be observed that mountainous countries are especially favorable for the defensive when the war is truly national, and when the roused populations defend their firesides with the obstinacy which enthusiasm for a holy cause gives ; then each step of the assailant is bought at the price of the greatest sacrifices.　But, in order that the struggle be crowned with success, it is always necessary that those populations be sustained by a more or less powerful disciplined army, without the support of which, brave inhabitants would soon succumb like the heroes of Stans and of the Tyrol.

The offensive against a mountainous country, presents also a double hypothesis ; shall it be directed against a belt of mountains terminating a vast échiquier of plains, or shall it be against a particular theatre wholly mountainous ?

In the first case there is scarcely but one precept to give : it is to make demonstrations against the whole periphery of a frontier, in order to oblige the enemy to extend his defensive, and to force afterwards a passage on the decisive point which shall promise the greatest results.　It is a cordon, feeble numerically, but strong by localities, which it is the object to break ; if it be forced upon a single point it is so upon the whole line. In reading the history of the Fort of Bard in 1800, or the taking of Leutasch, and Scharnitz in 1805 by Ney, who threw himself with fourteen thousand men upon Innspruck in the midst of thirty thousand Austrians, and succeeded, by seizing upon that central point, in obliging them to retreat in all directions, we may judge that with a brave infantry and bold chiefs, those famous mountain girdles will ordinarily be forced.

The history of the passage of the Alps, where Francis I. turned the army which awaited him at Susa, in passing by the steep mountains between Mt. Cenis and the valley of Queyras, is an example of *those insurmountable obstacles which are always surmounted.* In order to oppose it, it would have been necessary to have recourse to the cordon system, and we have already said what was to be expected from that. The position of the Swiss and Italians at Susa, engaged in a single valley was not wiser than a cordon, it was even less so, since it shut up the army in a cut-throat place, without guarding the lateral valleys. To push light corps into those valleys, to dispute the passes which are there found, and to place the bulk of the army near Turin or Carignano, is what strategy counselled.

When the tactical difficulties of a mountain warfare are considered, and the immense advantages which it seems to assure to the defense, we should be tempted to consider as a manœuvre of the highest temerity, the assembling of a considerable army in a single mass to penetrate by a single valley, and, we should be quite inclined to divide it also into as many columns as there should be practicable passages.

This is, in my opinion, one of the most dangerous of illusions ; we have only to recall the fate of the columns of Championnet at the battle of Fossano to be assured of it. If there exist five or six practicable roads upon the point menaced with invasion, to disquiet them all is necessary, but it is necessary to cross the chain at most in two masses ; yet the valleys which are to be passed over must not be in a divergent direction, for they will fail if the enemy is in the least condition to receive them at the outlets. The system followed by Napoleon in the passage of the St. Bernard seems the wisest, he formed the strongest mass at the centre, with two divisions on the right and left by Mt. Cenis and the Simplon, in order to divide the attention of the enemy and to flank his march.

The invasion of countries which have not only a mountainous belt, but the interior of which is still a continual series of mountains, is longer and more difficult than that where we can hope an early denouement by a decisive battle delivered in the plains ; because fields of battle suitable for deploying great masses scarcely ever being found thereon, such a war is an affair of partial combats. There it would perhaps be imprudent to penetrate upon a single point by a narrow and deep valley, of which the enemy could close the issues and place the army in a false position ; but we could penetrate by wings upon two or three lateral lines, the issues of which should not be at too great distances apart, by combining the marches in such a manner as to debouch at the junction of the valleys nearly at the same instant, and by taking care to repel the enemy from all the counterforts which separate them from each other. Of all entirely mountainous countries, Switzerland is incontestably that of which the tactical defense would be the easiest, if its militia were animated with one mind ; favored by the support of such a militia, a disciplined and regular army could defend itself against triple forces.

To give fixed precepts for the complications which are multiplied to infinity by those of the localities, by the resources of art, and by the enthusiasm of the populations and of the armies would be an absurdity ; history—but history well discussed and well presented—is the true school of mountain warfare. The narrative of the campaign of 1799, by the Arch-Duke Charles, that of the same campaigns which I have given in my critical history of the wars of the revolution ; the narrative of the campaigns of the Grisons by Ségur, and Mathieu Dumas ; that of Catalonia by St. Cyr and Suchet ; the campaign of the Duke De Rohan in the Valteline ; the passage of the Alps by Gaillard (History of Francis I,) are good guides for this study.

ARTICLE XXX

A FEW WORDS UPON GREAT INVASIONS AND DISTANT EXPEDITIONS.

Having already made mention of distant wars and invasions as connected with the policy of States, it remains to us to examine them succinctly under the military aspect. We feel some embarrassment in assigning to them their true place in this summary, because if on the one hand they seem to belong to poetry and to Homeric fictions much more than to strategic combinations, it may be said on the other that except the great distances which multiply the difficulties and the unfavorable chances of them, these adventurous expeditions offer nevertheless all the operations which are found in other wars ; in fact they have their battles, their combats, their sieges and even their lines of operations ; so that they enter more or less into the different branches of the art which make the subject of this work.   However as it is only the question here to consider them as a whole, and as they differ especially from other wars in regard to their lines of operations, we will place them at the end of the chapter which treats of them.

There are many kinds of distant expeditions ; the first are those executed across the continent as auxiliaries only, and of which we have spoken in Art. 5, upon wars of intervention ; the second are great continental invasions which have place across vast countries more or less friendly, neutral, doubtful or hostile ; the third are expeditions of the same nature, but executed in part by land and in part by sea with the concurrence of numerous fleets ; the fourth are expeditions beyond the sea, in order to found, defend or attack distant colonies ; the fifth are great descents less distant, but attacking great States.

We have already pointed out, in Article 5, some of the inconveniences to which auxiliary corps are exposed which are sent to a distance in order to succor powers with which we are connected by defensive treaties or by coalitions.   Without doubt, under the strategic point of view, a Russian army sent upon the Rhine or into Italy in order to act in concert with the Germanic powers, will be in a much stronger and more favorable situation than if it had penetrated to that distance by crossing hostile or even neutral countries ; its base, its lines of operations, its eventual points of support will be the same as those of its Allies ; it will have a refuge upon their lines of defense, provisions from their magazines, munitions from their arsenals ; whilst that in the contrary case it would only find those resources upon the Vistula or the Niemen, and might well experience the fate of those gigantic invasions which have badly succeeded.

However, notwithstanding the capital difference which exists between such an auxiliary war and a distant incursion undertaken in our own interest and with our own means, we could not dissemble the dangers to which those auxiliary corps are exposed, and the embarrassments which the generalissimo especially experiences, when he belongs to the power which plays the auxiliary part.   The campaign of 1805 furnishes a strong proof of this : General Kutusof advanced upon the Inn to the confines of Bavaria, with thirty thousand Russians ; the army of Mack with which he was to unite, is entirely destroyed, with the exception of eighteen thousand men which Kienmayer brought back from Donauwerth; the Russian general finds himself thus exposed, with less than fifty thousand combattants, to all the impetuous activity of Napoleon who has a hundred and fifty thousand, and in order to crown his misfortune a space of three hundred leagues separates Kutusof from his frontiers. Such a position would have been desperate if a second army of fifty thousand men had not arrived at Olmutz to receive him. Meanwhile the battle of Austerlitz, the result of a fault of the chief of staff, Weyrotha, compromised anew the Russian army far from its base; it came thus near becoming the victim of a distant alliance, and peace alone gave it time to regain its frontier.

The fate of Suwarof after the victory of Novi and especially in the expedition to Switzerland, that of the corps of Hermann at Bergen in Holland, are lessons which every chief called to such a command ought carefully to meditate. General Beningsen had less disadvantages in 1807, because, combatting between the Vistula and the Niemen, he supported himself on his own base and the operations depended in nothing upon his Allies. We recollect also the fate which the French experienced in Bavaria and Bohemia in 1742, when Frederick the Great abandoned them to their fate to make a separate peace. In truth those last made war as Allies and not as auxiliaries, but even in this last case, political ties are never closely enough drawn not to offer points of dissention which may compromise military operations; we have cited examples, in Article 19, upon political objective points.

With regard to remote invasions, across vast continents, it is from history alone that we can obtain lessons.

When Europe was half covered with forests; pasture-grounds and flocks; when there were necessary only horses and iron to transplant whole nations from one extremity of Europe to the other, the Goths, Visigoths, Huns, Vandals, Alians, Verangians, Franks, Normans, Arabs and Tartars, were seen to gain empires with rapidity. But since the invention of gun-powder and artillery, since the organization of formidable permanent armies, since, especially, civilization and policy have brought States nearer together, by enlightening them upon the necessity of reciprocally sustaining each other, such events could no longer be re-enacted.

Independently of the great migrations of people, the middle ages were remarkable for expeditions somewhat more military. Those of Charlemagne, almost contemporaneous with the invasion of Oleg and Igor carried to the gates of Constantinople, and the incursions of the Arabs to the banks of the Loire, give this epoch of the 9th and 10th centuries a peculiar physiognomy; as those events are as far from us by their date as by the elements which then constituted armies and nations; as there are beside more moral lessons than strategical precepts to be deduced from them, we shall content ourselves with tracing a short sketch thereof at the end of this work, if we have the leisure for so doing.

Since the invention of gun-powder, there have scarcely been but the incursions of Charles VIII, to Naples, and Charles XII, to Ukraine, which might be counted in the number of remote invasions, for the campaigns of the Spaniards in Flanders and of the Swedes in Germany were of a peculiar nature, the first belonging to civil wars, and the latter having appeared on the scene only as auxiliaries of the protestants. Besides, all those expeditions were executed with inconsiderable forces.

In modern times then, Napoleon alone has dared to transport the regular armies of the half of Europe, from the banks of the Rhine to the banks of the Volga; the desire to imitate him will not very soon be entertained. There would be wanting a new Alexander and new Macedonians, against the bands of Darius, to succeed in such enterprises : in truth the tender affection of modern societies for the enjoyments of luxury might well bring us armies like those of Darius; but where then shall we find Alexander and his phalanxes?

A few *Utopists* have imagined that Napoleon would have attained his end if, like a new Mahomet, he had put himself at the head of an army of political dogmas, and if, in place of the paradise of the Mussulmans, he had promised to the masses those sweet liberties, so fine in discourses and books, so difficult and so bordering upon license, when it is the question to apply them. Although it be permitted us to believe that the support of political dogmas is at times an excellent auxiliary, it must not be forgotten that the Koran even would gain no more than a province at this day, for in order to effect this, cannon, shells, balls, gunpowder and muskets are necessary; that with such encumbrances distances count for a great deal in combinations, and that nomadic excursions would no longer be in season.

An invasion carried two hundred leagues from one's base becomes now-a-days a hardy enterprise : those of Napoleon in Germany succeeded without the assistance of doctrines, because that directed against neighboring powers, and based upon the formidable barrier of the Rhine, they found in first line secondary States which, little united, ranged themselves under his banners; so that his base was all at once transported from the Rhine upon the Inn. In that of Prussia he took Germany on its weak side, after the events of Ulm, of Austerlitz and the peace of Schonbrunn, which left Berlin exposed to the whole weight of his power. As for what concerns the first war in Poland, already counted in the number of remote invasions, we have said elsewhere that his success was due to the hesitation of his adversaries, more still than to his own combinations, although they were as skillful as audacious.

The invasions of Spain and of Russia were less fortunate, but it was not for the want of fine political promises that those enterprises failed: the remarkable discourse of Napoleon to the deputation of Madrid in 1808, and his proclamations to the Russian people, equally warrant this belief.

With regard to Germany, quite full of confidence in the new political order which he had there founded, he was careful not to disturb its social order to please the popular masses, whose affections he lost for the rest by the ravages inseparable from great wars and by the sacrifices of the continental system much more than by his antipathy for radical doctrines.

As for what concerns France, he learned to his cost, in 1815, that it is dangerous to count upon political theories as upon a certain element of success; for if they are proper for raising storms, they could not direct their effect: his liberal homilies, insufficient for unchaining the popular masses, had no other result than to furnish the theorists and declaimers with arms for overthrowing him; for Lanjuinais, Lafayette and their journals, had no less part in his fall than the bayonets of his enemies.

He will be reproached perhaps for not having done enough to satisfy the popular pretensions; but he had too much experience of men and of affairs to be ignorant, that the unchaining of the political passions always leads to disorder and anarchy, and that doctrines which produce license bring about sooner or later that result. He believed that he had done enough in assuring and fixing the interests of democracy, without giving up the ship of State, all disabled, to the mercy of the heaving waves. Starting from this point of view, instead of reproaching him for not having done enough, it might be said with more reason that he did not know how, like Cardinal Richelieu, to employ in neighboring countries, those dangerous arms the use of which he feared in his own. But this is wandering too far from our subject, let us return to the military combinations of invasions.

As for the rest, apart from the chances which result from great distances, all invasions, when once the army has arrived on the theatre of war where it is to act, no longer offers combinations different from others. The great difficulty then consisting in the distances, one may recommend the maxims upon lines of operations lengthened in depth, and those upon strategical reserves or eventual bases, as the only useful ones, and it is especially on those occasions that their application becomes indispensable, although they are far from sufficient for parrying all dangers.

The campaign of 1812, so fatal to Napoleon, was nevertheless a model to cite of this kind : the care which he took to leave the prince de Schwartzenberg and Reynier upon the Bug, whilst that Macdonald, Oudinot and Wrede guarded the Dwina, that Bellune came to cover Smolensk, and that Augereau came to relieve him between the Oder and the Vistula, proves that he had neglected none of the humanly possible precautions, for basing himself suitably : but it proves also that the grandest enterprises perish through the magnitude even of the preparations which are made to secure their success.

If Napoleon committed faults in this gigantic struggle, they were those of having too much neglected political precautions; of not having united under a single chief the different corps left upon the Dwina and the Dnieper, of having remained ten days too long at Wilna; of having given the command of his right to a brother incapable of carrying such a burthen ; finally of having confided to prince Schwartzenberg a mission which the latter could not fulfil with the same devotion as a French general. I do not speak of the fault of having remained at Moscow after the conflagration, for then the evil was perhaps beyond remedy, although it would have been less serious if the retreat had been effected at once. He has been accused also of having too much despised distances, difficulties and men by pushing so foolish a point to the ramparts of the Kremlin. In order to condemn or absolve him, it would be very necessary to know the true motives which determined or constrained him to go beyond Smolensk, instead of halting and of passing the winter there, the project of which he ostentatiously announced ; finally it would be necessary to be assured whether it were possible to remain in position between that city and Witepsk, without having previously defeated the Russian army.

Far from wishing to set myself up as judge in so great a cause, I acknowledge that those who arrogate to themselves the right so to do are not always equal to such a mission, and want even the information necessary for accomplishing it. That which is most true in the whole affair, is that Napoleon forgot too much the resentments with which Austria, Prussia and Sweden were animated against him ; he counted too much upon a *denouement* between Wilna and the Dwina. A just appreciator of the bravery of the Russian armies, he was not the same of the national spirit, and of the energy of the people. Finally, above all, instead of securing to himself the interested and sincere concurrence of a great military power, the adjacent States of which would have procured a sure base for attacking the colossus which he wished to shake, he founded his whole enterprise upon the concurrence of a people brave and enthusiastic, but fickle and devoid of all the elements which constitute a solid power ; then, far from turning this ephemeral enthusiasm to the whole account of which it was susceptible, he paralyzed it still by unseasonable concealments.

The fate of all enterprises of this nature attests, in fact, that the capital point for assuring their success, and the only efficacious maxim which can be given, is, as we have said in Chapter I, Art. 6, never to attempt them without the assured and interested concurrence of a respectable power sufficiently near the theatre of operations for offering on the frontier a base suitable, as well for assembling beforehand thereon supplies of every kind, as for procuring a refuge in case of reverse, and new means for retaking the offensive at need.

With regard to the rules of conduct which should be sought in the precepts of strategy, it would be all the more rash to count upon them, as, without the above mentioned political precaution, the undertaking in itself would be but a flagrant violation of all strategical laws. For the rest, the divers precautions indicated in Articles 21 and 22, for the security of deep lines of operations, and for the formation of intermediate bases are, we repeat, the only military means proper for lessening the dangers of the enterprise ; we shall add thereto a just appreciation of distances, of seasons, of countries, in a word, sufficient accuracy in calculations and moderation in victory to know how to stop in time.

Moreover, far from us the thought that it is possible to trace precepts capable of assuring the success of great distant invasions ; in the space of four thousand years they have made the glory of five or six conquerors, and have been a hundred times the scourge of nations and armies.

After having exhausted nearly all that there is essential to say upon those continental invasions, there will remain for us a few remarks to make upon expeditions half continental, half maritime, forming the third series of those which we have indicated.

These kinds of enterprises have become very rare since the invention of artillery, and the crusades were, I believe, the last example that has been seen of them ; perhaps the cause of this must be attributed to the fact that the empire of the Seas, after having passed successively into the hands of two or three secondary powers, has got into those of an insular power, which possesses many squadrons, but not land forces necessary for those sorts of expeditions.

Be that as it may, from these two causes united, it evidently results that we are no longer in the times when Xerxes marched by land to the conquest of Greece, by causing himself to be followed by four thousand vessels of all dimensions, and when Alexander the Great marched from Macedonia by Asia Minor to Tyre, whilst his fleet coasted along the shore.

However, if those incursions are no longer made, it is not less certain that the support of a squadron of war and of a fleet of transports would always be an immense succor, when a great continental expedition could be effected in concert with so powerful an auxiliary.*

Meanwhile it must not be counted upon too exclusively; the winds are capricious; now a squall would suffice for dispersing, and even annihilating that fleet upon which we should have founded all our hopes. Successive transports would be less hazardous without being however, an over-certain resource.

I do not think it necessary to make mention here of invasions executed against a neighboring power, such as those of Napoleon against Spain and Austria; these are ordinary wars, pushed to a greater or less degree, but which have nothing peculiar, and the combinations of which are found sufficiently indicated in the different articles of this work.

The more or less hostile spirit of the populations, the greater or less depth of the line of operations, and the great distance of the principal objective point, are the only variables which may require modifications in an ordinary system of operations.

Indeed, for being less dangerous than a distant invasion, that which assails an adjacent power has also none the less its fatal chances. A French army which should go to attack Cadiz could, although well based upon the Pyrenees, with intermediate bases on the Ebro and the Tagus, find a tomb on the Guadalquivir. In the same manner, that which in 1809 besieged Komorn in the centre of Hungary, whilst others were warring from Barcelona to Oporto, might have succumbed in the plains of Wagram, without having any need of going so far as the Beresina. The antecedents, the number of disposable troops, the successes already gained, the state of the country, all have an influence upon the latitude which may be given to one's enterprises; the great talent of the general will be to proportion them to his means and to circumstances. With regard to the part which policy might exercise in those neighboring invasions, if it be true that it

---

* It will be said, perhaps, that after having blamed those who wish to base an army upon the sea, I seem to recommend this operation; the question is the means of supplying the intermediate bases which an army would take, and by no means the carrying of one's military operations upon the coasts.

is less indispensable than in remote incursions, it is necessary, meanwhile, not to forget the maxim which we have given out in Article 6, that there is no enemy, however insignificant he may be, with whom it would not be useful to become allied; the influence which the change of policy of the Duke of Savoy, in 1706, exercised upon the events of that epoch, also the declaration of Maurice of Saxony, in 1551, and of Bavaria in 1813, sufficiently proves that it is important to attach to one's self all the States adjacent to a theatre of war, in a manner to count, if not upon their co-operation, at least upon their strict neutrality.

There would remain no more for us but to speak of expeditions beyond the sea; but embarkation and debarkation being logistical and tactical operations rather than strategical, we refer them to Article 40, which treats specially of descents.

RECAPITULATION OF STRATEGY.

The task which I have imposed upon myself seems to me passably accomplished by the *exposé* which I have just made of all the strategical combinations which constitute ordinarily a plan of operations.

Meanwhile, as we have seen in the definition placed at the head of this Chapter, the greater part of the important operations of war participate at once of strategy for the direction in which it is suitable to act, and of tactics for the conduct of the action itself. Before treating of these mixed operations, it is proper then to present here the combinations of grand tactics, and of battles, as well as the maxims by the aid of which one may obtain the application of the fundamental principle of war. By this means we shall better comprehend the ensemble of those half strategical, half tactical operations: I shall be permitted merely to recapitulate in the first place the contents of the Chapter which we have just read.

From the fifteen articles of which it is composed, we may conclude, in my opinion, that the manner of applying the general principle of war to all possible theatres of operations, consists in what follows:

1. To know how to avail ourselves of the advantages which the reciprocal direction of the bases of operations could procure, according to what has been developed in Article 18 in favor of lines salient and perpendicular to the base of the enemy.

2. To choose between the three zones which a strategic field (*échiquier stratégique*), that one upon which we can direct the most fatal blows at the enemy, and where we ourselves run the least risks.

3. To establish and direct properly our lines of operations by adopting, for the defensive, the concentric examples given by the Arch-Duke Charles in 1796, and by Napoleon in 1814; or that of Marshal Soult in 1814, for retreats parallel to the frontiers.

In the offensive, on the contrary, we shall have to follow the system which assured the success of Napoleon in 1800, 1805 and 1806, by the direction given to his forces upon an extremity of the strategical front of the enemy, or else that of the direction upon the centre, which succeeded so well with him in 1796, 1809 and 1814. The whole according to the respective positions of the armies, and according to the divers maxims given in Article 21.

4. To choose well our eventual strategical lines of manœuvre, by giving them a direction suitable for being able to act with the better part of our divisions, and for preventing on the contrary, the parts of the hostile army from concentrating, or from reciprocally sustaining each other.

5. To combine properly, *in the same spirit of ensemble and centralization*, all the strategical positions, as well as all the great detachments which we should be called upon to make, in order to embrace the indispensable parts of the strategic field.

6. Finally, to impress upon our masses the greatest activity and the greatest possible mobility, to the end that by their successive and alternate employment upon the points where it is important to strike, we attain the capital end of putting in action superior forces against fractions merely of the hostile army.

It is by the vivacity of our movements that we multiply the action of our forces, in neutralizing on the contrary, a great part of those of our adversary; but if this vivacity suffices often to procure successes, its effects are centupled, if we give a skillful direction to the efforts which it would lead to, that is to say, when those efforts should be directed upon the decisive strategic points of the zone of operations, where they could carry the most fatal blows to the enemy.

Meanwhile, as we are not always in condition to adopt this decisive point, exclusive of every other, we can content ourselves at times with attaining in good part the object of every enterprise, by knowing how to combine the rapid and successive employment of our forces upon isolated parties, the defeat of which would be inevitable; when we shall unite the double condition of rapidity and vivacity in the employment of masses, with a good direction, we shall only be the more assured of victory and its great results.

The operations which best prove these truths are those so often cited of 1809 and 1814, as also that ordered at the end of 1793, by Carnot, already mentioned in Art. 24, and the details of which will be found in vol. 4, of my history of the wars of the Revolution. Forty battalions, transported successively from Dunkirk to Menin, to Mauberge and to Landan, by reinforcing the armies which were already found there, decided four victories which saved France.

The whole strategical science would have been found contained in this wise operation, if to that combination one had been able to add the merit of its application to the decisive strategic point of the theatre of war; but it was not so, for the Austrian army, being then the principal party of the coalition, and having its retreat upon Cologne, it was upon the Meuse that a general effort would have carried the severest blows. The committee provided for the most immediate danger, and the observation which I allow myself could diminish in nothing the merit of its manœuvre; it contains the half of the strategical principle, the other half consists precisely in giving to such efforts the most decisive direction, as Napoleon did at Ulm, at Jena and at Ratisbon. The whole art of strategical warfare is contained in these three different applications. I shall be pardoned for repeating so often these same citations, I have already given the motives for it.

It would be useless, I think, to add, that one of the great objects of strategy is to be able to secure advantages to the army, by preparing for it the most favorable theatre for its operations, if they have place in our own country; the situation of places, of intrenched camps, of têtes-de-ponts, the opening of communications upon great decisive direction, do not form the least interesting part of this science; we have indicated all the signs by which one may easily recognise those lines and those decisive points, whether permanent or eventual.

CHAPTER IV.

GRAND TACTICS, AND BATTLES.

Battles are the definitive shock of two armies which are contending for great questions of policy or of strategy. Strategy leads armies upon the decisive points of the zone of operations, prepares the chances of battle, and influences in advance its results; but it is for tactics, united to courage, to genius and to fortune, to gain them.

Grand tactics is then the art of well combining and well conducting battles; the directing principle of the combinations of tactics is the same as that of strategy, it is the carrying the weight of our forces upon a part only of the hostile army and upon the point which promises the greatest results.

It has been said that battles were difinitively the principal and decisive action of war; this assertion is not always exact, for we have seen armies destroyed by strategic operations without there having been battles, but only a series of small combats. It is true also that a complete and decisive victory may give the same results without there having been grand strategic combinations.

The results of a battle depend ordinarily upon a union of causes which are not always in the domain of the military art; the kind of order of battle adopted, the wisdom of its measures of execution, the more or less loyal and enlightened concurrence of the lieutenants of the generalissimo, the cause of the struggle, the enthusiasm, the proportions and the quality of the troops, the superiority in artillery or in cavalry, and their good employment, but above all the moral condition of armies and even of nations, are what give victories more or less decisive, and determine their results. Therefore has General Clausewitz advanced a great sophism in telling us that without turning manœuvres, a battle could not procure a complete victory. That of Zama saw perish in a few hours, the fruit of twenty years of glory and success of Hannibal, without any one having thought of turning him. At Rivoli the turners were completely beaten, and they were not more happy either at Stockach in 1799, or at Austerlitz in 1805. As will be seen in Art. 33, I am far from rejecting manœuvres tending to outflank and to turn a wing, for I have constantly insisted upon them, but it is important to know how to turn timely and skillfully, and I think that strategic manœuvres for seizing communications without losing one's own, are more sure than those of tactics.

There are three kinds of battles : the first are defensive battles, that is to say, those which an army delivers in an advantageous position where it awaits the enemy ; the second are offensive battles, delivered by an army for attacking the enemy in a chosen position ; the third are unexpected battles delivered by the two parties on the march. We shall examine successively the divers combinations which they present.

ARTICLE XXXI.

POSITIONS AND DEFENSIVE BATTLES.

When an army expects a combat, it takes position and forms its line of battle. It has been seen, by the general definition of operations given at the commencement of this work, that I have made a distinction between lines of battle and orders of battle, objects which have been until this day confounded.

I shall give the name line of battle to the position deployed, or composed of battalions in columns of attack, which an army will take, in order to occupy a camp and a ground where it may receive combat without a determinate aim, it is the denomination proper for a troop formed according to tactics, upon one or several lines, and which will make the more special object of Article 43. I shall call on the contrary, an order of battle that disposition of troops indicating a given manœuvre ; for example, the parallel order, the oblique order, and the order perpendicular upon the wings.

This denomination, although new, appears indispensable, in order to designate clearly two objects which it is necessary to guard against confounding.* From the nature of these two things, we see that the line of battle belongs more particularly to the defensive system, since the army which awaits the enemy, without knowing what he is going to do, truly forms a line of battle vague and without object. The order of battle indicating on the contrary, a disposition of troops formed with the intention for combat, and supposing a manœuvre decided upon in advance, belongs more especially to the offensive order. I do not pretend, however, that the line of battle is exclusively defensive, for a troop might very well attack a position in this formation ; in the same manner a defensive army might adopt an oblique order, or any other fit for the offensive. I speak only of the most frequent cases.

Without following absolutely what is called the system of a war of positions, an army may nevertheless, often await the enemy at an advantageous post, strong by nature, and chosen beforehand for receiving there a defensive battle. We can take such a post when we aim to cover an important objective point, such as a capital, grand depôts, or a decisive strategic point which commands the country, finally, when a siege is to be protected.

There are besides several kinds of positions, the strategical, of which we have spoken in Article 20, and the tactical. These last are subdivided in their turn ; there are first intrenched positions, selected for awaiting the enemy in a post sheltered, by works more or less connected, in a word, in intrenched camps ; we have treated of their relations with strategic operations in Article 27, and we shall treat of their attack and defense in Article 36. The second are positions strong from their nature, where armies

---

* It is not the pleasure of innovating which induces me to modify the received denominations for creating new ones ; to develop a science, it is important that the same word do not signify two altogether different things. If we adhere to naming *order of battle*, the simple distribution of troops in the line, then at least the names oblique order of battle, concave order of battle, must not be given to important manœuvres. In this case, it would be necessary to designate these manœuvres by the systematic terms of oblique battle, &c., but I prefer the denomination I have adopted ; the order of battle upon paper could be called plan of organization, and the ordinary formation upon the ground might take the name line of battle.

encamp for gaining a few days. The last finally are open positions, but chosen beforehand for receiving battle.

The qualities which should be sought in these, vary according to the object had in view ; it is important in the meanwhile, not to allow ourselves to lean to the prejudice too much in vogue, which causes to be preferred positions steep and difficult of access, very suitable perhaps for a temporary camp, but which are not always the best for delivering battle. Indeed, a position is not strong merely because it is composed of a steep ground, but rather when it is in harmony with the object which we propose in taking it, and when it offers the greatest possible advantages to the kind of troops which constitutes the principal strength of the army ; finally, when the obstacles of the ground are more injurious to the enemy than to the army which shall occupy that position. For example, it is certain that Masséna, taking the strong position of the Albis, would have committed a grave fault if he had been superior in cavalry and in artillery ;- whilst, for his excellent infantry, it was exactly what he needed. For the same reason, Wellington, whose whole strength consisted in his weight of fire, chose well the position of Waterloo, all the avenues of which he swept to a distance by a rasant fire. Moreover, the position of the Albis was rather a strategic position, that of Waterloo a position for battle. The maxims which must ordinarily be observed for these last are :

1. To have outlets more easy for falling upon the enemy when the moment is judged favorable, than the latter would have for approaching the line of battle.

2. To assure to the artillery all its defensive effect.

3. To have a ground advantageous for concealing the movements that might be made, from one wing to the other, with a view of directing masses upon the point judged suitable.

4. To be able, on the contrary, to discover easily the movements of the enemy.

5. To have an easy retreat.

6. To have the flanks well supported, in order to render an attack upon the extremities impossible, and to reduce the enemy to an attack upon the centre, or at least upon the front.

This last condition is difficult to fulfil ; for if the army is supported by a river, by mountains or impracticable forests, and experiences the least check, it may be changed into a complete disaster, since the broken line would be thrown back upon those same obstacles which were believed suited to protect it. This incontestable danger authorizes the belief that posts of an easy defense are better, on a day of battle, than insurmountable obstacles, since it suffices to have posts where we can maintain ourselves for a few hours by the aid of simple detachments.*

A defect of support for the flanks is remedied sometimes by crotchets in rear. This system is dangerous, inasmuch as a crotchet inherent to the line constrains the movements, and the enemy, by placing cannon upon the angle of the two lines, would cause in them great ravages. A double reserve, disposed in deep order behind the wing which we should wish to secure from insult, seems better to accomplish the object than a crotchet ; localities ought to determine the employment of these two means. We shall give more ample details of them in the battle of Prague, (Chapter 2d of the Seven Years War.)

7. It is not only the flanks that we should seek to cover in a defensive position, it often happens that the front offers obstacles upon a part of its development, so as to necessitate the enemy to direct his attacks upon the centre. Such a position will always be one of the most advantageous for a defensive army, as the battles of Malplaquet and Waterloo have proved. To attain this object, immense obstacles are not necessary, the least accident of ground sometimes suffices ; it was the miserable stream of Papelotte which forced Ney to attack the centre of Wellington, instead of assailing the left as he was ordered.

When such a post is to be defended, it is necessary to render movable a part of the wings thus sheltered, in order that they may participate in the action, instead of remaining idle witnesses thereof.

It cannot be dissembled, nevertheless, that all these means are but paliatives, and that the best of all for an army which awaits the enemy defensively, is to know how to retake the initiative when the moment has arrived for doing so with success.

We have placed in the number of qualities requisite for a position, that of offering an easy retreat ; this leads us to the examination of a question raised by the battle of Waterloo. Would an army, backed against a forest, when it should have a good road in rear of the centre and each of

---

* The park of Hougoumont, the hamlet of la Haie-Sainte, and the stream of Papelotte, presented to Ney obstacles more serious than the famous position of Elchingen, where he forced the passage of the Danube in 1805, upon the remnant of a burnt bridge. The courage of the defenders could, in fact, not have been absolutely equal in the two circumstances ; but, apart from this chance, it must be owned that the difficulties of a ground, when they are turned to good account. need not be insurmountable. in order to baffle any attack. At Elchingen. the great elevation and the steepness of the banks, rendering the effect of the fire almost null, was more injurious than useful to the defense.

the wings, be compromised as Napoleon has pretended, if it chanced to lose the battle? As for myself I believe, on the contrary, that such a position would be more favorable for a retreat than a ground wholly uncovered, for the beaten army could not traverse a plain without being exposed to the greatest danger. Doubtless, if the retreat should degenerate into a complete rout, a part of the artillery left in battery before the forest would probably be lost, but the infantry, the cavalry and the remainder of the artillery would retire as well as across a plain. If the retreat, on the contrary, is made in order, nothing could better protect it than a forest; well understood, nevertheless, that there exist at least two good roads behind the line, that one does not allow himself to be pressed too near, without considering upon the measures necessary for the retreat, and that no lateral movement be permitted the enemy in advance of the army at the issue of the forest, as took place at Hohenlinden. The retreat would be all the more sure if, as was the case at Waterloo, the forest formed a concave line in the rear of the centre, for this reentrant would become a veritable place of arms for collecting the troops and giving them time to file successively upon the grand route.

We have already indicated, in speaking of strategic operations, the divers chances which the two systems, offensive and defensive, procure an army, and we have seen, that in strategy especially, he who took the initiative, had the great advantage of directing his masses, and of striking where he judged agreeable to his interests to do so; whilst he who waits in position, anticipated everywhere, and often taken by surprise, was always forced to subject his movements to those of his adversary. But we have recognized equally that in tactics, those advantages are less positive, because the operations not being upon so vast a circuit, he who has the initiative could not conceal them from the enemy who, discovering him instantly, can, by the aid of good reserves, remedy it upon the spot. Besides that, he who marches upon the enemy, has against him all the disadvantages resulting from obstacles of the ground which he has to overcome, in order to approach the line of his adversary; however flat a country may be, there are always inequalities in the ground, little ravines, small forests, hedges, farm houses, and villages to gain or to pass; add to these natural obstacles, hostile batteries to carry, and the disorder which always introduces itself more or less in a troop long exposed to the fire of artillery or musketry, and we shall be convinced that at least, the advantage of the initiative is balanced.

However incontestable these truths may be, there is another which rises above them, and which is demonstrated by the greatest events of history.

It is that in the long run, every army which awaits the enemy in a fixed post, will end by being forced, whilst that by profiting at first of the advantages of the defensive, in order to seize afterwards those which the initiative procures, it may hope for the greatest successes. A general who waits for the enemy like an automaton, without taking any other part than that of fighting valiantly, will always succumb when he shall be well attacked. It is not so with a general who awaits with the firm resolution of combining great manœuvres against his adversary, to the end of retaking the moral advantage which the offensive impulse gives, and the certainty of placing his masses in action upon the most important point, which in the simple defensive never has place.

In fact, if he who awaits is found in a well chosen post, where his movements may be free, he has the advantage of seeing the enemy arrive ; his troops well disposed beforehand according to the ground, and favored by batteries placed in such a manner as to obtain the greatest effect, may make his adversaries pay dear for the ground which separates the two armies ; and when the assailant, already shaken by sensible losses, shall be vigorously assailed himself at the moment when he believed himself within reach of victory, it is not probable that the advantage will remain on his side, for the moral effect of such an offensive return on the part of the enemy who was considered beaten, is calculated to shake the most audacious.

A general may then employ with the same success, for battles, the offensive or defensive system ; but it is indispensable to this effect :

1st. That, far from limiting himself to a passive defense, he should know how to pass from the defensive to the offensive when the moment has arrived ;

2d. That he should have a sure *coup d'œil* and much calmness ;

3d. That he command troops upon whom he can count ;

4th. That in retaking the offensive he should not neglect to apply the general principles which would have presided over his order of battle, if he had commenced by being the aggressor ;

5th. That he direct his blows upon the decisive points.

The example of Bonaparte at Rivoli and at Austerlitz, that of Wellington at Talavera, at Salamanca and at Waterloo, prove these truths.

ENSIVE.

here is an attacking party and the party attacked, each battle will then
the one and defensive for the other

of battle most appropriate to the mode which shall be preferred.

ENSIVE

a
k
t
p
p
c

as
c
th

wl

be

--- defensive for the other party attacked, each battle will then of those heights seems the most advantageous tactical point; but it may happen, nevertheless, that these heights are of a very difficult access, and situated precisely at the least important point relatively to strategic views. At the battle of Bautezen, the left of the Allies was supported by the steep mountains of Bohemia, then rather neutral than hostile; it seemed then that, tactically, the side of those mountains would be the decisive point to carry, and it was just the opposite; because that the ground was very favorable there to the defense, that the allied army had only a single line of retreat upon Reichenbach and Gorlitz, and that the French, by forcing the right in the plain, seized upon this line of retreat, and threw the allied army into the mountains, where it would have lost all its *matériel* and a great part of its *personnel*. This last course offered then more facilities of ground, more immense results, and less obstacles to vanquish.

From all that precedes, we can, I believe, deduce the following truths : 1st. The topographical field of battle is not always the tactical key. 2d. The decisive point of a field of battle is unquestionably that which unites the strategic advantage with the most favorable localities. 3d. In the case where there are not too formidable difficulties of ground upon the strategic point of this field of battle, that point is ordinarily the most important. 4th. However, it happens also that the determination of this point depends above all upon the position of the respective forces; thus, in lines of battle too extended and cut up, the centre will be always the most essential to attack; in close lines the centre is on the contrary, the strongest point, since independently of the reserves which are found there, it will be easy to cause it to be sustained by the wings; then the decisive point will be on the contrary, upon one of the extremities. With a great superiority of forces, we may attack the two extremities at the same time, but not with forces equal or inferior. It is seen then that all the combinations of a battle consists in employing our forces in such a manner that they obtain the greatest possible action upon that one of the three points which offers the most advantages, a point which it will be easy to determine, by submitting it to the analysis which we have just explained.

The aim of an offensive battle can only be to dislodge and break the enemy, unless by strategic manœuvres the entire ruin of his army has been prepared; now an enemy is dislodged, either by overthrowing his line upon some point of his front, or by outflanking it, in order to take it in flank or in reverse, or in making the two means concur at the same time, that is to say, by an attack in front at the same time that an acting wing should double and turn the line.

In order to attain these various ends, it is necessary to choose the order of battle most appropriate to the mode which shall be preferred.

There are counted at least twelve kinds of orders of battle, viz: 1st. The simple parallel order; 2d. The parallel order with the defensive or offensive crotchet; 3d. The order reinforced upon one or two wings; 4th. The order reinforced upon the centre; 5th. The oblique order, either simple or reinforced upon the assailing wing; 6th and 7th. The order perpendicular upon one or both wings; 8th. The concave order; 9th. The convex order; 10th. The order in echelon upon one or both wings; 11th. The order in echelon upon the centre; 12th. The order combined of a strong attack upon the centre and upon one of the extremities at the same time. (See plate opposite, figures 1 to 12.)

Each of these orders may be employed simply or be combined, as has been said, with the manœuvre of a strong column destined to turn the hostile line. In order to judge of the merit of each of them, it is necessary to be assured of their relations with the general principles which we have laid down.

We see, for example, that the parallel order (No. 1) is the worst; for there is no skill in causing the two parties to fight with equal chances, battalion against battalion; it is the absence of all tactics. There is, nevertheless, an important case in which this order is suitable; it is when an army having taken the initiative of grand strategic operations, shall have succeeded in carrying itself upon the communications of its adversary, and in cutting him off from his line of retreat while covering its own; then when the definitive shock between the armies has place, he who is found upon the rear may deliver a parallel battle, since having made the decisive manœuvre before the battle, his whole aim consists in repelling the effort of the enemy to open himself a passage; except this case the parallel order is the least advantageous. Nevertheless, that is not saying that a battle cannot be gained by adopting it, for it is necessary that some one should gain it, and the advantage will remain then to him who shall have the best troops, who shall know best how to engage them at the proper time, who shall manœuvre best with his reserves, or finally who shall be favored by fortune. The parallel order with a crotchet upon the flank, (fig. 2) is taken most ordinarily in a defensive position; it may, however, be also the result of an offensive combination, but then it will be found in advance of the line, whilst in the defensive it is in rear. There may be seen in the battle of Prague, one of the most extraordinary examples of the fate which such a crotchet may experience when it is well attacked.

The parallel order (No. 3,) reinforced upon one of the wings, or that (No. 4,) reinforced upon the centre, in order to pierce that of the enemy, are much more favorable than the two preceding, and are also much more conformable to the general principle which we have pointed out, although with an equality of forces, the part of the line which should be weakened, in order to reinforce the other, might also be compromised, if it were placed in battle parallelly to the enemy.

The oblique order (No. 5,) is that which suits the best an inferior army, which attacks a superior ; for, while offering the advantage of carrying the mass of the forces upon a single point of the enemy's line, it procures two others equally important ; in fact, we do not only refuse the weakened wing, by keeping it beyond the blows of the enemy, that wing fulfills still the double destination of holding in respect the part of the line which it is not wished to attack, and in the mean time of being able to serve as reserve at need to the acting wing. This order was employed by the celebrated Epaminondas at the battle of Leuctra and Mantinea ; but we shall present the most brilliant example of the advantages of this system, which was given by Frederick the Great at the battle of Leuthen. (See Chapter 7, Treatise of Grand Operations.)

The order perpendicular upon one or both wings, such as is presented in figures 6 and 7, should only be considered a theoretical form to indicate the tactical direction upon which we should direct our efforts. Never would two armies be found in positions relatively perpendicular, such as we see them traced on the plate, for if the army B took in fact its first direction in a perpendicular line upon one or both of the extremities of the army A, the latter would change immediately the front of a part of its line, and even the army B, when it should have attained or passed the extremity, would not fail to change the direction of its columns to the right or to the left, in order to approach the enemy's line, so that the part C would take it in reverse, and there would result two true oblique lines like those pointed out in figure 6. It must be inferred hence, that a single division of the assailing army should be carried perpendicularly upon the enemy's flank, whilst that the remainder of this army should approach the other extremity, in order to disquiet it, which would lead to one of the oblique dispositions indicated by figures 5 and 12.

Besides, the attack upon two wings, whatever form we may give it, may be very advantageous, but it is when the assailant is found very superior in number ; for if the fundamental principle consists in carrying the major part of the forces upon the decisive point, an inferior army would violate this principle in forming a double attack against a single superior mass ; we shall demonstrate this truth in the course of the work.

The order, concave upon the centre, (No. 8,) has found partisans, since Hannibal owed to it the signal victory of Cannæ. This order may be, in fact, very good when it is taken in consequence of the events of the battle, that is to say, when the enemy engages in the centre which yields before him, and when he allows himself to be enveloped by the wings. But if this formation is taken before the battle, the enemy, instead of throwing himself upon the centre, would only have to fall upon the wings which would of themselves present their extremities, and would be thus in the same situation as if they were found assailed upon a flank. Therefore, this position is seldom taken, except against an enemy who should himself be formed in convex order to deliver battle, as will be seen hereafter.

In truth, an army will rarely form a semi-circle, and will rather take a broken line reentrant towards the centre, (like figure 8 bis.) If we believe several writers, it was such a disposition which caused the English to triumph on the celebrated days of Crecy and Agincourt. It is certain that this order is better than a semi-circle, because it does not lend the flank so much, allows the marching in advance by echelon, and preserves with that all the effect of concentration of fire. However, its advantages disappear if the enemy, instead of throwing himself madly in the concave centre, confines himself to observing it from a distance, and throw himself with the mass of his forces upon one wing only. The battle of Essling, in 1809, offers still an example of the advantage of a concave line; but it cannot be inferred that Napoleon did badly in attacking its centre; we cannot judge an army fighting with the Danube at its back, and not having the power to move without uncovering its bridges, as if it had had full liberty of manœuvering.

The convex order salient at the centre, (No. 9,) is taken for fighting immediately after the passage of a river, when we are forced to refuse the wings, in order to rest on the river and cover the bridges, or better still, when we fight defensively, backed against a river, in order to repass it and cover the defile as at Leipsig; finally we can take it naturally, in order to arrest an enemy who forms a concave line. If the enemy directed his effort upon the salient, or upon one of the extremities alone, that order would cause the ruin of the army.* The French took it at Fleurus in 1794, and succeeded, because the Prince of Coburg, instead of attacking in force the centre, or a single extremity, divided his efforts upon five or six divergent rays, and especially upon the two wings at the

---

* An attack upon the two extremities might succeed well also in some circumstances, either when one should have sufficient forces to attempt it, or when the enemy should be unable to uncover his centre in order to sustain his wings. But as a general thing, a false attack, in order to hold the centre and a grand effort upon a single extremity, would be especially the most favorable against such a convex line.

same time. It was nearly in the same convex order that they fought at Essling, as well as on the second and third days of the famous battle of Leipsig ; it had, on the last occasions, the infallible results which it ought to have.

The order of echelons upon the two wings (No. 10) is in the same case as the perpendicular order ; (No. 7); it must be observed nevertheless that the echelons approaching towards the centre, where would be held the reserve, this order would be better than the perpendicular, since the enemy would have less facility, space and time to throw himself in the interval of the centre and direct there a menacing counter-attack.

The order of echelons upon the centre only (No. 11) might especially be employed with success against an army which should occupy a line broken and too much extended, because his centre being found then isolated from the wings in a manner to be overcome separately, this army, cut thus in two, would probably be destroyed. But by the application of the same fundamental principle this order of attack would be less certain against an army occupying a compact and united position, for the reserves being found ordinarily within reach of the centre and the wings being able to act either by a concentric fire or by taking the offensive against the first echelons, could easily repulse them.

If this formation offers some resemblance to the famous triangular wedge or *caput porci* of the ancients and with the column of Winkelried ; it differs from them however essentially, because in place of forming a full mass, which would be impracticable in our days on account of the artillery, it would offer on the contrary a great open space in the middle, which would facilitate the movements. This formation suitable, as has been said, for piercing the centre of a too extended line, could equally succeed against a line which should be condemned to immobility ; but if the wings of the line attacked know how to act seasonably against the flanks of the first echelons, it would not be without its inconveniences. A parallel order considerably reinforced upon the centre would perhaps be better, (figures 4 and 12) for the parallel line, in this case would have at least the advantage of deceiving the enemy upon the true point of the projected effort and of preventing the wings from taking in flank the echelons of the centre.

This echelon order was adopted by Laudon for the attack of the intrenched camp of Burzelwitz (Treatise of Grand Operations Chapter 28). In such a case it is really suitable, since we are sure then that the defensive army being forced to remain in its intrenchments, there would be no attack to fear on his part against the flanks of the echelons. However this formation having the inconvenience of indicating to the enemy the point of the line which he wishes to attack, it would be indispensable to make upon the wings simultaneous attacks strong enough to mislead the enemy upon the real point where the effort should be directed.

The order of attack in columns upon the centre and upon one extremity at the same time (No. 12) is more suitable than the preceding, especially when it is applied to a continuous hostile line ; it may even be said that of all the orders of battle it is the most rational ; in fact the attack upon the centre seconded by a wing that outflanks the enemy, prevents the latter from doing as Hannibal and Marshal Saxe did ; that is to say, from rushing upon the assailant taking him in flank ; the hostile wing which is formed pressed between the attack of the centre and that of the extremity, having almost the whole of the assailing masses to combat, will be overwhelmed and probably destroyed. This was the manœuvre which caused Napoleon to triumph at Wagram and at Ligny ; it was what he wished to attempt at Borodino and which only succeeded imperfectly on account of the heroic defense of the troops of the left wing of the Russians, that of the division Paskevitch in the famous redoubt of the centre, then by the arrival of the corps of Baggavout upon the wing which he hoped to outflank. Finally he employed it also at Bautzen where he would have obtained unexampled success but for an incident which deranged the manœuvre of his left destined to cut off the route of Wurschen, and which had already everything disposed for that purpose.

We should observe that those different orders could not be taken literally as the geometrical figures indicate them. A general who should wish to establish his line of battle with the same regularity as upon paper, or upon a field of exercise, would unquestionably be deceived in his expectations and beaten, especially after the present method of making war. In the times of Louis XIV, and Frederick the Great, when armies encamped under tents, almost always united ; when one found himself several days face to face with the enemy, when he had leisure to open marches or symmetrical roads in order to cause his columns to arrive at uniform distances ; then a line of battle could be formed almost as regular as the figures traced. But now that armies bivouac, that their organization into several corps renders them more moveable, that they approach each other in consequence of orders given out of the visual ray and often without even having had time to reconnoitre exactly the position of the enemy, finally that the different arms are found mingled in the line of battle : then all orders drawn by compass must necessarily be found at fault. Therefore those kinds of figures have ever served only to indicate an approximate disposition.

If armies were compact masses which could be moved in a single body by the effect of a single will and as rapidly as thought, the art of gaining battles would be reduced to choosing the most favorable order of battle, and we might count upon the success of manœuvres combined previous to the combat. But it is quite otherwise : the greatest difficulty in the tactics of battles will ever be to assure the putting in simultaneous action all those numerous fractions which should concur in the attack upon which the hope of victory is founded, or more properly speaking, the execution of the capital manœuvre which, according to the primitive plan, should bring about success.

The precise transmission of orders, the manner in which the lieutenants of the general-in-chief shall conceive and execute them ; the too great energy of some, the laxity or the defective *coup d'œil* of others ; all may hinder that simultaneous action, without speaking of fortuitous accidents which may suspend the arrival of a corps.

From thence result two incontestible truths, the first is that the more simple a decisive manœuvre shall be, the more certain will be its success ; the second is that the seasonableness of sudden dispositions, taken during the combat, is of more probable success than the effect of manœuvres combined in advance ; unless the latter reposing upon interior strategic movements, have led the columns which are to decide the battle, upon points where their effect will be assured. Warterloo and Bautzen attest this last truth ; from the moment when Bulow and Blucher had arrived upon the height of Frischermont, nothing could have prevented the loss of the battle by the French, they could struggle only to render the defeat more or less complete. In the same manner at Bautzen as soon as Ney had arrived at Klix, the retreat of the Allies on the night of the 20th of May, would alone have been able to save them, for on the 21st it was no longer time, and if Ney had better executed what he was advised, the victory would have been immense.

With regard to manœuvres for breaking a line, by counting upon the co-operation of columns departing from the same front as the rest of the army, to the end of operating by great circular movements around a hostile wing, their success is always doubtful, for it depends upon a precision of calculation and of execution which is seldom met with ; we shall speak of them in Article 33.

Independently of the difficulty of counting upon the exact application of a premeditated order of battle, it often happens that battles commence without determinate objects, even on the part of the assailant, although the shock was anticipated. This uncertainty results either from the precedents of the battle or from want of knowledge of the position of the enemy and of his projects, or finally from the waiting for a portion of the army which might yet be in rear.

Hence many people have concluded against the possibility of reducing the formations of orders of battle into different systems, and against the influence which the adoption of such or such another of those orders could exercise upon the issue of a combat; a false conclusion, in my opinion, even in the cases before cited. Indeed, in those battles commenced without a decided plan, it is probable that at the commencement of the action the armies are found in line nearly parallel to each other, more or less reinforced upon one or the other point; the defender ignorant upon what side the storm will burst, will hold a good part of his forces in reserve to guard against events; he who is resolved to attack will do the same at first in order to have his masses disposable; but as soon as the assailant shall have determined the point upon which he shall decide to strike, then his masses will be directed, either upon the centre, or upon one of the wings, or upon both at the same time. Now, whatever may happen there will ever result approximately one of the dispositions prescribed in the different figures of the preceding plate. Even in unexpected rencounters the same thing would happen, which will demonstrate, I hope, that this classification of the various systems or orders of battle is neither chimerical nor useless.

Indeed there is nothing even in the battles of Napoleon which does not prove this assertion, although they are less than all others susceptible of being figured by lines traced with the compass; we see, for example, that at Rivoli, Austerlitz, Ratisbon, he concentrated his forces upon the centre in order to watch the moment for falling upon that of the enemy. At the Pyramids he formed an oblique line in echelon squares; at Essling, at Leipsic, at Brienne, he presented a kind of convex order nearly like that in figure 7, at Wagram we see him adopt an order quite like that in figure 12, directing two masses upon his centre and his right, refusing his left, which he wished to repeat at Borodino, as well as at Waterloo before the arrival of the Prussians. At Eylau, although the encounter was almost unforeseen on account of the unlooked for offensive return of the Russian army, he outflanked the left almost perpendicularly, whilst upon another side he sought to break the centre; but there was no simultaneousness in those attacks, that of the centre being already repulsed at eleven o'clock, whilst Davoust was not actively engaged upon the left until towards one o'clock.

At Dresden he attacked by the two wings, for the first time perhaps in his life, because his center was sheltered by a fort and an intrenched camp; moreover, the attack of his left was combined with that of Vandamme upon the line of retreat of the Allies.

At Marengo, if Napoleon himself is to be trusted, the oblique order which he took in resting his right upon Castel Ceriolo, saved him from an almost inevitable defeat. Ulm and Jena were battles gained strategically, before being delivered even, and tactics had but little part in them; at Ulm there was not even a battle.

I think then I can conclude that, if it be absurd to expect to draw upon the ground rectilinear orders of battle such as are traced upon a plan, a skillful general can nevertheless have recourse to dispositions which would produce a distribution of the acting masses, similar very nearly to what it would have been in one or another of the orders of battle indicated. He should apply himself in those dispositions, whether foreseen or unexpected, to judge soundly of the important point of the field of battle, which he will be able to do by comprehending the relations of the hostile line with the decisive strategic directions; he will then direct his attention and efforts upon that point, by employing a third of his forces to hold in check or to observe the enemy, then by throwing the other two-thirds upon the point the possession of which would be the pledge of victory. Acting thus he will have fulfilled all the conditions that the science of grand tactics can impose upon the most skillful captain; he will have obtained the most perfect application of the principles of the art. We have already indicated in the preceding chapter the means of recognizing easily those decisive points.

Since I have given the definition of the ten orders of battle above mentioned, the thought has occurred to me to reply to some assertions in the memoirs of Napoleon published by General Montholon, which refer to this subject:

The great Captain seems to suppose that the oblique order is a modern conception, an inapplicable utopia, which I equally deny, for the oblique order is as ancient as Thebes and Sparta, and I have seen it applied under my own eyes; those assertions will appear all the more astonishing that Napoleon, as we have just said, has himself boasted of having applied with success, at Marengo, this same order the existence of which he denies.

If we took the oblique system in the absolute sense which General Ruchel gave to it in the Academy of Berlin, certainly Napoleon would be right in regarding it as an hyperbole: but I repeat, a line of battle was never a perfect geometrical figure; and if we have used such figures in tactical discussions, it was in order to put in force an idea and to explain it by a symbol. It is certain nevertheless that every line of battle which should neither be parallel nor perpendicular to that of the enemy, would of necessity be oblique. Now if an army attacks an extremity of the enemy, by reinforcing the wing charged with the attack and refusing the enfeebled wing, the direction of its line will be in reality a little oblique, since one extremity will be more removed from the hostile line than the other. The oblique order is so far from a chimera, that every order in echelons upon a wing will always be oblique (pl. 2, fig. 10,) now I have seen more than one combat thus disposed in echelons.

As for the other figures traced upon the same plate, it could not be contested that at Essling, as well as at Fleurus, the general disposition of the Austrians was concave, and that of the French convex. But those two orders may form parallel lines as well as two right lines : now these orders would be systematically parallel if no part of the line were not more reinforced nor brought nearer to the enemy than another.

As for the rest, let us leave geometrical figures, and acknowledge that the true scientific theory of battles will always be limited to the following points :

1. The offensive order of battle should aim to dislodge the enemy from his position by every rational means.

2. The manœuvres which the art indicates are to overwhelm a wing only, or else the centre and a wing at the same time. The enemy may also be dislodged by manœuvres for outflanking and turning him.

3. We shall succeed all the better in these enterprises if we are able to conceal them from the enemy until the moment of assailing him.

4. To attack the centre and the two wings at the same time, without having very superior forces, would be a total absence of the art, unless we should reinforce considerably one of the attacks, taking care not to compromise the others.

5. The oblique order is nothing else but a disposition tending to unite the half at least of one's forces in order to overwhelm a wing, holding the other fraction out of the reach of the enemy, either by echelons, or by the inclined direction of the line (figs. 5 and 12, pl. 2).

6. The divers formations, convex, concave, perpendicular, &c., all present the same combination of attacks parallel or reinforced, upon a portion only of the hostile line.

7. The defense desiring the contrary of the attack, the dispositions of defensive order should have for their object, to multiply the difficulties

of the approach, then to provide strong reserves well concealed, in order to fall, at the decisive moment, where the enemy should expect to find but a feeble point.

8. The best mode to employ for constraining a hostile line to quit its position is difficult to determine in an absolute manner. Every order of battle or of formation which could combine the advantages of fire with those of the impulsion of attack and the moral effect it produces, would be a perfect order. A skilfull mixture of deployed lines and of columns, acting alternately according to circumstances, will ever be a good system. As regards its practical application, the *coup d'œil* of the chief, the *moral* of the officers and soldiers, their instruction in all kinds of manœuvres and fires, the localities or the nature of the ground, will always have a great influence upon the variables which might present themselves.

9. The essential object of an offensive battle being to force the enemy from his position, and especially to cut him up as much as possible, it will be our especial duty ordinarily to count upon the employment of material force as the most efficacious means for succeeding in it.

It happens however that the chances for the employment of force alone, would be so doubtful, that we would succeed more easily by manœuvres tending to outflank and to turn that one of the wings which should be nearest to the line of retreat of the enemy, which would decide him to a retrograde movement for fear of being cut off.

History abounds in examples of the success of like movements, especially against generals of a feeble character: and although victories obtained by this means only are less decisive, and the hostile army is never seriously broken up by them, those half-successes suffice to prove that such manœuvres ought not to be neglected, and that a skilfull general should know how to employ them at the proper time, and especially to combine them as much as possible with attacks by main force.

10. The union of these two means, that is to say, the employment of material force upon the front, seconded by a turning manœuvre, will give more surely the victory than if we limited ourselves to employing them separately; but in both cases it is necessary to guard against movements too disconnected, in the face of the least respectable enemy.

11. The various means of carrying a hostile position, that is to say of breaking its line and compelling it to retreat by the use of material force are, to shake it at first by the effect of a superior artillery fire, to introduce into it some confusion by a well directed and timely cavalry charge,

then to approach finally this line thus shaken, with masses of infantry preceded by skirmishers and flanked by a few squadrons.*

In the meanwhile admitting the success of an attack so well combined against the first line, it will remain yet to conquer the second, and even the reserve : now it is here that the embarrassment of the attack would be more serious, if the moral effect of the defeat of the first line did not often carry with it the defeat of the second, and did not cause the general attacked to lose his presence of mind.

In fact, in spite of their first success, the assailing troops would also be a little disunited on their side ; it will often be very difficult to replace them by those of the second line, not only because the latter do not always follow the march of the acting masses under the fire of musketry, but above all because it is ever embarrassing to replace one division by another in midst of a combat, and at the instant when the enemy might combine his greatest efforts to repel the attack.

Everything then induces the belief that, if the troops and the general of the defensive army did equally well their duty and displayed equal presence of mind, if they were not menaced on their flanks and their line of retreat, the advantage of the second shock would almost always be on their side : but for that purpose it is necessary to seize, with a sure and rapid *coup d'œil* the instant when it is proper to throw the second line and the cavalry upon the victorious battalions of the adversary, for a few minutes lost may become irreparable, to such a degree that the troops of the second line would be carried away with those of the first.

12. From what precedes, there results for the attacking party the following truth : " it is that the most difficult as well as the most sure of all " the means of success, is to cause the line already engaged to be well sustained by the troops of the second line, and the latter by the reserve; " then to calculate accurately the employment of masses of cavalry and " that of batteries, to facilitate and to second the decisive effort against " the second hostile line, for here is presented the greatest of all the problems of the tactics of battles."

It is in this important act that theory becomes difficult and uncertain, because it is found then insufficient and will never be equal to natural genius for war, nor the instructive *coup d'œil* which experience in combats will give to a general brave and of a tried *sang-froid*.

---

* At the moment when I decide to republish this article, I receive a pamphlet from General Okouneff, upon the employment of artillery for breaking a line. I shall say a few words upon it in Art. 46.

The simultaneous employment of the greatest possible number of forces, of all the arms combined, except a small reserve of each of them, which it is proper always to have on hand,* will be then, at the decisive moment of the battle, the problem which every skilfull general will apply himself to resolve, and which should make his rule of conduct. Now this decisive moment is very generally that when the first line of one of the parties should be broken, and when the efforts of the two adversaries should tend, either to complete the victory or to wrest it from the enemy. There is no need of saying that in order to render the decisive blow more sure and more efficacious a simultaneous attack upon a flank of the enemy would have the most powerful effect.

13. In the defensive the fire of musketry will always play a greater part than in the offensive where the object is to march if we wish to carry a position ; now to march and to fire are two things which skirmishers alone can do at the same time : it is necessary to renounce it for the principal masses. The object of the defender not being to carry positions, but to break and put in disorder the troops which advance against him, artillery and musketry will be the natural arms for his first line ; then when the enemy shall press the latter too closely, it will be necessary to launch against him the columns of the second with a part of the cavalry ; every thing leads to the belief that he will be repulsed.

I could not, without entering into vague theories, which would besides pass the limits of this treatise, say any thing more upon battles, unless it be to offer a sketch of the combination of the formation and the employment of the three arms, which will make the subject of Chapter 7.

With regard to details of application and execution of the various orders of battle, nothing more complete could be recommended than the work of the Marquis de Tiernay ; it is the remarkable part of his book. Without believing that all which he indicates can be practiced in presence of an enemy, yet it is just to acknowledge that it is the best tactical work that has been published in France up to this day.

---

* The grand reserves should naturally also be engaged when it is necessary, but it is well always to keep two or three battalions and five or six squadrons in hand. General Moreau decided the battle of Eugen with four companies of the 58th regiment, and it is known what the 9th Light and the cavalry of Kellerman did at Marengo.

ARTICLE XXXIII.

TURNING MANŒUVRES, AND TOO EXTENDED
MOVEMENTS IN BATTLES.

We have spoken, in the preceding article, of manœuvres undertaken for turning the enemy in the day of battle, and of the advantage that might be expected from it. It remains for us to say a few words upon the too extended movements to which those manœuvres often give place, and which have caused the failure of so many projects in appearance well concerted.

In principle, every movement sufficiently extended to give the enemy time to beat separately half of the army whilst it is being operated, is a loose and dangerous movement. In the meanwhile as the danger which may result from it depends upon the rapid and sure *coup d'œil* of the adversary, as well as upon his habitual system of warfare, it is easily comprehended why so many similar manœuvres have failed against some, and succeeded against others, and why such a movement which would have been too extended before Frederick, Napoleon or Wellington, has had entire success against mediocre generals, wanting tact to take the initiative or habituated themselves to disconnected movements. It appears very difficult to trace an absolute rule of conduct, there exists no other than that " of holding the weight of our forces in hand in order to cause them to act at the opportune moment, but without falling into the contrary excess of too much accumulating them : we shall be sure then of always being in condition to meet events. But if the affair is with an adversary of little skill, or inclined to extend too much, we can then venture more."

A few examples taken from history will be the best explanations for rendering these truths more sensible, and cause to be appreciated the difference which exists in the results of like movements, according to the army and the general with which we are to be measured.

We have seen in the Seven Years War, Frederick gain the battle of Prague, because the Austrians had left a feeble interval of from a thousand to twelve hundred yards between their right and the rest of their army, and because this remainder of the army continued immoveable whilst that the right was overwhelmed; this inaction was all the more extraordinary as the left of the imperialists had much less distance to make in order to succor their own, than Frederick to attain the right, which, formed in crotchet, compelled a semi-circular movement

Frederick came near on the contrary losing the battle of Torgau for having made with his left, a movement too extended and loose, (near two leagues), to the end of turning the right of Marshal Daun.* The affair was re-established by a concentric movement of the king's right, which Mollendorf conducted upon the heights of Siptitz in order to re-unite with him.

The battle of Rivoli was one of the kind: it is known that Alvinzi and the chief of his staff Weyrother wished to surround the little army of Napoleon, concentrated upon the plateau of Rivoli, and how their centre was beaten whilst the left was accumulated in the ravine of the Adige, and that Lusignam with the right gained by a long circuit the rear of the French army, where he was soon surrounded and taken. The splendid map and the narratives which I have published of it, are the best study that can be made upon this kind of battles.

No person can have forgotten the battle of Stockach where General Jourdan conceived the unfortunate idea of causing to be attacked an army of sixty thousand combattants, by three small divisions from seven to eight thousand men, distant from each other several leagues, whilst that Saint-Cyr with the third of the army (ten thousand men), was to pass the right flank at four leagues distance upon the rear of those sixty thousand men, which could not fail to be victorious over these scattered fractions and to capture that one which wished to cut off their retreat, a fate from which Saint-Cyr escaped by a miracle.

It is recollected how the same General Weyrother, who had wished to surround Napoleon at Rivoli, designed to do the same at Austerlitz, in spite of the severe lesson which he had received without profit to him. It is known how the left of the Allies, wishing to outflank Napoleon's right, in order to cut him off from the road to Vienna, (where he did not desire to return,) by a circular movement of about two leagues, left an opening of half a league in its line, from which Napoleon profited by falling upon the isolated centre, and surrounding afterwards that left, thrust between the lakes of Tellnitz and Melnitz.

Finally, it is known how Wellington gained the battle of Salamanca by a manœuvre nearly similar, because the left of Marmont, which wished to

---

* See for these two battles, Chapts. 2 and 25, of the Treatise of Grand Military Operations

cut him off from the route to Portugal, left a gap of half a league, from which the English general profited for beating that wing stripped of its support.

The narratives of ten wars which I have published, are full of similar examples, of which it would be superfluous to multiply here the number. Since it can add nothing to what we have already said for causing to be appreciated the dangers, not only of turning manœuvres, but of every gap left in the line of battle, when we have to fight an enemy accustomed to play a close game.

It will be readily judged, that if Weyrother had had to do with Jourdan, at Rivoli as at Austerlitz, he would perhaps have ruined the French army, instead of sustaining himself, a total defeat. For the general who attacked at Stockach a mass of sixty thousand men with four little masses, isolated and unable to second each other, would not have known how to profit by the two extended movements attempted against him. In the same manner, Marmont was unlucky at Salamanca, in having to struggle against an adversary whose best acknowledged merit was a tried and rapid tactical *coup d'œil* ; before the Duke of York or More he would probably have succeeded.

Among the turning manœuvres which have succeeded in our day, Waterloo and Hohenlinden were those which had the most brilliant results ; but the first was almost a strategic movement, and accompanied by a host of fortunate circumstances, the concurrence of which is rarely presented. As regards Hohenlinden, we should vainly seek in military history for another example where a single brigade adventured in a forest in the midst of fifty thousand men, produces there all the miracles which Richepanse operated in that cut-throat place of Matenpöt, where it was much more probable that he would be obliged to lay down his arms.

At Wagram, the turning wing of Davoust had a great part in the success of the day ; but if· the vigorous attack executed on the centre by Macdonald, Oudinot and Bernadotte had not opportunely seconded it, it is not certain that it would have been so.

So many examples of opposite results might cause it to be concluded that there is no rule to give upon this matter, but this would be wrong, for it appears to me on the contrary evident : "That by adopting in general a system of battles very compact, and well connected, we will be found in condition to meet every contingency, and will leave little to chance ; but it is important, nevertheless, above all, to judge accurately of the enemy whom we are to combat, in order to measure the boldness of our enterprises after his character, and the system which he shall be known to follow.

"That in case of numerical superiority, we can, as well as in that of moral superiority, attempt manœuvres, which, in an equality of numerical forces and of capacity in the chiefs, would be imprudent.

"That a manœuvre for outflanking and turning a wing, ought to be connected with the other attacks, and sustained in time by an effort which the remainder of the army should make upon the enemy's front, either against the wing turned, or against the centre.

"Finally, that strategic manœuvres for cutting an army off from its communications before battle, and thus attacking it in reverse, without losing our own line of retreat, are of a much more sure and much greater effect, and moreover do not require any disconnected manœuvre in the combat."

For the rest, this is sufficient upon the chapter of combined battles, it is time to pass to those which are unforeseen.

ARTICLE XXXIV

RENCOUNTER OF TWO ARMIES IN MARCH.

One of the most dramatic acts in war, is that which results from this kind of unforeseen collision of two armies.

In the greater part of battles, it happens that one of the parties awaits the enemy at a post determined beforehand, and that the other army goes to attack it thereon, after having reconnoitred that position as well as possible. But it also frequently happens, especially in the modern system, and in the offensive returns of one of the parties, that two armies march each upon the other, with the reciprocal intention of making an unexpected attack; then there results a kind of mutual surprise, for the two parties are equally deceived in their combinations, since they find the enemy where they in no wise expected to meet him. Finally, there are also cases where one of the two armies allows itself to be attacked in march by its adversary who prepares for it this surprise, as happened to the French at Rosbach.

It is on those great occasions that all the genius of a skillful general, of a warrior capable of governing events, displays itself; it is where we recognize the seal of the great captain. It is always possible to gain a battle with brave troops, without the chief of the army being able to arrogate to himself the least part in the success of the day, but a victory like those of Lutzen, of Luzzara, of Eylau, of Abensberg, can be the result only of a great character, joined to great presence of mind, and to wise combinations.

There is too much of chance and too much of poetry in these kinds of rencounters, easily to give positive maxims upon them; however, it is, especially in this case, that it is necessary to be well penetrated with the fundamental principle of the art and of the different modes of applying it, in order to make tend to that end all the manœuvres which we will be in the condition to order on the instant even, and in the midst of the tumult of arms. What we have said of impromptu manœuvres, in Article 32, is the only rule then to give for those unforeseen circumstances; it will suffice to combine them with the antecedents and with the physical and moral condition of the two parties.

Two armies marching, as they did formerly, with all the equipage of the encampment, and meeting each other unexpectedly, would have doubtless nothing better to do than to deploy at first their advanced guards to the right or to the left of the routes they pass over. But each of them should at the same time assemble the bulk of its forces, in order to launch them afterwards in a suitable direction, according to the object it should have in view; a grave fault would be committed in deploying the whole army behind the advanced guard, because even in the case where we should succeed in it, it would never be any thing but the formation of a defective parallel order, and if the enemy pushed the advanced guard somewhat vigorously, there might result from it the rout of the troops which should be in movement in order to form. (See the battle of Rosbach, Treatise on Grand Operations.)

In the modern system, with armies more moveable, marching upon many routes, and forming as many fractions capable of acting independently of each other, these routs will be less to be feared, but the principles remain the same. It is necessary always to halt and form the advanced guard, then to unite the mass of our forces upon the suitable point, according to the end which is proposed in putting them in march; whatever may be the manœuvres of the enemy, we will find ourselves prepared for everything.

ARTICLE XXXV.

SURPRISES OF ARMIES.

We do not intend to examine here those petty surprises of detachments which constitute the war of partisans, or of light troops, and for which the Russian and Turkish light cavalry have so much superiority. We mean to speak of the surprises of entire armies.

Before the invention of fire-arms, these surprises were more easy, because the explosion of artillery and musketry scarcely permit in our day the entire surprise of an army, unless it forget the first duties of the service, and allow the enemy to arrive in the midst of its ranks, for the want of advanced posts which should do their duty. The Seven Years War offers the memorable surprise of Hochkirch, as an example worthy enough of being pondered upon ; it proves that the surprise does not consist positively in falling upon sleeping and badly guarded troops, but also in combining an attack upon one of their extremities, in such a manner as to surprise them, and to outflank them at the same time. In effect, the question is not the seeking to take the enemy so much at fault, that one could burst upon his isolated men in their tents, but rather to arrive with his masses, without being perceived, upon the point where he should desire to assail the enemy before the latter have time to make counter dispositions.

Since armies no longer encamp in tents, surprises combined in advance are more rare and more difficult, for, in order to premeditate them, it is necessary to know precisely the situation of the hostile camp. At Marengo, at Lutzen, at Eylau, there were a kind of surprises, but these were in reality only unexpected attacks to which this name cannot be given. The only great surprise that we could cite, is that of Taroutin, in 1812, where Murat was assailed and beaten by Benningsen ; in order to justify his want of prudence, Murat alleged that he reposed upon a tacit armistice, but there existed no such convention, and he allowed himself to be surprised by an unpardonable negligence.

It is evident that the most favorable manner of attacking an army, is to fall upon its camp a little before day, at the moment when it is expecting nothing of the kind; confusion will then be inevitable, and if to this advantage is joined that of being well acquainted with the localities, and of giving to the masses a suitable tactical and strategic direction, we may flatter ourselves with a complete victory, barring unexpected events. This is an operation of war which must not be despised, although it is more rare and less brilliant than great strategic combinations which assure victory, thus to speak, before having fought.

For the same reason that it is necessary to profit of every occasion for surprising our adversary, it is important also to take every necessary precaution for securing ourselves against such enterprises. The standing regulations of every country have provided against them; it only remains to follow them exactly.

ARTICLE XXXVI.

ATTACK BY MAIN FORCE OF FORTIFIED PLACES, OF INTRENCHED CAMPS OR LINES, AND *COUPS-DE-MAIN* IN GENERAL.

There exist many strong-holds which, without being regular fortresses, are reputed secure from a *coup-de-main*, and which are however, susceptible of being carried by escalade, either at the first onset, or by breaches as yet little practicable, whose slope would require always the employ-ment of ladders, or other means of arriving at the parapet.

The attack of these kinds of posts presents nearly the same combinations as that of intrenched camps, for it enters like the latter in the category of grand *coups-de-main*.

These kinds of attacks vary naturally according to circumstances; 1st, e strength of the works; 2d, the nature of the ground upon which they are situated ; 3d, their connection or isolation ; 4th, the moral condition of the two parties. History does not lack examples for all the species.

For example, the intrenched camps of Rehl, of Dresden, of Warsaw ; the lines of Turin, and of Mayence; the strong intrenchments of Feldkirch, of Scharnitz, of the Assiette; here are ten events, the conditions of which vary like the results. At Kehl, (1796,) the intrenchments were more connected and better finished than at Warsaw ; they were almost a *tête-de-pont* in permanent fortification, for the Arch-Duke believed it his duty to pay them the honors of a regular seige, and, in fact, he could not think of attacking them by main force without running great risks. At Warsaw the works were formed isolated, but meanwhile of a very respectable relief, and they had for redoubt a great city surrounded with crenated walls, armed, and defended by a body of desperate men.

Dresden had for redoubt in 1813, a bastioned *enceinte*, but the front of which, already dismantled, had only a field parapet ; the camp, properly speaking, was composed only of simple redoubts far removed from each other, and of very incomplete execution, the redoubt alone made its strength.*

At Mayence and at Turin there were continuous lines of circumvallation ; but if the first were strongly traced, we could not say as much of the latter which, upon one of the important points, offered but a bad parapet of three feet above the ground and a proportionate ditch. Moreover, at Turin, the lines, turned and attacked from without, were found taken between two fires, since a strong garrison attacked them in reverse, at the moment when the Prince Eugene assailed them on the side of their line of retreat. At Mayence they were attacked in front, a slender detachment only outflanked the right.

The practicable measures to take in these kinds of attacks against field works, are of small number. If you think yourself able to attempt the surprise of a work by attacking it a little before day, nothing is more natural than to try it ; but if this operation is the most advisable for a detached post, it is difficult to suppose that an army, established in a great intrenched camp, in presence of the enemy, would do its duty so badly as to allow itself to be surprised ; the more so as the rule of every service is to be under arms at the break of day. As it is probable then that the attack will always be made by main force, it results, from the nature even

---

* At Dresden the number of defenders was the first day, (25th August,) twenty-four thousand men, the next day there were already sixty-five thousand, and the third day upwards of a hundred thousand.

of the operation, that the following precautions are indicated as the most simple and the most rational.

1st. To extinguish at first the fire of the works by a formidable artillery, which fulfills at the same time the double object of shaking the *moral* of the defenders.

2d. To provide the troops with all the necessary objects, (as fascines and small ladders,) in order to facilitate the filling up of the ditch, and the mounting of the parapet.

3d. To direct three small columns upon the work which it is wished to carry, seconding them by skirmishers, and holding reserves in sustaining distance.

4th. To profit by all the accidents of the ground for putting the troops under shelter, and uncovering them only at the last moment.

5th. To give precise instructions to the principal columns as to what they will have to do when the work shall be carried, and that it will be the object to charge the enemy's forces which occupy the camp ; finally to designate the corps of cavalry which are to assist in the attack with those forces, if the ground permit it. After these recommendations there is only one thing more to do, this is to launch one's troops with all the vivacity possible upon the works, whilst that a detachment shall then turn them by the gorge, for the least hesitation is worse in such a case than the most audacious temerity.

We shall add, nevertheless, that gymnastic exercises for familiarizing the soldiers with escalades and the attacks of barricaded posts, would be as useful at least as all the exercises that could be prescribed to them ; and that modern balistics might well exercise the mind of the engineers, for finding the means of facilitating, by portable machines, the crossing of a field ditch and the escalade of a parapet.

the assault of Warsaw, and of the intrenched camp of Mayence are the best

Of all the dispositions which I have read upon these matters, those of conceived. Thielke gives us a disposition of Laudon for the attack of the camp of Bunzelwitz, which was not executed, but which is not the less a good example to offer.

The attack of Warsaw especially may be cited as one of the most splendid operations of this kind, and does as much honor to Marshal Paskevitch as to the troops which executed it. Here is an example of what it is suitable to do. With regard to the examples of what it is necessary to shun, we can cite nothing worse than the dispositions prescribed for the attack of Dresden in 1813. Those who were the authors of it could not have done better if they had wished to prevent the taking of the camp; those dispositions may be seen in the work of General Plotho, although they are there already revised and corrected.

By the side of attacks of this nature, may be placed the memorable assaults or escalades of Port Mahon, in 1756, and of Bergen-Op-Zoom, in 1747; both, although they were preceded by a seige, were not the less brilliant *coups de main*, since there was not a sufficient breach for a regular assault. The assaults of Praga, Oczakoff and Ismaiel, can also be ranged in the same class, although in the latter cities the earthen parapets, partly fallen in, favored the escalade, there was not the less merit in the execution.

As for continuous intrenched lines, although they seem better connected than isolated works, they are yet more easy to carry, because constructed upon an extent of many leagues, it is almost impossible to prevent the enemy from penetrating upon some one point; the taking of those of Mayence, and Wissemburg, which we have reported in the history of the wars of the Revolution, (Chap. 21, and 52,) that of the lines of Turin, by Prince Eugene of Savoy, in 1706, are great lessons to study.

This famous event of Turin, which we have already often cited, is too well known for us to recall its circumstances, but we could not dispense with observing that never was a triumph bought so cheaply, nor more difficult to conceive. In truth, the strategic plan was admirable; the march from the Adige by Placentia upon Asti by the right of the Po, leaving the French upon the Mincio, was perfectly combined; but as for the operations under Turin, it must be owned that the conquerors were more fortunate than wise. The Prince Eugene had no need of a great effort of genius to draw up the order which he gave his army, and he must have cruelly despised his adversaries to execute the march which was to direct thirty-five thousand allies of ten different nations, between eighty thousand French and the Alps, marching for forty-eight hours around their camp, by the most famous flank march which has ever been attempted. Besides that, the disposition for the attack was, in itself, so laconic and so little instructive, that any officer of the staff would in our day give one more satisfactory. To prescribe the formation of eight columns of infantry by brigades in two lines, to give the order to crown the intrenchments, and to make therein practicable openings, in order that the columns of cavalry which followed could penetrate into the camp, is all the science which the Prince Eugene could call to the assistance of his audacious enterprise. It is true that he had chosen well the feeble point of the intrenchment, for it was so miserable that it was not three feet above the ground, and did not cover its defenders to the middle.

With regard to the generals who commanded this camp of Turin, their panegyric has been given by one of the historians of the Prince Eugene; M. de M * * , without fearing to diminish the glory of his heroes, exclaims against the court of France, *which eulogised generals whose conduct would, in all justice, have merited the scaffold*. Doubtless he wished only to speak of Marsin, for every body knows that the Duke of Orleans had protested against the idea of awaiting the enemy in the lines, and that two wounds disabled him from the commencement of the attack; as for the truly culpable person he expiated, by an honorable death, a fault which nothing could justify*.

But I am carried away by my subject, and it is necessary to return to the measures most suitable for an attack against lines. If these are of a relief sufficiently strong to render their assault dangerous, and if on the contrary there are means for outflanking or turning them by strategic manœuvres, this course would ever be more suitable than a doubtful attack. In the contrary case, and if you have some motive for preferring this, a point upon one of the wings would be necessary, because it is natural enough that the centre is more easy to sustain. However it has been seen, that an attack upon a wing being regarded with reason by the defender as the most probable, you might succeed in deceiving him by directing a somewhat strong false attack upon that side, whilst that the true, made upon the centre would succeed precisely because it was not probable. In these kinds of combinations, the localities and the spirit of the generals ought to decide as to the best mode to follow.

Moreover, as regards the execution of the attack, we can scarcely employ other means than those recommended for intrenched camps. Meanwhile as these lines, heretofore at least, often had the relief and proportions of permanent works, it may happen that their escalade be difficult except for earthen works already rather old, the slopes of which might be the worse for time and accessible to a somewhat dexterous infantry.

Such were, as we have already said, the ramparts of Ismaiel and of Prague; such was also the citadel of Smolensk which General Paskevitch defended with so much glory against Ney, because he preferred to defend the ravines which were in front of it rather than take refuge behind a parapet scarcely 30 degrees inclined.

If a line is supported by a river, it seems absurd to think, even, of penetrating upon that wing, because the enemy, collecting his forces, the weight

---

* Albergotti was not less culpable than Marsin; placed with forty battalions on the right bank of the Po, where there was no attack, he refused to march to the succor of Marsin, which always happens in such cases, each troubling himself only about the point which he occupies.

of which would be near the centre, could overturn the columns which should advance thus between them and the river, in such a manner that their total loss would be certain. Meanwhile this absurdity has been seen to succeed, because the enemy, forced behind his lines, rarely thinks of an offensive return, however advantageous it may appear; for a general and soldiers who seek a refuge in lines are already half conquered, and the idea of taking the offensive does not happen to them when their intrenchments are found already invaded. However, it would be impossible to counsel the trial of such a manœuvre; the general who should expose himself by it, and who should experience the fate of Tallard at Hochestaedt, could not complain of it.

Considering the defense of intrenched camps and of lines, there are not many maxims to give: the first is unquestionably to assure one's self two good reserves, placed between the centre and each of the wings, or, more properly speaking, upon the right of the left wing, and upon the left of the right wing. By this means, you can run to the succor of the point which should be forced with all the promptitude possible, which a single central reserve would not permit. It has been thought even that three reserves would not be too many, if the intrenchment were very extended; as for myself, I should incline for having but two. A recommendation not less essential, is to thoroughly impress the troops with the idea that an affair would not be desperate because the line should be found crossed upon a point. If you have good reserves which take the initiative seasonably, you will be none the less victorious, by preserving your presence of mind in order to engage them well at the suitable point and moment.

The troops which shall defend the ditch and the parapet will conform to instructions given by the engineers according to the usages practiced in sieges; however, it must be acknowledged, a good work upon the details of the infantry service in sieges and intrenched camps, which may be within the reach of the officers of that arm, is a work yet to make; such an enterprise has nothing in common with this treatise, for it should be the object of a regulation and not of a dogmatic book.

COUPS DE MAIN.

Coups de main are hardy enterprises which a detachment of an army attempts for seizing a more or less important or more or less strong post.* They participate at the same time of surprises and of attacks by main force, for we employ equally those two kinds of means in order to arrive at our ends. Although in appearance these kinds of enterprises seem to belong almost exclusively to tactics it cannot be concealed nevertheless that they draw all their importance from the relations which the posts taken would have with the strategic combinations of the operations. Thus we have already been called to say some words of them in Art. 28, in speaking of detachments : but however troublesome these repetitions may be we are obliged to make mention of them here for what concerns their execution which enters into the domain of attacks of intrenchments.

It is not nevertheless that we pretended to subject them to tactical rules, since a *coup de main*, as the name implies, is in some sort an enterprise outside of all ordinary rules. We wish only to cite them here for reference, directing our readers to the various historical or didactic works which might make mention of them.

We have already pointed out the nature of the results, often very important, which may be promised from them. The taking of Sizipoli in 1828 ; the unsuccessful attack of General Petrasch upon Kehl in 1796 ; the singulor surprises of Cremona in 1702, of Gibralter in 1704, and of Bergen-op-Zoom in 1814, as well as the escalades of Port Mahon and Badajos, may give an idea of the different kinds of *coups de main*. Some are the effect of surprise, others are made by main force ; address, ruse, terror, audacity, are elements of success for these kinds of enterprises.

In the present mode of making war, the carrying of a post, however strong it may be from its situation, would no longer have the importance formerly attached to it, unless it offered a strategic advantage susceptible of influencing the results of a great operation.

The taking or the destruction of an intrenched bridge, that of a grand convoy, that of a small fort barring important passages, like the two attacks which took place in 1799 upon the Fort of Lucisteig in the Grisons ; the taking of Leutasch and of Sharnitz by Ney in 1805 ; finally

---

* It is necessary to distinguish between the importance and the strength of a post, for a strong post is far from always being an important one.

the carrying of a post not fortified even but which should serve as grand depôt for provisions and munitions indispensable to the enemy, such are the enterprises which may recompense the risk to which a detachment would be exposed for their execution.

The Cossacks at times also attempted *coups de main* in the late wars ; the attack of Laon by Prince Lapoukin, those of Cassel and of Chalons, had advantages, but enter altogether nevertheless into the class of secondary enterprises the positive effect of which is to harrass and disquiet the enemy.

Whatever instruction could be given upon these kinds of enterprises in general, the memoirs of Moutluc and the strategems of Frontin, those old histories which one would believe of another world, will give more information than I can in this chapter ; the escalade, the surprise and the panic do not admit of being reduced to maxims.

Some have carried posts by filling up the ditches, sometimes with fascines, sometimes with wool sacks, even dung has been employed for it : others have succeeded by the means of ladders without which such an enterprise is rarely attempted ; finally they have used also cramp hooks attached to the hands and the shoes of the soldiers for climbing the rocks which command an entrenchment. Others have introduced themselves by the sewers, like the Prince Eugene at Cremona.

It is in the reading of these facts that we must seek, not precepts, but inspirations, if however, what has succeeded with one may serve as a rule for another. It would be desirable that some studious officer would apply himself to unite in one detailed historical abstract, all the most interesting *coup-de-mains ;* this would be rendering a signal service not only to the generals, but to each of the subordinates who may have to co-operate in like attempts, where often the intelligence of a single person may lead to success.

As for what concerns us, we have accomplished our task by indicating here their principal relations with the ensemble of operations. We refer besides to what has been said in the commencement of this article upon the manner of attacking field intrenchments, the only military operation which has any analogy to those *coups-de-main*, when they are made by main force.

CHAPTER V.

OF DIFFERENT MIXED OPERATIONS, WHICH PARTICIPATE AT THE SAME TIME OF STRATEGY AND OF TACTICS.

ARTICLE XXXVII.

PASSAGES OF STREAMS AND RIVERS.

The passage of small streams, upon which a bridge is found established, or where one can easily be thrown, does not present combinations which belong to grand tactics or to strategy; but the passage of great streams or rivers, such as the Danube, the Rhine, the Po, the Elbe, the Oder, the Vistula, the Inn, the Ticino, &c., are operations worthy of being studied.

The art of throwing bridges is a special knowledge, which belongs to the officers of pontooneers or sappers. It is not under this aspect that we shall treat these passages, but as an attack of a military position, and as a manœuvre of war.

The passage, in itself, is a tactical operation, but the determination of the point where it ought to be made, is connected with the grand operations which embrace the whole theatre of war. The passage of the Rhine by General Moreau in 1800, of which we have already spoken, may still serve as an example for causing to be appreciated this assertion. Napoleon, more skillful in strategy than his lieutenant, wished him to pass in mass at Schaffhausen to take in reverse the whole army of Kray, to anticipate it at Ulm, to cut it off from Austria, and to drive it back upon the Maine. Moreau, who had already a *tête de pont* at Basle, preferred to pass more commodiously upon the front of the enemy, to turning his extreme left, the tactical advantage appeared to him more sure than all the strategical; he preferred a certain half success to the chance of a victory which would have been decisive, but exposed to greater hazards. In the same campaign, the passage of the Po by Napoleon offered another example of the strategic importance which is attached to the choice of the point of passage; the army of reserve, after the combat of the Chiusella, could march by the left of the Po to Turin, or pass the river at Crescentino and march direct to Genoa; Napoleon preferred to pass the Ticino, to enter Milan, to unite there with Moncey, who came with twenty thousand men by the St. Gothard, then to pass the Po at Placentia, persuaded that he would more surely precede Melas upon that point, than if he changed direction too soon upon his line of retreat. The passage of the Danube at Donanwerth and Ingolstadt, in 1805, was an operation nearly of the same kind; the direction chosen became the first cause of the destruction of the army of Mack.

The suitable point in strategy is easily determined, after what we have said in Article 19, and it is not useless to recollect that in a passage of a river, as in every other operation, there are permanent or geographical decisive points, and others which are relative or eventual, since they result from the situation of the hostile forces.

If the point chosen unite strategic advantages to the tactical convenience of localities, this choice will leave nothing to be desired; but if it present local obstacles almost insurmountable, then it would be necessary to choose another, having care to prefer that which might be the nearest to the strategic direction which it would be important to attain. Independently of those general combinations, which should have an influence upon the choice of the point of passage, there is still another, which has reference to the places themselves. The best place will be that where the army, after having passed, shall be able to take its front of operations and its line of battle perpendicularly to the river, at least for the first marches, without being forced to divide itself into several corps upon different directions. This advantage will save it equally from the peril

of receiving battle with the river behind, as happened to Napoleon at
Essling.

This is enough upon the strategic combination which should decide
passages ; it is time to speak of their execution.   History is the best school
for studying the measures proper for securing their success.   The ancients
have made a marvel of that of the Granicus, which is but a rivulet.   In
this respect the moderns have greater actions to cite.

The passage of the Rhine at Tolhuys, by Louis XIV, is not the one
which has made the least noise, and it must be owned that it is worthy
of remark.

In our day, General Dedon has celebrated the two passages of the
Rhine at Kehl, and that of the Danube at Hochstaedt in 1800 : his work
should be consulted as classic for details ; now, precision in details is
everything for these kinds of operations.

Finally, three other passages of the Danube, and the ever-celebrated
one of the Beresina, surpassed all that had been seen until then of this
kind.   The first two were those which Napoleon executed at Essling and
at Wagram, in presence of an army of a hundred and twenty thousand
men, provided with four hundred pieces of artillery, and upon one of the
points where the bed of the river is the broadest ; it is necessary to read
the interesting narrative of it by General Pelet.   The third is that which
was executed by the Russian army at Satounovo in 1828 : although it
could not be compared with the preceding, it was very remarkable from
the excessive·difficulties which the localities presented, and from the nature of the efforts which it was necessary to make in order to surmount
them.   With regard to that of the Beresina,it was in every respect miraculous.   My object not being to enter here into historical details, I refer
my readers·to the special accounts of these events, and I shall give a summary of the general rules relative to those passages.

1st. It is essential to deceive the enemy as to the point of passage, in
order that he may not accumulate there his means of resistance.   Besides strategical demonstrations, there will yet be necessary false attacks
in proximity with the passage, in order to divide the means which the
enemy will there have assembled ; to this effect half of the artillery should
be employed in making a great noise upon every point where it is not
designed to cross ; whilst that the greatest silence should reign at the real
point where all the serious preparations should be directed.

2d. We ought as much as possible to protect the construction of
bridges, by directing the troops in boats upon the opposite banks, in

order to dislodge the enemy which should impede the works ; those troops should immediately take possession of villages, woods, or other obstacles in proximity.

3d. It is important also to place strong batteries of large calibre, not only for sweeping this opposite bank, but for silencing the artillery which the enemy would bring with the intention of battering the bridge as fast as it should be constructed ; to this end it is proper that the bank from whence the assailant is to depart should command a little the opposite bank.

4th. The neighborhood of a large island, near the hostile bank, offers great facilities to troops for debarking, as well as to the workmen. The neighborhood also of a small tributary stream, gives the means of uniting and concealing the preparations for the boats.

5th. It is well to choose a place where the river forms a reentrant bend or elbow, to the end of being able to assure the troops a certain landing, protected by batteries whose fire, crossed upon the avenue, would prevent the enemy from falling upon the batallions as they should pass.

6th. The placé fixed upon for throwing bridges ought to be in proximity with good routes upon the two banks, in order that the army may find easy communications after the passage, as well as for assembling. To this effect points where the slopes should be too steep, especially on the side of the enemy, should be avoided.

With regard to the defence of a passage, its rules should be of the same nature with those of the attack ; they ought then to have for their object the opposing of the measures above indicated ; the essential thing is to cause the course of the river to be watched by light corps, without pretending to defend it everywhere ; then to concentrate rapidly upon the menaced point, in order to burst upon the enemy when a part only of his army shall have crossed. It is necessary to do like the Duke of Vendôme at Cassano, and as did the Arch-Duke Charles on a larger scale at Essling in 1809—a memorable example, which cannot be too strongly recommended, although the conqueror did not derive from it all the fruit he expected.

We have already pointed out in article 21, the influence which the passages of rivers at the commencement of an enterprise or of a campaign may exercise upon the direction of lines of operations, it remains for us to examine that which they may have upon the strategical movements which might immediately follow them.

One of the greatest difficulties which present themselves after the passages, is to cover the bridges against the enemy without meanwhile cou straining too much the enterprises which the army might wish to undertake. When they have place, with a great numerical superiority, or at the end of great victories already gained, the thing is not so embarrassing ; but when they are executed at the beginning of a campaign, in presence of an enemy almost equal in forces, the case is different.

If a hundred thousand French pass the Rhine at Strasburg, or at Manheim, in presence of a hundred thousand Germans, the first thing they will have to do will be to push the enemy in three directions, the first to the front of them, even to the mountains of the Black Forest ; the second to the right, for covering the bridges on the side of the Upper Rhine ; and the third to the left, to cover those on the side of Mayence and of the Lower Rhine. This necessity leads to a deplorable parceling of forces ; but in order to diminish its inconvenience it is necessary to guard against thinking it incumbent to divide the army into three equal parts, or that it is necessary to keep up those detachments beyond a few days needful for being assured of the place of re-assembling of the hostile forces.

It cannot, however, be dissembled that this is one of the most delicate situations for a general-in-chief ; for, if he divides his army in order to cover his bridges, he may with one of these fractions encounter the bulk of the enemy's masses, which would overwhelm it ; if he unites his forces upon a single direction, and the enemy deceive him as to the point of his assembling, he might be exposed to see his bridges carried or destroyed, and to find himself compromised before having had time to gain a victory.

The most sure remedies will be to place his bridges near a city which can rapidly be put in condition to protect their defence, then to give his first operations all the vigor and rapidity possible by throwing himself successively upon the fractions of the hostile army, and punish them in such a manner as to remove from them the desire of troubling the bridges. In some cases we can add to those means the system of eccentric lines of operations ; if the enemy has divided his hundred thousand men into several corps, spread in a position of observation, and we move with an equal mass upon a single point in the vicinity of the centre of this cordon, the hostile corps which should find itself isolated at the centre, being quickly overthrown, we could then without risk form two masses of fifty thousand men, which, by taking a divergent direction, would surely disperse the isolated hostile fractions in an exterior direction, prevent them henceforward from re-uniting, and would remove them thus farther and farther from the bridges. But if the passage were effected, on the contrary, upon one of the extremities of the strategic front of the enemy by changing direction briskly upon that front which would be attacked in its whole extent, as Frederick attacked the Austrian line tactically at Leuthen in all its length, the army would have its bridges behind it, and would cover them in all its forward movements. It was thus that Jourdan, having passed at Dusseldorf (1795) upon the extreme right of the Austrians, could advance in all security upon the Maine; if he was repulsed it was because the French having a double and exterior line of operations, left a hundred and twenty thousand men paralyzed from Mayence to Basle, whilst Clair-fayt repulsed Jourdan upon the Lahn. But this circumstance could alter in nothing the evident advantage which a point of passage procures, established upon an extremity of the strategic front of the enemy. The generalissimo could adopt this system or that explained above for central masses at the moment of the passage, then afterwards excentric, according to the situation of the frontiers and of the bases, finally according to the positions of the enemy. These combinations, of which we have already said something in the article on lines of operations, have not appeared to me misplaced in this, since their relations with the position of bridges makes the principal point of the discussion.

It happens at times that superior reasons determine the attempt of a double passage upon the extent of the same front of operations, as occurred to Jourdan and to Moreau in 1796. If we gain by it on one side the advantage of having in need a double line of retreat, we have the inconvenience by operating thus upon the two extremities of the enemy's front, of forcing him so to speak, to assemble upon the centre, which would put him in condition to ruin separately the two armies. Such an operation will ever have deplorable consequences, when the affair shall be with a general capable of profiting from this violation of principles.

All that can be recommended upon the subject is to diminish the inconveniences of the double passage, by directing the weight of the forces at least upon that one of the two points which should then be decisive, then to bring the two corps towards each other as soon as possible in an interior direction, to prevent the enemy from overwhelming them separately. If Jourdan and Moreau had followed this maxim, and had united at Donanwert instead of moving exteriorly—far from being thrown back upon the Rhine, they would probably have obtained great successes in Bavaria.

As for the rest, this enters into double lines of operations, upon which we are not to return.

A·RTICLE XXXVIII.

ˋRETREATS AND PURSUITS.

Of all the operations of war, retreats are incontestably the most difficult. It is so true that the celebrated Prince de Ligne said, with his accustomed spirit, that he did not see how an army succeeded in retiring. When we reflect, indeed, upon the physical and moral condition in which an army finds itself when it fights retreating, in consequence of a lost battle, upon the difficulty of maintaining order in it, upon the disastrous chances which the least disorder may lead to, we comprehend why the most experienced generals have so much difficulty in resolving upon it.

What system is to be advised for a retreat? Is it necessary to combat desperately until the approach of night, to be able to execute it by favor of the darkness? Is it better not to wait until the last extremity, and to quit the field of battle when we can yet do it with a good countenance? Ought we to take, by a forced night march, the greatest possible start of the enemy, or rather to halt in good order at a half march, making a show of accepting anew the combat? Each of these modes, suitable in certain cases, might in others cause the total ruin of the army, and if the theory of war is impotent in some respects, it is certainly in that which relates to retreats.

If you wish to fight desperately until night, you may expose yourself to a complete defeat before this night has arrived; and then, if a forced retreat were to be made at the moment when darkness begins to envelope everything in its veil, how are you to prevent the decomposition of the army which no longer knows nor sees what it does? If, on the contrary, we quit the field of battle in open day, and without awaiting the last extremity, we may expose ourselves to losing the game at the moment when the enemy himself might renounce the continuance of his attacks, which might cause the troops, ever disposed to blame those prudent chiefs who fight in retreat before being evidently constrained to it, to lose all confidence. Moreover, who could guarantee that a retreat, executed in open day, before a somewhat enterprising enemy, may not degenerate into a rout?

When the retreat is finally commenced, it is not less embarrassing to decide whether it is necessary to force a march for gaining all the start possible, since this precipitation may accomplish the loss or safety of the army. All that it is possible to affirm upon this subject, is that, with a considerable army, it is better to make, in general, a slow retreat, with short marches and in good echelon order; because, then one has the means of forming rear guards sufficiently numerous for maintaining themselves a part of the day against the heads of the hostile columns. We shall return for the rest to these rules :—

Retreats are of divers kinds, according to the motive which determines them.

You retreat voluntarily before having fought, in order to lead the enemy upon a point less advantageous for him than that where he is found; it is a prudent manœuvre rather than a retreat. It was thus that Napoleon retired, in 1805, from Wischau upon Brunn, in order to lead the allies upon the point which suited him. It was thus that Wellington retreated from Quatre-Bras upon Waterloo. Finally, it was what I proposed to do before the attack of Dresden, when we had been informed of the arrival of Napoleon. I represented the necesssity of a march upon Dippodiswalde for choosing an advantageous field of battle; this idea was confounded with a retreat, and a chivalrous point of honor prevented a retrograde movement without fighting, which would nevertheless have avoided the catastrophe of the following day, (26th Aug., 1813.)

You retire also without being defeated in order to fly to a point menaced by the enemy, whether upon the flanks, or upon the line of retreat. When you march far from your depôts, in an exhausted country, you may be obliged to decamp in order to draw near to your magazines. Finally, you retire by compulsion after a lost battle, or at the end of an unsuccessful enterprise.

These different causes are not the only ones which modify the combinations of retreats, they vary according to the nature of the country, the distances to be passed over, and the obstacles which the enemy may oppose to them. They are especially dangerous when they are made in hostile countries; the farther the point of departure is removed from the frontiers, and from the base of operations, the more painful and difficult is the retreat.

From the famous retreat of the ten thousand, so justly celebrated, until the catastrophe which overwhelmed the French army in 1812, history does not offer a great abundance of remarkable retreats. That of Anthony, repulsed from Media, was more painful than glorious. That of the Emperor Julian, harrassed by the same Parthians, was a disaster. In more modern times, that which Charles VIII executed on returning from Naples, by cutting through the Italian army at Fornoua, was not of the least glorious.   The retreat of M. de Bellisle from Prague, does not merit the eulogies which have been lavished upon it.   Those which the King of Prussia executed after the raising of the siege of Olmutz, and after the surprise of Hochkirch, were very well directed, but could not count among distant retreats.   That of Moreau, in 1796, exalted by party spirit, was honorable, without being extraordinary.*   That which the Russian army executed, without allowing itself to be broken, from the Nieman to Moscow, in a space of two hundred and forty leagues, before an enemy like Napoleon, and a cavalry like that which the active and audacious Murat conducted, can certainly be placed above all the others. Doubtless it was facilitated by a multitude of circumstances, but that detracts nothing from its merit, if not as regards the strategic talent of the chiefs who directed the first period of it, at least as respects the steadiness and the admirable firmness of the body of troops which executed it.

Finally, although the retreat from Moscow was for Napoleon a bloody catastrophe, it cannot be denied that it was glorious for him and for his troops, at Krasnoi as at the Beresina ; for the skeleton of the army was saved, whilst not a man ought to have returned.   In this memorable event, the two parties covered themselves with equal glory, the chances alone differed like the results.

The magnitude of the distances and the nature of the country to be passed over, the obstacles to be dreaded from the enemy upon the flanks and rear, the superiority or inferiority that may be had in cavalry, the spirit of the troops; such are the principal causes which influence the fate of retreats, independently of the skillful dispositions which the chiefs may make for assuring them.

An army, falling back upon its line of magazines, may preserve its troops together, maintain order among them, and make its retreat with more security than one which has to canton, to subsist, and to extend itself to find cantonments.   It would be absurd to pretend that a French army, falling back from Moscow upon the Nieman, without any resources in provisions, wanting cavalry and draught horses, could do so with the same order and the same steadiness as the Russian army, well provided with everything, marching in its own country, and covered by an immense light cavalry.

---

* The retreat of Laccmbe from the Engadine to Altorf, and that of MacDonald by Pontremoli, after the defeat of the Trebbia, were as well as that of Suwaroff from the Muttenthal to Coire, glorious feats of arms, but partial and of short duration.

There are five ways of combining a retreat.

The first is to march en mass upon a single route;

The second is to echelon upon a single route, in two or three corps, marching at a day's distance from each other, in order to avoid confusion, especially in the *materiel ;*

The third consists in marching upon a same front, by several parallel routes leading to the same end ;

The fourth is to depart from two points distant from each other towards a concentric end ;

The fifth would be to march, on the contrary, by several excentric routes.

I do not speak of the particular dispositions of the rear guard ; it is understood that a good one ought to be formed and be sustained by a part of the reserves of cavalry. These kinds of dispositions are common to all sorts of retreats, and the question here is only the strategic points of view.

An army which falls back intact, with the intention of fighting when it shall have attained an expected reinforcement, or a strategic point at which it aims, ought to follow in preference the first system, because it is that which assures the most compactness to the different parts of the army, and allows it to sustain a combat whenever it wishes ; to that effect it only has to halt its heads of columns, and to form the remainder of the troops as they arrive.

This is not saying, nevertheless, that the army, adopting this system, ought to march as a whole, upon the grand routes, when it may find small lateral roads which would facilitate its movement.

Napoleon, in retiring from Smolensk, adopted the second system (by echelons at an entire march from each other,) and committed in that a fault, so much the more serious, that the enemy did not follow in his trail, but rather in a lateral direction, and chanced to fall almost perpendicularly in the midst of his isolated corps ; the three days of Krasnoi, so fatal to his army, were the result of it. This system of echelons upon the same route, can only have for its object to avoid being encumbered ; now it suffices that the interval between the time of departure of the corps be sufficiently great for the artillery to file off; it is useless to place an entire march between them ; it suffices to divide the army into two masses and a rear guard, at a half march from each other ; these masses, moving successively, and placing an interval of two hours between the departure of their army corps, would march without encumbrance at least in ordinary countries. At the St. Bernard and the Balkan other calculations were doubtless necessary.

I apply this idea to an army of from one hundred and twenty to one hundred and fifty thousand men, which shall have a rear guard of twenty or twenty-five thousand men, at about half a march distant, and of which the remainder will be divided into two masses of about sixty thousand each, equally camped in echelons, at the distance of three or four leagues from each other.

The two or three army corps of which each of these masses will be composed could be thus in echelons in the direction of the route, or else formed upon two lines across the route. In either case, if one corps of thirty thousand men is placed in march at 5 o'clock in the morning, and the other at 7 o'clock, there will be no fear of encumbering each other, except by extraordinary accident ; for the second mass, departing at the same hours at four leagues farther in rear, will arrive only at 12 or 2 o'clock in the positions quitted long since by the first.

When there are cross roads practicable at least for infantry and cavalry, it will diminish the interval so much the more. There is no need of adding, that in order to march thus, provisions are necessary, that the march of the third kind is in general preferable, since we march in order of battle ; finally, that, in long days and in warm countries, it is necessary to march alternately at night and at early morning. Moreover it is one of the most difficult branches of logistics to know how to combine well the starting and the halts of troops ; in retreats especially it is a capital point.

Many generals neglect to regulate the mode and time of halts, which is the cause of numberless disorders, in marches ; each division or brigade believing itself able to halt when its soldiers are a little fatigued, or find an agreeable bivouac. The more considerable the army, the more compactly it marches, the more important it is to regulate well the departures and halts, especially when night marches are decided upon. An untimely halt of a part of the column may do as much evil as a rout.

If the rear-guard be somewhat pressed, the army should be made to halt for relieving it by a fresh corps from the second mass, which will take position to this effect. The enemy seeing eighty thousand men formed, will think of halting, in order to unite his columns, then the retreat must recommence in the night, in order to regain ground.

The third method of retreat, that of following several parallel routes, is very suitable when those routes are sufficiently near to each other. But if they are too far removed apart, each of the wings of the army, separated from the others, might be separately compromised, if the enemy, directing the weight of his forces upon it, obliged it to receive battle.

The Prussian army, coming in 1806, from Magdeburg to gain the Oder, furnishes proof of this.

The fourth system, which consists in following two concentric routes, is without doubt the most suitable, when the troops are found removed from each other at the moment when the retreat is ordered ; nothing is then better than the rallying of one's forces, and the concentric retreat is the only means of succeeding in it.

The fifth mode indicated, is nothing else than the famous system of ex-centric lines, which I have attributed to Bulow, and combatted with so much earnestness in the first editions of my works, because I believed that there was no misunderstanding the sense of his text, nor the object of his system. I understood from his definition, that he recommended retreats starting from a given point, to be divided upon several divergent directions, as much for avoiding more easily the pursuit of the enemy, as for arresting him by menacing his flanks and his own line of operations. I have sternly censured such a system, for the reason that a beaten army is already feeble enough in itself, without weakening it still more by an absurd dispersion of its forces in presence of a victorious enemy.

Bulow has found defenders who have affirmed that I badly compre-hended the sense of his words, seeing that, by excentric retreats, he did not mean retreats made upon several divergent directions, but rather retreats, which, instead of being directed towards the centre of the base of opera-tions or towards the centre of the country, should lead in an excentric di-rection from this focus of operation by prolonging themselves upon the circumference of the frontier.

It is possible that I am indeed deceived as to his intention ; in that case my criticism would fall of itself, since I have strongly approved those kinds of retreats which I have, in truth, named parallel retreats. In fact, it seems to me that an army, quitting the convergent line which leads from the circle of the frontiers to the centre of the State, in order to direct itself to the right or to the left, would march rather in the direction nearly parallel with its frontiers, or with its front of operations and its base. Hence it seems also more rational to give the name parallel re-treats, to those which follow this latter direction, leaving the name ex-centric retreats for those which should depart from the front of operations in divergent directions.

However it may be concerning this dispute of words, for which the ob-scurity of the text of Bulow might be the only cause, I intend only to censure the divergent retreats, executed upon several radii, under the pretext of covering a greater extent of frontiers, and of menacing the enemy upon both of his flanks.

With those great words flanks, an air of importance is given to systems the most contrary to the principles of the art. An army in retreat is always inferior physically and morally, because it retires only in consequence of a series of reverses, or from its numerical inferiority. Must it be weakened then still more by disseminating it ? I do not combat retreats executed in several columns for rendering them more easy, when those columns shall be able to sustain each other; I speak of those which would be effected upon divergent lines of operations. I will suppose an army of forty thousand men in retreat before another of sixty thousand. If the first form four isolated divisions of about ten thousand men, could not the enemy, manœuvering with two masses of thirty thousand men each, turn, envelope, disperse and ruin successively all those divisions? What means will they have of escaping their fate? *that of concentrating.* Now this means being opposed to a divergent disposition, this system falls of itself.

I will invoke, to the support of my reasoning, the great lessons of experience. When the first divisions of the army of Italy were repulsed by Wurmser, Bonaparte reassembled them all at Roverbello, and although he had only forty thousand men, he defeated sixty thousand, because he had to fight isolated columns only. If he had made a divergent retreat, what would have become of his army and his conquests? Wurmser, after this first check, made an excentric retreat, by directing his two wings towards the extremities of his line of defense. What happened? The right, although favored by the mountains of the Tyrol, was beaten at Trente; Bonaparte directed himself afterwards upon the rear of the left, and destroyed it at Bassano and at Mantua.

When the Arch-Duke Charles yielded to the first efforts of the two French armies in 1796, would he have saved Germany by an excentric manœuvre ? Is it not on the contrary to the concentric direction of his retreat that Germany. owed its safety? Finally, Moreau, who had marched upon an immense development by isolated divisions, perceived that this inconceivable system was good for effecting his destruction when it was the question to fight and especially to retire; he concentrated his scattered forces, and all the efforts of the enemy were wasted before a mass which it was necessary to observe upon every point of a line of eighty leagues. After such examples, it seems to me that nothing could be said in reply.*

There are scarcely but two cases where divergent retreats could be admitted as extreme resources; the first, is when an army should have experienced a great check in its own country, and its disunited fractions should seek a powerful shelter under its fortifications. The second is in a national war, when each fragment of the army thus scattered would retire to serve as a nucleus to the rising of a province; but in a war truly military, it is an absurdity.

There is another combination of retreats, which has respect especially to strategy; it is to determine the case in which it is proper to make them perpendicularly, departing from the frontier towards the centre of the country, or to direct them parallelly to the frontier.† For example, Marshal Soult, abandoning the Pyrenees in 1814, had to choose between a retreat upon Bordeaux, which would have led him to the centre of France, or a retreat upon Toulouse by moving along the frontier of the Pyrenees. In the same manner Frederick, in retiring from Moravia, marched upon Bohemia, instead of regaining Silesia.

These parallel retreats are often preferable, inasmuch as they turn the enemy from a march upon the capitol of the State and upon the centre of its power; the configuration of the frontiers, the fortresses which are found there, the greater or less space which an army would find for moving, and re-establishing its direct communications with the centre of the State, are so many considerations which influence the opportuneness of these operations.

Spain, amongst others, offers very great advantages for this system. If a French army penetrate by Bayonne, the Spaniards have the choice of basing themselves upon Pampeluna and Saragossa, or upon Leon and the Asturias, which would make it impossible for their adversary to direct himself towards Madrid, leaving his narrow line of operations at the mercy of the Spaniards.

The frontier of the Turkish empire upon the Danube, would offer the same advantage for that power, if it knew how to profit by it.

France is equally very proper for this kind of war, especially when there does not exist in the country two political parties which may aspire to

---

* Ten years after the publication of this chapter, the concentric retreat of Barklay, and of Bagration saved the Russian afmy; although it did not prevent at first the success of Napoleon, it was the first cause of his loss.

† Those parallel retreats, if the defenders of Bulow must be believed, could be none other than those he has, it is said, recommended under the name excentric.

the possession of the capitol, and render its occupation decisive for the enemy. If the latter penetrate by the Alps, the French can act upon the Rhone and Saone, turning on the frontier to the Moselle on the one side, or to Provence on the other. If it penetrate by Strasburg, Mayence or Valenciennes, it is the same; the occupation of Paris would be impossible, or at least hazardous, so long as a French army intact should remain based upon its girdle of strong places. It is, for the rest, the same for all countries having double fronts of operations.*

Austria would not perhaps have the same advantages, because of the direction of the Rhetian and Tyrolean Alps and the course of the Danube; in truth Lloyd, considering Bohemia and the Tyrol as two bastions of which the line of the Inn forms the formidable curtain, seems on the contrary to present this frontier as the more advantageous for being defended by lateral movements. This assertion has received, as we have said, cruel denials in the campaigns of 1800, 1805 and 1809, but as the lateral defense has not been precisely well attempted there, the question is still susceptible of controversy.

All depends in my opinion upon respective situations and antecedents; if a French army coming from the Rhine by Bavaria, found the Allies upon the Lech and the Iser and should be in force, it would be very delicate to throw all the Austrian army into the Tyrol or into Bohemia, with the idea of arresting thus its direct march, for it would be necessary always to leave the half of this Austrian army upon the Inn in order to cover the approaches to the capitol; then there would be a fatal division in the forces, and if it were decided to concentrate the whole army in the Tyrol, leaving the route of Vienna open, the plan would be very dangerous in presence of an enterprising enemy. In Italy beyond the Mincio the lateral defense would be easy on the side of the Tyrol, and in Bohemia also against an enemy coming from Saxony.

But it is especially in applying it to Prussia that this system of parallel retreats offers all the variations of which it is susceptible, for it would be perfect against an army debouching from Bohemia upon the Elbe or upon the Oder, whilst that it would be altogether impossible, against a French army coming from the Rhine, or against a Russian army coming from the Vistula, unless Prussia should be allied to Austria. The cause of this difference is in the geographical configuration of the country,

---

* In all these calculations I suppose the forces nearly equal, if the invading army is twice as strong. then it may follow with the half of its troops that which retires parallelly, and carry the other half upon the capital; but with equal forces that would be impossible.

which permits and which even favors lateral movements in the direction of its great depth (from Memel to Mayence) but which would render them disastrous in the direction of the small space which the country offers from south to north (from Dresden to Stettin).

When an army puts itself in retreat, whatever may be the motive, there is also necessarily a pursuit.

A retreat, even the best ordered, executed with an army intact, gives always an advantage to him who pursues; but it is especially after a defeat and in distant countries that the retreat becomes always the most difficult operation of war, and its difficulties increase in proportion to the skill which the enemy displays in the pursuit.

The audacity and activity of the pursuit will be naturally influenced by the more or less enterprising character of the chiefs, but also by the physical and moral state of the two armies. It is difficult to give rules upon all the cases which a retreat may present but it is necessary to recognize :

1st. That in general it is advantageous to direct it upon the flank of the columns rather than upon the rear, especially when one is in his own country and can without danger take a diagonal direction or even one perpendicular to the line of operations of the adversary. However it is necessary not to allow one's self to be drawn into too wide movements, which might cause the trace of the enemy to be lost.

2d. That it is generally suitable to throw into the pursuit the greatest possible activity and audacity, especially when it is the result of a battle gained, because demoralization involves the loss of the beaten army.

3rd. That there are few cases where it is wise to make a bridge of gold to the enemy, although thus says the old Roman adage ; that could scarcely happen except in occasions where an army inferior in forces should have obtained an almost unhoped for success.

We cannot add anything to what we have just said of retreats, as connected with grand combinations. It remains for us to point out the tactical measures which may facilitate their execution.

One of the surest means of well executing a retreat is to familiarize the officers and soldiers with the idea that from whatever side the enemy may come, they run no more risk in fighting him by the rear than by the front, and to persuade them that the maintenance of order is the only means of saving a troop harrassed in a retrograde march. It is especially on those occasions that we can appreciate the advantages of a strong discipline which will ever be the best guaranty of the maintenance of order ; but to exact discipline it is necessary to assure subsistence, in order to prevent the troops dispersing for marauding.

It is well to place with the rear guard a chief gifted with a grea *sang-froid*, and officers of the staff who could reconnoitre in advance the favorable points where the rear guard might make a stand in order to suspend the march of the enemy, to the end of placing there the reserve of the rear guard with artillery.* It is necessary to relieve successively the echelon in such a manner as never to allow them to be pressed too closely.

The cavalry being able to rally rapidly on the main body, it will be comprehended that good masses of this arm facilitate much a slow and methodical retreat and give also the means of well scouting and flanking the route in order to prevent the enemy coming unawares to disturb the march of the columns and cut off a part of them.

It suffices generally that the rear guard hold the enemy at a half march from the main body; to expose it further off would be hazardous and useless; nevertheless when it shall have defiles behind it, and when they shall be well guarded by its troops it will be able to prolong a little its sphere of operations and remain a march from the army, for defiles equally facilitate a retreat when one is master of them, as they render it difficult when the enemy has seized them. If the army be very numerous and the rear guard strong in proportion, then it may well remain a march in rear; that depends on its strength, the nature of the country, and on the enemy with whom we have to do. If the latter becomes too pressing, it would be important not to allow ourselves to be crowded too close, especially if the army were yet in tolerably good order. It is proper in this case to halt from time to time and to fall unexpectedly upon the advanced guards of the enemy, as the Arch-Duke Charles did in 1796 at Neresheim, Moreau at Biberach and Kleber at Ukerath. Such a manœuvre almost always succeeds by the surprise which this offensive return causes in a troop which expects only to gather easy trophies.

Passages of rivers in retreat also offer combinations which are not without interest : if it be a small stream with permanent bridges, it is only a passage of an ordinary defile ; but if it be a river which has to be crossed upon bridges of boats, it is a more delicate manœuvre. All the precautions which can be prescribed, are limited to causing the parks to be taken

---

* The qualities which distinguish a good general of a rear guard are not common, especially in southern armies. Marshal Ney was the most perfect type which one could desire of this kind; the Russian army is favored in this respect, for the general spirit of its troops is necessarily partaken by the chiefs.

in advance in order not to be encumbered with them; this measure sufficiently indicates the propriety of the army halting at a half march at least
from the river. In this case, it will be well also that the rear guard be
held a little farther distant from the main body than usual, as far as the
localities of the country and the respective forces would permit. By this
means the army will have time to defile without being too closely pressed ;
it will be necessary only to combine the march of the rear guard in such
a manner that it be in position in advance of the bridges, when the last
troops of the main body shall effect their passage. This decisive moment
will appear without doubt suitable for relieving the rear guard by a fresh
corps, which should be disposed beforehand upon well reconnoitered ground ;
then the rear guard will traverse the intervals of this corps, in order to
pass the river before it; and the enemy astonished at finding troops fresh
and disposed to receive him well, will not attempt to press them : the night
will thus be gained without check, and the new rear guard will be able in
turn, to pass and to break the bridges.

It is understood that the troops, as they have passed, should form at
the issues of the bridges, and post their batteries in such a manner as to
protect the corps left to hold out against the enemy.

The dangers of such a passage in retreat, and the nature of the precautions which may facilitate it, sufficiently indicate that the best mode
of favoring it would be to take in advance one's measures for constructing an intrenched tête-de-pont upon the point where the bridges will have
been thrown. In the case where time would not permit the construction
of a regular one, they will be able to supply it by a few redouts well
armed, which will be of great utility for protecting the retreat of the last
troops.

If the passage of a great river offers so many delicate chances when
one is followed in rear by the enemy, it is an affair much more difficult
still when the army finds itself assailed at the same time in front and rear,
and the river to be crossed is guarded by an imposing corps.

The doubly celebrated passage of the Beresina,.by the French, is one
of the most remarkable examples of such an operation ; never was an
army found in a more desperate situation, and extricated itself from it
more gloriously and more skillfully. Pressed by famine, overwhelmed by
the cold, removed five hundred leagues from its base, assailed in front and
rear on the banks of a marshy river, and in the midst of vast forests, how
could it hope to escape ? Doubtless it paid dearly for that honor ; doubtless the fault of Admiral Tschitchagoff contributed powerfully to extricate it from its embarrassment, but the army made none the less heroic

efforts to which we should render homage. We do not know which to admire most, the plan of operations which brought the Russian armies from the depths of Moldavia, from Moscow and Polotsk, upon the Beresina, as to a rendezvous of peace—a plan which came near bringing about the capture of their formidable adversary, or the admirable constancy of the lion thus pursued, and who succeeded in opening himself a passage.

Not to allow ourselves to be pressed too closely, to deceive the enemy as to the point of passage, to burst upon the corps which bars our retreat, before that which follows in rear can rally to its assistance, are the only precepts to give. There may be added thereto that of never placing ourselves in a similar position, for it is rare that we can extricate ourselves from it.

If the retreating army ought to do everything to secure its bridges from insult, either by a regular *tête-de-pont*, or by a line of redouts which protect at least the rear guard, it is natural also that the pursuing enemy take every possible measure for destroying the bridges. When the retreat is made descending the course of a river, he may throw upon it wooden buildings, fire ships, mills, as the Aurtrians did against the army of Jourdan, in 1796, near Neuweied upon the Rhine, where they came near compromising the army of the Sambre and Mense. The Arch-Duke Charles did as much in 1809 at the famous passage at Essling. He broke the bridge of the Danube, and brought Napoleon to the brink of ruin.

There are few means of placing a bridge secure from such attacks, unless we have time to prepare stockades of piles. We may also anchor, by cables, a few boats for arresting the materials thrown upon the current, and for having the means of extinguishing the fire ships.

ARTICLE XXXIX.

CANTONMENTS AND WINTER QUARTERS.

So much has been written upon this matter, and it pertains so indirectly to our subject, that we shall say but a few words upon it.

Cantonments in open war are, in general, a rather delicate operation ;

however compactly they may be made, it is always difficult to have them sufficiently so not to be exposed to the enemy. A country where there is an abundance of large cities, like Lombardy, Saxony, the low countries, Arabia, old Prussia, presents more facilities for establishing quarters therein than countries where cities are rare. Not only are resources there found for the subsistence of troops, but shelters are found near to each other, which permit the maintaining divisions together. In Poland, in Russia, in a part of Austria and France, in Spain, in Southern Italy, it is more difficult to establish ourselves in winter quarters.

Formerly, each party entered them respectively at the end of October, and contented themselves with taking reciprocally a few battalions too isolated at advanced posts; it was a partisan warfare.

The surprise of the Austrian winter quarters by Turenne, in Upper Alsacé, in 1674, is one of the operations which best indicate what can be undertaken against hostile cantonments, and the precautions which should be taken on our side, in order that the enemy do not form the same enterprises.

To establish cantonments very compactly, and upon a space as extended in depth as in breadth, to the end of avoiding too long a line, always easy to pierce and impossible to rally; to cover them by a river or by a first line of troops barracked and supported by field works; to fix upon places of concentration which may in every case be attained in advance of the enemy; to cause the avenues to the army to be scoured by permanent patrols of cavalry; finally, to establish alarm signals for the case of a serious attack. These are, in my opinion, the best maxims that could be given.

In the winter of 1807, Napoleon cantoned his army behind the Passarge in the face of the enemy; the advanced guards alone were barracked in proximity with the cities of Gutstadt, Osterode, &c. This army exceeded a hundred and twenty thousand men, and there was much skill necessary to maintain and nourish it in this position until the month of June. The country favored, it is true, this system, and we do not find everywhere one as suitable.

An army of a hundred thousand men may find compact winter quarters in countries where cities abound, and of which we have spoken above. When the army is more numerous, the difficulty is increased; it is true, however, that, if the extent of quarters is augmented in proportion to the numerical force, it must be owned also that the means of resistance to oppose to a hostile irruption is increased in the same progression: the essential point is to be able to unite fifty or sixty thousand men in four and twenty hours; with this force, and the certainty of seeing it augmented still, continually, we may resist until the assembling of the army, however numerous it may be.

In spite of that, it must be admitted that it will ever be a delicate affair to canton when the enemy, remaining united, should wish to obstruct it, and hence it should be concluded that the only sure means for the repose of an army during winter, or in the midst of a campaign, is to have its quarters secured by a river or an armistice.

ARTICLE XL.

DESCENTS.

Descents are one of the operations of war the most rarely to be seen, and which may be ranged in the number of the most difficult, when they take place in the presence of a well prepared army.

Since the invention of artillery, and the changes which it has necessarily produced in the Navy, transport vessels are too subordinate to colossal three deckers, armed with a hundred thunderbolts of war, to be able to effect descents without the assistance of a numerous fleet of men-of-war, which keep the sea at least until the moment of debarkation.

Before this invention, vessels of transport were at the same time vessels of war; they moved at need by the oar, were light, and could run along the coasts; their number was proportioned to the troops to be embarked, and apart from the chance of tempests, we could almost combine the operations of a fleet like those of an army. Therefore does ancient history offer the example of greater debarkations than modern times.*

Who does not recall the great armaments of the Prussians in the Black Sea, the Basphorus and the Archipelago? Those innumerable armies of Xerxes and Darius, transported to Thrace, to Greece; the numerous expeditions of the Carthagenians and the Romans, to Spain and

---

* I have given, in the preceding expedition, a long notice of the principal expeditions beyond the sea; if space permits, I will reproduce it at the end of this volume.

to Sicily ; the expedition of Alexander to Asia Minor; those of Cæsar to England and to Africa ; those of Germanicus to the mouths of the Elbe ; the Crusades ; the expeditions of the people of the north to England, to France, and even to Italy ?

Since the invention of cannon, the too celebrated *Armada* of Philip II was the only colossal enterprise until that which Napoleon formed against England in 1803. All the other expeditions beyond the sea were partial operations ; those of Charles V, and of Sebastian of Portugal, upon the Coast of Africa ; several descents, like those of the French upon the United States of America, upon Egypt and St. Domingo ; those of the English upon Egypt, Holland, Copenhagen, Antwerp, Philadelphia, all enter into the same category. I do not speak of the project of Hoche against Ireland, for it did not succeed, and it shows all the difficulty of these kinds of enterprises.

The large armies which the great States keep up at this day, does not admit of their being attacked by descents of thirty or forty thousand men. We can then only form similar enterprises against secondary States, for it is very difficult to embark a hundred or a hundred and fifty thousand men, with the immense equipment of artillery, munitions, cavalry, &c.

Meanwhile, we have been on the point of seeing resolved in our day this immense problem of *grand descents*, if it be true that Napoleon ever really entertained the serious project of transporting his hundred and sixty thousand veterans from Boulogne into the bosom of the British Islands ; unfortunately, the non-execution of that colossal project has left an impenetrable veil over this grave question.

It was not impossible to unite fifty French vessels-of-the-line in La Manche, deceiving the English; this *rëunion* was on the eve of being effected, hence it was not then impossible, if the wind favored the enterprise, for the flotilla to pass in two days, and to effect the debarkation. But what would have become of the army if a gale of wind dispersed the fleet of war vessels, and if the English, returned in force in *La Manche*, defeated it or constrained it to regain its ports ?

Posterity will regret, for the sake of the example to ages to come, that this immense enterprise had not been brought to its close, or at least attempted. Doubtless many a brave man would have perished in it ; but have not those brave men been less usefully destroyed on the plains of Suabia, of Moravia, of Castile, in the mountains of Portugal, or in the forests of Lithuania? What mortal would not be glorified for contributing to the decision of the greatest cause that has ever been debated between two great nations? At least will our posterity find, in the preparations which were made for this descent, one of the most important lessons which this memorable age has furnished for the study of military men and statesmen. The labors of every kind performed on the coasts of France from 1803 to 1805, will be one of the most extraordinary monuments of the activity, foresight and skill of Napoleon; they cannot be too highly commended for the study of young military men. But admitting the possibility even of succeeding in a great descent, undertaken upon a coast as neighboring as Boulogne is to Dover, what success could be promised from it, if such an *Armada* had a longer navigation to make to attain its end? What means are there of moving such a multitude of small vessels, even for two days and two nights? and to what chances would not one be exposed by engaging in such a navigation in a high sea, with light pinnaces? Besides that, the artillery, the munitions of war, equipments, provisions, the fresh water necessary to be embarked with this multitude of men, require an immense preparation and equipage.

Experience has demonstrated the difficulties of a distant expedition, even for a corps which does not exceed thirty thousand men. Hence it is evident that a descent can be effected with such a force only in four hypotheses :—

1st. Against colonies, or isolated possessions ;

2d. Against powers of the second rank, which could not be immediately sustained

3d. In order to effect a temporary diversion, or to seize a post, the occupation of which for a given time would have a high importance ;

4th. For a diversion, at the same time political and military, against a State already engaged in a great war, and whose troops should be employed far from the point.

These kinds of operations are difficult to subject to rules : to deceive the enemy as to the point of debarkation ; to choose an anchorage where it can be done simultaneously ; to exercise all the activity possible, and to seize promptly upon a point of support in order to protect the successive development of the troops ; to land immediately the artillery, to give assurance and protection to the troops disembarked ; this is nearly everything which can be recommended to the assailant.

The great difficulty of such an operation arises from the fact that the transport vessels never being able to approach the shore, it is necessary to place the troops on the few shallops which follow the fleet, so that the descent is long and successive, which gives the enemy great advantages, however little he may be prepared. If the sea be the least rough, the fate of the disembarking troops will be much hazarded; for what can infantry do, huddled in the shallops, battered by the waves, generally tried by sea sickness, and nearly out of condition to use their arms?

With regard to the defender, he can only be advised not to divide his forces too much in order to cover everything. It is impossible to furnish all the shores of a country with coast batteries, and with battalions to defend them; but it is necessary, at least, to cover the approaches to those points where there are great establishments to protect. It is necessary to have signals in order to know promptly the point of debarkation, and to unite, if it be possible, all our means before the enemy has taken solid footing with all his.

The configuration of the coast will as much influence upon the descent as upon the defense. There are countries where coasts are steep, and offer few points accessible at the same time to vessels and to the troops which it is the question to land; then those known points, being few in number, are more easy to watch, and the enterprise on that account becomes more difficult. Finally, descents offer a strategic combination which it is useful to point out. It is, that the principle which forbids a continental army to direct its principal forces between the sea and the hostile army, requires, on the contrary, that the army which operates a descent, preserve always its principal force in communication with the shore, which is at the same time its line of retreat and base of supply. For the same reason his first care should be to assure himself of a fortified port, or, at least, of a tongue of land easy to intrench, and in reach of a good anchorage, so that, in case of reverse, the re-embarkation can be made without too much precipitation and loss.

CHAPTER VI.

LOGISTICS, OR THE PRACTICAL ART OF MOVING ARMIES.

ARTICLE XLI.

A FEW WORDS UPON LOGISTICS IN GENERAL.

Is logistics merely a science of detail, or is it on the contrary a general science, forming one of the most essential parts of the art of war? or finally might it be only an expression consecrated by use, to designate vaguely the different branches of the staff service, that is to say, the divers means of applying the speculative combinations of the art, to effective operations?

These questions will appear singular to those who are in the firm persuasion that there is nothing more to say upon war, and that it is wrong to seek new definitions when all seems to them so well defined. As for myself, who am persuaded that good definitions lead to clear conceptions, ·I own that I am almost embarassed to resolve those questions in appearance so simple.

In the first editions of this work, I have, after the example of many military men, ranged logistics in the class of details of execution of the staff service, which make the object of the regulations of the field service, and of a few special instructions upon the corps of quarter-masters. This opinion was the result of prejudices consecrated by time; the word logistics is derived, as we know, from that of *major general des logis*, (translated in German by that of *Quartiermeister*,) a kind of officers whose functions were formerly to lodge or encamp the troops, to direct the columns, and to place them upon the ground. This was the limit of logistics which, as we see, embraced nevertheless ordinary castrametation. But after the new manner of making war without camps, movements were more complicated, and the staff had also more extensive attributes. The chief of the staff was charged with transmitting the thoughts of the generalissimo upon the farthest removed points of the theatre of war, to procure him all the documents for basing his operations. Associated in his combinations, called upon to transmit them, to explain them, and even to watch over their execution as a whole, as well as of their least details, his functions extend necessarily to all the operations of a campaign.

From that time, the science of a chief of staff was to embrace also the different parts of the art of war, and if it be this which is designated under the name of logistics, the two works of the Arch-Duke Charles, the voluminous treatise of Guibert, of Laroche-Aymon, Bousmard, and of the Marquis de Ternay, would scarcely suffice to sketch the incomplete course of such a *logistique*, for it would be nothing less than the science of the application of all the military sciences.

From what precedes, it seems to result naturally that the ancient logistics could no longer suffice to designate the science of the staff, and that the present functions of this corps would still require to be reduced to form, partly into a body of doctrines, partly into regulating dispositions, if it were wished to give it any instruction which should fully respond to its object. It would be for governments to take the initiative, by publishing well considered regulations, which, after having traced all the duties and the attributes of the chiefs and officers of the staff, would be followed by clear and precise instructions for tracing for them also the methods most proper for fulfilling those duties.

The Austrian staff had formerly such regulating instructions; but somewhat superanuated, it was found more appropriate to the old methods than to the new system.

This work is for the rest, the only one of that kind which has reached me; I do not doubt that there exist others, either published, or secret; but I frankly own my ignorance upon this subject. A few generals, like

Grimoard and Thieubaut, have brought to light staff manuels; the new royal corps of France has caused to be printed several partial instructions, but a satisfactory whole exists yet nowhere. I believe that General Boutourlin has the project of publishing soon an instruction addressed to his officers when he was quarter-master general, and we can only wish that it be realized without delay, for it cannot fail to throw much light upon this interesting subject, upon which there yet remains much to say.

If it be acknowledged that the ancient logistics was only a science of details for regulating every-thing material in regard to marches; if it be asserted that the functions of the staff embrace at this day the most elevated functions of strategy, it must be admitted also that logistics is no longer merely a part of the science of the staff, or rather that it is necessary to give it another development, and to make of it a new science, which will not only be that of the staff, but that of generals-in-chief.

In order to be convinced of this, let us enumerate the principal points that it ought to embrace, in order to comprehend all that which relates to the movements of armies, and to the enterprises which result from them.

1. To cause to be prepared beforehand all the material objects necessary for putting the army in motion, that is to say, for opening the campaign. To draw up the orders, instructions and routes, (*Marschroute*) for assembling it and putting it afterwards in action.

2. To draw up all the orders of the general-in-chief for the different enterprises, also the plans of attack for anticipated or premeditated combats.

3. To concert with the chiefs of engineers and artillery, the measures to be taken for putting in security the different posts necessary to the establishment of the depôts, as also those which it would be proper to fortify to the end of facilitating the operations of the army.

4. To order and direct the reconnoisances of every kind, and to procure as well by this means as by espionage, information as exact as possible of the positions and movements of the enemy.

5. To take all measures for combining the movements ordered by the general-in-chief. To concert the marches of the different columns, to the end that they be made with order and harmony, to be assured that all the means used for rendering these marches at the same time easy and certain, be prepared to that effect; to regulate the mode and time of halts.

6. To compose and direct well by good instructions the advanced and rear guards, as well as the corps detached, either as flankers or with other

destinations. To provide those different corps with all the objects necessary for accomplishing their mission.

7. To resolve upon the forms and instructions to the chief of corps or their staffs, for divers methods of distributing the troops of the columns within reach of the enemy, also for forming them the most suitably when it shall be necessary to get into line for combat, according to the nature of the ground and the kind of enemy to be encountered.*

8. To indicate to the advanced guards, and other detached corps, points of assembling well chosen, for the case in which they should be attacked by superior forces, and to cause them to know what support they may expect to find at need.

9. To order and to watch over the march of the parks of equipage of munitions, of provisions and ambulances, as well in the columns as in the rear, in such a manner that they do not constrain the troops, at the same time remaining in proximity with them; to take measures of order and of security, either in march or in quarters and *wagenburg,* (barricades of wagons.)

10. To look to the successive arrival of convoys destined to replace the provisions or munitions consumed. To assure the assembling of all the means of transport, as well of the country as of the army, and to regulate their employment.

11. To direct the establishment of camps, and to regulate the service for their security, order and police.

12. To establish and to organize the lines of operations and staple lines of the army, as well as the communications of detached corps with those lines. To designate officers capable of organizing and commanding the rear of the army ; to watch over the security of the detachments and convoys ; to provide them with good instructions ; to watch also over the maintainance of the means of communication between the army and its base.

13. To organize, upon this line, the depôts of convalescents, of disabled, of the feeble, the movable hospitals, the workshops ; to provide for their safety.

14. To keep an exact note of all the detachments formed, either upon the flanks or upon the rear ; to watch over their fate and their return, so soon as they shall be no longer necessary ; to give them at need a centre of action, and to form of them strategic reserves.

15. To organize marching battalions, or companies for collecting together isolated men, or small detachments going from the army to the base of operations, or from this base to the army.

---

* The question is here general instructions and forms, and not repeated for each daily movement. This would be impracticable.

16. In case of sieges, to order and watch over the service of the troops in the trenches, and to concert with the chiefs of engineers upon all the labors to be prescribed to those troops, and upon their conduct in sorties, as well as in assaults.

17. To take in retreats, the precautionary measures necessary for assuring their order ; to place relay troops, whose duty it shall be to sustain and relieve those of the rear guard ; to charge intelligent officers of the staff with the reconnoissance of all the points where the rear gurds will be able to resist with success, in order to gain time ; to provide in advance the movement of the *impedimenta*, to the end of abandoning nothing of the *materiel;* to maintain in them a strict order, and to take precautions for watching over their security.

18. For cantonments, to make the distribution of them between the different corps, to indicate to each of the army corps the place of general rendezvous in the event of an alarm, to prescribe measures of *surveillance*, and to see that the regulations are punctually executed.

Upon the examination of this vast nomenclature, which might still be increased by many minute articles, every one will exclaim that all these duties are as much those of the generalissimo as those of the staff ; this is a truth which we have just this moment proclaimed, but it is incontestable also that it is precisely in order that the general-in-chief may be able to devote all his care to the supreme direction of operations, that he has been given a staff charged with the details of execution ; hence all their attributes are necessarily in common, and woe to the army when those authorities cease to make but one ; that happens meanwhile only too frequently, first, because generals are men, and have all their defects, and then because there is not wanting in the army, interests or pretentions in rivalry with the chiefs of the staff.*

There could not be expected in our summary a complete treatise for regulating all the points of this almost universal science of the staff ; for in the first place, every country assigns to this corps a more or less extended sphere of action, so that there would be necessary a different treatise for every army ; then many of those details are found as much in the works above cited as in that of Colonel Lallemand, entitled Treatise on the Secondary Operations of War ; in that of Marquis de Ternay ; finally, in the first work of the Arch-Duke, entitled *Grundsatze der hohern Kriegskunst.*

---

* The chiefs of the artillery, of the engineers and of the administration, all pretend to work with the general-in-chief, and not with the chief of the staff. Doubtless nothing should prevent the direct relations of those authorities with the general-in-chief; but he ought to labor with them in presence of the chief of the staff, and to send him all their correspondence ; otherwise there would be confusion.

I will limit myself then to presenting a few ideas on the first articles of the nomenclature which precedes.

1. The measures which the staff should take to prepare for the entrance into the field, embrace all those which are of a nature to facilitate the success of the first plan of operations. We ought naturally to be assured by inspection of the different services, that all the *materiel* is in good condition; the horses, the carriages or caissons, the teams, the harness, the shoeing ought to be examined and completed. The pontoon train, the chests of engineer implements, the *materiel* of the artillery, the siege train, if it is to be moved, that of the field hospital, in a word, all that constitutes the *materiel* ought to be verified and put in good condition.

If the campaign be opened in the neighborhood of great rivers, it will be necessary to prepare beforehand gun boats and flying bridges, to cause to be collected all the means of embarkations on the points and at the bank where it is desired to use them. Intelligent officers will reconnoitre the points the most favorable, as well for the embarkation as for the debarkation, preferring the localities which offer the most certain chances of success, for a first establishment upon the opposite bank.

The staff will indicate all the routes which will be necessary to lead the different corps of the army upon the points of assembling, applying themselves especially to directing the marches in such a manner as to do nothing to warn the enemy relative to the enterprises that it should be designed to form.

If the war is offensive, one will confer with the chiefs of engineers upon the labors to be executed in proximity with the base of operations, in the case where têtes-de-ponts or intrenched camps should there be constructed.

If the war is defensive, those labors will be ordered between the first line of defense and the second base.

2. An essential part of logistics is, without contradiction, that which concerns the drawing up of dispositions for marches or attacks, resolved upon by the general-in-chief, and transmitted by the staff. The first quality of a general, after that of knowing how to form good plans, will, unquestionably be to facilitate the execution of his orders by the lucid manner in which they shall be written. Although this is in reality the business of his chief of staff, it will ever be from the commander-in-chief that will emanate the merit of his dispositions if he be a great captain; in the contrary case the chief of staff will supply this as much as possible, by concerting well with the responsible chief.

I myself have seen employed two quite opposite systems for this important branch of the service ; the first, which may be called the old school, consists in giving every day, for the movements of the army, general dispositions filled with minute and, in some instances, scholastic details, all the more misplaced, as they are ordinarily addressed to chiefs of corps sufficiently experienced not to be conducted in leading strings, like sub-lieutenants just from school.

The other system is that of the isolated orders given by Napoleon to his marshals, prescribing to each what concerned him particularly, and limiting himself at most to giving them a knowledge of the corps destined to operate in common with them, either to the right or to the left, but never tracing for them the ensemble of the operations of the whole army.* I have had reason to be convinced that he acted thus systematically, either for covering the *ensemble* of his combinations by a mysterious veil, or from the fear that orders more general happening to fall into the hands of the enemy would aid the latter to defeat his projects.

Doubtless it is very advantageous to keep one's enterprises secret, and Frederick the Great said with reason that if his night-cap knew what he had in his head, he would throw it into the fire. This secresy might be practicable in times when Frederick encamped with all his army lying around him ; but upon the scale on which Napoleon manœuvred, and with the present mode of making war, what harmony could be expected on the part of generals who should be absolutely ignorant of what passes around them.

Of these two systems, the last appears to me preferable ; however, a medium might be adopted between the laconism often carried to excess by Napoleon, and the minute verbiage which prescribed to experienced generals such as Barclay, Kleist and Wittgenstein, the manner in which they should break by platoons, and reform on arriving at their positions ; a puerility all the more lamentable that it became impracticable in the face of the enemy.† It will suffice, in my opinion, to give to the generals

---

* I think that at the passage of the Danube before Wagram, and at the beginning of the second campaign of 1813, Napoleon deviated from his custom by sketching a general order.

† I shall be reproached, perhaps, for interdicting here to chiefs of the general staff, those same details which I place above in the number of their important duties; which would be unjust. Those details are, in fact, within the range of the staff, which is not saying that the Major General cannot confide them to the delegates in each of the army corps marching separately. He will have sufficient to do to direct the whole, and to watch particularly over the marches of the main body which ordinarily accompany the general headquarters of the army. We see then that there is no contradiction.

special orders for what concerns their army corps, and to join to them a few lines in cipher to indicate to them, in a few words, the *ensemble* of the operation, and the part which is reserved to them. In default of this cypher, a verbal order will be .confided to an officer capable of rightly conceiving it, and of rendering it exactly. Indiscretion would no longer be feared, and the *ensemble* of the operations would be assured.

Be this as it may, the draughting of those dispositions is in itself a very important thing, although it does not always accomplish what might be expected from it; every one writes his instructions according to his views, his character, his capacity, and nothing could better indicate the degree of merit of the chiefs of an army, than the attentive perusal of the instructions which they have given to their lieutenants—it is the best biography that could be desired.

But it is time to quit this digression, in order to come to the article upon marches.

3. The army being assembled, and wishing to set about any enterprise whatever, the question will be to put it in motion with all the harmony and precision possible, taking all the measures in use for keeping it well informed, and covering it in its movements.

There are two kinds of marches, those which are made out of view of the enemy, and those which have place in his presence when the question is to retire, or attack him. These marches, especially, have undergone great changes in the late campaigns. Formerly, armies seldom attacked each other until after having been several days in presence; then the attacking party caused to be opened by the pioneers parallel roads for the different columns. Now they attack more promptly, and are contented with existing roads. It is essential, however, when an army is in march, that pioneers and sappers follow the advanced guards to mutiply the issues to overcome difficulties, to throw at need small bridges over the streams, and to assure frequent communication between the various army corps.

In the present manner of marching, the calculation of time and of distances has become more complicated; the columns of an army all having different spaces to pass over, it is necessary to know how to combine the moment of their departure and their instructions :—1st, with the distances which they have to traverse ; 2d, with the more or less considerable *materiel* that each will drag in its train ; 3d, with the more or less difficult nature of the country ; 4th, with the reports as to the obstacles which the enemy may oppose to them ; 5th, with the degree of importance there should be as to their march being concealed or open.

In this condition of things, the means which appear the most sure and the most simple for ordering the movements, either of great corps forming the wings of the army, or of all those which should not march with the column where the general headquarters are found, will be to trust for their details to the experience of the generals commanding these corps, having care to habituate them to a great punctuality. Then it will suffice to indicate to them the point and the object which they seek to attain, the route which they are to take, and the hour at which it is expected that they will arrive in position. Well understood that they are to be made acquainted with the corps which should march either with them or upon the lateral routes to the right and to the left, in order that they may be able to regulate themselves accordingly; finally they will be informed of what is known as to the presence of the enemy, and will have indicated to them a direction of retreat, if they should be constrained to one.*

All the details which should here tend to prescribe daily to the chiefs of those corps the manner of forming their columns and of putting them in position, are pedantries more injurious than useful. To require that they march habitually according to all the rules or usages adopted, is a necessary thing; but they must be left the latitude of organizing their movements so as to arrive at the hour and the point indicated, under pain of sending them from the army if they fail in it by their fault or their ill will. In retreats, nevertheless, which should be made in echelons upon a single route, it would be necessary to take precise measures for departures and halts.

As a matter of course, each column should have its small advanced guard and its flankers, in order to march according to the requisite precautions, and it is proper, even when they should march as a second line, that at their head there be found always a few pioneers and sappers of the divisions, with implements for opening the necessary marches, or to repair the accidents which might happen; some of these workmen should be assigned to each column of the park. For the same reason a light equipage of trestles, for throwing small bridges, will always be of great utility.

4. An army often marches preceded by a general advanced guard, or what is more frequent in the modern system, the main body and each of the wings have their particular advanced guard. It is rather common

---

* Napoleon never did it, because he pretended that one ought never to believe beforehand in the possibility of being beaten. In many marches it is, in fact, a useless precaution, but in very many cases it is indispensable.

for the reserves and the centre to march together with the general head-quarters, and according to every probability the general advanced guard, where there shall be one, will follow the same direction, so that half of the army will be thus agglomerated upon the central route. It is in those circumstances especially that it is necessary to know well how to take measures for avoiding encumbrance. It also happens, at times, that great blows, requiring to be directed upon a wing, the reserves and the general headquarters, even sometimes the general advanced guard are transported to the same side; in this case, all that which is indicated for the movements of the centre will be equally practicable and advisable.

It is essential that the advanced guards be accompanied by good officers of the staff, capable of judging well of the movements of the enemy, and of rendering an account of them to the general-in-chief in order to enlighten his resolutions, which the commandant of the advanced guard will also do on his part. Of course, a general advanced guard ought to be composed of light troops of all arms; some choice troops as a main body, a few dragoons equipped for fighting on foot, horse artillery, pontoniers, sappers, &c., with light trestles and pontoons for passing small rivers, a few carbiniers, good marksmen, will not be misplaced; and a topographical officer should equally follow to take a rough sketch of the country to a half league or more, from each side of the route. Finally, it is indispensable to add to it the irregular cavalry as scouts, as much for sparing the good cavalry, as because the irregular troops are the most apt at this service.

5. In proportion as the army advances and is removed from its base, the laws of a good *logistique* indicate the necessity of organizing the line of operations and staple lines, which should serve as a bond between the army and this base. The staff will divide these storehouses into districts, of which the chief place shall be in the city the most important for its resources in lodgings and in supplies of every kind; if there be a military post, the principal place will be established there in preference.

The storehouses placed at the distance of from five to ten leagues, according to existing cities; but, on an average of seven or eight leagues, would thus be to the number of fifteen upon a line of one hundred leagues, and would form from three to four magazine brigades. Each one of them would have a commander with a detachment of troops or of convalescent soldiers, for regulating the quarters, and to serve at the same time as a protection to the authorities of the country, (when they remain;) they will furnish safeguards to the post relays, and the necessary escorts; the commandant will see to the good condition of the routes and bridges.

As much as possible there ought to be made small magazines, and a park of a few wagons, in each of the depôts, or at least at the principal places of the brigades.

The command of the territorial divisions will be confided to provident and capable general officers, for upon their operations often depend the security of the communications of the army.* Those divisions can even, according to circumstances, be transformed into strategic reserves, as we have said in Article 24; some good battalions, aided by detachments unceasingly going from the army to its base, and from the base to the army, will almost always suffice for keeping up the communications.

6. With regard to measures half logistical, half tactical, by means of which the staff should bring the troops from the order of march to the different orders of battle, it is a study as important as it is minute. The three works which we have cited, have sufficiently sifted this matter to dispense with our following them on grounds so arduous; those questions could only be treated by taking up those details which make the merit of these works, and which are altogether beyond the limits of this. Besides, what would remain to us to say after the two volumes which M. de Ternay and Colonel Koch, his commentator, have devoted to the demonstration of all the logistical combinations of the movements of troops, and of the different processes of formation? And if many of those processes are very difficult to put in practice before an enemy, their utility will be acknowledged, at least, for the preparatory movements executed out of his reach; thanks to that excellent manual, to the treatise of Guibert, and to the first work of the Arch-Duke (*Gransatze der hoheren Kriegskunst*) we may easily instruct ourselves in all those logistical operations which are not permitted to us to pass over in silence, but which it suffices for our plan to point out.

Before quitting this interesting subject, I think it my duty to refer to some remarkable events in order to cause to be appreciated all the importance of good logistics : the one is the miraculous assembling of the French army in the plains of Gera in 1806 ; the second is the opening of the campaign in 1815.

In both of these events Napoleon knew how to collect together, with

---

* It will be objected that in national wars these magazines are impracticable. I shall say, on the contrary, that in such they will often be hazardous; but that it is in such precisely that they should be established upon a greater scale, and that they are the most necessary. The line from Bayone to Madrid had a similar staple line, which resisted four years all the attacks of the guerrillas, although some convoys were taken; it was even extended for a time to Cadiz.

an admirable precision, upon the decisive point of the zone of operations, his columns which had departed from the most divergent points.

The choice of this decisive point was a skillful strategic combination, the calculation of the movements was a logistical operation which emanated from his closet. For a long time it was pretended that Berthier was the author of those instructions conceived with so much precision, and communicated generally with so much lucidity. I have had a hundred occasions to be assured of the falsity of this assertion. The Emperor was himself the true chief of his staff, furnished with a compass opened at a scale of from seven to eight leagues in a right line, (which supposes always nine or ten leagues, at least, by the sinuosities of the routes,) leaning over and sometimes lying down upon his map, where the positions of his army corps and the presumed positions of the enemy were marked with pins of different colors, he ordered his movements with an assurance of which it would be difficult to form a just idea. Moving his compass with vivacity upon this map, he judged in the twinkling of an eye of the number of marches necessary to each of his corps for arriving at the point where he wished to have it at a given day; then placing his pins in those new positions, and combining the rapidity of the march which it would be necessary to assign to each of the columns with the possible epoch of their departure, he dictated those instructions which of themselves alone would be a title to glory.

It was thus that Ney, coming from the borders of Lake Constance, Lannes from Upper Suabia, Soult and Davoust from Bavaria and the Palatinaté, Bernadotte and Augereau from Franconia, and the imperial guard arriving from Paris, were found in line upon three parallel routes debouching at the same time between Saalfeld, Gera and Plauen, when no person in the army, nor in Germany, conceived anything of those movements in appearance so complicated.*

In the same manner, in 1815, when Blucher cantoned peaceably between the Sambre and the Rhine, and Wellington gave or received *fêtes* at Brussels, both awaiting the signal to invade France, Napoleon, whom they believed at Paris quite occupied with ostentatious political ceremonials, accompanied by his guard, which had just scarcely been reformed at the capital, burst like lightning upon Charleroi and upon the quarters of Blucher, with columns converging from all points of the horizon, to arrive, with rare punctuality, the 14th June in the plains of Beaumont

---

* I except, however, a small number of officers capable of penetrating them by analogy with precedents.

upon the borders of the Sambre, (Napoleon had not departed until the 12th from Paris.)

The combinations of those two operations reposed upon a skillful strategic calculation; but their execution was undeniably a *chef d'œuvre* of logistics. In order to appreciate the merit of similar measures, I would refer, in opposition to them, to two circumstances where faults of logistics came near becoming fatal. Napoleon recalled from Spain in 1809, by the preparations of Austria, and certain of having war with that power, despatched Berthier to Bavaria with the delicate mission of assembling the army, all dispersed from Strasburg to Erfurt.

Davoust returned from this city, Oudinot from Frankfort, Massèna *en route* for Spain, retrograded by Strasburg upon Ulm; the Saxons, the Bavarians and Wurtembergers quitted their respective countries. Immense distances separated thus those corps, and the Austrians, united a long time since, were able easily to pierce this web and to destroy or disperse the parts of it. Napoleon, justly uneasy, ordered Berthier to collect the army at Ratisbon, if the war had not commenced at his arrival, but in the contrary case to unite it farther in rear near Ulm.

The cause of this double alternative was not difficult to penetrate; if the war had commenced, Ratisbon was found too near the frontier of Austria to be designated as the place of rendezvous, for the corps might arrive and throw themselves separately in the midst of two hundred thousand enemies, by fixing the union at Ulm; the army would be sooner concentrated, or at least the enemy would have five or six marches more to make in order to reach it, which was a capital point in the respective situation of the two parties.

It did not require to be a genius to comprehend the thing. Meanwhile, hostilities having commenced only a few days after the arrival of Berthier at Munich, this too celebrated major general had the simplicity to adhere literally to the order received, without perceiving its manifest meaning; he not only persisted in endeavoring to unite the army at Ratisbon, but he even caused Davoust to return to that city, who had the good sense to fall back from Amberg in the direction of Ingolstadt.

Happily, Napoleon, advised in twenty-four hours of the passage of the Inn, by telegraph, arrived like lightning at Abensberg, at the moment when Davoust was about to find himself invested, and the army cut in two or scattered by a mass of a hundred and eighty thousand enemies. It is known by what prodigies he rallied it, and triumphed in the five glorious days of Abensberg, of Siegenburg, of Landshut, of Eckmuhl, and of Ratisbon, which repaired the faults of the miserable logistics of his chief of the staff.

We shall terminate these citations by the events which preceded and accompanied the passage of the Danube, before Wagram; the measures for causing to arrive at a given point on the island of Lobau, the corps of the Viceroy of Italy coming from Hungary, that of Marmont coming from Styria, and that of Bernadotte coming from Linz, are less astonishing still than the famous resolution or imperial decree of thirty-one articles which regulated the details of the passage and of the formation in the plains of Enzersdorf, in the presence of a hundred and forty thousand Austrians, and of five hundred pieces of artillery, as though it had been a military fête. All those masses were found united on the island the evening of the 4th of July, three bridges were thrown in the twinkling of an eye upon an arm of the Danube a hundred and forty yards wide, in the darkest of nights and in the midst of torrents of rain; a hundred and fifty thousand men there defiled in presence of a formidable enemy, and are formed before noon in the plain, at a league in advance of the bridges, which they covered by a change of front; the whole in less time than would have been necessary for doing it in a manœuvre of instruction several times repeated. In truth, the enemy had resolved to dispute the passage but feebly; but this was not known, and the merit of the dispositions made was none the less manifest.

Meanwhile, by an oversight the most extraordinary, the major general had not perceived, in dispatching ten copies of the famous decree, that by mistake the bridge of the centre had been assigned to Davoust, although he should have formed the right wing, whilst the bridge of the right had been assigned to Oudinot, who was to form the centre. These two corps thus crossed each other during the night, and but for the intelligence of the regiments and their chiefs, the most horrible disorder might have prevailed. Thanks to the inaction of the enemy, they were allowed to pass for a few detachments which followed corps to which they did not belong; what was more astonishing, is that after such a blunder, Berthier should have been decorated with the title of Prince of Wagram—this was the most cruel of epigrams.

Doubtless the error had escaped Napoleon in the dictation of his decree; but a chief of staff dispatching twenty copies of this order, and charged with the office of superintending the formation of the troops— should he not have perceived such a mistake?

Another example not less extraordinary, of the importance of good logistical measures was given at the battle of Leipzig. In receiving this

battle, backed against a defile like that of Leipzig, and wooded prairies
cut up by small streams and gardens, it would have been important to
throw a great number of small bridges, to open roads for arriving at
them, and to mark out those roads ; that would not have prevented the
loss of a decisive battle, but a considerable number of men, cannon and
caissons would have been saved which were abandoned for the want of
order and issues for retiring.   The inconceivable explosion of the bridge
of Lindenau was equally the result of an unpardonable neglect on the
part of the staff, which, for the rest, no longer existed in the army except
in name, thanks to the manner in which Berthier composed it and treated
it.   Besides, it must be acknowledged that Napoleon, who perfectly understood logistics for organizing an irruption, had never thought of a
measure of precaution in case of defeat, and when he was present, everybody reposed upon the Emperor as though he himself had ordered everything and foreseen everything.

Here is sufficient for causing to be appreciated all the influence which
good logistics can have upon military operations.

In order to complete what I had proposed to say in writing this article,
I should have to speak also of reconnoissances.   They are of two kinds.
The first are purely topographical and statistical ; they have for object
the acquiring of ideas upon the country, its accidents of ground, its
routes, defiles, bridges, &c., of ascertaining its resources and its means of every
kind.   At this day, geography, topography and statistics have made so
much progress that these reconnoissances are less necessary than formerly;
meanwhile they will always be of great utility, so long as Europe shall not
be registered : now it is probable she will never be so.   There exist many
good instructions upon these kinds of reconnoissances, to which I must
refer my readers.

The others are those which are ordered for assuring ourselves of the
movements of the enemy.   They are made by detachments more or less
strong ; if the enemy is formed in presence, it is the generals or chiefs of
the staff who should go in person and reconnoiter him.   If he be in
march, whole divisions of cavalry may be pushed for piercing the curtain
of posts with which he is surrounded.

These operations are sufficiently well pointed out in a host of elementary works, especially that of Colonel Lallemand, and in the regulations
for field service ; besides, we believe it our duty to reserve for the article
following all that we have to say on the various means of penetrating
what the enemy is doing.

ARTICLE XLII.

RECONNOISSANCES, AND OTHER MEANS OF ASCERTAINING CORRECTLY THE MOVEMENTS OF THE ENEMY.

One of the most important means of well combining skillful manœuvres of war, would unquestionably be never to order them except upon an exact knowledge of what the enemy might be doing. Indeed, how are we to know what we ourselves ought to do, if we be ignorant of what the adversary is doing? But, as decisive as this knowledge might be, to the same degree it is difficult, not to say impossible, to acquire; and this is precisely one of the causes which render the theory of war so different from the practice.

It is from this that come all the miscalculations of generals, who are educated men only, without having the natural genius for war, or without supplying it by the practical *coup d'œil* which a long experience and a great habit of directing military operations can give. It is always easy in leaving the walls of an academy, to make a project for outflanking a wing, for menacing the communication of the enemy, where you act for both parties at the same time, and where you dispose of them to your liking, either upon a geographical map or upon a fictitious plan of ground, but when you have to do with a skillful, active and enterprising adversary, all of whose movements are an enigma, then the embarrassment commences, and it is here that all the mediocrity of an ordinary general shows itself.

I have acquired so many proofs of this truth in my long career, that if I had to test a general, I should esteem much more him who should make just suppositions upon the movements of the enemy, than him who should make a display of theories so difficult to make well, but so easy to apprehend when one finds them all made.

There are four means of attaining a judgment as to the operations of a hostile army; the first is that of an *espionage* well organized and lib-

erally paid,* the second is that of reconnoissances made by skillful officers
and light corps, the third consists in the information which could be obtained from prisoners of war, the fourth is that of establishing with one's
self the hypotheses which may be the most probable from two different
bases. I shall explain this idea farther on. Finally, there is a fifth mode,
that of signals, although it is applied rather to indicate the presence of
the enemy than to judge of his projects, it may be ranged in the category with which we are occupied.

For all that passes in the interior of the hostile army, espionage seems
the most sure, because a reconnoissance, however well made it may be,
can give no notion of what passes beyond the advanced guard. That is
not saying that they must not be made, for it is necessary to try all the
means of being well instructed, but it means that the result must not be
counted upon. It is the same with reports of prisoners of war, they are
often useless, and it would oftener be dangerous to give credit to them.
In every case, a skillful staff will not fail to choose certain instructed officers, who, charged with this especial service, will be able to direct their
questions in such a manner as to distinguish among the replies what may
be important to know. The partisans which are thrown as scouts in the
midst of the lines of operations of the enemy, without doubt could learn
something of his movements ; but it is almost impossible to communicate
with them, and to receive information from them. Spying, it is conceived, upon a large scale, will more generally succeed ; however, it is difficult for a spy to penetrate to the closet of the enemy's general, and be able to
wrest from him the secret of his enterprises ; he will limit himself oftener
to indicating the movements of which he is a witness, or those which he
shall learn through public rumor, and when one shall receive the information of those movements, he will know nothing of those which supervene
in the interval, nor of the ulterior end which the enemy proposes to himself ; he will know well, for example, that such a corps has passed
through Jena, directing itself upon Weimar—such another has passed
through Gera, directing itself towards Naumburg ; but where will they
go ? What do they wish to undertake ? This is what will be very difficult to learn even from the most skillful spy.

When armies encamped in tents, almost wholly united, then news of
the enemy was more certain, for parties could be pushed even within sight
of their camp, and spies could become instructed of all the movements

---

* To recommend spying will appear an impious work to visionary philanthropists, but
I pray them not to forget that the question is to spy the movements of an army, and not
of delation.

of those camps. But with the present organization into army corps, which canton or bivouac, the thing has become more complicated, more embarrassing, and in result almost nothing.

Espionage may render, nevertheless, good service when the army of the adversary is conducted by a great captain or a great sovereign, marching always with the major part of his forces and reserves. Such were, for example, the Emperor Alexander and Napoleon. When it could be known where they had passed, and what direction they took, without stopping at the details of other movements, the project they had in view could be nearly calculated.

A skillful general may supply the inefficiency of all these means by hypotheses well laid down and well resolved in advance, and I may say it with a certain satisfaction, this means has seldom failed me, and I am rarely deceived in having recourse to it. If fortune has never put me at the head of an army, I have been, at least, chief of staff of nearly a hundred thousand men, and called many times to the councils of the greatest sovereigns of our day, in which it was the question to direct the masses of the whole of armed Europe, and I have been deceived but two or three times in the hypotheses I have laid down, and in the manner of resolving the questions which resulted from them. I am even convinced that every question well laid down, is almost always easy to resolve when one has a sound judgment. Now, as I have already said, I have constantly observed that an army being able to operate only upon the centre or upon one of the extremities of its front of operations, there are scarcely ever more than three or four possible chances to foresee. Hence a mind well penetrated with these truths, and embued with good principles of war, can always adopt a course which provides beforehand the most probable chances. I shall allow myself to cite a few examples of them taken in my own experience.

When, in 1806, they were yet undecided in France upon the war with Prussia, I made a memoir upon the probabilities of the war, and the operations which would have place in that contingency.

I established the three following hypotheses :—1st, the Prussians will await Napoleon behind the Elbe, and will make defensive war to the Oder, in order to await the concurrence of Russia and Austria ; 2d, in the contrary case, they will advance upon the Saale, resting their left upon the frontier of Bohemia, and defending the outlets from the mountains of Franconia ; 3d, or else, expecting the French by the grand route of Mayence, they will advance imprudently to Erfurt.

I do not think there were any other possible chances to suppose, unless it were believed that the Prussians were so badly advised as to divide their forces, already inferior, upon the two directions of Wesel and of Mayence ; a useless fault, since upon the first of those routes there had not appeared a French soldier since the seven years war.

Well, those three hypotheses thus laid down, if it were asked the course which best suited Napoleon to adopt, was it not easy to conclude " that the weight of the French army, being already assembled in Bavaria, it was necessary to throw it upon the left of the Prussians by Gera and Hoff, for whatever hypotheses they should adopt, there was the Gordion knot of the whole campaign."   ╲

Did they advance upon Erfurt? By falling upon Gera they were cut off from their line of retreat and thrown back upon the Lower Elbe, to the North Sea. Did they rest upon the Saale ? By attacking their left by Hoff and Gera, they were partially overwhelmed, and could yet be anticipated by Leipsic at Berlin. If they remained finally behind the Elbe, it was always in the direction of Gera and Hoff that it was necessary to seek them.

Hence what importance was it to know the detail of their movements, since the interest was always the same ? Thus well convinced of these truths, I did not hesitate to announce—*a month before the war*—that it would be what Napoleon would undertake, and that if the Prussians passed the Saale, it would be at Jena and at Naumburg that they would fight.

What suppositions did the Duke of Brunswick and his counsellors make at the same instant that I saw so accurately? In order to credit it, it is necessary to read them in the works of MM. O. de W. and Ruhle de Lilienstern, (*Operations plan an Bericht eines Augenzeugen..*)

If I recall this circumstance, already more than once cited, it is not a feeling of vanity which leads me to it, because I would have other citations of this nature to make ; but I have only desired to demonstrate that we may often act in war after problems well considered, without pausing too long at the details of the movements of our adversary. If General Clausewitz had been as often as myself in the position to weigh these problems, and see them resolved, he would not so much have doubted the efficacy of the theories of war founded upon principles, for it is those theories which alone will be able to serve as a guide for such solutions. His three volumes upon war prove evidently that in a situation like that in which the Duke of Brunswick was found in 1806, he would have been quite as embarrassed as he was as to the course which it was necessary to take. Irresolution must be the accompaniment of minds which doubt everything.

Returning to our subject I must confess that espionage has been singularly neglected in many modern armies, and in 1813 among others the staff of the Prince of Schwartzenburg not having a sou at its disposition for this service, the Emperor Alexander had to furnish funds from his chest to give to that staff the means of sending agents into Lusace to learn where Napoleon was. General Mack at Ulm and the Duke of Brunswick in 1806 were no better informed ; and the French generals in Spain often paid dear for the impossibility of having spies and information upon what was passing around them.

For information which can be obtained from flying corps, the Russian army is better off than any other, thanks to its Cossacks and the intelligence of its partizans.

The expedition of the Prince Koudacheff, sent after the battle of Dresden to the Prince of Sweden, and who after having swam the Elbe, marched in the midst of the French columns near Wittenburg, is an historical monument of those kinds of excursions. The information furnished by the partisans of Generals Czernitcheff, Benkendorf, Davidoff and Seslawin, have rendered eminent services of the same nature. We recollect that it was a despatch of Napoleon to the Empress Maria Louisa, intercepted near Châlons by the Cossacks which advised the Allies of the project formed by the French Emperor for throwing himself upon their communications with all his united forces, by basing himself on the belt of strong places of Lorraine and Alsace. This precious information decided the union of the armies of Blucher and Schwartzenburg, which all seeming strategic remonstrance had never succeeded in making act in concert, excepting at Leipsic and Brienne.

It is known also that it was information given by Seslawin to General Doctoroff, which prevented the latter from being overwhelmed at Borowsk by Napoleon who had just left Moscow with all his army to commence his retreat. He was not at first believed and it was necessary that Seslawin, piqued, should go and carry off an officer and some soldiers of the guard, in the midst of the French bivouacs, to confirm his report. This information which decided the march of Kutusoff upon Malo-Jaroslawitz, prevented Napoleon from taking the route of Kalouga, where he would have found more resources, where he would have avoided the disasters of Krasnoi and of the Beresina, which for the rest, would have diminished the catastrophe without preventing it entirely.

Such examples however rare they may be suffice to give an idea of what can be expected from good partisans conducted by capable officers.

To conclude I would sum up this article with the following truths :

1st. That a general ought to neglect nothing in order to be informed of the movements of the enemy and employ to this effect reconnoissances, spies, light corps conducted by capable officers, signals, finally, instructed officers charged with directing at the advanced guards the interrogation of prisoners.

2nd. That by multiplying reports however imperfect and contradictory they may be, we often succeed in separating the truth even from the midst of their contradictions.

3rd. That it is necessary nevertheless to distrust these means and not to count too much upon them for the combination of our operations.

4th. That in default of sure and exact information a capable general ought never to put himself in march without having two or three courses taken upon the probable hypotheses which the respective situations of the armies would offer, and that those hypotheses be founded upon principles.

I could guaranty that in this case nothing very unexpected could come to surprise him, and cause him to lose his senses as often happens : for unless he be altogether incapable of commanding an army he ought to be able to make the most probable suppositions upon what the enemy will undertake, and to adopt in advance a course upon the one of those suppositions, which should happen to be realized.* I could not too frequently repeat, that it is in like suppositions well laid down, and well resolved, that we recognize the true seal of military genius ; and although the number of them be always very restricted, it is inconceivable to what degree this powerful means is neglected.

In order to complete this article it remains for us to say also, what may be obtained by the aid of signals.

There are several kinds of them, and at the head of all we should naturally place telegraphs. It was to the idea he had of establishing a telegraphic line between his head quarters and France, that Napoleon owed his astonishing success at Ratisbon in 1809. He was found yet at Paris when the Austrian army passed the Inn at Braunau, for invading Bava-

---

* I shall not be accused I think of meaning that there never happens an event in war which is not foreseen ; the surprises of Cremona, Bergen-op-Zoom, Hochkirch, will suffice to prove the contrary. I believe merely that those events approach always more or less one of the hypotheses adopted or anticipated, so that one could remedy them by the same means.

ria and piercing his cantonments. Informed in twenty-four hours of what passed at two hundred and fifty leagues from him, he threw himself instantly into his carriage and eight days afterwards he was conqueror in two battles under the walls of Ratisbon ; without the telegraph the campaign would have been lost : this fact suffices for appreciating its importance.

It has been imagined also to use the portable telegraph, and to my knowledge, the first idea of it belonged to a Russian merchant who had brought it from China. These telegraphs manœuvred by men on horseback posted upon heights, seem to be able to carry in a few minutes orders, from the centre to the extremities of a line of battle, as well as the reports of the wings to head quarters. Repeated trials were made, but the project was abandoned without my knowing the reasons for it. Those communications could be in truth but very brief, and cloudy weather might make them sometimes uncertain : meanwhile as the vocabulary of similar reports could be reduced to a score of phrases, for which it would be easy to have conventional signs, I think that the mode should not be despised, though even we should be obliged to send the duplicate of its transmissions, by officers capable of well rendering verbal orders. We would always gain rapidity thereby.

A trial of another nature was attempted in 1794, at the battle of Fleurus, where General Jourdan employed an aëronaut for reconnoitering and making signals of the movements of the Austrians. I do not know whether he had occasion to congratulate himself on this trial, which was not again renewed, although it was pretended at the time that it had assisted in the victory, which I very much doubt. It is probable that the difficulculty of having an aëronaut all ready to make his ascension at the moment when it should be opportune, that of observing well what passes below when one has thus ventured in the air, and the instability of the winds may have caused this renunciation of the means. By maintaining the balloon at an inconsiderable elevation, by placing in it an officer capable of judging of the movements of the enemy, and by perfecting a small number of signals which might be expected from it, are circumstances in which we might perhaps obtain some fruit from it. The smoke of the artillery however, the difficulty of distinguishing to which party belong the columns that one sees moving like troops of Lilliputians, will always render those reports very uncertain : an aëronaut would have been sufficiently embarrassed to decide at the battle of Waterloo if it were Grouchy or Blucher who arrived by St. Lambert ; but in cases where armies are less mingled and more distinct, it seems that this means might be sometimes

turned to account.   What is certain is that I was convinced upon the
steeple of Gautsch, at the battle of Leipsic of the fruits which one may
derive from such an observation ; and the aid de camp of the Prince de
Schwartzenburg whom I conducted there, could not deny that it was our
solicitations which decided the prince to leave the confined place between
the Pleisse and the Elster.   Doubtless one is more at his ease upon a steeple than in a frail ærial car, but one does not always find steeples situated
in such a manner as to be able to overlook the whole field of battle, and
they cannot be transported at will.   It would besides remain for Messrs.
Green or Garnerin to tell us how objects are seen at five or six hundred
feet of perpendicular elevation.

There is a kind of signals more substantial, which are those given by
fires lighted upon the elevated points of a country : before the invention
of the telegraph they had the merit of being able to bear rapidly the news
of an invasion, from one end of the country to the other.   The Swiss use
them for calling the militia to arms.   They are also used sometimes for giving
the alarm to winter cantonments, in order to assemble them more promptly :
they are used all the better to this end that two or three variations in
the signals suffice for indicating to the *corps d'armée*, upon which side the
enemy menaces the quarters most seriously, and upon what point they
ought to effect their rendezvous.   For the same reasons these signals might
be suitable upon the coasts against descents.

Finally there is a last species of signals which are given to troops in ac.
tion by the aid of military instruments ; as they do not bear directly upon
the subject we treat, I shall limit myself to observing that they are better
perfected in the Russian army than any where else.   But at the same time
acknowledging of what importance it would be to find a sure means of im-
pressing a spontaneous and simultaneous movement upon a mass of troops
in accordance with the sudden will of its chief, it must be owned that this
will yet be a long time a difficult problem to resolve : and apart from the
case of a general hurrah impressed upon the whole line by the charge step
repeated gradually it will ever be difficult to apply signals by instruments.
to other use than to skirmishers : even these general hurrahs are rather the
effect of a transport of the troops than the result of an order : I have
seen but two examples of them in thirteen campaigns.

CHAPTER VII.

THE FORMATION OF TROOPS FOR COMBAT,* AND THE SEPARATE OR COMBINED EMPLOYMENT OF THE THREE ARMS.

Two essential articles of the tactics of battles remain for us to examine : the one is the manner of disposing the troops in order to conduct them to combat, the other is the employment of the different arms. Although these objects belong to logistics and to secondary tactics, it must be owned meanwhile that they form one of the principal combinations of a general-in-chief when it is the question to deliver battle ; hence it necessarily enters into the plan that we have proposed to ourselves.

Here doctrines become less fixed, and one falls back of compulsion into the field of systems : it is not therefore without astonishment that we have seen quite recently one of the most celebrated modern writers, pretend that tactics is fixed, but that strategy is not, whereas it is the contrary.

Strategy is composed of invariable geographic lines, the relative importance of which is calculated upon the situation of the hostile forces, a sit-

---

* All that which concerns formations belongs rather to logistics than to tactics ; but I have thought this chapter thus written seven years ago, could well remain as it was, for the formation depends upon the employment, and the employment depends also a little upon the formation most familiar to an army.

uation which can never lead but to a small number of variations, since the hostile forces are found divided or collected either upon the centre, or upon one of the extremities. Nothing is more possible than to subject ele. ments so simple to rules derived from the fundamental principle of war, in spite of the efforts of fastidious writers to perplex the science in endeavoring to render it too abstract and exact. It is the same with the combinations of orders of battles, which can be subjected to maxims equally referable to the general principle. But the means of execution that is to say the tactics properly so called, depend upon so many circumstances, that it is impossible to give rules of conduct for the innumerable cases which may present themselves. To be assured of this, it is sufficient to read the works which succeed each other every day upon these portions of the military art without any being able to agree; and if we bring together two distinguished generals of cavalry or of infantry, it is very rare that they succeed in having a perfect understanding as to the most suitable method of executing an attack. Add to this the enormous difference which exists in respect to the talents of chiefs in their energy in the *moral* of the troops, and we shall be convinced that the tactics of execution will forever be reduced to contrary systems, and that it will be a great deal if one succeeds in laying down a few regulating maxims, which prevent the introduction of false doctrines into the systems that shall be adopted.

ARTICLE XLIII.

THE POSTING OF TROOPS IN LINE OF BATTLE.

After having defined in Article 31, what should be understood by the line of battle, it is proper to say in what manner they are formed, and how the different troops should be distributed in them.

Before the French revolution, all the infantry, formed by regiments and brigades, were found united into a single battle corps, subdivided into first and second lines which had each their right and left wings. The cavalry was ordinarily placed on the two wings, and the artillery, yet very heavy at this epoch, was distributed upon the front of each line (they dragged sixteen pounder guns, and there was no horse artillery). Then the army always encamping united, put itself in march by lines or by wings, and as there were two wings of cavalry and two of infantry, if they marched by wings they formed thus four columns. When they marched by lines, which was especially suitable in flank marches, then they formed but two columns, unless, through local circumstances, the cavalry or a part of the infantry had encamped in a third line, which was rare.

This method simplified logistics, since the whole disposition consisted in saying : " You will march in such a direction, by lines or by wings, by the right or by the left." They seldom deviated from this monotonous, but simple formation, and in the spirit of the system of war they followed it was the best they could do.

The French determined at Minden, to try a different logistical disposition, by forming as many columns as brigades, and opening roads for conducting them abreast upon a given line, which they could never form.*

If the labors of the staff were facilitated by this mode of encamping and marching by lines, it must be owned that, applied to an army of a hundred or a hundred and fifty thousand men, this system would produce columns without end, and that routs would often occur like that of Rosbach.†

The French Revolution brought about the system of divisions, which broke the too great unity of the old formation, and gave fractions capable of moving on their own account upon all kinds of ground, which was a real benefit, although they fell perhaps from one extreme into another, by returning almost to the legionary organization of the Romans. Those divisions, composed ordinarily of infantry, artillery and cavalry, manœuvred and fought separately ; whether they were extended beyond measure for causing them to live without magazines, or whether they had the mania for prolonging their line, with the hope of outflanking that of the enemy, we often see seven or eight divisions of which an army is composed, march abreast upon as many routes at four or five leagues from each other ; the head-quarters was placed at the centre without other reserve than five or six slender regiments of cavalry of three or four thousand horses ; so that if the enemy chanced to unite the bulk of his forces upon one of those divisions and defeat it, the line was found pierced, and the general-in-chief, having no infantry reserve in hand, saw no other resource than to put himself in retreat to rally his scattered forces.

---

* Chapter 15 of the treatise upon grand operations.
⊥ Chapter 4 of the same work.

Bonaparte, in his first Italian war, remedied this inconvenience as much by the mobility and rapidity of his manœuvres, as in uniting always the bulk of his divisions upon the point where the decisive blow was to be directed.

When he was placed at the head of the State, and saw each day increase the sphere of his means and that of his projects, Napoleon comprehended that a stronger organization was necessary; he took then a mean term between the ancient and the new system, at the same time preserving the advantage of the division organization. He formed in the campaign of 1800, corps of two or three divisions, which he placed under lieutenant generals for forming the wings, the centre or the reserve of the army.*

This system was definitively consolidated at the camp of Boulogne, where were organized permanent army corps, under marshals who commanded three divisions of infantry, one of light cavalry, and from thirty-six to forty pieces of artillery, with sappers. They were as many little armies proper to form, at need, any enterprise by themselves. The heavy cavalry was united into a strong reserve, composed of two divisions of cuirassiers, four of dragoons, and one of light cavalry. The grenadiers united and the guard formed a fine reserve of infantry; later, in 1812, the cavalry was organized into corps of three divisions, in order to give more unity to the ever increasing masses of this arm.

It must be owned, this organization left little to be desired, and that grand army, which effected such great things, was soon the type upon which all Europe was modeled.

Some military men, dreaming of the perfectibility of the art, would have desired that the infantry division, called sometimes to fight by itself, were increased from two brigades to three, because this number, gives a centre and two wings, which is of a manifest advantage, since without it the number two gives for centre an opening, an interval, and that the fractions forming the wings, deprived of central support, could not operate separately with the same security. Besides that, the number three permits two brigades to be engaged, and have one in reserve which evidently augments the disposable forces for the decisive shock. But if thirty brigades, formed in ten divisions of three brigades each, are better than distributed into fifteen divisions of two brigades, it would be neces-

---

* Thus the army of the Rhine was composed of the right wing, under Lecourbe, three divisions; of the centre, under St. Cyr, three divisions; and of the left, under St. Susanne, two divisions; the general-in-chief had besides three divisions as a reserve, under his immediate orders.

sary, to obtain this division organization, *par excellence*, to augment the infantry by a third, or to reduce the divisions of the *corps d'armée* to two instead of three, which would be a more real evil, since the *corps d'armée* being oftener called to fight alone than a division, it is to it especially that the number three is the most suitable.*

As for the rest, the best organization to give to an army entering the field, will be for a long time a logistical problem to resolve, because of the difficulty that is experienced in maintaining it in the midst of the events of the war, and the incessant detachments which they more or less necessitate.

The grand army at Boulogne, which we have just cited, is the most evident proof of it. It seemed that its perfect organization should have secured it from every possible vicissitude. The centre under Marshal Soult, the right under Davoust, the left under Ney, the reserve under Lannes, presented a regular and formidable battle corps of thirteen divisions of infantry, without counting those of the guard and of the united grenadiers. Besides that, the corps of Bernadotte and Marmont, detached to the right, and that of Augereau detached to the left, were disposable for acting upon the flanks. But from the passage of the Danube at Donauwert, all was disordered; Ney, at first reinforced to five divisions, was reduced to two; the main body was dislocated, part to the right, a part to the left, so that this fine order of battle became useless.

It will ever be difficult to give an organization at all stable; meanwhile events are not always as complicated as those of 1805, and the campaign of Moreau in 1800, proves that the primitive organization can, to a certain point, be maintained, at least for the bulk of the army. To this end it seems that the organization of the army into four fractions, viz: two wings, a centre, and a reserve, is the only rational one; the composition of those fractions may vary according to the strength of the army, but in order to be able to maintain it, it will be indispensable to have a certain number of divisions out of line, to furnish the necessary detachments. Those divisions whilst they are detached, could reinforce the one or the other of those fractions which should be the most exposed to receive or to strike great blows; or else they would be employed either upon the flanks of the main body, or to double the reserve. Each of the

---

* Thirty brigades formed into fifteen divisions of two brigades each, would engage only fifteen brigades as a first line; whilst that those thirty brigades, formed into ten divisions of three brigades. would give twenty brigades as a first line, and ten as a second. But then it is necessary to diminish the number of divisions, and to have only two in each *corps d'armee*, which would be objectionable, since the army corps are oftener required to manœuvre alone than the division.

four grand fractions of the main body may only form a single corps of three or four divisions, or else be divided into two corps of two divisions. In this last case we should have seven corps, by counting but one for the reserve; but it would be necessary that the latter should always have three divisions, in order that the centre and the wings have each their reserve.

In forming thus seven corps, if we had not always some out of line for detachments, it would often happen that the corps of the two extremities would be found detached, so that there would remain for each wing but two divisions, from which it would be necessary even at times to detach still a brigade to flank the march of the army, in such a manner that there would remain no more than three brigades, which does not constitute a very strong order of battle.

These truths lead to the belief that an organization of the line of battle into four corps of three divisions of infantry and one of light cavalry, besides three or four divisions destined for detachments, would be less subject to variations than one of seven corps of two divisions.

For the rest, as all depends in these kinds of arrangements, on the strength of the army and the units which compose it, as much as on the nature of its enterprises, there result many variations which it would take too much space to detail here, and I will confine myself to tracing on the accompanying plate, the principal combinations which a formation would present, according as the divisions should be of two or three brigades, and the corps of two or three divisions. I have traced there the formation for two corps of infantry upon two lines, either one behind the other, or one by the side of the other. The latter leads us to examine if it can ever be suitable to place thus two corps the one behind the other, as Napoleon has often done, especially at Wagram. I believe that with the exception of the reserves, this system could only be applied to a position of expectation, and by no means to an order of combat; for it is much preferable that each corps have in itself its second line and its reserve, than to accumulate several corps under different chiefs. However well disposed a general may be to sustain one of his colleagues, it will ever be repugnant to him to divide his forces to that effect, and when, instead of a colleague, he shall see in the commander of the first line but an envied rival, as happens only too often, it is probable that he will not furnish with haste the succors of which it might be in need. Besides that, a chief whose command is spread upon a long extent, is much less sure of his operations, than if he had only embraced half of this front, and when he would find in exchange in greater depth, the support which might be necessary to him.

battalions it would be necessary at least that the battalions should have 1000 men.

four
thre
In t
rese
tl
r

d
w
t
s
tl
a

i
s
j

g
n
t
a
p
t
f
o
e
F
e
o
p
t
d
,

Finally, in order to complete this sketch, it will be seen by the table hereafter,* how much this question of the best formation is subordinate to the strength of the army, and how complicated it is.

We can scarcely be regulated now a days, by the enormous masses put action from 1812 to 1815, where we have seen one army form fourteen rps which had from two to five divisions. With such forces, it is incontable that nothing can be imagined better than an organization by y corps of three divisions; eight of these corps would be destined for line of battle, and there would remain six as well for detachments as reinforcing such points of this line as should be judged suitable. But apply this system to armies already very respectable of one hundred d fifty thousand men only, we can scarcely employ divisions of two gades, where Napoleon and the Allies employed entire army corps.

In effect, if we destine nine divisions to form the main body, that is to y, the two wings and the centre, and design six others for the reserve d the eventual detachments, there would be necessary fifteen divisions thirty brigades, which would number one hundred and eighty battalions, the regiments are of three battalions each. Now this supposes already mass of a hundred and forty-five thousand foot, and an army of two undred thousand combattants.

With regiments of two battalions it would require, it is true, but a undred and twenty battalions, or ninety-six thousand foot, but if the egiments have only two battalions, then the force of the latter ought to be increased to a thousand men, which would always give an hundred and twenty thousand foot, and an army of a hundred and sixty thousand men. These calculations alone prove how much the system of formation of inferior fractions influence that of the grand fractions.

---

* Every army has two wings, a centre, and a reserve, in all four principal fractions, besides eventual detachments.
These are the various formations which can be given to infantry:

1st. In Regiments of two Battalions of 800 men each.

	Divisions	Brigades	Battalions	
Four corps of two divisions besides 3 divisions for detachments, -	11	22	88	= 72,000 men
Four corps of three divisions besides 3 divisions for detachments, -	15	30	120	= 96,000 men
Seven corps d'armee of two divisions, an eighth for detachments,	14 / 2	28 / 4	} 128	=103,000 men

2nd. In Regiments of three Battalions, Brigades of six Battalions.

	Divisions	Brigades	Battalions	
Four corps of two divisions besides detachments,	11 Divisions	22 Brigades	132 Battalions	=105,000 men
Four corps of three divisons do. do.	15 "	30 "	180 "	=144,000 "
Eight corps of two divisions,	16 "	32 "	192 "	=154,000 "

If to these figures there is added a quarter for cavalry, artillery and sappers, the force necessary for these various formations may be calculated.

It is necessary only to observe that regiments of two battalions of 800 men would be very weak at the end of two or three months campaign. If they have not three battalions it would be necessary at least that the battalions should have 1000 men.

If an army does not exceed a hundred thousand men, the formation in divisions, as in 1800, would be better perhaps than that by corps.

After having sought the best mode for giving a somewhat stable organization to battle corps, it will not be out of place to examine whether this stability is desirable, and whether we do not better deceive the enemy by frequently changing the composition of corps and their position.

I do not deny this last advantage, but it is possible to harmonize it with that which procures approximate stability in the order of battle. If we unite the divisions destined for detachments with the wings and the centre, that is to say, if we compose those fractions of four divisions, instead of three, and if at times we add one or two divisions to that one of the wings which should be the most probably destined to the principal shock, we shall have at the wings corps which will be nominally of four divisions, but which by detachments will ordinarily have but three, and at times might be reduced to two, whilst that the opposite wing, reinforced by a part of the reserve until the concurrence of five divisions, would present a sufficiently marked difference, in order that the enemy should never know exactly the real force of the fractions of the main body which he would have before him. There would be by this means more unity in the orders of movements of the staff, more facility for daily expeditions, and in the mean time not enough regularity to allow the enemy to know always precisely with whom he would have to do. I perceive, however, that I am engaged too far in an arena into which I ought not even to enter. It is for governments to decide those questions which merit a mature examination, and ought to make the object of an instruction for the staff; instruction, nevertheless, which should not impose absolute chains on the generalissimo, who ought always to have the power to regulate his forces according to his particular views, and the extent of the enterprises which he should form.

Definitively whatever may be the force and the number of the subdivisions or fractions of the army, the organization by *corps d'armée*, will remain probaby a long time the normal type with all the great continental powers, and it is on this truth that the line of battle should be calculated.

If the distribution of the troops in them is different from what it formerly was, the line of battle itself has also undergone some changes which result from the reserves, and the light cavalry attached to the various corps of infantry. Formerly it was composed ordinarily of two lines, now it is composed of two lines, with one or several reserves. But in latter times the European masses which encountered each other became, so considerable, that the *corps d'armée*, themselves formed upon two lines, being found often placed the one behind the other, formed thus four lines; and the corps of reserve being formed also in the same manner, there resulted frequently, even six lines of infantry, and several of cavalry, a formation good perhaps for a preparatory position, but which is too deep for battle.

However that may be, the classic formation, if this name can be given it, is still, for the infantry, that upon two lines; the more or less confined extent of the field of battle, and the forces of the armies could well give rise sometimes to a deeper formation, but this will always be an exception, or used for a last effort, for the order upon two lines besides the reserves, appearing to suffice for solidity, and giving more forces fighting at a time, seems also the most suitable.

When the army possesses a permanent corps as an advanced guard, this corps could also be formed in advance of the line of battle, or withdrawn to the rear for augmenting the reserve,* but as has already been said elsewhere, that rarely happens after the manner of the present formations, and the mode of combining the marches they require; each wing of the army has its own advanced guard, and that of the main body finds itself quite naturally furnished by the troops of the army corps which should march in front; when the army arrives in presence, those divisions reenter into their respective battle positions. Often even the reserves of cavalry are found almost entirely in the advanced guard, which does not prevent their taking the post assigned them, at the moment of delivering battle, either from the nature of the ground, or from the views of the general-in-chief.

After what we have just explained, our readers will be assured that the methods followed since the revival of the art of war and the invention of gunpowder until the French Revolution, have undergone great changes through the present organization, and that in order to appreciate well the wars of Louis XIV, of Peter the Great, and of Frederick II, it is necessary to refer them to the system adopted in their time.

However, a part of the ancient methods can still be employed, and if, for example, the position of the cavalry on the wings is no longer a fundamental rule, it might be good for an army of fifty or sixty thousand men, especially when the centre is found upon a ground less suitable to this arm than the one or the other of the extremities. It is generally the cus-

---

* The advanced guard being every day exposed in face of the enemy, and forming even the rear guard, when it is the question to retrograde, it seems but just, at the moment of the battle, to give it a less exposed post than that in front of the line of battle.

tom to attach one or two brigades of light cavalry to each of the infantry corps ; those in the centre place it in preference behind the line, those of the wings may place it upon their flanks.   With regard to the reserves of this arm, if it be sufficiently strong for organizing three corps, to the end that the centre and each of the wings have its reserve, it would be an order as perfect as could be desired.   In default of that, we could dispose this reserve in two columns, the one at the point where the centre is connected with the right, the other between the centre and the left ; these columns could thus arrive with the same facility upon every point of the line which should be menaced.*

The artillery, now more movable, is indeed as formerly distributed upon the whole front, since each division has its own.   Meanwhile it is well to observe that, its organization being perfected, we can better distribute it according to need, and it is ever a great fault to scatter it too much.   There exists, for the rest, few positive rules upon this distribution of artillery, for who would dare to counsel, for example, to block up a gap in a line of battle, by placing a hundred pieces in a single battery, far from the whole line, as Napoleon did with so much success at Wagram ?   Not being able here to enter into all the details of this arm, we will limit ourselves to saying :

1. That horse artillery ought to be placed upon the ground where it can be moved in every direction.

2. That foot artillery, especially that of position, would be better posted, on the contrary, upon a point where it would he covered by ditches, or by hedges which would secure it against a sudden charge of cavalry.   I need not say that, in order to preserve to it its greatest effect, we should be careful not to post it upon too elevated eminences, but rather upon flat grounds or slopes like a glacis ; this is what every sous-lieutenant ought to know.

3. If the horse artillery be principally joined to the cavalry, it is well, however, that each army corps have its own, for gaining rapidly a point essential to occupy.   Besides that, it is proper that there be some of it in the artillery reserve, in order to be able to direct it with more promptitude to the succor of a menaced point.   General Benningsen had cause to congratulate himself at Eylau for having united fifty-eight pieces in reserve, for they contributed powerfully to re-establishing affairs between the centre and the left where his line chanced to be broken.

---

* It is well understood that this position supposes a ground favorable for that arm, a first condition of every well combined order of battle

4. If one be on the defensive, it is proper to place a part of the batteries of heavy calibre upon the front, instead of holding them in reserve, since it is the object to batter the enemy at the greatest possible distance, in order to arrest the impulsion of his attack and to scatter confusion in his columns.

5. In the same condition it seems suitable, that apart from the reserve, the artillery be equally distributed upon the whole line, since one has an equal interest in repelling the enemy upon every point; this, meanwhile, is not rigorously true, for the nature of the ground, and the evident projects of the enemy, might necessitate the carrying of the bulk of the artillery upon a wing or upon the centre.

6. In the offensive it may be equally advantageous to concentrate a very strong artillery mass upon a point where we should wish to direct a decisive effort, to the end of making a breach in the hostile line, which would facilitate the grand attack upon which might depend the success of the battle.

Having to treat here only of the distribution of the artillery, we shall speak farther on of its employment in combats.

ARTICLE XLIV.

THE FORMATION AND EMPLOYMENT OF INFANTRY.

The infantry is, without contradiction, the most important arm, since it forms the four-fifths of an army, and it is it which carries positions or defends them. But if it must be admitted that next to the talent of the general it is the first instrument of victory, it must be owned also that it finds a powerful support in the cavalry and artillery, and that without their assistance it would often find itself much exposed, and able only to gain half successes.

We shall not evoke here the old disputes upon the shallow and the deep order, although the question, which was thought to be decided, is far from being exhausted, and placed in a point of view which permits the resolving it by examples and probabilities, at least. The war with Spain and the battle of Waterloo have renewed the controversies relative to the ad vantages of fire, or the shallow order, over the impulsion of columns of attack, or the deep order; we shall express our opinion farther on.

In the meantime we must not be misunderstood; it is no longer the question now to dispute whether Lloyd was right in wishing to give to the infantry a fourth rank armed with pikes, to the end of offering a greater shock in moving upon the enemy, or more resistance in receiving his attack; every experienced military man acknowledges in our day, that there is already sufficient difficulty in moving with order, battalions deployed in three closed ranks, and that a fourth rank would add to this embarrassment, without adding the least thing to their strength. It is astonishing that Lloyd, who had made war, should have insisted so much upon this material force; for the contact is very rarely sufficiently close, in order that this mechanical superiority be put to the test; and if these ranks turn their backs, it is not the fourth that will restrain them. This augmentation of a rank diminishes, in the defensive, the front and the fire, whilst that in the offensive, it is far from offering the mobility and the impulsion which are the advantages of columns of attack. We might affirm even that it will diminish that impulsion, for it is more difficult to cause eight hundred men to march in line of battle with four full ranks than in three, although there be a quarter less extent of front: the difficulty of the jointing of the two middle ranks, amply makes up for this slight difference.

Lloyd has not been much more happy in the choice of the means which he proposes for diminishing the inconvenience of narrowing the front; it is so absurd that we cannot conceive how a man of genius could have imagined it. He would deploy twenty battalions, leaving between each of them a hundred and fifty yards, that is to say, an interval equal to their front; we may imagine what would become of those battalions all disunited and isolated at such a distance, leaving between them twenty gaps where cavalry could penetrate in strong columns, to take them in flank, and sweep them like dust before the wind.

The question, we have said, no longer consists in discussing upon the augmentation of the number of ranks of a line, but merely to decide whether it ought to be composed of deployed battalions, acting only by their fire, or rather of columns of attack formed, each of a battalion ployed upon the two platoons of the centre, and acting only by their impulsion and their impetuosity.

Several modern writers have treated these matters with sagacity, without any one of them succeeding to present any thing conclusive, because in tactics all is much more subjected to unexpected events, to sudden inspirations, to the *moral,* and to individualities. Guibert was the most dred victo-

eloque
ries of
Cham

under the
cumulated. In France M. Jaquinot has also given a good elementary course.

vant

whi
fro
cou
twe
equ
talic
then
take
Th
augn
whet
their
ploye
pulsio
Sev
out an
in tact
pirati

..., and to individualities. Guibert was the must

eloquent advocate of the shallow order and of fires, and a hundred victories of the late wars has given it a hundred denials. The Marquises of Chambray and Ternay have approached the same questions, and have given birth to doubts without resolving them. The course of tactics of the latter presents nevertheless, for orders of battle especially, valuable developments, not for prescribing absolute rules, but for familiarizing us with the different combinations which may result from them; this is all the advantage that can be promised from a tactical work.*

General Okounief, in his argued disquisition upon the three arms, has not shown less penetration, nor obtained less success. Perhaps he has not been sufficiently conclusive and has allowed yet some uncertainty to hover over the solution of the problem. Like his predecessors, he has not enquired whether the French columns, repulsed by the fire of the deployed English, were not masses much too deep, instead of being merely columns of a single battalion, like those of which we have just made mention, which would constitute a capital difference.

I shall resume the points of view which the question presents.

There exist, in fact, but five modes in forming troops for encountering the enemy.

1. As skirmishers;
2. Into deployed lines, either continuous or checker-wise, (*en échiquier;*)
3. In lines of battalions ployed upon the centre of each battalion;
4. In deep masses;
5. In small squares

The skirmishers are an accessorary, for they ought only to cover the line properly so called by favor of the ground, to protect the march of the columns, to fill up the intervals, or defend the approaches of a post.

These divers modes of formation are thus reduced to four systems: the shallow order, or the one deployed into three-ranks: the half deep order, formed of a line of battalions in columns of attack upon the centre, or of squares by battalions; the mixed order where the regiments should be in part deployed, and partly in columns; finally, the deep order, composed of heavy columns of battalions, deployed the one behind the other.

The order deployed upon two lines, with a reserve, was formerly generally used, it is especially useful in the defensive. Those deployed lines may be continuous, formed checker-wise, (*en échiquier,*) or in echelons.

---

* The Prussian Major Decker, has written in German, a work equally good to consult, under the title of Tactics of the Three Arms; but it presents a system of masses too accumulated. In France M. Jaquinot has also given a good elementary course.

The order by which each battalion of a line is found formed in column of attack by divisions upon the centre, is more concentrated; it is in some sort a line of small columns, (like the figure 5 of the opposite plate.)

In the present regulation of three ranks, the battalion having four divisions,* this column would present twelve ranks in depth, which gives perhaps too many non-combattants, and too much exposure of artillery. To diminish these inconveniences, it has been proposed, whenever it should be desired to employ infantry in columns of attack, to form it into two ranks, to place but three divisions of each battalion behind each other, and to deploy the fourth as skirmishers in the intervals of the battalions and upon the flanks, but to rally them behind the three divisions, if the enemy's cavalry chanced to charge. (See figure 6.) Each battalion would have by this means two hundred more shots, besides those which the increase, by a third, of the front would give by putting the third rank in the first two. Thus there would be in fact but a depth of six men, and we should obtain one hundred files front, and four hundred shots for each column of attack of a battalion.

There would thus be strength and mobility united.† A battalion of eight hundred men, formed, after the method in use, into column of four divisions, presents about sixty files to each division, and the first alone firing by two ranks, there would be but one hundred and twenty shots to furnish for each of the battalions thus placed in line, whereas, according to the mode proposed, there would be four hundred delivered.

But whilst seeking the means of obtaining more fire at need, it is important to recollect also that the column of attack is not destined to fire, and that it ought to reserve this means for a desperate case; for, if it commences to fire in marching upon the enemy, its impulsion will become null, and the attack will fail. Besides that, this reduced order would be advantageous only against infantry, for the column of four sections of three ranks, forming a kind of solid square, is better against cavalry. The Arch-Duke Charles was fortunate at Essling, and especially at Wa-

---

* The word *division*, employed to express four or five regiments, as well as for designating two platoons of the same battalion. creates a confusion in tactical language which it would be important to abolish. It is to the regulations alone that this right is reserved.

† In the Russian army, they take the skirmishers from the third rank of each company or division, which reduces the column to eight ranks instead of twelve, and procures more mobility. But for facility in rallying the skirmishers in column, perhaps it would be better to employ for them the entire fourth division; one would then have nine ranks, or three divisions of three ranks each, against infantry, and the full column of twelve ranks against cavalry.

gram, in having adopted this last order, which I proposed in my chapter upon the general principles of war published in 1807 ; the brave cavalry of Bessieres could do nothing against those little masses.*

In order to give more solidity to the column proposed, we could in truth call in the skirmishers and reform the fourth section ; but there would always be but two ranks, which would present much less resistance against a charge principally upon the flanks. If for diminishing this inconvenience, we wish to form square, many military men think that in two ranks it would offer less consistency still than the column. Meanwhile the English squares were of only two ranks at Waterloo, and in spite of the heroic efforts of the French cavalry, there was but a single battalion broken.

I have explained all the parts of the process ; it remains for me to observe that if it were desired to adopt the formation in two ranks for the column of attack, it would be difficult to preserve that in three ranks for deployed lines, an army being scarcely able to have two modes of formation, or at least to employ them alternately on the field of battle. Hence what European army (if we except the English) could be risked to deploy in lines of two ranks? It would be necessary in this case never to move but in column of attack.

I conclude from thence that the system employed by the Russians and the Prussians, that of forming the column of four divisions in three ranks, of which one could at need be employed as skirmishers, is that which is generally applicable to all situations, whilst that the other of which we have spoken is suitable only in certain cases, and would require a double mode of formation.

Independently of the two orders above mentioned, there exists a mixed, which Napoleon employed at the Tagliamento, and the Russians at Eylau ; their regiments of three battalions deployed one in first line, and formed the other two behind this one, upon the platoons of its extremities, (fig. 2, same plate.)

This regulation, which belongs also to the semi-profound order, is suitable, in fact, for the offensive-defensive, because the troops deployed in first line resist a long time by a murderous fire, the effect of which always somewhat shakes the enemy ; then the troops, formed in column,

---

* M. de Wagner seems to call in question that I contributed to the adoption of this formation. His Royal Highness, the Arch-Duke himself, assured me of it in the meanwhile, in 1814 ; for, in the Austrian as well as in the French regulations. it was used only for the attacks of posts, and not for lines of battle.

can debouch through the intervals and throw themselves upon him with success. Perhaps we could augment the advantage of this formation by placing the two battalions of the wings upon the same line as that of the centre, which would be deployed in such a manner that the first divisions of those battalions would be in line. There would thus be a half battalion more for each regiment in the first line, which for fire would not be inconsiderable; but it might be feared that those divisions putting themselves in condition for firing, the two battalions kept in column to be launched upon the enemy would be less easily disposable. However, there are many cases where such an order would be advantageous, it is sufficiently so for rendering it a duty to indicate it.

The order in very deep masses is certainly the least suitable, (fig. 3.) We have seen in the late wars, divisions of twelve battalions deployed and compressed behind each other, forming thirty-six crowded and accumulated ranks. Such masses are exposed to the ravages of artillery, diminish mobility and impulsion, without adding any strength. This was one of the causes of the small success of the French at Waterloo. If the column of Macdonald succeeded better at Wagram, it paid dearly for it, and but for the success of the attacks of Davoust and of Oudinot upon the left of the Arch-Duke, it is not probable that it would have came out victorious from the position in which, for a moment, it saw itself placed.

When it is decided to risk such a mass, it is necessary, at least, to take care to establish upon each flank a battalion marching by files, in order that if the enemy chanced to charge in force upon those flanks, it would not oblige the column to halt, (see fig. 3 ;) protected by those battalions which will face to the enemy, it will be able at least to continue its march to the object assigned it, otherwise this great mass, battered by converging fires to which it has no means of opposing even a proper impulsion, will be put in disorder like the column at Fontenoi, or broken as the Macedonian phalanx was by Paulus Æmilius.

Squares are good in plains and against an enemy superior in cavalry. They were made formerly very large, but it is acknowledged that the square by regiment is the best for the defensive, and the square by battalion for the offensive. We can, according to circumstances, form them into perfect squares or into long squares, in order to present a greater front, and obtain more fire on the side from whence the enemy is expected to come, (see fig. 8 and 9.) A regiment of three battalions would easily form a long square by breaking the middle battalion and causing each half battalion to move, the one to the right, and the other to the left.

In the wars with Turkey, squares were almost exclusively employed,

because hostilities took place in the vast plains of Bassarabia, of Moldavia and of Wallachia, and the Turks had an immense cavalry. But, if
operations have place in the Balkan or beyond, and if their feudal cavalry give place to an arm organized in the European proportions, the importance of squares will diminish, and the Russian infantry will show all
its superiority in Romelia.

Be that as it may, the order in squares by regiments of battalions appears suitable to every kind of attack, whenever there is a superiority in
cavalry, and we manœuvre on even ground, favorable to the charges of
the enemy. The long square, applied especially to a battalion of eight
platoons, of which three should march abreast, and one upon each of the
sides, would be better for moving to the attack than a deployed battalion ;
it would be less suitable than the column proposed farther back, but there
would be less wavering and more impulsion than if it marched in a deployed line ; it would have, moreover, the advantage for being in condition
against cavalry.

It would be difficult to affirm that each of those formations are always
good, or always bad ; but it will be admitted, at least, that it is an incontestable rule that, for the offensive, there is necessary a mode which should
unite *mobility, solidity*, and *impulsion*, whilst for the defensive there is
wanted *solidity* united *to the greatest possible fire.*

This truth admitted, it will remain to decide whether the bravest offensive troops, formed in columns and deprived of fire, will hold out long
against deployed troops having twenty thousand musket shots to send it,
and able to deliver it two or three hundred thousand in five minutes.

In the late wars, we have often seen Russian, French and Prussian
columns, carry positions at the support arms, without firing a shot ; it is
the triumph of impulsion and of the moral effect which it produces, but
against the murderous fire and the *sang froid* of the English infantry,
columns have not had the same success at Talavera, at Busaco, at Fuente
di Onor, at Albuera, and still less at Waterloo.

Meanwhile, it would be imprudent to conclude from thence that this
result should cause the balance to incline decidedly in favor of the shallow
order and of fire ; for, if the French were accumulated in all these affairs
into masses too profound, as I have more than once seen with my own
eyes, it is not astonishing that enormous columns, formed into deployed
and wavering battalions, battered in front and flank by a murderous fire,
and assailed on all sides, have experienced the fate which we have pointed
out above. But would the same result have taken place with columns

of attack formed each of a single battalion ployed upon the centre according to rule? I do not think so, and in order to judge of the decided
superiority of the shallow or firing order, over the half deep order, or that
of offensive impulsion, it would be necessary to witness repeatedly what
would happen to a deployed line which should be boldly attacked by an
enemy thus formed, (fig. 6 of plate 2.) As for myself, I can affirm that, in all
the actions in which I have been, I have seen these little columns succeed.

Moreover, is it easy to adopt another order for marching to the attack
of a position? Is it possible for this purpose to conduct an immense line
in deployed order and firing? I believe that every one will pronounce
. for the negative : to throw twenty and thirty battalions in line, executing
a fire by file or by platoon, with the object of crowning a position well
defended, is to arrive there in disorder like a flock of sheep, or rather it
is never to succeed.

What ought we to conclude from all that we have just said? 1st, That
if the deep order is dangerous, the semi-profound order is excellent for
the offensive. 2d, That the column of attack by battalions is the best order
for carrying positions, but that is is necessary to diminish as much as possible its depth, to give more fire at need, and to diminish the effect of the
enemy's fire ; it is proper, moreover, to cover it by many skirmishers, and
to sustain it by cavalry. 3d, That the deployed order as first line, with
the second in column, is that which is the best suited to the defensive.
4th, That the one and the other may triumph according to the talent a
general shall have for employing seasonably his disposable forces, as we
have said in treating of the initiative, in Article 16 and Article 31.

In truth, since this chapter was written, the numerous inventions which
have had place in the art of destroying men would be able to militate in
favor of the deployed order, even for moving to the attack. However, it
would be difficult to anticipate the lessons which it is necessary to look
for from experience alone, for despite all that rocket batteries, the howitzers of Schrapnel or of Bourman, and even the guns of Perkins, could
offer redoubtable ; I own that I should have difficulty in conceiving a
better system for leading infantry to the assault of a position, than that
of the column by battalions. Perhaps it will even be necessary to give
back to the infantry the casques and cuirasses that it wore in the fifteenth
century, before throwing it upon the enemy in deployed lines. But if we
return decidedly to this deployed system, it would be necessary, at least,
in marching to the attack to find a more favorable means than that of
long continuous lines, and to adopt either columns at distances for deploying on arriving at the enemy's position, or lines broken *en échiquier*, or

finally the march in battle by the flank of platoons, operations all more or less dangerous in front of an adversary who knows how to profit from them. Meanwhile, as we have said, a skillful general can, according to circumstances and localities, combine the employment of the two systems.

If experience has proved to me long since that one of the most diffi-cult problems of the tactics of war was the best mode of forming troops for going to combat, I have found out also that to resolve this great pro-blem in an absolute manner, and by an exclusive system, is a thing im-possible.

In the first place, the nature of countries differ essentially. There are those where we can manœuvre two hundred thousand men deployed, as in Champagne ; there are others, like Italy, Switzerland, the valley of the Rhine, the half of Hungary, where we could scarcely deploy a division of ten battalions. The degree of instruction of the troops in all kinds of manœuvres, their armament and their national character, could also have an influence upon formations.

By favor of the great discipline of the Russian infantry, and of its in-struction in manœuvres of every species, it is possible that they may suc-ceed in moving it in great lines with sufficient order and harmony for causing it to adopt a system which would, I think, be impracticable with the French or the Prussians at this day. My experience of this kind has taught me to believe everything possible, and I am not of the number of orthodox persons who admit but one same type and one same system for all armies, as for all countries.

In order to approach the nearest possible to the solution of the pro-blem, it seems to me then that we ought to seek—

(a) The best mode of moving in sight of the enemy, but still out of reach of his shot ;

(b) The best mode of advancing to the attack ;

(c) The best order of defensive battle.

Whatever solution may be given to these questions, it appears to me suitable, in every case, to exercise the troops :—

1. In the march in columns of battalions upon the centre, for deploy-ing, if desired, within reach of the musket, or for advancing on the enemy, even with the columns, if it be necessary ;

2. In the march in deployed and continuous lines, by eight or ten bat-talions at a time ;

3. In the march en échiquier of battalions deployed, which offer broken lines more easy to move than long continuous lines ;

4. In the march in advance by the flanks of platoons;

5. In the march in advance by small squares, either in line or *en échi-quier;*

6. In the changes of front, by means of these various methods of marching;

7. In the changes of front executed by columns of platoons at full distances, in order to reform without deployment; a means which is more expeditious than the other modes of changing front, and which is better adapted to all kinds of ground.

Of all the modes of moving in advance, the march by flanks of platoons would be the easiest if it did not offer some danger; on level ground it answers marvellously, on rough ground it is the most convenient. It has the inconvenience of much fracturing the line; but by habituating the chiefs and the soldiers to it, by dressing well the guides of platoons, and the directing colors, all confusion could be avoided. The only objection which could be offered to it would be the fear of exposing the disjointed platoons to the danger of a rush of cavalry. I do not deny the danger, but it can be avoided either by being well watched by the cavalry, or by not employing this order too near the enemy, but only for crossing the first part of a great space which should separate the two armies. At the least sign of the approach of the enemy, the line could be reformed in a second, since there would only be necessary the time required for a platoon to place itself by file in line at the marching step. However, whatever precautions we may take, it must nevertheless be confessed that this manœuvre could only be employed with troops well disciplined and well exercised, but never with militia or young soldiers. I have never seen it used before the enemy, but only in manœuvres; and for the changes of front especially, it was employed with success. We could always try it in the great annual manœuvres.

I have also seen tried, marches in lines of battalions deployed *en échi-quier;* these marches did very well, whilst those in full or continuous lines were always horribly bad. The French, especially, have never known how to march well in deployed lines. Perhaps those marches *en échiquier* would be found also dangerous in case of an unexpected charge of cavalry; we could, however, employ them for the first moment of the march, to the end of rendering it more easy, then the second *échiquiers* could enter in line with the first before assailing the enemy. Besides, by placing but a small distance between the *échiquiers* it would be always easy to form the line at the instant of a charge, for it must not be forgotten that the *échiquiers* do not constitute two lines, but a single one, which has been divided in order to avoid the wavering and the disorder of a march in continuous line.

The best formation for charging seriously the enemy is not less difficult to point out. Of all the trials which I have seen made, that which appeared to me to succeed the best was the march of twenty-four battalions upon two lines of columns by battalions formed upon the centre for deploying; the first line went at the charge step upon the enemy's line, and arrived within twice the range of musketry, it deployed in the march. The company of voltigeurs of each battalion was deployed as skirmishers, the others were formed, then commenced a sustained fire by file; the second line of columns followed the first, and the battalions which composed it threw themselves at the charge step through the intervals of the companies which were firing. This was done, in truth, without an enemy, and it seemed that nothing could have resisted this double effect of the fire and of the column.

Besides those lines of columns, there are yet three other means of moving to the attack in semi-deep order.

The first is that of lines mingled with deployed battalions and battalions in column upon the wings of those deployed, of which we have spoken at page 297. The deployed battalions and the first divisions of those in column would fire at half musket range, and afterwards throw themselves upon the enemy.

The second is to advance with the deployed line, and firing, to within half musket range, then to throw the columns of the second line through the intervals of the first.

The third is the echelon order, mentioned on page 213, and in figure 11 of plate 1.

Finally, the last mode is to advance entirely in deployed order, by the sole ascendant of the fire until one of the two parties retreat, which appears almost impracticable.

I cannot affirm which of those modes would be the most suitable, for I have seen nothing of the like in the field. In fact, in war, I have never seen anything in the combats of infantry, but battalions deployed beforehand, which commence firing by platoon, then engaging by degrees a fire by file; or else by columns marching fiercely upon the enemy, which fled without awaiting the shot, or which repulsed those columns before the actual meeting, either by its firm continuance or by its fire; or, finally, by taking, itself, the offensive by advancing to the rencounter.* It is scarcely but in villages and defiles that I have seen real melées of infantry in column, the heads of which encountered with the bayonet ; in battle position I have never seen the like.

However it may be with regard to these controversies, we could not too often repeat, it would be absurd to reject the fire of musketry, as well as to renounce semi-profound columns, and the imposing an absolute system of tactics for all countries and against all nations indiscriminately, would be to ruin an army. It is less the mode of formation than the well combined employment of the different arms which will give the victory ; I except from it, nevertheless, columns too deep, which should be proscribed by all theories.

We will terminate this dissertation by recalling, that one of the most essential points for conducting infantry to the combat, is to secure our troops from the fire of the enemy's artillery as much as possible ; not in withdrawing them unseasonably, but by profiting by the inequalities of the ground, or other accidents which are found before them, in order to shelter them from the batteries. When we have arrived under the fire of musketry, then shelters are not to be calculated upon ; if we be in condition to assail, we must do so ; shelters are suitable only, in this case, for skirmishers and for defensive troops.

It is sufficiently important, generally, to defend villages which are upon the front, or to seek to carry them if we be the assailant ; but it is equally necessary not to attach an undue importance thereto, forgetting the famous battle of Hochstaedt : Marlborough and Eugene seeing the bulk of the French infantry buried in the villages, forced the centre and took twenty-four battalions, sacrificed to guard those posts.

For the same reason it is useful to occupy clumps of trees or copses, which may give a support to that one of the two parties which is the master of them. They shelter the troops, conceal their movements, protect those of the cavalry, and hinder that of the enemy from acting in their proximity.

The skeptic Clausewitz was not afraid to sustain the contrary maxim, and under the singular pretext that he who occupies a wood acts blindly, and discovers nothing of what the enemy is doing, he presents their defense as a fault of tactics. Blinded himself, probably, by the results of

---

*I have often seen, also, great combats where the half of the infantry was engaged by platoon as skirmishers; but that enters into the category of battalions engaged in an irregular file firing.

the battle of Hohenlinden, the author is too prone to confound here the occupation of a wood in the line of battle with the fault of throwing a whole army in a vast forest without being master of the issues, either of the front or of the flanks ; but he must never have seen a combat who denies the incontestable importance of the possession of a wood situated in proximity with a line that he wishes to defend or attack. The part which the park Hougeumont played in the battle of Waterloo is a great example of the influence that a post well chosen and well defended can have in a combat; in advancing his paradox, M. Clausewitz had forgotten the importance which woods had in the battles of Hochkirch and of Kollin. But we have already dwelt too long upon this chapter of the infantry, it is time to speak of other arms.

ARTICLE XLV.

THE CAVALRY.

The formation of the cavalry, subjected to nearly the same controversies as that of the infantry, has been subjected also to the same uncertainty, and the too much vaunted treatise of the Count de Bismark, has not done much to clear them up. As we have been scarcely better settled upon its employment, I shall be permitted to submit what I think of it to the decision of generals habituated to conducting it.

The employment which a general-should make of cavalry, naturally depends a little on the relative strength of that of the enemy, either in number or in quality. Nevertheless, whatever modification those variations may induce, a cavalry inferior, but well conducted, may always find occasions to do great things, so decisive is the proper moment in the employment of this arm.

The numerical proportion of the cavalry to the infantry has much varied. It depends upon the natural disposition of nations, whose inhabitants are more or less fit to make good horsemen ; the abundance and the quality of the horses also exercise a certain influence. In the wars of the revolution, the French cavalry, though disorganized, and very in-

ferior to that of the Austrians, served marvellously. I saw, in 1796, in
the army of the Rhine, what they pompously called the reserve of cavalry, and which formed scarcely a feeble brigade, (fifteen hundred horses.)
Ten years afterwards I saw those same reserves fifteen or twenty
thousand horses strong, so much had ideas and means changed.

As a general thing, we may admit that an army in the field ought to
have a sixth of its force in cavalry; in mountainous countries, a tenth
is sufficient.

The principal merit of the cavalry lies in its rapidity and its mobility;
we might add even in its impetuosity, if it were not feared to see a false
application made of the last quality.

However important it may be in the ensemble of the operations of a
war, the cavalry could not defend a position without the assistance of
infantry. Its principal object is to prepare or to finish the victory, to
render it complete by taking prisoners and trophies, by pursuing the
enemy, by rapidly carrying succor to a menaced point, by breaking the
shaken infantry, finally by covering the retreats of the infantry and the
artillery. This is why an army, wanting in cavalry, rarely obtains great
successes, and why its retreats are so difficult.

The mode and the moment most suitable for engaging the cavalry, belongs to the *coup d'œil* of the chief, to the plan of battle, to what the enemy
is doing; and to a thousand combinations too numerous to mention
here. We shall indicate then their principal features.

It is acknowledged that a general attack of cavalry against a line in
good order, could not be attempted with success unless sustained by infantry and much artillery, at least at a certain distance. It was seen
at Waterloo how much it cost the French cavalry for having acted
against this rule, and the cavalry of Frederick experienced the same
fate at Kunersdorf. We may, nevertheless, find ourselves called upon to
engage the cavalry alone ; but, in general, a charge upon a line of infantry which should already be found engaged with the adverse infantry, is
that from which we could expect the most advantages ; the battles of
Marengo, of Eylau, of Borodino, and ten others, have proved this.

Meanwhile there is a case in which the cavalry has a decided superiority over infantry ; it is when there falls a beating rain or snow, which
wets the arms and deprives the infantry of its fire; the corps of Augereau had a cruel proof of it at Eylau, and the left of the Austrians experienced the same fate at Dresden.

Great charges are also executed with success against infantry, when we should have already succeeded in shaking it by a fearful fire of artillery, or in any other manner. One of the most remarkable charges of this kind was that of the Prussian cavalry at Hohenfriedberg, in 1745, (see Treatise of Operations.) But every charge against squares of good infantry not broken, must fail. Great charges are made for carrying the batteries of the enemy, and facilitating for the masses of infantry the means of crowning his position; then it is necessary that the infantry be in condition to sustain them without delay, for a charge of this nature has but an instantaneous effect, of which it is necessary to profit briskly before the enemy drive back your cavalry disunited. The fine charge of the French upon Gosa, at the battle of Leipsic, 16th of October, is a great example of this kind. Those which they executed at Waterloo with the same object, were admirable, but without results, for want of support. In the same manner the audacious charge of the feeble cavalry of Ney upon the artillery of the Prince Hohenloe, at the battle of Jena, is an example of what may be done in such a case.

Finally, general charges are made against the enemy's cavalry for driving it from the field of battle and returning afterwards against his battalions with more liberty.

The cavalry could be launched with success for taking the hostile line in flank or in reverse, at the moment of a serious attack, which the infantry should execute in front. If it be repulsed, it can return at a gallop, and be rallied upon the army; if it succeed, it may cause the ruin of the hostile army. It is rare that it is given this destination, and I do not see, nevertheless, what obstacle there could be to it, for cavalry well conducted could not be cut off, even when it should find itself in rear of the enemy. For the rest, this is the part which belongs especially to irregular cavalry.

In the defensive, the cavalry can equally obtain immense results, by engaging at the proper moment a hostile body of troops, which, having approached the line should be ready to penetrate it, or which should already have pierced it; it could in this case re-establish affairs, and cause the destruction of an adversary shaken and disunited even by its first successes; a fine charge of the Russians at Eylau, and the English cavalry at Waterloo proved this. Finally, the especial cavalry of the army corps make timely charges, either for favoring an attack, or for profiting from a false movement of the enemy, or in order to finish his defeat in a retrograde movement.

It is not so easy to determine the best mode of attack, it depends upon the object that is proposed, and other circumstances which have an influence upon the choice of the moment. There are four modes of charging ; in columns at distance, in lines at the trot,* in lines at the gallop, finally at a helter-skelter, (*a la débandade :*) all may be employed with success. In the charge *en muraille* or in line, the lance offers incontestable advantages ; in melées, the sabre is better, perhaps :· hence comes the idea of giving the lance to the first rank which is to break, and the sabre to the second, which is to finish by partial struggles. The firing with the pistol is suited only to advanced posts in a charge as foragers, or when the light cavalry wishes to harrass the infantry and draw its fire, in order to favor a more serious charge. As for carbine firing, we scarcely know what it is good for, since it requires the whole troop to halt in order to fire deliberately, which will expose it to a certain defeat if it be attacked boldly. It is skirmishers only who are able to fire running.

We have just said that all the modes of charging could be equally good. Meanwhile it is necessary to guard against believing that impetuosity is always decisive in a shock of cavalry against cavalry. The fast trot on the contrary appears to me the best gait for charges in line, because here everything depends upon harmony, steadiness and order, conditions which we do not find in charges at a gallop. These are suitable especially in charges against artillery, because it is more important to arrive quickly than to arrive in order. For the same reason, with cavalry armed with sabres, we may throw ourselves at a gallop at two hundred paces against a hostile line which awaits us steadily. But if we have a cavalry armed with lances, the fast trot is the true gait, for the advantage of this arm depends above all upon the preservation of order ; as soon as there is a melée, the lance loses all its value.

When the enemy comes upon you at a fast trot, it does not seem prudent to run upon him at a gallop, for you arrive all disunited against a compact and close mass, which will pass through your disjointed squadrons. There would only be the moral effect produced by the apparent audacity of your charge which would be favorable to you ; but if the enemy appreciate it at its just value you will be lost, for in the physical and natural order, success ought to be for the compact mass against horsemen galloping without harmony.

In charges against infantry, the Mamelukes and the Turks have sufficiently proved the importance of impetuosity ; where the lancers or the

---

* When I speak here of charges in lines, there is no contradiction with what I have advanced elsewhere; it is comprehended that the question here is not great deployed lines, but brigades, or divisions, at the most. A corps of several divisions will form upon the ground in several echelon columns, the head of which for each will be two or three regiments deployed for the charge.

cuirassiers at the trot will not penetrate, no cavalry will pierce. It is only against infantry much shaken, or whose fire could not be kept up, that the impetuous charge can have any advantage over the trot.* In order to force good squares, cannon and lancers are necessary, better still cuirassiers armed with lances. For charges as foragers or helter-skelter, so frequent in the daily recounters, it is necessary to imitate the Turks or the Cossacks : these are the best examples that can be taken : we shall return to this subject.

Whatever system is employed for going to the shock, a recognized truth for all possible charges is, that one of the best means of succeeding is to know how to throw at the proper time some squadrons on the flanks of the enemy's line which is to be assailed in front. But in order that this manœuvre should obtain a full success, in charges of cavalry against cavalry especially, it is necessary that it be executed only at the instant when the lines come to be engaged, for a minute too soon or too late the effect would probably be nothing : thus it is that the greatest merit of an officer of cavalry consists in this exact and rapid *coup d'œil.*

The armament and the organization of cavalry have been the subject of many controversies, which it would be easy to reduce to a few truths. The lance is, as has just been said the offensive arm for a troop of horsemen charging in line, for it attains an enemy that could not approach them ; but it may be well to have a second rank or a reserve armed with sabres, more easy to handle when in a melée, and when the ranks cease to be united. Perhaps it would even be better still to cause a charge of lancers to be sustained by an echelon of hussars, who penetrating the hostile line after them, would better finish the victory.

The cuirass is the defensive arm *par excellence.* The lance, and the cuirass of strong leather doubled, or a buffalo hide, seems to me the best armament for the light cavalry ; the sabre and the iron cuirass for that the heavy cavalry. Some experienced military men incline even to arming the cuirassiers with lances, persuaded that such a cavalry, very similar to

---

* M. Wagnen opposes to me the opinion of experienced horsemen who prefer the full gallop commenced at two hundred yards. I know that many horsemen think so, but I know also that the most distinguished generals of that arm incline for charges at the trot. Lasalle, one of the most skillful of those generals, said one day in seeing the enemy's cavalry runing up at a gallop—"These are lost people!" and those squadrons were indeed overwhelmed at a slow trot. As for the rest, personal bravery has more influence upon shocks and melees than the different gaits ; the full gallop has against it only, the leading to dispersion and the change of the shock into a melee, which can be avoided with the char ges at a trot. On the other hand the much talked of momentum, the only advantage of the gallop, is but a phantom to frighten inexperienced troopers.

the ancient men at arms, would overturn all before it. It is certain that a lance would suit them better than the musketoon, and I do not see what should prevent giving them weapons similar to those of the light cavalry.

With regard to the amphibious troop, dragoons, opinion will ever be divided ; it is certain that it would be useful to have some battalions of mounted infantry, which could anticipate the enemy at a defile, to defend it in retreat, or to scour a wood ; but to make cavalry of infantry, or a soldier who would be equally proper for either arm, appears a difficult thing : the fate of French foot dragoons would seem to have sufficiently proved it, if on the other side the Turkish cavalry had not fought with the same success on foot as on horseback. It has been said that the greatest inconvenience of dragoons arises from the circumstance that you are obliged to preach to them in the morning that a square cannot resist their charges, and to teach them in the evening that a footman armed with a gun ought to overcome all possible horsemen : this argument is more specious than true, for instead of preaching to them maxims so contradictory, it would be more natural to tell them, that if brave horsemen can break a square, brave infantry can also repulse that charge ; that the victory does not depend always upon the superiority of the arm, but rather upon a thousand circumstances ; that the courage of the troops, the presence of mind of the chiefs, a seasonably made manœuvre, the effect of the artillery and the fire of musketry, the rain, the mud even, have contributed to checks or successes ; but that in general, a brave man on foot or on horseback ought to beat a poltroon. By inculcating these truths to dragoons, they will be able to believe themselves superior to their adversary, either when employed as infantry or when charging as horsemen. It is thus that the Turks and Circassians act, whose cavalry often dismount to fight in the woods or behind a shelter gun in hand. Meanwhile, it cannot be concealed, good chiefs and good soldiers are necessary to carry the education of a troop to that degree of perfection.

However that may be, a regiment of dragoons attached to each *corps d'armée* of infantry or cavalry, as well as to an advanced or rear guard, could be very useful ; whilst that forming whole divisions of dragoons is reducing them to the impossibility of being employed as infantry in the small number of unexpected cases where that would become necessary. It would then be better to make lancers of them.

All that has been said in respect to the formation of infantry may be applied to the cavalry, saving the following modifications.

1. Lines deployed checkerwise, or in echelon are much more suitable to cavalry than full lines ; whilst that in the infantry the order deployed *en*

échiquier would be too broken, and dangerous if cavalry chanced to penetrate and take the battalions in flank ; the disposition *en échiquier* is sure only for preparatory movements previous to the contact with the enemy, or for lines in columns of attack able to defend themselves alone in every direction against cavalry. Whether we form the *echiquier*, or prefer full lines, the distance between the lines ought to be sufficiently great in order that they should not reciprocally drag each other on in case of a check, in view of the rapidity with which they are rallied if the charge is unfortunate. It is merely well to observe that, in the echiquier, the distance may be less than in the full line. In no case, could the second line be full. It ought to be formed in columns by divisions, or at least to leave in it openings for two squadrons which we ploy in columns on the flanks of each regiment, in order to facilitate the passage of the troops rallied.

2. In the order in columns of attack upon the centre, the cavalry should be by regiments, and the infantry only by battalions. To comply well with this order, regiments of six squadrons are then necessary, in order that in ploying upon the centre by divisions they may be able to form three. If they have only four squadrons, they would then only form two lines.

3. The column of attack of cavalry should never be compact like that of infantry, but at full or half squadron distance, with a view to having ground for separating and charging. This distance is only intended for troops thrown out to'combat ; when they are in repose behind the line they can be closed together in order to cover less ground and to diminish the space which they would have to pass over in order to engage, provided. nevertheless, that those masses shall be under shelter or out of reach of cannon.

4. An attack on the flank being more to be feared in cavalry than in a combat of infantry against infantry, it is necessary to establish, upon the extremities of a line of cavalry, some squadrons in echelon by platoons, in order that they be able to form, by a right wheel or a left wheel against the enemy who should come to disturb the flank.

5. For the same motive it is essential, as has already been said, to know how to throw seasonably some squadrons upon the flanks of a line or cavalry which we are about to attack ; if there be irregular cavalry present, it is especially for that we ought to use it in the combat, because for this use it is worth as much and perhaps more than the regular.

An important observation also is that, in the cavalry especially, it is well that the commander-in-chief extend in depth rather than in length. For example, in a division of two brigades which should deploy, it would not be expedient that each brigade should form a single line behind the other, but rather that each brigade should have a regiment in first line, and one in the second : thus each unit of the line will have its own reserve behind it, an advantage which cannot be misunderstood, for events pass so quickly in charges, that it is impossible for a general officer to be master of two deployed regiments.

It is true that in adopting this mode each general of brigade will have the disposition of his reserve, and that it would be well, nevertheless, to have one for the whole division; for this reason it is believed that five regiments for a division is very suitable for cavalry. If it is wished to engage in line by brigades of two regiments, the fifth serves as general reserve behind the centre. If it is wished, we may also have three regiments in line, and two in column behind each wing.

Is it preferred, on the contrary, to take a mixed order by deploying but two regiments at a time, keeping the remainder in column, in this case, we have also a suitable order, since three regiments formed by divisions behind the line cover the flanks and the centre, at the same time leaving intervals for passing the first line if it is beaten. (See fig. 10, plate 3.)

Two essential maxims are generally admitted for combats of cavalry against cavalry : the one is, that every first line ought to be sooner or later led back, for, in the supposition even that it should have made the most fortunate charge, it is probable that the enemy, by opposing to it fresh squadrons, will force it to rally behind the second line. The other maxim is, that with equal merit in the troops and chiefs, the victory will remain to him who shall have the last squadrons in reserve, and who shall know how to launch them at the proper moment upon the flanks of the hostile line, already engaged with his.

It is upon these two truths we shall be able to form a just idea of the system of formation most suitable for conducting a heavy body of cavalry to the combat. Whatever order may be adopted, it is necessary to guard against deploying large bodies of cavalry in full lines; for they are masses difficult to handle, and if the first is driven back, the second will be dragged along with it without being able to draw a sabre. To the number of a thousand proofs that the late war has give us of this, we will cite the attack executed by Nansouty in columns by regiments, upon the Prussian cavalry deployed in advance of Chateau-Thierry.

In the first edition of this treatise I opposed the formation of cavalry upon more that two lines ; but I have never intended to exclude several lines *en echiquier* or in echelon, nor reserves formed in columns ; I wished to speak only of cavalry deployed for charging *en muraille*, and the lines of which uselessly accumulated the one behind the other, would be swept away as soon as the first should chance to retreat.*

For the rest, in cavalry more still than in the infantry, the moral ascendancy does a great deal ; the *coup d'œil* and the *sang froid* of the chief, the intelligence and bravery of the soldier, whether in the melée, or for rallying, procure victory oftener than such or such another formation. Meanwhile, when we can unite these two advantages, we are only the more sure of conquering, and nothing could legitimize the adoption of a mode recognized as vicious.

The history of the late wars (1812 to 1815) has renewed also ancient controversies for deciding if cavalry fighting in line can triumph in the long run over irregular cavalry, which avoiding all serious engagement flies with the speed of the Parthian, and returns to the combat with the same vivacity, limiting itself to harrassing the enemy by individual attacks. Lloyd has pronounced for the negative, and several exploits of the Cossacks against the excellent French cavalry seems to confirm his judgment ;† but we must not be deceived, and think that it would be possible to execute the same things with disciplined light cavalry, which we should launch as foragers against squadrons well united. It is the constant habit of moving in disorder which causes irregular troops to know how to direct all their individual efforts towards a common end ; the best exercised hussars will never approach to the natural instinct of the Cossack, of the Tscherkès or of the Turk.

If experience has proved that irregular charges may bring about the defeat of the best cavalry in partial combats, it is necessary to acknowledge also the impossibility of counting upon helter-skelter charges in

---

* M. Wagner, in order to combat this assertion, cites the battle of Ramilies, where Marlborough conquered by a grand cavalry charge in lines, without intervals, against the French *en echiquier*. But, if my memory serves me, I think that the allied cavalry was at first formed *en echiquier* on two lines ; the true cause of the success was that Marlborough, seeing that Villeroi had paralyzed the half of his army behind Anderkirch and the Gette, had the good sense to draw thirty-eight squadrons from that wing in order to reinforce his left, which had thus twice as many cavalry as the French. As for the rest, I willingly admit many exceptions to a maxim which I do not give as more absolute than all other maxims of cavalry tactics, a tactics as changeable as that arm.

† When I speak of the excellent French cavalry, I mean to speak of its impetuous bravery, and not of its perfection ; for it does not approach the Russian or the German cavalry, either in equitation, in organization, or in the care of its horses.

pitched battles, upon which depends often the fate of a whole war. Such a charge could without doubt aid an attack in lines, but alone it would produce nothing important. We ought then to consider those irregular charges as a powerful auxiliary in the daily rencounters of cavalry, and as a useful accessory in decisive shocks.

From all that which precedes, we ought to conclude, in my opinion, that for battles, a regular cavalry, furnished with long arms, and for petty warfare, an irregular cavalry armed with excellent pistols, with lances and with sabres, will ever be the best organization for this important branch of the service of war.

For the rest, whatever system we adopt it appears not less incontestable that a numerous cavalry, whatever be its nature, ought to have a great influence upon the results of a war; it can carry to a distance terror into the ranks of the enemy; it captures convoys, blockades the army, thus to speak, in its positions; renders its communications difficult, if not impossible; disturbs all harmony in its enterprises and in its movements. In a word it procures almost the same advantages as a rising in mass of the people, by carrying confusion upon the flanks and upon the rear of an army, and by making it impossible for its general to calculate anything with certainty.

Every organization, then, which should tend to double the strength of the cavalry, in case of war, by incorporating militia into it, would be a good system; for those militia, aided by a few good squadrons, will be able at the end of some months' campaign, to make good partizans. Without doubt those militia will not have all the qualities which the warlike and wandering populations possess who pass, thus to speak, their lives on horseback, and whose first instincts are those of petty warfare; but they will supply them in part. In this respect Russia has a great advantage over all her neighbors, as much by the number and quality of her horses of the Don, as by the nature of the irregular militia which she can raise at a moments' warning.

The following is what I wrote twenty years ago in Chapter 35 of the Treatise of Grand Military Operations, upon this same subject :—

"The immense advantages which the Cossacks have given to the Russian armies are incalculable. Those light troops, insignificant in the shock of a great battle, (unless it be for falling upon the flanks,) are terrible in the pursuit and in a war of posts; this is the most redoubtable enemy for all the combinations of a general, because he is never sure of the arrival and execution of his orders, his convoys are always exposed, and his operations uncertain. So long as an army has a few half regular regiments of them, their whole utility is not recognized; but when the number of them is increased to fifteen or twenty thousand, their importance is felt, especially in countries where the people are not hostile to them.

" When a convoy is carried away by them, it is necessary to escort all such, and that the escort be numerous and well conducted. We are never certain of making a tranquil march, because we know not where our enemies are; these labors require considerable forces, and the regular cavalry is soon rendered unserviceable by fatigues which it is not able to sustain.

" For the rest, I believe that hussars or volunteer lancers, raised or organized at the moment of the war, well conducted, and moving where bold chiefs conduct them at their will, would accomplish nearly the same object; but it is necessary to regard them as independent, for if they were to receive orders from the headquarters, they would no longer be partizans. They would not, perhaps, have all the qualities of good Cossacks, but they might approach them."

Austria has also in the Hungarians, the Transylvanians and the Croats, resources which other States have not; however, the services rendered by the mounted *landwehr* prove that we can draw also upon this species of cavalry, were it only for relieving the regular cavalry in the accessory services which abound in all armies, as escorts, despatches, detachments for conducting convoys, flankers, &c. Mixed corps of regular and irregular cavalry can often render more real services than if they were composed only of cavalry of the line, for the fear of compromising and ruining the latter, often prevents launching it into audacious movements which may produce immense results.

I would not terminate this article without noticing the by far too passionate attacks of which it has been the object on the part of General Bismark, and with which, unfortunately, I have become acquainted too late for replying to them as I ought to do. The passage which seems to have especially excited his wrath, is that in which I have advanced, after many others, that cavalry could not defend a position by itself. The General, who doubtless pretends that cavalry can make war of itself alone, and that it could hold a position quite as well as infantry, thinks to justify such sophisms in going for examples even to the war of Hannibal upon the Ticino, as if musketry, shells and grape shot had brought about no change in the employment of this arm! Proud of his equestrian erudition, he treats as ignorant all who do not think like him.

Without being a Seydlitz or a Laguérinière, one may very well reason upon the employment of cavalry in war, and although I have no pretension to being a trooper, I can say that the most experienced of generals in our day have partaken of my ideas upon the cavalry, and that in many battles I have often judged of it better than those who have commanded large masses of it.

The only one of my maxims which has excited some controversies, is that relative to the gait of the trot for charges against cavalry. Whatever may have been said of it, I believe still, at the moment at which I am writing, that success depends much upon the maintenance of order until the instant of the shock; and that for lancers especially, the shock of a *mass well in hand* and at the trot, would triumph over a troop scattered by the gallop.

As for the rest, to maintain order as much as possible in the shock, to endeavor to have it seconded at the opportune moment by a flank attack; to be able to give moral impulsion to one's troop, and to have an echelon ready for support, are the only elements of success which I have ever recognized as practicable in the charges of cavalry against cavalry, for all the fine maxims in the world vanish in a struggle rapid as the lightning, where the most skillful professors would only have time to parry sabre cuts, without even being in condition to give an order which could be heard and executed.

With regard to the good employment of the cavalry, in the whole of a battle as in that of the whole of a war, I believe that no experienced general would repudiate the ideas which I have advanced upon this subject.

I have never denied that cavalry would not concur in the defense of a position; but that it would defend it by itself, I shall ever deny. Posted on a position, behind a hundred pieces of artillery, it will be able to maintain itself there if one be contented with cannonading it, as the French cavalry so bravely defended itself at Eylau; but let infantry and artillery march upon it after having paralyzed its batteries, and you will see if the position will be defended.

For the rest, the true cause of the great wrath of General B**** is easy to divine. I have had the imprudence to say that his Treatise upon the Cavalry, albeit very erudite, had not caused much progress to be made in this arm. This judgment has doubtless appeared to him severe, and in spite of the wrongs of the author in regard to myself, I agree that it was pronounced in too absolute a manner. Meanwhile, after the teachings we have been able to receive from the cavalry of Seydlitz and

of Napoleon, I do not know whether that which M. B**** would organize and conduct according to his doctrines, would do much better ;
here lies the question.   For having dared to resolve it negatively, I am
but an ignoramus ; there is good criticism for you ! If opinions be free,
cannot one discuss them without injuries ? As for myself, I recognize
in M. B**** much mind and erudition ; perhaps he has even too much
for the subject he treats.   When wit sparkles and the passions speak,
reason and judgment sleep.   As for the rest, I have already observed in
the notice which precedes this work, that it was not in serious books that
a military man ought to reply to personalities especially after having
been ignorant of them for six years.

ARTICLE XLVI.

THE EMPLOYMENT OF THE ARTILLERY.

The artillery is at the same time an offensive and defensive arm, equally
formidable.

As an offensive means, a great battery, well employed, crushes a hostile line, shakes it, and facilitates to the troops which attack it the
means of breaking it.   As a defensive arm, it must be acknowledged
that it doubles the strength of a position, not only by the harm it does
an enemy from afar, and by the moral effect which it produces at a long
distance upon troops which march to the attack, but yet by the local
defense which it will make of the position itself, and within grape shot
range.   It is not less important in the attack and defense of places, or of
intrenched camps, for it is the soul of modern fortification.

We have said a few words upon its distribution in the line of battle,
but we are more embarrassed in speaking of the mode in which it should
be made to act in combat.   Here the chances multiply in such a man-
mer, by reason of the particular circumstances of the affair, of the
ground and of the movements of the enemy, that we cannot say that
the artillery has any action independent of that of the other arms.   In
the meanwhile we have seen Napoleon at Wagram throw a battery of a

hundred pieces in the gap occasioned in his line by the departure of the corps of Masséna, and thus to hold in check all the efforts of the Austrian centre; but it would be very dangerous to set up as a maxim such an employment of the artillery.

We shall limit ourselves then to presenting here a few fundamental data, observing that they are based upon the condition of this arm, such as it existed in the late wars; the employment of the new discoveries not being yet well determined could not find place here.

1. In the offensive, we ought to unite a certain mass of artillery upon the point where we are preparing to direct our heaviest blows; we will employ it at first for shaking by its fire the hostile line, in order to second the attack of the infantry and cavalry.

2. There are necessary, besides, a few batteries of horse artillery, for following the offensive movement of the columns, independently of the light foot batteries which have the same object. We must not, however, throw too much foot artillery in an offensive movement; it can be placed in such a manner as to attain the object without following the columns.

3. We have already said that the half, at least, of the horse artillery ought to be united in reserve, in order to be directed rapidly wherever its services shall be most required.* To this effect it is necessary to place it upon the most open ground, where it can be moved in every direction. We have also mentioned the best post for the artillery of position.

4. Batteries, although spread in general over the whole of a defensive line, ought to know how to direct their attention upon the point where the enemy would find more advantages and facilities to penetrate; it is necessary then that the general commanding the artillery should know the strategic and the tactical point of a field of battle, as well as the ground itself, and that every distribution of the reserves be calculated upon this double data.

5. Every one knows that artillery posted on level ground, or in the midst of declivities gently inclined *en glacis*, is that whose effect, in

---

* Since this chapter was first published. several powers have adopted the system of placing the artillerists on the train. instead of putting them on horseback; this saves many horses. and the embarrassment of holding them during the firing of the batteries; but it will never equal, for mobility, the superb horse artillery of the Russians. which surpasses every idea which one seeks to form of it. Many other inventions of ordnance have had place, but they are not yet sufficiently known to find a place here, it will be for experience to demonstrate the manner of employing them.

direct or ricochet firing, will be the most murderous. No person is ignorant, either, that the concentric fire is the most suitable.

6. Artillery of every kind employed in battles ought never to forget that its principal destination is to batter the troops of the enemy, and not to reply to his batteries. Meanwhile, as it is well not to leave the field free to the action of the hostile artillery, it is useful to combat it for drawing its fire ; a third of the disposable pieces may be destined to that object, but two thirds at least ought to be directed upon the·cavalry and the infantry.

7. If the enemy advance in deployed lines, the batteries should seek to cross their fires in order to take those lines obliquely ; those which could place themselves upon the flanks, and batter the lines in their prolongation, would create a decisive effect.

8. When the enemy advances in columns, they can be battered in front ; that is to say, in their depth. However, it is not less advantageous to batter them obliquely, and especially in flank or in reverse. The moral effect produced upon troops by artillery taking them in reverse, it incalculable. It is rare that the most valiant soldiers are not astonished and shaken. The fine movement of Ney upon Preitiz (battle of Bautzen) was neutralized by a few pieces of Kleist, which took his columns in flank, arrested them, and decided the Marshal to change his good direction. A few pieces of light artillery, thrown at every risk upon the flanks for obtaining a like result, would never be ventured without utility.

9. It is acknowledged that batteries should be constantly sustained by infantry or cavalry, and that it is advantageous to support them properly upon the flanks. Meanwhile many cases present themselves when it is necessary to deviate from this maxim, and the example of Wagram, of which we have spoken, is one of the most remarkable of them.

10. It is very important that, in the attacks of cavalry, the artillery do not allow itself to be frightened, and that it fire with ball, but especially with grape shot, as long as possible.* In this case, the infantry charged with protecting batteries ought to be formed in squares in proximity, in order to give refuge to the horses, and afterwards to the cannoniers ; long squares, proportioned to the extent of the front of the battery, seem the most proper for accomplishing this object, when the infantry is in rear of the pieces. If it be found at the side, perfect

---

* The newly invented shell, giving the means of carrying these projectiles two thousand yards. with an insensible parabola, will be a terrible arm against cavalry.

squares will be preferable. We are assured that rocket batteries can be employed against cavalry, the horses of which they frighten ; but I repeat, this is still an experiment to make, and we could base no maxim upon data so uncertain.

11. In the attacks of infantry against artillery, the maxim to fire as long as possible, without, nevertheless, commencing at too great a distance, is yet more rigorous than in the case above mentioned. The cannoniers will always have the means of securing themselves from infantry, if they are properly sustained. Here is one of the cases for engaging the three arms at the same time, for if the hostile infantry be shaken by the artillery, a combined attack of the infantry and cavalry will cause its destruction.

12. The proportions of the artillery have considerably varied in the late wars. Napoleon went to the conquest of Italy in 1800, with forty or fifty pieces, and succeeded completely ; whilst in 1812 he invaded Russia with twelve hundred pieces, and did not succeed. This sufficiently proves that no absolute rule could fix those proportions. It is generally admitted that three pieces to a thousand combattants are sufficient, and even in Turkey, as well as in the mountains, this is a great deal too much.

The proportions of heavy artillery, the reserve, so called, with those of lighter artillery, equally vary. It is a great fault to have too much heavy artillery, for in battles six or eight pounder guns produce nearly the same effect as twelve pounders, and there is meanwhile a great difference in the mobility and the accessory embarrassments of these calibres. For the rest, one of the most notable proofs which can be cited for appreciating the influence of the proportions of the armament upon the success of armies, was given by Napoleon after the battle of Eylau ; the cruel losses which his troops sustained by the fire of the numerous artillery of the Russians, made him feel the necessity of increasing his own. With an activity difficult to conceive, he set all the arsenals at work in Prussia, on the line of the Rhine, and even at Metz, to increase the number of his pieces, and to cast new ones, for turning to account the munitions which he had captured in the campaign. In three months he doubled, at four hundred leagues from his frontiers, the *personel* and the *materiel* of his artillery, a thing unheard-of in the annals of war.

13. One of the most suitable means for obtaining the best possible employment of the artillery, would be always to give the superior command of this arm to a general of artillery who is at the same time a good tactician and strategician ; this chief would have the faculty of

disposing not only of the artillery reserve, but even of half of the pieces attached to the different corps or divisions.

He could thus concert with the generalissimo as to the moment and the place where considerable masses of artillery could best contribute to the victory ; but he will never make such a union of masses without having taken previously the orders of the commander-in-chief.

At the moment when I was about to publish this article for the second time, I received a pamphlet from General Okounieff upon the importance of the artillery. However interesting it may be, it could not decide me to change what I have said upon this arm.

The author avows, with a laudable frankness, that he had not sufficiently appreciated that importance in his work upon the employment of the three arms ; and as if to make reparation to the artillery, he sustains now that it is henceforth to decide battles, and to become for that purpose even the principal arm of European armies.

As I have recognized at all times the part that a well employed artillery may have in victories, I am very much disposed to admit with the author, that its influence would be greater if it were known always how to realize from it the part of which it is susceptible. I acknowledge, also, that several quite recent inventions, which will augment its effect whether for ricochet firing, or for grape at long range, are of a nature to call the attention of generals who shall be at liberty to make use of them, and who have at command the means of trying their effects, as also finding the means of securing themselves against them.

The pamphlet of General Okounieff would then have already attained an important end in in opening this vast quarry ; but after having rendered him justice, I shall be permitted to say that the author has rather overstepped the mark, for if it were necessary to believe all he advances, there would no longer be required in an army anything but cuirassiers, artillerists, and the infantry necessary for holding enclosed posts, for the rest would be but food for projectiles. Setting out with this dominant idea, M. Okounieff concludes from it by a very natural consequence, that the means of gaining battles will be reduced to breaking the centre of an army by dint of cannon shots, and in having masses prepared to fall upon this breach ; a means which he finds very preferable to those he calls *movements of conversion*, and which to this day, according to his own confession, have gained very many battles.

Here, I own, I am obliged to contend that there is something too absolute in these assertions. In the first place, I do not perfectly compre-

hend those movements of conversion ; they are doubtless attacks for outflanking a wing at the same time that a part of the front is assailed. If
I am not deceived, these kinds of manœuvres are not always movements
of conversion ; at best it is but a quarrel of definition, which is really
of little importance ; that which I do not consider well founded, is the idea
that an exclusive manœuvre can be adopted as an universal panacea, and
that it is necessary to renounce all other tactics than that of immense
batteries and heavy masses piercing centres. For my part, if I had to
combat an enemy professing such exclusive ideas, I should be no wise
embarrassed in opposing to him means which would defeat his favorite
attacks. At first I should employ that which M. Okounieff himself cites
on page 35, as having been adopted with success by the Prince de Lich-
tenstein at the battle of Wagram, against the famous column of Macdonald ; the system employed at Cannae by Hannibal, could all the
better find here its application, as such a mass battered by the concentric fires of an artillery equal in number, and disposed in a concave line,
like that of the Arch-Duke Charles at Essling, would be much compromised. Finally, in order to avoid cutting the army in two parts, who
knows if one of those movements of conversion which the author would
repudiate, would not be an excellent means to oppose to his system, since
it would transport the decisive effort of the combat on quite another
point than the centre ?

Far be the thought from me of contesting all merit in a strong attack
upon the centre ; I have often recommended it, but especially when it
should be combined with an attack upon the extremity of the line (agree-
ably to figure 12 of plate 1, page 210,) or where it should be made on a
rather too extended line.

Be that as it may, it appears to me that the author has rather lost sight
of the fact that the moral of the troops, the character and genius of the chiefs
have also a great influence upon the issue of battles. These are batteries
less murderous, but not less efficacious. It must not be forgotten either
that all fields of battle and all countries do not offer the same advantages
to artillery ; in Italy, in Switzerland, in Vendée, in many parts of Germany, in every very broken country, in a word, we do not find fields of
battle like Wagram and Leipsic.

As for the rest, there are useful lessons in his pamphlet, to which no
other reproach could be made than that of having drawn him from one
extreme to the other. The author has without doubt wished to imitate
those advocates who, after a fine defense, draw exaggerated conclusions,
certain that the judges will always abate the half of them ; wise men

will be able to take what they find in them true and useful, and give him credit for them.

The first result of this treatise should be to awaken the attention of men who have the mission of influencing the destinies of armies, that is to say, of governments and generals. The second will be, perhaps, the doubling of the *materiel* and *personel* of the artillery, and the adoption of all improvements capable of augmenting its destructive effect. And as artillerists will be in the number of the first victims, it will be very necessary to engage in instructing in the infantry, men chosen to serve the pieces at need, and to fill even the vacancies which battles would leave in the ranks of the artillery. Finally, it will be necessary to endeavor to find the means of neutralizing the effects of this carnage, and the first which occur seem to be the modification in the armament and the equipment of troops, then the adoption of a new tactics which will render results as prompt as possible. This task will be for the rising generation, when we shall have tested by experience all the inventions with which we are occupied in the schools of artillery, whilst awaiting better. Happy will be those who, in the first rencounters, shall have a plenty of schrapnel howitzers, many guns charged at the breech, and firing thirty shots a minute ; many pieces richocheting at the height of a man, and never failing their mark upon one or another part of the field of combat ; finally, the most improved rockets—without counting even the famous steam guns of Perkins, reserved to the defense of ramparts, but which, if the written statement of Lord Wellington is to be believed, will yet be able here to make cruel ravages. * * * What a beautiful text for preaching universal peace and the exclusive reign of railroads !

I shall be pardoned if I terminate a discussion so grave, by a phrase bordering upon pleasantry. But we must take a less sombre view of the future with which so many brave men menace us, who by a cruel foresight combine the means of rendering war still more bloody than it is, and that, too, in the hope of assuring the triumph of their banners. A terrible but indispensable emulation, if we would remain on an equality with our neighbors so long as the law of nations shall not have placed limits to those inventions.

ARTICLE XLVII.

OF THE COMBINED EMPLOYMENT OF THE THREE ARMS.

In order to terminate entirely this summary, it would remain to speak of the combined employment of the three arms : but how many minute variations would not this subject present if one pretended to penetrate into all the details which the application of the general maxims indicated for each of those arms in particular, require ?

Several works, and the German particularly, have sounded this bottomless abyss, and have obtained passable results, but by multiplying to infinity examples taken in the small partial combats of the late wars. Those examples in effect supply maxims, when experience demonstrates that it would be impossible to give fixed ones. To say that the commander of a corps composed of the three arms, ought to employ them in such a manner that they naturally support and second each other, would seem a truism ; and it is, nevertheless, the only fundamental dogma which it is possible to establish, for to wish to prescribe to that chief the manner in which he ought to go to work in every circumstance, would be to engage in an inextricable labyrinth. Now, as the objects and the limits of this sketch do not allow me to touch such questions, I can do no better than to refer officers to the special works which have treated them with the most success.

To place the different arms according to the ground, according to the object which is proposed, and that which may be supposed of the enemy, to combine their simultaneous action according to the characteristic qualities of each—this is all that the art can advise. It is in the study of wars, and especially in the practice, that a superior officer will be able to acquire these notions, as well as the *coup d'œil* which inspires their seasonable application. I think I have fulfilled the task which I have imposed upon myself, and I am going to pass successively to the narration of the memorable wars, in which my readers will find at each step occasion to be assured that military history, accompanied by sound criticism, is indeed the true school of war.

CONCLUSION

We have endeavored to retrace the principal points which have appeared to us susceptible of being presented as fundamental maxims of war. War, however, in its ensemble, is not a science, but an art. If strategy, especially, can be subjected to dogmatic maxims which approach the axioms of positive sciences, it is not the same as a whole with the operations of a war, and combats among others will often escape all scientific combinations, to offer us acts essentially dramatic, in which personal qualities, moral inspirations, and a thousand other causes, will play at times the first part. The passions which shall agitate masses, called to hurl themselves against each other—the warlike qualities of those masses—the character, energy and the talents of their chiefs—the greater or less martial spirit, not only of nations, but even of epochs*— in a word, all that which may be called the poetry and the metaphysics of war, will ever have an influence upon its results.

Is it saying, for all that, that there are no tactical rules, and that no tactical theory could be useful? What reasonable military man would dare pronounce such a blasphemy? Will it be believed that Eugene and Marlborough have triumphed only by inspiration, or by the moral superiority of their battalions? Will there not be found, on the contrary, in the victories of Turin, of Hochstaedt, of Ramillies, manœuvres which resemble those of Talavera, of Waterloo, of Jena, or of Austerlitz, and which were the causes of victory? Now, when the application of a maxim, and the manœuvre which has been its result, have a hundred times given the victory to skillful captains, and offer in their favor all the

---

* The famous Spanish proverb. *he was brave on such a day*, may be applied to nations as well as to individuals. One could not compare the French at Rosback with those at Jena nor the Prussians at Prenzlow with those at Dennewitz.

probable chances, will their occasional failure be sufficient for denying
their efficacy, and for disputing all influence of the study of the art; will
every theory be vain because it will procure but three fourths of the
chances of success?

If the *moral* of an army and of its chiefs have also an influence upon
these chances, is it not definitively because it will produce a physical action subjected, like the combination of tactics, to laws common to *military statics?* The impetuous attack of twenty thousand electrified brave
men upon the extremity of a hostile line, will more surely give the victory than the manœuvre of forty thousand demoralized men against that
same extremity, because the first will exercise a real action, and the latter
will remain passive, if they do not even fly.

Strategy, as we have said, is the art of conducting the greatest part
of the forces of an army upon the most important point of the theatre
of war, or of a zone of operations.

Tactics is the art of using those masses upon the point where well
combined marches will have brought them; that is to say, the art of
putting them in action at the moment and at the decisive point of the
field of battle upon which the definitive shock is to have place. When
troops think more of flying than of fighting, they are no longer acting
masses, in the sense we give to this expression.

A general instructed in theory, but devoid of *coup d'œil*, of *sang froid*
and of skill, may make a fine strategic plan, and be at fault in all the
laws of tactics, when he finds himself in the presence of the enemy; then
his projects will be baffled, and his defeat probable. If he have character, he will be able to diminish the bad consequences of his check; if he
lose his wits, he will lose his whole army.

The same general may on the contrary be as good a tactician as he
has been strategician, and may have prepared victory by every means
in his power; in this case when he shall be ever so little seconded by his
troops and lieutenants, he will probably gain a signal victory; but if
on the contrary he command but an undisciplined rabble, wanting in
order and courage, if he be envied and deceived by perfidious lieutenants,* he will doubtless see vanish all his hopes, and his most splendid

---

* It oftener happens than is thought, that a general-in-chief is deceived by his lieutenants, who, listening but to their egotism, forget that they are betraying at the same time
the country and the army, through the effect of the basest jealousy and the most con-
temptible ambition. The unskillfulness of a lieutenant, who should be incapable of conceiving the merit of a prescribed manœuvre, and should commit grave faults of execution, would have the same results in overturning the finest combinations.

combinations will be able but to diminish the disasters of an almost inevitable defeat. This defeat would be all the more sure when with such instruments he should have to combat an adversary, perhaps less skillful than himself, but having troops inured to war, or enthusiasts for their cause.

No tactical system could guarantee the victory when the *moral* of the army is bad, and even when it should be excellent, victory may depend upon an incident like the rupture of the bridges of the Danube at Essling. A systematic general could prohibit columns from adopting the shallow or firing order, or else confine it to purely defensive means, in order to adopt exclusively the semi-profound columns, without being sure, nevertheless of success.

These truths do not prevent the existence of good maxims of war which, with equal chances, will be able to procure victory; and if it be true that these theories could not teach with a mathematical precision what it would be suitable to do in every possible case, it is certain at least that they will always point out the faults that are to be avoided: now this would already be an immense result: for such maxims would thus become, in the hands of generals commanding brave troops, more or less certain pledges of success.

The correctness of this assertion being incontestible, it remains then but to know how to recognize the good maxims from the bad; it is in that, it is true, which consists all genius for war, but there are meanwhile directing principles for arriving at this knowledge. Every maxim of war will be good when it shall have for result, the assuring the employment of the largest sum of means of action at the opportune moment and point. We have presented in chapter III, all the strategic combinations which can lead to this result. As for what concerns the tactical, the principal of those combinations will ever be the choice of the most suitable order of battle, considering the project that shall be had in view. Afterwards, when it comes to the local action of the masses upon the ground, those means of action may be equally well, a charge of cavalry seasonably made, a strong battery posted and unmasked at the proper moment, a column of infantry charging with impetuosity, or a division deployed furnishing, with steadiness and sang-froid, a murderous fire, finally tactical movements which should menace the enemy in flank and reverse, as well as every manœuvre which should shake the *moral* of one's adversaries. Each of these acts may, according to circumstances, become the cause of victory; to determine the cases in which it would be necessary to give the preference to either, would be an impossible thing.

In order to play well this great drama of war, the first of duties then will be to become well acquainted with the theatre upon which we are to act, to the end of judging of the advantages of the double *échiquier* upon which the two parties shall move, appreciating the advantages of the enemy as well as those of our own party. This knowledge acquired, we must consider as to the means of preparing a base of operations; afterwards it will be the object to choose the most suitable zone upon which to direct our principal efforts, and to embrace this zone in a manner the most conformed to the principles of war, by choosing well our lines and front of operations. The assailing army should especially attach itself to breaking up seriously the hostile army, by adopting to this end skillful objective points of manœuvre; it will then take for the objective of its enterprises, geographical points proportioned to the successes which it shall have obtained.

The defensive army, on the contrary, should calculate all the means of neutralizing this first impulsion of its adversary, by procrastinating operations, as much as possible without compromising the fate of the country, and by putting off the decisive shock, until the moment when a part of the hostile forces should be found broken down by fatigues, or scattered for occupying the invaded provinces, masking fortifications, covering sieges, protecting the line of operations and the depôts, &c.

Until then, all that we have just said may be the object of a first plan of operations: but that which no plan could foresee with any certainty, is the nature and issue of the definitive shock which will result from those enterprises. If your lines of operations have been skillfully chosen, your movements well disguised; if the enemy, on the contrary, make false movements which permit you to fall upon the yet dispersed fractions of his army, you will be able to conquer without pitched battles, by the sole ascendancy of your strategic advantages. But if the two parties find themselves in equally good condition at the moment when the rencounter shall have place, then there will result one of those great tragedies like Borodino, Wagram, Waterloo, Bautzen, and Dresden, in which the precepts of grand tactics indicated in Chapter IV, will certainly be able to exercise a notable influence.

If certain obstinate military men, after having read this book, after having studied attentively the discussed history of a few campaigns of the great masters, maintain still that there are neither principles nor good maxims of war, then one could only pity them and reply to them by the famous saying of Frederick the Great: " A mule which should have made twenty campaigns under Prince Eugéne, would be none the better tactician therefor."

Good theories founded upon principles, justified by events, and joined to discussed military history, will be, in my opinion, the true school for generals. If these means do not form great men, who are always formed by themselves when circumstances favor them, they will at least make generals sufficiently skillful to hold the second rank among the great captains.

later to march upon Rome. Beaten in his turn, and repulsed upon Beneventum, he repassed into Epirus with the nine thousand men which re-remained to him.

Carthage, which had prospered for a long time, profited by the ruin of Tyre and of the Persian Empire. The Punic wars between this African republic and that of Rome, which became preponderant in Italy, were the most celebrated in the maritime annals of antiquity. The armaments made by the Romans and the Carthagenians were especially worthy of remark for the rapidity with which the first perfected and augmented their navy. In the year 488, (264 B. C.,) they had scarcely canoes for passing into Sicily, and eight years afterwards we see them under Regulus, conqueror at Ecnona, with three hundred and forty large vessels, carrying each three hundred oarsmen and one hundred and twenty combattants, forming a total of one hundred and forty thousand men. The Carthagenians were, it is said, still stronger by twelve or fifteen thousand men and fifty vessels.

This great victory of Ecnona, more extraordinary perhaps than that of Actium, was the first step of the Romans towards the empire of the world. The descent which followed into Africa, was composed of forty thousand men; but the conquerors, having committed the fault of recalling the greater part of those forces to Sicily, the remnant was overwhelmed, and Regulus, made prisoner, became as celebrated by his death as by his famous victory.

The great fleet armed for avenging him, and victorious at Clypea, was destroyed on its return by a tempest; that which succeeded it had the same fate at Cape Palinurus. Beaten at Drepana, (year 249,) the Romans lost twenty-eight thousand men and more than a hundred vessels. Another fleet is entirely swallowed up the same year at Cape Pactyrus, in going to besiege Lilybæum.

Disgusted with so many disasters, the Senate renounced at first holding the sea; but seeing that the empire of Sicily and of Spain would depend on its maritime superiority, it armed anew, and in the year 242, (B. C.) Lutatius was seen to depart with three hundred galleys and seven hundred transport vessels for Drepana, and to gain the battle of the Aegates islands, where the Carthagenians lost one hundred and twenty vessels; this event put an end to the first Punic war.

The second having been signalized by the expedition of Hannibal to Italy, gave a less maritime turn to the operations. Scipio carried meanwhile the Roman eagles before Carthage, and by the conquest of that place, ruined forever the empire of the Carthagenians in Spain. Finally, he carried the war into Africa with an armament that did not even equal that of Regulus, which did not prevent him from triumphing at Zama, from imposing upon Carthage a shameful peace, and from burning five hundred of its vessels. Later, the brother of this great man crossed the Hellespont with twenty-five thousand men, and went to gain at Magnesia the celebrated victory which gave up the kingdom of Antiochus to the mercy of the Romans. This expedition was favored by a naval victory, gained at Myonnesus in Ionia by the Romans, united to the Rhodians against the fleet of Antiochus.

From that time the Romans, having no more rivals, augmented their power with all the influence which the empire of the sea assures. Paulus Æmilius made a descent upon Samothrace at the head of twenty-five thousand men, (168 years B. C.,) conquered Persia and subjected Macedonia.

Twenty years later, the third Punic War decided the fate of Carthage ; the important port of Utica having given itself up unreservedly to the Romans, an immense armament, departed from Lilybaeum, and immediately transported there eighty thousand infantry and four thousand horse ; siege was laid to Carthage, and the son of Paulus Æmilius, adopted by the great Scipio, had the glory of finishing the victory of his fathers, by destroying that bitter rival of the Romans.

After this triumph, Rome ruled in Africa as well as in Europe ; but its empire was momentarily shaken in Asia by Mithradates ; this great king, after having successively seized small neighboring States, commanded not less than two hundred and fifty thousand men, and had a fleet of four hundred vessels, three hundred of which were decked. He fought the three Roman generals who commanded in Cappadocia, invaded all Asia Minor, caused eighty thousand Roman subjects to be massacred, and even sent a powerful army to Greece. Sylla descended with a reinforcement of twenty-five thousand Romans, and retook Athens ; but Mithradates sent successively two great armies by the Bosphorus or by the Dardanelles ; the first, of a hundred thousand men, was destroyed at Chaeronea ; the second, of eighty thousand, had the same fate at Oorchomenus. At the same time, Lucullus assembled all the maritime forces of the cities of Asia Minor, those of the isles, and especially of the Rhodians, and came to take the army of Sylla at Cestas, for conducting it into Asia ; Mithradates frightened, made peace.

In the second war, made by Muraena, and in the third conducted by Lucullus, there were no more descents operated. Mithradates, pushed by degrees as far as Colchis, and no longer holding the sea, conceived the project of turning the Black Sea by the Caucasus, in order to return by Thrace against Rome, a project difficult to conceive on the part of a man who could not defend his States against fifty thousand Romans.

Cæsar made a descent upon England for the second time, with six hundred vessels, carrying nearly forty thousand men. In the civil wars he transported thirty-five thousand men into Greece. Anthony, departing from *Brindes*, in order to join him with twenty thousand men, in pasing through the naval forces of Pompey, was as much favored by the fortune of Cæsar as by the dispositions of his lieutenants.

Later, Cæsar transported sixty thousand men into Africa, but these latter only arrived there successively, and at several different times.

The greatest armament which signalized the latter days of the Roman republic, was that of Augustus, which transported eighty thousand men and twelve thousand horses destined to fight Anthony in Greece ; for, independently of the number of transport vessels for a like army, he had two hundred and sixty vessels of war for protecting them. Anthony had superior forces upon land, and committed the fate of the world to that of a naval battle ; he had a hundred and seventy vessels of war, besides sixty Egyptian galleys from Cleopatra, the whole carrying twenty-two thousand choice infantry besides the complement of oarsmen.

Later, Germanicus conducted to the mouths of the Ems a grand expedition, composed of a thousand vessels departing from the mouths of the Rhine, and carrying at least sixty thousand men. The half of this fleet was destroyed on its return by a tempest, and it is not conceived why Germanicus, master of the two banks of the Rhine, exposed himself to the hazards of the sea for so short a journey, which he could have executed by land in a few days.

When the Roman empire had extended its limits from the Rhine to the Euphrates, maritime expeditions were rare, and the great struggle which followed with the people of the North after the division of the empire, caused to be directed all the forces of the State to the side of Germany and of Thrace. The Eastern empire, preserved, nevertheless, a great marine, for which the islands of the Archipelago created the necessity and furnished the means.

The first five centuries of the Christian era offer then little interest under the maritime aspect. The Vandals were the only people who, masters of Spain, made a descent on Africa under Genseric, to the num-of eighty thousand; they were afterwards conquered by Belisarius; but their marine, mistress of the Balearic islands and of Sicily, commanded for a moment the Mediterranean.

At the same time at which the people of the East were overrunning Europe, those of Scandinavia began to visit the coast of England. Their operations are scarcely better known than those of the barbarians; they were lost in the mysteries of Odin. Bards of Scandinavia accord two thousand five hundred ships to Sweden; less poetical calculations give nine hundred and seventy to the Danes, and three hundred to the Norwegians, who often acted in concert.

The Swedes naturally turned their incursions towards the northern extremity of the Baltic, and pushed the Varangians upon Russia. The Danes, situated more in reach of the North Sea, directed themselves towards the coasts of England and of France.

If the enumeration cited by Depping is exact, it is certain at least that the better part of those ships were but fishermens' barks carrying a score of men. There were also *snekars* with twenty benches of rowers, which would make forty oars for the two sides. The chiefs moved in *dragons* with thirty-four benches of rowers. The incursions of the Danes, who ascended far up the Seine and Loire, incline us to believe that the major part of those vessels were very small. However, Hengist, invited in 449, by the Breton Wortiger, conducted five thousand Saxons into England, with eighteen vessels only, which would prove that there were also large ones, or that the marine of the borders of the Elbe was superior to that of the Scandinavians.

From 527 to 584, three new expeditions, under Ida and Cridda, placed England in the power of the Saxons, who formed of it seven kingdoms. It is only at the end of three centuries (833) that this Heptarchy is united into a single State under Egbert.

By a movement the reverse of that of the Vandals, the African populations, visited in their turn the South of Europe. The Moors crossed in 712 the Straits of Gibraltar, under the conduct of Tarik. Invited by Count Julian, they came at first only to the number of five thousand, and far from experiencing a strong resistance, they were favored by the numerous enemies of the Visigoths. Then was the fine time of Califs, and the Arabs could indeed pass for liberators in comparison with the oppressors of the North. The army of Tarik, soon increased to twenty thousand men, conquered king Rodrigo at Xeres de la Frontera, and subjected the kingdom. By degrees, several millions of inhabitants from Mauritania, passed the sea to establish themselves in Spain, and if their numerous migrations cannot figure precisely in the number of descents, they nevertheless form one of the most imposing pictures as well as the most curious of history, placed between the invasions of the Vandals in Africa, and the Crusades in the East.

A revolution not less important, and which left more durable traces, signalized in the North the establishment of the vast empire which bears at this day the name of Russia. The Varangian princes, invited by the Novogorodians, and of which Ruric was the first, soon signalized themselves by great expeditions.

In 902 Olig embarked, it is said, upon the Deieper, with two thousand barks carrying eighty thousand men, who crossed the cataracts of the river, debouched into the Black Sea, whilst their cavalry moved along the coast, presented themselves before Constantinople, and forced Leo, the philosopher, to pay them tribute.

Forty years afterwards Igor took the same route with an armament which the chronicles fix at ten thousand barks. Arrived near Constantinople, his fleet, frightened by the terrible effects of the Greek fire, is driven upon the coast of Asia, lands troops there which are repulsed, and the expedition returns home.

Far from being discouraged, Igor re-establishes his fleet and his army, descends to the mouth of the Danube, where the Roman Emperor, Lapucenus, sends to demand of him peace, and renews the tributes (943).

Scarcely a quarter of a century has passed, when Swatoslaus, favored by the disputes of Nicephorus with the king of the Bulgarians, embarks sixty thousand men (967), debouches into the Black Sea, ascends the Danube, and seizes Bulgaria. Recalled by the Patzinacites, who men. aced Kiew, he allies himself with them, returns to Bulgaria, breaks his alliance with the Greeks, then, reinforced by Hungarians, crossed the Balkan and goes to attack Adrianople. The throne of Constantine was then occupied by Zimisces, who was worthy of it; instead of ransoming himself like his predecessors, he raises a hundred thousand men, arms a respectable fleet, repulses Swatoslans from Adrianople, obliges him to retire upon Silistria, and causes the capitol of the Bulgarians to be re-taken by assault. The Russian prince marches to meet the enemy, gives him battle not far from Silistria, but is forced to re-enter into the place, where he sustained one of the most memorable seiges of which history makes mention.

In a second battle, still more bloody, the Russians perform prodigies, and are forced anew to yield to numbers. Zimisces knowing how to honor courage, finally makes with them an advantageous treaty. About the same time the Danes are attracted to England, by the hope of pillage; we are assured that Lothaire also invited their king Ogier, into France, to avenge himself upon his brothers. The first success of those pirates augmented their taste for adventures : every five or six years they vomit upon the coasts of France and Bretagne, bands which devastate every thing. Ogier, Hastings, Regner, Sigefroi, conduct them sometimes to the mouths of the Seine, sometimes to those of the Loire, finally to those of the Garonne. It is pretended even that Hastings entered the Mediterranean, and ascended the Rhone as far as Avignon, which is at least doubtful. The strength of their armaments is not known, the largest appears to have been three hundred sail.

At the commencement of the tenth century, Rollo, descending at first upon England, finds in Alfred a rival who leaves him little hope of success, he allies himself with him, makes a descent upon Nuestria, in 911, and marches by Rouen upon Paris ; others corps advance from Nantes upon Chartres. Repulsed from this city, Rollo extends himself into the neighboring provinces and ravages every thing. Charles the Simple, sees no better means of delivering his kingdom from this continual scourge, than of offering to cede to Rollo his beautiful province of Nuestria, on condition of marrying his daughter and becoming a christian, which was eagerly accepted.

Thirty years later, the grand son of Rollo, disturbed by the successors of Charles, calls the king of Denmark to his assistance. The latter makes a descent with considerable forces, defeats the French, makes their king prisoner, and secures Normandy for ever to the son of Rollo.

In the same interval, from 838 to 950, the Danes showed the same bitterness against England, and treated her still worse than France, although the conformity of language and of manners being then nearer the Saxons than the French. Iwar established his race in Northumberland, after having sacked the kingdom ; Alfred the Great, at first conquered by the successors of that chief, succeeded in reconquering his throne, and constrains the Danes to submit to his laws.

Affairs change their face ; Swenon, more fortunate still than Iwar, after having overrun England, as much her devastator as her conqueror, twice sells her peace for gold, and returns to Denmark, leaving a part of his army in the country.

Ethelred, who disputed with him without talents, the remnants of the Saxon power, believes he cannot better disembarrass himself of his importunate guests than by ordering the simultaneous massacre of all the Danes left in the island, (1002.) But Swenon reappears in the following year with an imposing force ; three fleets operated successively, from 1003 to 1007, as many debarkations, which ravage anew unhappy England.

In 1012, Swenon made a descent upon the mouths of the Humber, overruns the country a second time like a torrent, and the English, tired of obeying princes who are not able to defend them, recognize him as king of the North. His son, Canute the Great, had to dispute the throne with a rival more worthy of it, (Edmund Ironsides.) Returning from Denmark with considerable forces, and seconded by the perfidious Edric, Canute ravaged the southern part and menaced London. A new division took place, but Edmund having been assassinated by Edric, Canute was finally recognized king of all England, departed afterwards to subject Norway, returned to attack Scotland, and died, dividing his kingdoms between his three children, according to the usage of the times.

Five years after his death, the English restored the crown to their Anglo-Saxon princes; but Edward, on whom it devolved, was better calculated for a monk than for saving a country the prey of such intestine broils. He died in 1066, leaving Harold a crown which the chief of the Normans established in France contested with him, to whom Edward had, it is said, ceded it; and unfortunately for Harold, this competitor was an ambitious and a great man.

This year, 1066 was signalized by an extraordinary double expedition. Whilst that William the Conqueror made ready in Normandy a formidable armament against Harold, the brother of the latter, driven from Northumberland for his crimes, seeks support in Norway, departs with the king of this country and more than thirty thousand men, borne by five hundred vessels, which made a descent upon the mouths of the Humber. Harold destroys them almost entirely in one bloody battle, delivered near York; but at the same instant a more furious storm is about to fall upon him. William profited by the moment when the Anglo-Saxon king was fighting the Norwegians, to set sail from St. Valery with one of the most considerable armaments of the age; (Hume affirms that it contained three thousand transport vessels, others reduce its numbers to twelve hundred, carrying sixty or seventy thousand combattants.) Harold, hastened from York, delivering him near Hastings a decisive battle, in which the king of England finds an honorable death, and his happy rival soon subjects the whole country to his dominion.

At the same instant at which this passed, another William, surnamed Iron-arm, Robert Guiseard and his brother Roger, go to the conquest of Calabria and of Sicily, with a handful of brave men, (1058 to 1070.)

Thirty years have scarcely passed since those memorable events, when an enthusiastic priest animates all Europe with a fanatical infatuation, and precipitates it upon Asia to conquer the Holy Land.

Followed at first by a hundred thousand men, then by two hundred thousand badly armed vagabonds, who perished in part by the sword of the Hungarians, Bulgarians, and of the Greeks, Peter the Hermit succeeded at last in crossing the Bosphorus, and arrived before Nice with fifty or sixty thousand men, who were entirely destroyed or taken by the Saracens.

A more military expedition succeeded this campaign of Pilgrims; a hundred thousand French, Lorrains, Burgundians and Germans, conducted by Godfrey of Bouillen, directed themselves by Austria upon Constantinople; a like number, under the Count of Toulouse, marched by Lyons, Italy, Dalmatia and Macedonia. Bohemond, Prince of Tarentum, with Normans, Sicilians and Italians, embarked, in order to follow the route by Greece upon Gallipoli.

This grand migration recalls the fabulous expeditions of Xerxes; the Genoese, Venitian and Greek fleets are freighted for transporting those swarms of crusaders into Asia, by passing the Bosphorus and the Dardanelles; more than four hundred thousand men were united in the plains of Nice, and avenged there the fate of their predecessors; Godfrey, conqueror, conducted them then across Asia and Syria to Jerusalem, where he founded a kingdom.

All the maritime means of Greece, and of the flourishing republic of Italy were employed, either in transporting those masses beyond the Bosphorus, or in supplying them during the seige of Nice; and the grand movement which this impressed upon the maritime powers of Italy, was perhaps the most happy result of the crusades.

This momentary success became the cause of great disasters; the Mussulmans, divided between themselves, rallied always when it was the question to fight the infidels; and division passed in its turn into the camp of the crusaders. A new expedition was necessary to secure the kingdom, which the valiant Noureddin menaced. Louis VII, and the Emperor Conrad, departed at the head, each, of a hundred thousand crusaders, and took, like their predecessors, the route of Constantinople, (1142.) But the Greeks, frightened by the reiterated visits of those menacing hosts, conspired their ruin.

Conrad, who had wished to take the advance, fell into the snares of the Turks, warned by Manuel Comnenus, and was defeated in detail by the Sultan of Iconium. Louis, more fortunate, conquered the Turks upon the borders of the Maeander; but his army, deprived of the support of Conrad, harrassed by the enemy, partially defeated in the passage of the defiles, and lacking every thing, saw itself confined at Attalia upon the coast of the Pamphilia, where it sought the means of embarking; the Greeks furnished their wants insufficiently, and scarcely fifteen or twenty thousand men succeeded in reaching Antioch with their king; the rest perished, or fell into the hands of the Saracens.

These feeble succors, soon devoured by the climate and daily combats, although reinforced by the small successive bodies of troops which the Italian marine brought from Europe, were ready to succumb anew under the blows of Saladin, when the Court of Rome succeeded in uniting the Emperor Frederick Barbarossa with the kings of France and of England, for saving the Holy Land.

The Emperor, departed the first at the head of a hundred thousand Germans, clears a passage by Thrace, in spite of the formal resistance of the Greeks, then governed by Isaac Angelus. Frederick, victorious, marches to Gallipoli, crosses the Dardanelles, seizes Iconium, and dies for having imprudently bathed in a river that has been pretended to be the Cydnus. His son, the Duke of Suabia, harrassed by the Musselmans, prostrated by disease, brings scarcely six thousand men to Ptolemais.

At the same time, Richard Cœur-de-Lion, and Philip-Augustus, better inspired,* took the way by sea, departing from Marseilles and Genoa with two large fleets, (1190.) The first took Cyprus, and both made a descent afterwards on Syria, where they would have probably triumphed but for the rivalry which arose between them and brought Philip back to France.

Twelve years afterwards, a new crusade was decided upon, (1203;) a part of the crusaders embarked from Provence and Italy; others, under the Count of Flanders and the Marquis of Montferrat, take the route of Venice, with the intention of doing the same. But these last, seduced by the skillful Dandolo, unite themselves with him, in order to attack Constantinople, under the pretext of sustaining the rights of Alexius Angelus, son of that Isaac Angelus, who had combatted the Emperor Frederick, and successor of those Comnenian princes, who favored the destruction of the armies of Conrad, and of Louis VII.

Twenty thousand men dare to attack the ancient capital of the world, which numbers at least two hundred thousand defenders. They made a double assault upon it by sea and by land, and carried it. The usurper

---

* Richard departed from England with twenty thousand infantry and five thousand horsemen, and debarked in Normandy, from whence he went by land to Guinne. and from there to Marseilles. We are ignorant what fleet carried him to Asia. Philip embarked at Genoa in Italian ships, with, at least. as considerable forces.

fled ; Alexius Angelus, replaced upon his throne, cannot maintain himself ; the Greeks rise in favor of Mourzoufle, but the Latins make a more bloody assault than the first, seize Constantinople, and place on the throne their chief, the Count Baldwin, of Flanders. This empire lasts half a century ; the remnant of that of the Greeks took refuge at Nice and Trebizond.

A sixth expedition was directed upon Egypt, by John of Brienne, and spite of the success of the horrible siege of Damietta, he was obliged to yield before the ever increasing efforts of the Musselman population ; the remnant of his brilliant army, near being submerged in the waters of the Nile, were too happy in buying permission to re-embark for Europe.

The Court of Rome, which found it to its interest to keep up the ardor of the christians for these expeditions, from which it alone drew the fruit, stimulated the German princes to sustain the tottering kingdoms of Jerusalem. The Emperor Frederick, and the Landgrave of Hesse, embark at *Brindes*, 1127, at the head of forty thousand choice soldiers. But this Landgrave, and afterwards Frederick himself, having fallen ill, the fleet put into Tarentum, whence the Emperor, irritated by the pride of Gregory IX, who dared to excommunicate him, because he did not obey promptly enough his behests, departed again later with ten thousand men, thus yielding to the terror which the pontifical thunders inspired.

Louis IX, animated by the same spirit, or guided, if Ancelot is to be believed, by motives of a more elevated policy, departed from Aigues-Mortes in 1248, with one hundred and twenty large vessels, and fifteen hundred small boats, hired from the Genoese, Venitians and Catalans, for France, although washed by two seas, had yet no marine. This king made a descent upon Cyprus, rallied there still some forces, and departed, says Joinville, with more than eighteen hundred vessels, to descend upon Egypt. His army must have had about eighty thousand men, for, although the half was dispersed and thrown upon the coast of Syria, it marched some months after upon Cairo, with sixty thousand combattants, of which twenty thousand were horse. It is true that the Count of Poitiers had operated a second debarkation of troops coming from France.

It is sufficiently well known what a sad fate this brilliant army experienced, which did not prevent, twenty years afterwards, the same king from attemping the hazards of another crusade, (1270.) He made a descent this time upon the ruins of Carthage, and besieged Tunis ; but the plague destroyed the half of his army in a few weeks, and he himself was the victim of it. The king of Sicily debarked with powerful reinforcements at the moment of the death of Louis, wishing to bring back the remnant of the army to his island, experienced a tempest which swallowed up four thousand men and twenty large vessels. This prince did not less meditate the conquest of the Greek empire and of Constantinople, as a prey more useful and more sure. But Philip, son and successor of Saint Louis, pressed to return to France, rejected this proposition. This effort was the last; the christians, abandoned in Syria, were there destroyed in the memorable attacks of Tripoli and Ptolemais; some remnants of the religious orders took refuge at Cyprus, and established themselves at Rhodes.

The Musselmans passed in their turn the Dardanelles at Gallipoli, 1355, and seized successively the European Provinces of the Eastern Empire, against which the Latins themselves had struck the last blow.

Mahomet II, besieging Constantinople, (1453,) caused, it is said, his fleet to pass by land, in order to introduce it into the canal, and to close the port; it is even said that it was considerable enough to carry twenty thousand choice infantry. Reinforced after the taking of this capital, by all the means of the Greek navy, Mahomet placed, in a little time, his empire in the first rank of maritime powers. He ordered attacks against Rhodes, and even against Otranto, whilst he goes to Hungary in search of a rival more worthy of him, (Huniades.) Repulsed and wounded at Belgrade, the Sultan throws himself on Trebisond with a numerous fleet, subjects that city, and goes with four hundred sail to debark at the island of Negropont, which he takes by assault. A second attempt upon Rhodes, executed, it is said, with a hundred thousand men, by one of his best lieutenants, is repulsed with loss. Mahomet got ready to go there in person, at the head of an immense army, assembled upon all the coasts of Ionia, and which Vertot fixes at three hundred thousand men, when death surprises him in this project.

About the same epoch, England commenced also, to show herself formidable to her neighbors upon land as well as upon sea; and the Hollanders, rescuing their country from the waves of the ocean, formed the germ of a still more extraordinary power than that of Venice.

Edward III, debarked in France, and besieged Calais with eight hundred vessels and forty thousand men.

Henry V made two descents, in 1414 and 1417; he had, it is said, one thousand five hundred vessels, and only thirty thousand men, six thousand of whom were cavalry.

But, up to this epoch, and the taking of Constantinople, all the events that we have just related had had place before the invention of gunpowder; for, if Henry V had a few cannon at Agincourt, as is pretended, it is certain that they were not yet used in the marine. From that time all the combinations of armaments changed, and this revolution had place, thus to speak, at the same instant when the discovery of the mariner's compass, of the Cape of Good Hope and of America, were about to change also all the combinations of maritime commerce, and crèate an absolutely new colonial system.

We shall not speak here of the Spanish expeditions to America, nor of those of the Portuguese, of the Hollanders and of the English in India, by doubling the Cape of Good Hope. In spite of their great influence upon the commerce of the world, in spite of the genius of the Gamas, of the Albuquerques, of the Cortez, those expeditions undertaken by little corps of two or three thousand men, against tribes bordering on the sea, who were not acquainted with fire-arms, offer no interest as operations of war.

The Spanish marine, carried to a high degree of splendor, in consequence of this discovery of the new world, flourished under Charles V ; meanwhile the glory of the expedition to Tunis, which this Prince conquered at the head of thirty thousand choice men, carried by five hundred Genoese and Spanish vessels, was balanced by the disaster which an expedition of the same strength sustàined, undertaken against Algiers (1541) in a too advanced season, and in spite of the wise advice of Admiral Doria. Scarcely debarked, the Emperor saw one hundred and sixty of his vessels, and eight thousand men swallowed up by the waves, and the rest saved by the skill of Doria, reunited at Cape Metafuz, where Charles V rejoined him not without danger or trouble.

During these transactions the successors of Mahomet had not misapprehended all the advantages which the dominion of so many fine maritime provinces promised them, which, at the same time causing them to appreciate the importance of the empire of the seas, furnished immense means for arriving at it. At this epoch, artillery and the military art were not less advanced among the Turks than the Europeans. Their grandeur was carried to its height under Solyman I, who besieged and took Rhodes, (1522,) with an armament which has been estimated at a hundred and forty thousand land troops, and which would still be considerable in reducing it by a half. In 1565, Mustapha and the celebrated Dragut made a descent at Malta, where the knights of Rhodes had made a new establishment ; they conducted thirty-two thousand Janizaries, with a hundred and forty vessels. It is known how John of Vallette immortalized himself by repulsing him.

A more formidable armament, which is estimated at two hundred galleys and fifty-five thousand men, was directed in 1527 against the island of Cyprus, where it took Nicosia, and laid siege to Famagousta. The horrible cruelties committed by Mustapha augmented the alarm which his progress. inspired. Spain, Venice, Naples and Malta, united their naval forces for succoring Cyprus. But Famagousta had already succumbed spite of the heroic defense of Barberiego, whom Mustapha had the baseness to have flayed alive, to avenge the death of forty thousand Turks who had perished during two years in the island.

In the meantime, the combined fleet, conducted by two heroes, Don Juan of Austria, brother of Philip II, and Andrew Doria, attained that of the Turks at the entrance of the Gulf of Lepanto, near the same promonitory of Actium, where was in former times decided the empire of the world between Anthony and Augustus. They destroyed it almost entirely; more than two hundred boats and thirty thousand Turks were captured or sunk, (1571.) This victory did not put an end to the supremacy of the Ottomans, but it arrested their progress; however, they made such great preparations that a fleet as considerable as the other retook the sea—peace placed a limit to so many ravages.

The bad success of Charles V against Algiers, did not prevent Sebastian of Portugal from wishing to attempt the conquest of Morocco, where a Moorish Prince, despoiled of his estates, called him. Making a descent upon the coasts of this kingdom, at the head of twenty thousand men, this young Prince was killed and his army cut in pieces at the battle of Alcazar, by Muley Abdelmeleck, in 1578

Philip II, whose pride had been increased since the naval battle of Lepanto, by the success which his machiavelism and the blindness of the leaguers procured him in France, did not believe that anything could resist his arms. He thought to subject England. The invincible Armada destined for that object, and which made so much noise in the world, was composed of an expedition departing from Cadiz to the number of a hundred and thirty-seven ships of war, according to Hume, of two thousand six hundred and thirty pieces of bronze ordnance, and carrying twenty thousand soldiers, besides eleven thousand sailors. To those forces were to be joined an army of twenty-five thousand men, which the Duke of Parma should bring from the Low countries by Ostend. A tempest and the English did justice to this armament, a considerable one for the epoch, but which, far from meriting the pompous epithet which had been given it, lost thirteen thousand men and the half of its vessels, without having approached the coasts of England.

After this expedition, that of Gustavus Adolphus to Germany first presents itself, (1630.) The army was composed only of fifteen or eighteen thousand men; the fleet numbered nine thousand sailors; but it is without doubt through error that M. Ancillon affirms that it carried eight thousand cannon. The debarkation in Pomerania met with little opposition from the imperialists, and the King of Sweden found a great point of support in the people of Germany. His successor made an expedition of quite an extraordinary nature, and of which there is found in history but a single other example; we allude to the march of the King of Sweden, Charles X, crossing the Belt upon the ice in order to repair to Schleswig by the island of *Fionie* upon Copenhagen, (1658.) He had twenty-five thousand men, of which nine thousand were cavalry, and a proportionate artillery. This enterprise was so much more audacious, as the ice was not safe, since many pieces of ordnance, and the carriage even of the King, broke through.

After seventy-five years of peace, the war between Venice and the Turks had recommenced (1645). The latter carried an army of fifty-five thousand men with three hundred and fifty galleys or vessels to Candia, and seized the important post of Cannae, before the republic dreamed of succoring it. Although Venice had commenced to lose the qualities which had made its grandeur, it still possessed some brave men. Morosini, Gremani, and Mocenigo struggled several years against the Turks, to whom their numerical superiority and the possession of Cannae gave great advantages.

The Venitian fleet had acquired nevertheless under Gremani a marked ascendency, when a horrible tempest destroyed two-thirds of it, with the admiral himself.

In 1648 commenced the siege of Candia, Jussuf attacks it with fury at the head of thirty thousand men, two assaults are repulsed, an immense breach permits a third to be attempted; the Turks penetrate into the place, Mocinigo throws himself upon them to seek death; a brilliant victory crowns his heroism, he repulses them and fills the ditches with their bodies.

Venice would have been able to drive away the Turks by sending twenty thousand men to Candia; but Europe sustained her feebly, and the republic had put forth all the true warriors she had remaining.

The siege recommenced sometime after, lasted longer than that of Troy: each campaign was signalized by new attempts of the Turks to carry succors to their army, and by naval victories of the Venitians who, keeping up with the progress which naval tactics made in Europe, had over the stationary musselmans a marked superiority, and made them pay dearly for every attempt they made to come out of the Dardanelles. Three Morosinis and several Mocinigos distinguished themselves in this long quarrel.

Finally the celebrated Kionperti, placed by his merit at the head of the Ottoman ministry, resolved to conduct, himself, a war which had dragged on for so long a time; he repaired to the island where his successive transports brought fifty thousand men, at the head of which he actively pushed the attacks (1667).

The Turks displayed in this memorable siege more art than they had shown until that time; their artillery, of an enormous calibre, was well saved, and they made use for the first time of trenches, invented by an Italian engineer.

The Venitians, on their side, perfected their defense by mines; never was seen more bitterness in destroying one another by combats, mines, assaults. This heroic resistance gave the garrison the means of gaining the winter; in the Spring, Venice sent it re-inforcements, and the Duke de la Feuillad brought some hundreds of French volunteers.

The Turks having equally received powerful re-inforcements, redoubled their energy, and the siege drew to its close when six thousand French, conducted by the Duke de Beaufort and Navailles, arrived to their succor (1669). However a sortie badly conducted discouraged that presumptuous youth, and Navailles at the end of two months, disgusted with the sufferings of the siege, took upon him to bring back the remnant of his troops to France. Morosini having then no more than three thousand exhausted men, for defending a place open on all sides, consented at last to evacuate it by a convention which became a formal treaty of peace. Candia had cost the Turks twenty-five years of efforts, more than a hundred thousand men killed in eighteen assaults and several hundred sorties; it is estimated that thirty-five thousand christians of all nations perished in that honorable defense.

The struggle between Louis XIV, Holland and England, offers great maritime operations, but no notable descent. That of James II to Ireland (1660) was composed only of six thousand French, although the fleet of Tourville numbered seventy-three ships of the line, carrying five thousand eight hundred pieces of artillery and twenty-nine thousand sailors. It was a grave fault not to have thrown at least twenty thousand men into Ireland with such means. Two years afterwards Tourville having been conquered at the famous battle of the *Hogue*, the remnant of disembarked troops were compelled to return in consequence of a treaty of evacuation.

At the commencement of the eighteenth century, the Swedes and Russians made two very different expeditions.

Charles XII, wishing to succor the Duke of Holstein, made a descent upon Denmark at the head of twenty thousand men, carried by two hundred transports and protected by a strong squadron ; in truth he was seconded by the English and Dutch marine ; but the expedition was not less remarkable for the details of debarkation. The same prince made a descent upon Livonia to succor Narva, but he landed in a Swedish port.

Peter the Great having reason to complain of the Persians and wishing to profit by their discords, embarked in 1722 upon the Volga ; he debouched into the Caspian Sea with two hundred and seventy ships, carrying twenty thousand foot, and goes to make a descent upon Agrakan at the mouths of the *Koissou* where he awaits his cavalry which, nine thousand dragoons and five thousand cossacks strong, comes to join him by land, crossing the Caucasus. The czar then goes to seize Derbent, he besieges Backou, then he treats finally with one of the parties which rent the empire of the Sophis, causing to be ceded to himself Astrabad, the key of the Caspian Sea, and in some sort, that of the Persian monarchy.

The age of Louis XV was signalized only by secondary expeditions, not excepting that of Richelieu against Minorca, very glorious as an escalade, but less extraordinary as a descent.

The Armerican war (1779) was the epoch of the greatest maritime efforts of France ; Europe did not see, without astonishment, that power send at the same time Count D'Estaing to America with twenty-five vessels of the line, whilst that M. Orvilliers, with sixty-five Franco-Spanish vessels of the line, was to protect a descent operated by three hundred transport vessels and forty thousand men united at Havre and St. Malo.

This new Armada cruised for two months without undertaking anything ; the winds drove it at last into its ports.

More fortunate D'Estaing gained the ascendancy in the Antilles and debarked in the United States six thousand French under Rochambeau, who, followed later by another division, contributed in investing the small army of Cornwallis in New York (1781) and in fixing thus the independence of America. France would have triumphed perhaps forever over her implacable rival, if, by the aid of those parades in La Mariche, she had sent ten vessels and seven or eight thousand men more with Governor Suffren into India.

The attempt of Hoche against Ireland, with twenty-five thousand men, was dispersed by the winds, and had no other consequenees, (1796.)

Later, the expedition of Bonaparte, carrying twenty-three thousand men to Egypt, with thirteen ships, seventeen frigates, and four hundred transports, obtained at first successes, soon followed by cruel reverses. It is known that, in the hope of driving him from thence, the Turks debarked at Aborikir to the number of fifteen thousand, and that in spite of the advantage of that peninsular for intrenching themselves and awaiting reinforcements, they were all driven into these a or taken : a memorable example of the defensive to imitate in like cases.

The considerable expedition directed in 1802 against St. Domingo, was remarkable as a descent ; it failed afterwards by the ravages of the yellow fever.

After their successes against Louis XIV, the English attached themselves rather to destroying rival fleets and to conquering colonies, than to making great descents. Those which they attempted in the eighteenth century against Brest and Cherbourg, with corps of ten and twelve thousand men, could do nothing in the heart of a State as powerful as France. The astonishing conquests which gained them the empire of Hindostan, were successive. Possessors of Calcutta, and afterwards of Bengal, they were reinforced there by degrees by partial detachments, and by the Sepoys whom they disciplined to the number of a hundred and fifty thousand.

The Anglo-Russian expedition against Holland, in 1799, was executed by forty thousand men, but by several successive debarkations ; it is, nevertheless, interesting from its details.

In 1801, Abercrombie, after having disquieted Ferrol and Cadiz, made a descent with twenty thousand English upon Egypt ; every one knows the result.

The expedition of General Stuart to Calabria, (in 1806,) after some successes at Maida, had to regain Sicily. That against Buenos-Ayres, more unfortunate, was terminated by a capitulation.

In 1807, Lord Cathcart made a descent with twenty-five thousand men at Copenhagen, besieged and bombarded it ; he took possession of the Danish fleet, the object of his enterprise.

In 1808 Wellington made a descent on Portugal with fifteen thousand men. It is known how, victorious at Vimiero, and supported by the insurrection of all Portugal, he forced Junot to evacuate that kingdom. The same army increased to twenty-five thousand men under the orders of Moore, wishing to penetrate into Spain for succoring Madrid, was driven back upon Corunna, and forced to re-embark with great loss. Wellington debarked anew in Portugal with some reinforcements, having united thirty thousand English and as many Portuguese, avenged that defeat by surprising Soult at Oporto, (May, 1809,) and by going afterwards as far as the gates of Madrid to fight Joseph at Talavera.

The expedition to Antwerp, made the same year, was the most considerable which England had undertaken since Henry V. It numbered not less than seventy thousand men, forty thousand of which were land troops, and thirty thousand sailors; it failed to attain its end because of the little genius of him who commanded it. A descent of altogether a similar nature to that of the King of Sweden, Charles X, was one of thirty Russian battalions crossing, in five columns, the Gulf of Bothnia upon the ice, with their artillery, in order to go to the conquest of the islands of Aland, and to spread terror even to the gates of Stockholm, whilst another division passed the gulf at Umeo, (March, 1809.)

General Murray made, in 1813, a well combined descent near Tarragona to cut off Suchet from Valencia; however, after some successes, he was obliged to re-embark.

The armament which England made in 1815 against Napoleon, returned from the island of Elba, was remarkable for the immense *materiel* which it debarked at Ostend and Antwerp. The troops amounted also to sixty thousand Anglo-Hanoverians; but the one came by land, and the others landed on the soil of a powerful ally, so that it was a successive and pacific descent rather than a military expedition.

Finally, the English made, in the same year, 1815, an enterprise which may be ranked among the most extraordinary; we allude to that against the capital of the United States of America. There was seen, to the astonishment of the world, a handful of seven or eight thousand English, descend in the midst of a State of ten millions of souls, to penetrate sufficiently far to seize the capitol, and to destroy thereat all the public establishments—results for which one seeks in vain another example in history. One would be tempted to reproach for it the republican and anti-military spirit of the inhabitants of those provinces, if we had not seen the militia of Greece, of Rome and of Switzerland, defend their firesides better against aggressions much more powerful; and if in that same year an English expedition, more numerous than the other, had not been totally defeated by the militia of Louisiana, under the orders of General Jackson:

The perhaps rather fabulous armaments of Xerxes and of the Crusades excepted, nothing of all that has been done, particularly since war fleets carried a formidable artillery, can sustain the least comparison with the colossal project and the proportionate preparations which Napoleon had made for throwing a hundred and fifty thousand disciplined veterans upon England, by means of three thousand pinnaces, or large gun boats, protected by sixty ships-of-the-line.

We see also how different it is to attempt such descents when only an arm of the sea of some leagues is to be crossed, or when one is to direct himself in open sea to great distances. The number of operations made by the Bosphorus is explained by this difference, which is decisive in these kinds of enterprises.

---

* Six months after the first publication of this work, thirty thousand French embarked at Toulon, made a descent upon Algiers, and, more fortunate than Charles V, took possession of that place in a few days, and of all the regency. This expedition, as well conducted by the marine troops as by those of the land, did honor to the army as well as to its chiefs.

NOTE

ON INTRENCHED CAMPS.

To the article on intrenched camps already written in 1835, (page 173,) I had added a few words upon that of Linz, of which I had only a superficial hear-say knowledge ; the number of the Military Spectator which makes mention of it, having afterwards fallen into my hands, I think it my duty to rectify what I have said inexact upon that camp. It is composed of thirty-two towers, of which eight are on the left bank, with a square fort commanding the Perlingsberg. Of the twenty-four towers which are found on the right bank, seven are only half towers. The circumference of this line is about twenty-one thousand yards, (about twelve miles.) The towers are nearly five hundred and twenty-five yards from each other, and will hereafter be connected, in case of war, by a palisaded covered way. They are in masonry and of three stories, in addition to a terrace which constitutes the principal defense, since it contains eleven twenty-four pounders ; two howitzers are besides placed in the upper story. Those towers are placed, as I have said, in the excavation of a broad and deep ditch, the earth of which has furnished an elevated glacis that places, it is said, the tower secure from direct shots, which I think, nevertheless, difficult for the platform where the artillery is found.

We have been assured that this great work had cost almost three-fourths of what an entirely bastioned enciente would have cost, which would have made of Linz a place of the first rank ; others affirm that it has cost no more than a fourth of the expense which an enciente would have required, and that it fulfills quite another object. If those works be considered as made for resisting a regular siege, it is certain that they would be very defective. But, considered as an intrenched camp, for giving a refuge and an outlet upon the two banks of the Danube to a considerable army, it is certain also that they would fulfill sufficiently well this design, and that they would be of great importance in case of a war like that of 1809. If they had existed at this epoch, they would probably have saved the capitol.

In order to complete a great system, it would have been better, perhaps, to surround Linz with a regular bastioned line, then to establish a line of from seven to eight towers between the eastern salient of the place and the mouth of the Traun, in a direct extent of four thousand yards only, to the end of reserving as an intrenched camp only the great bend formed by the Danube between Linz and the Traun. There would thus be had the-double advantage of a fortress of the first rank, and a camp under the shelter of its ramparts; if it had been a little less vast, it would have sufficed nevertheless, for a great army, especially if they had preserved the eight towers of the left bank and the fort of Perlingsberg.

I shall not speak of the defects of this camp, for there would be necessary an exact plan of the ground upon both banks of the Danube, and although I have passed Linz many times, I do not recollect the environs sufficiently well to judge of them. What astonishes me is, that there is not at least a redoubt-around Linz, to favor a retreat if the camp chanced to be forced. It will be said, perhaps, that no army could penetrate between those towers, even after the fire of some of them had been extinguished; this is not unanswerable, for in such a case it would not be easy for the adjacent towers to fire upon two armies engaged in so narrow a space, without doing as much harm to the defenders as to the enemy himself; besides, if I am well informed, the batteries could not be directed against the interior. Now, if, after having paralyzed the fire of the four towers, from 7 to 10, strong masses were pushed to Linz, God knows what a melée might have place, if one had to do with a Suwarof or a Ney, with the soldiers of Ismail, or of Friedland.

I have not comprehended, either, the necessity of the nine towers, 21 to 29, which are placed upon the Danube; could a debarkation in boats in the midst of a hundred thousand men be feared? Could they be for replying to the hostile field batteries placed on the left bank? Land batteries would have well sufficed, guarded by a ditch like the Danube!

For the rest, the interesting notice of Captain Allard upon those towers, proves that they are well conceived for obtaining the greatest possible fire, upon the whole periphery of attack with a small number of artillerists, although there is a manifest error in the enumeration which he has made of them. In mountainous places like Genoa, (where they are employed for the first time upon a different model,) as well as Besançon, Grenoble, Lyons, Béfort, Briançon, Verona, Prague, Salsburg, and the forts covering the gorges of mountains, they would be valuable. With regard to the *tracé* of the camp which seems somewhat extensive, the space of from eighteen to twenty thousand yards, to be garnished completely upon a single line with a reserve, would require a hundred and fifty battalions at least; but it would rarely occur that both banks would require to be defended at the same time, the same also of the side along the Danube; now, the true defense would scarcely comprise but the distance of eight thousand yards, from the mouth of the Traun to the Danube above, so that with eighty battalions the camp would be well guarded. Denuded of troops, it would always require a garrison of five thousand men for the occupation of the towers; but those men, scattered into thirty-two small detachments, would be unable to make sorties.

Definitively, if Vienna still possessed its ancient *enciénte*, and its garrison were resolved to make good use of it, the enemy would think twice before braving two such establishments, and march without being disturbed by them upon that capital by the valley of the Danube. It could be done only by the route through Carinthia, except after having totally defeated the army as at Ulm, at Jéna, and at Waterloo, or after having reduced the camp of Linz.

LOGISTICS.
